THE ARCHAEOLO(

Also available from Bloomsbury

Dura-Europos by J. A. Baird
Early Islamic North Africa by Corisande Fenwick
Narrating Heritage: Rights, Abuses and Cultural Resistance by Veysel Apaydin

THE ARCHAEOLOGY OF AMAZONIA

A HUMAN HISTORY

José Iriarte

BLOOMSBURY ACADEMIC
LONDON • NEW YORK • OXFORD • NEW DELHI • SYDNEY

BLOOMSBURY ACADEMIC
Bloomsbury Publishing Plc
50 Bedford Square, London, WC1B 3DP, UK
1385 Broadway, New York, NY 10018, USA
29 Earlsfort Terrace, Dublin 2, Ireland

BLOOMSBURY, BLOOMSBURY ACADEMIC and the Diana logo are trademarks of Bloomsbury Publishing Plc

First published in Great Britain 2024

Cover image: Demoledores rock art panel, Serranía de la Lindosa,Colombia. Photograph by José Iriarte

A catalogue record for this book is available from the British Library.

Library of Congress Cataloging-in-Publication Data
Names: Iriarte, José, Ph. D., author.
Title: The archaeology of Amazonia: a human history / José Iriarte.
Description: London; New York, NY: Bloomsbury Academic, 2024. |
Includes bibliographical references and index.
Identifiers: LCCN 2023059704 (print) | LCCN 2023059705 (ebook) |
ISBN 9781350270732 (paperback) | ISBN 9781350270749 (hardback) |
ISBN 9781350270756 (pdf) | ISBN 9781350270763 (ebook)
Subjects: LCSH: Amazon River Region–History. | Amazon River Region–Antiquities. | Archaeology–Amazon River Region. |
Human ecology–Amazon River Region.
Classification: LCC F2546 .I75 2024 (print) | LCC F2546 (ebook) |
DDC 980/.00909–dc23/eng/20240407
LC record available at https://lccn.loc.gov/2023059704
LC ebook record available at https://lccn.loc.gov/2023059705

ISBN: HB: 978-1-3502-7074-9
PB: 978-1-3502-7073-2
ePDF: 978-1-3502-7075-6
eBook: 978-1-3502-7076-3

Typeset by RefineCatch Limited, Bungay, Suffolk
Printed and bound in Great Britain

To my family, Cecilia, Iñaki and Maria Clara

CONTENTS

ILLUSTRATIONS

PREFACE

A synthesis of Amazonian archaeology is a difficult undertaking because of the vastness of the region, its long human history, the heterogeneous nature of its ecosystems and the flurry of recent discoveries. Larger than Europe, and inhabited by humans from as early as 13,000 years ago, the Amazon is extremely diverse, with landscapes ranging from humid evergreen, seasonal and flooded forests, to wetlands and savannahs. All these factors have resulted in one of the world's most ethnically diverse regions. The Amazon is home to more than 300 ethnic groups, with protected indigenous lands covering about 4 million kilometres^2 (Chapter 2).

Most people when they think of the Amazon, picture a vast, unspoilt jungle. For many, it recalls scenes of 'Fitzcarraldo: The Wrath of God', where the hard, machete-wielding conquistadors stride through uninhabited places and face a seemingly impenetrable tangle of forest. However, as we will see in this book, archaeology has shown that beyond the rivers, the Amazon was full of land roads interconnecting different places (Chapters 7 and 8).

Vast swathes of the Amazon's forests remain archaeologically unexplored. As Patricia Lyon (1974) famously stated, Amazonia is the least known region of 'the least known continent'. However, things are rapidly changing. During my academic career, the rapid documentation of archaeological cultures has radically changed our understanding of the Amazonian past. The geoglyphs, the Amazonian garden cities, the sun villages and the Amazonian 'Stonehenge' are just a few examples of the evocative and grandiose names applied to these newly discovered archaeological traditions. It has been a period of tremendous technological change. We can now fly over any place in the Amazon virtually, with Google Earth, while developments such as lidar – our 'lasers in the sky' – allow us to peer beneath the forest canopy (Chapter 7). As a result, entire new regions with complex archaeological cultures have been uncovered. Evidence from a previously unexplored 800 kilometre stretch of the upper basin of the Tapajós River, for example, has demonstrated that the entire southern rim of Amazonia was once inhabited, with an estimated population of between half and one million people (Chapter 7).

As an anthropological archaeologist, I am living in a privileged time, a time of change and discoveries. The rate at which fresh archaeological findings are made is so rapid that it is likely that a novel archaeological tradition will be defined by the time this book goes to print. Unfortunately, much of this new knowledge is coming to light at a time when tropical forests and their native residents are rapidly disappearing. As an archaeologist and archaeobotanist (researching plant remains from archaeological sites), I have increasingly realized that the role of archaeological evidence relating to plants is underestimated. Plant evidence is very often applied solely to an investigation of diet in the past, with its broader potential frequently overlooked. Archaeobotanical studies have an important contribution to make in relation to other crucial questions in archaeology and anthropology, and in increasing our understanding of how the wellbeing of modern societies could be enhanced. They have shown, for example, that the forest can be intensively cultivated causing minimal deforestation, that controlled fires prevent massive megafires, and that some pre-Columbian raised-field farmers had fire-suppression practices that are key for ensuring sustainable Amazonian futures, as we will see in Chapter 10. We are currently experiencing significant turning points in Amazonian archaeology. Long neglected, considered marginal in relation to the Andean and Mesoamerican states and chiefdoms, native Amazonian cultures are revealing their complexity, ingenuity and sophistication because of recent research. For example, new findings are showing that Amazonia contributed some of the most important crops to the world (Chapter 4). The Neotropics and the Amazon are now established as a region with multiple independent plant cultivation and domestication centres, comparable to the other major world centres of plant domestication, beginning during the late Pleistocene and early Holocene. However, until recently, documentation of plant domestication in the tropics was not an easy feat. I had the opportunity to witness first-hand the 'micro-botanical revolution', mainly led by Dolores Piperno and Deborah Pearsall, which has arguably freed us from the limitations of relying solely on the few sites where macro-botanical remains are preserved. For example, we are now able, thanks to advancements in techniques of micro-botanical analysis, to document the cultivation and domestication of many tubers in ways that were previously inaccessible because of their fragile nature as macrobotanical remains (Chapter 4). Similarly, fossil starch grains, ancient DNA and chemical biomarkers have revealed the cultivation and potential domestication of cacao during the middle Holocene, while phytolith analysis has shown that rice domestication took place during the middle Holocene in the Amazon basin (Chapter 5). It is important to note that in Amazonia, as in other tropical regions of the world, current data imply a very particular relationship between people and plants. This suggests that the traditional approaches to how we conceptualize plant domestication, based on evidence from the Near East, do not apply to Amazonia.

The singularity of Amazonia is also reflected in the type of early urbanism developed in the region. Areas of Amazonia, such as the Llanos de Mojos and the Upano River, are exhibiting a distinct form of social aggregation known as low-density urbanism. This phenomenon has been identified in other locations with a hyper-seasonal climate and with significant investments in agricultural infrastructure (Chapter 8). Collectively, the weight of the evidence means we have reached a point where we can compare Amazonia with the societies of the Old World Antiquity and ask, as Michael Heckenberger usually puts it in television documentaries: 'Why not civilizations in the Amazon?'

It is a time when perspectives are shifting on how we conceive the relationship between humans and tropical forests. Tropical forests are no longer seen as a barrier to the dispersal of hunter-gatherers; rather, we now understand that they played a significant role in peopling the world. Amazonia is no exception (Chapter 3). The conventional view of 'tropical forest cultures', whereby people are seen as passively adapting to their surroundings, or heavily influenced by the constraints of the environment, is also changing. The methodology of the palaeo sciences is advancing our understanding of this issue (Chapter 3). In my career, I have also witnessed a transition in the use of palaeoecology, from solely reconstructing vegetation histories to documenting plant domestication, land use and the impact of human activity on forests. The typical attitude when I first started in archaeology was that 'everything in Amazonia is natural until we prove human agency'. Now, balanced and nuanced debates are taking place about the role of humans in shaping today's forests. Vast databases of forest plots overlaid with archaeological data are being used to investigate the potential human impact on forest composition. For example, of the estimated 16,000 tree species that grow in the Amazon, only 222, known as 'hyperdominants', cover 50 per cent of its area. More telling, Carolina Levis discovered that plants edible to humans are five times more likely than non-edible plants to be hyperdominant, underscoring the human footprint on Amazonian forests. Historical ecology approaches have reintroduced humans into the equation as niche modellers and keystone species in shaping Amazonia.

Although it would be foolish to dismiss the natural processes at work across millions of years in this natural marvel, dubbed the 'Magic Web' by Ziegler and Leigh (2016), we no longer imagine a wild, pristine forest but rather a cultivated landscape rich in the history of human interaction with the land. We now acknowledge that it is as important to preserve 'pristine' forests as well as preserving 'cultural forests' containing an immensely rich bio-cultural heritage. Investigations are now undertaken by large interdisciplinary teams, with historical ecology complemented by a deep-time perspective provided by the palaeo sciences. Collectively, these works document the human presence across the Amazon basin while recognizing the heterogeneity of the scale and nature of the human impact on the landscape. Even areas long thought to be pristine refugia or sparsely inhabited, such as the aseasonal montane forests of Ecuador, are now revealing urban-scale societies (Chapter 8). Many geometrically ditched enclosures, known as 'geoglyphs' exist, similar in size to the Neolithic henge of Avebury. When I give presentations in the UK, I often wonder aloud about the condition of prehistoric Essex if there were more than 500 Avebury henges found in this region. Would anyone be discussing its pristine state?

All these developments have been accompanied by huge growth in the practice of archaeology in Amazonia. During the past two decades, the number of archaeologists working in the region has increased dramatically, pioneered in large part by the Central Amazon Project (Neves, 2022) and Projeto Geoglifos (Ranzi and Pärssinen, 2021; Schaan et al. 2010), among many others (Chapter 7), and substantial funding from the Brazilian government, as well as the establishment of numerous new departments of archaeology in the Brazilian Amazon universities. The growth of Amazonian archaeology was materialized in the first *Encuentro Internacional de Arqueología Amazónica* in 2008, which attracted hundreds of archaeologists from Latin America, the United States and Europe, and has continued to grow exponentially since then.

It is crucial to approach the study of the Native Amazonian past with respect and deference. We are currently seeing a significant change in anthropology and archaeology programmes in the Amazon, with the inclusion of indigenous actors. This encourages an entirely new way of looking at the past (Chapter 10), and is significant because the lessons learned from Amazonia's archaeology can also benefit people worldwide. Understanding the who, what, where, how and why of changes that occurred in the past, and are occurring now, will help us navigate our collective future.

On a personal note, I must admit that Amazonia didn't sweep me off my feet at first. I am a first-generation of Basque immigrants transplanted to the vast grassy pampas of Uruguay –'Rivers of the Birds' in Tupi-Guarani – who enjoys sharing a conversation with his endearing group of friends (*la barra*), drinking the native *mate* (*Ilex paraguayensis*), served on a bottle gourd overlooking an 'asado en la parrilla'. My initial impressions of the tropical forest were of the typical green curtain experienced by foreigners. Over time, I developed an appreciation for the tropical flora's richness, subtleties and the legacy of past human impact. By flying across Amazonia numerous times in small Cesna planes to reach remote field locations, one develops an eye for determining which processes are responsible for creating the vegetation patterns we see, from the yellow, pink and white flowers of *Ipê* trees to the concentrations of palms and Brazil nut trees, likely created by humans and growing on top of Amazonian anthrosols. I am no longer irritated by sweat dripping over the pages of my notebooks, and I enjoy the comfortable, cool shade under the canopy, the air pungent with the smells of blossom and decay.

I started in the academic world with the solid foundations of the Department of Anthropology at Universidad de la República (Uruguay) and the University of Kentucky (US). I was fortunate to have four, first-rate academic mentors, Tom Dillehay, Dolores Piperno, Doyle McKey and José María López Mazz. Although we do not always agree, they instilled in me a rigorous approach, curiosity and a distance from parochialisms. They also demonstrated to me the hardships and challenges, but more significantly, the rewards of working across different fields. The European-funded PAST project team of brilliant PhD students and early career researchers provided me with some of the most energetic and stimulating intellectual environments I have ever experienced. They are now colleagues and the results of our collaboration are largely summarized in this book.

The Amazon forest and its people are in crisis. As Eduardo Neves emphasizes in public talks, the Anthropocene in the Amazon is not a geological golden spike to be found thousands of years ago, but a political process that is happening now, destroying forest livelihoods. Commercial interests, population growth, climate change and reduced environmental regulations threaten biodiversity, indigenous heritage and community identity. Across the world, other forests, such as those in Indonesia and Madagascar, are suffering a similar fate. The South American Atlantic biome has lost 95 per cent of its 'monkey-puzzle' *Araucaria* forest, which was planted in part by the Je indigenous people during the late Holocene (Robinson et al. 2018). We are now rapidly losing the Amazon, the largest tropical forest on Earth, vital for its role in cooling the planet. The Amazon stores and captures more carbon than any other ecosystem. As well as providing food and medicines, it is a reservoir of biodiversity, containing more kinds of plants than the entire European continent. More than 90 per cent of the world's poorest people depend on forests to maintain their livelihoods and cultures, while about half of the world's population will live in the tropics by the year 2050 (Penny et al. 2020). Revitalizing forest livelihoods is critical. In the Amazon, forest areas protected by their residents suffer a rate of deforestation eleven times lower than that of the surrounding areas. About 22 per cent of the Brazilian Amazon, representing 27 per cent of its carbon stocks, is managed by forest residents (e.g., FAO and UNEP, 2020; Forest Trends, 2017; Nepstad, 2006; Walker et al. 2014). As the map in Figure 10.2 shows, by superimposing deforestation patterns with indigenous lands, it is clear to see that deforestation occurs only outside indigenous territories. As Michael Heckenberger (2009a) reminds us: 'Protecting forest residents and the forest are one and the same thing.'

I have the humbling and privileged opportunity to work with traditional Amazonian people. Research is only possible with their assistance, which ranges from guiding us in and out of the forest, to teaching us their learned ancestral understandings about these areas from generations past. I am aware I represent a Western paradigm of doing science that extracts knowledge from indigenous communities. To reciprocate their generosity and support, I have endeavoured to help revitalize their forest livelihoods by running workshops, co-writing books and developing diplomas for community-based local tourist guides with no academic background.

Developing sustainable land use practices and alternative solutions to destructive industries is crucial for protecting the Amazon forest and securing the global future. I believe, as I will show in Chapter 10, that the deep-time perspective provided by archaeology can offer valuable lessons for sustainable Amazonian futures. Methods of crop cultivation have been identified, for example, which could be practiced without clearing large patches of forest, such as closed-canopy forest enrichment, limited clearing for crop cultivation and low-severity fire management intensive cultivation. Unlike the situation in the moorlands of Britain, where areas deforested during the European Neolithic and Bronze Age have not recovered, the Amazon forest has been preserved. It appears that the forests that fascinated European botanists during the Age of Discovery, were not, after all, the result of large-scale regrowth following the Columbian Encounter, but had always been there.

Finally, I have had the privilege over the past five years of studying the unique and remarkable rock art in the Serrania de la Lindosa region of the Colombian Amazon (Chapter 3). This region boasts one of South America's largest and oldest concentrations of rock art, dating back at least to the beginning of the Holocene and likely representing some of the first forms of graphic communication among Amazonian peoples. The paintings on the walls of the mesa-top hills, called *tepuis*, reveal fascinating details about the people who created them and the environment they inhabited. Inspired by nature, they used animals, plants, rivers, rocks and mountains as symbols to express their ways of seeing and behaving in the world (Iriarte et al. 2022a). As Javier Aceituno points out, these painters acted as biologists, recording the details of plants and animals, as geographers mapping rivers and mountains, as anthropologists recording their own shamanic dances, ceremonies and rituals, and as historians preserving group memories in the form of pictures.

The Uruguayan writer Eduardo Galeano, my neighbour and my father's companion at *tertulias*, wrote of these graphisms: 'The Indians say that these are works of the gods, to guide their steps and illuminate their ceremonies. Painted bodies are vaccines of beauty against sadness' (*Los indios dicen que esan son obras de los dioses, para guiar sus pasos e iluminar sus ceremonias. Los cuerpos pintados son vacunas de la belleza contra la tristeza).* But, the importance of La Lindosa's paintings goes far beyond their artistic value. They are more than a wonderful spectacle. They represent a tapestry of human history, the roots of a way of life in indigenous Amazonia, based on thousands of years of communities coexisting with the jungle and maintaining its ecological balance. An archive of knowledge and culture, irreplaceable among Amazonian peoples, they signify a prosperous and long-term relationship with the natural world that dates back more than 13,000 years. Indigenous peoples, together with their ways of life and their understanding of ecology, are critically threatened by contemporary human activities. But their culture and experience in managing Earth's resources are essential for the survival of the Amazon rainforest's enormous biodiversity and, in turn, the future of humanity itself. La Lindosa, deeply rooted as it is in indigenous human-nature relationships, provides us with valuable lessons for the contemporary present. As Stephen Rostain (2012:132) tells us: 'Although the pre-Columbian history of America's indigenous peoples may not be written in books, it is nevertheless present in its soils, stones, trees and rivers; it is everywhere in the Amazon. And it is the task of archaeologists to rediscover and restore this rich past.' I am engaged in this fabulous task.

The peoples of Amazonia had a special relationship with the largest and most diverse tropical forest in the world. Over many centuries they created new plants, such as manioc, which today make up the breadbasket of the world (Chapter 4). They were the first to savour cacao. They buried their loved ones in urns shaped like seated humans; they built henges of standing megaliths and some were obsessed with geometry, constructing enclosed areas in regular shapes and lived in villages shaped like a drawing of the sun. They built cities with plentiful forest gardens, and huge pyramids, comparable in size to Tiawanaku's Akapana (Chapter 8). They engineered landscapes to perfection, without destroying tropical forests (Chapters 6 and 10). In the following pages, I invite you on a journey through 13,000 years of human history to meet these remarkable people.

ACKNOWLEDGEMENTS

I could not have undertaken this ambitious project without the support of different institutions and funding bodies that supported my research. First and foremost, I am indebted to the University of Exeter and the European Research Council Horizon 2020 grants PAST (616179) and LASTJOURNEY (834514), upon which most of my research presented here is based on. Projects of this magnitude, which involve multiple disciplines, are only made possible thanks to the support of the European Commission. I also received the generous support of the Leverhulme Trust, the British Academy, Newton Fund, UKRI Impact Acceleration funds, the National Geographic Society, Wenner-Gren Foundation and CRNS.

I would like to thank my colleagues at the EarthMovers project in French Guiana, Doyle McKey, Stephen Rostain, Nicolas Guillaume-Gentil, Bruno Glaser, Jago Birks and Jenny Watling. I gained valuable knowledge about interdisciplinary collaboration between various disciplines, which will stay with me forever. I am grateful to collaborators Denise Schaan, Per Stenborg and Lilian Rebellato on the Brazilian-Swedish 'Cultivating Wilderness' project in Santarém. Losing Denise at such a young age is a significant loss to Amazonian archaeology, but her legacy lives on within all of us.

I learned a great deal from palaeoecologists Bron Whitney and Frank Mayle, as well as archaeobotanist Ruth Dickau during our Leverhulme Trust project 'Pre-Columbian land use and impact in the Bolivian Amazon' (F/00158/Ch). I want to thank botanists Izais Brasil da Silva, Edemar de Oliveira, Daniel Soto and Ezequiel Chavez who endured many long, hot days under the forest canopy rolling out measuring tapes, scratching and sniffing the bark of trees, pulling down flowers and pressing plants until late at night. INPA, Noel Kempff Museum and Cayenne Herbarium kindly provided us with pollen and phytolith samples to build our reference collections. Denise Schaan, Alceu Ranzi and Antonia Damasceno kindly opened up the doors of Acre state to work in a collaborative way. Carla Jaimes and Heiko Prümers have kindly invited me to participate on the Mojos 3D Lidar project. Integrating and testing the lidar sensor into so many flying devices was truly a rollercoaster of emotions. Thanks to Luis Aragão, Salman Khan, Nei da Silva and Mark Robinson for their hard work and patience during these bumpy experiences.

The LASTJOURNEY project, the result of collaboration and friendship with Francisco Aceituno, Gaspar Morcote Rios, Patrick Roberts, Mikkel Pedersen and Alan Outram, is one of the most exciting projects I have ever worked on.

Many individuals made the fieldwork possible and gratifying in the Amazon. They are too numerous to mention, but I thank them all for their efforts, enthusiasm and support. Local communities kindly hosted us in different places across the Amazon. A few of them, with whom we have created 'un cariño especial', deserve a special mention: the families of Silvia and Jose Velásquez in Versalles, José Noe Rojas in Cerro Azul and

Nelson Castro in Raudal del Guayabero. We have been safely guided into and out of the most remote regions of the Colombian forest by Edgar Osorio, 'El Barbas'. Together we shared great conversations over tasty fish, turtle steaks and cold beers. These families clearly understand the value of studying and preserving the archaeological sites. Along with their communities, they have been excellent stewards of the Amazonian bio-cultural heritage, ensuring professional archaeologists' access to it as well as the wider community.

I am also grateful for the scholarly generosity of several 'Amazonists' colleagues who allowed me to use their photographs, as well as for the several interesting conversations over the years including (in no particular order) Daiana Alves, Jennifer Watling, Yoshi Maezumi, Mark Robinson, Umberto Lombardo, Carla Jaimes Betancourt, Lautaro Hilbert, Cristiana Barreto, Manuel Arroyo-Kalin, Gustavo Politis, Javier Aceituno, Gaspar Morcote Rios, Martinj van del Bel, Alejandra Sánchez Polo, Antonia Damasceno, Carolina Levis, Sonia Zarrillo, Bruna Rocha, Heiko Prümers, Doyle McKey, Eduardo Neves, Stephen Rostain, William Balée, João Saldanha, Fernando Santos Granero, Fernando Urbina, Christian Gutierrez, Oscar Saavedra, Renato Kipnis, Fernando Montejo and Francisco Cruz. Special thanks to Jonas Gregorio de Souza for creating the maps. His extensive knowledge of Amazonia is evident in their detail. Patrick Roberts kindly reviewed the manuscript and provided me with valuable constructive comments. I would also like to thank Jess Collins who edited the manuscript for clarity and Ana Marcela García Agudelo for her proficiency and patience with drafting the figures.

On a more personal note, special thanks goes to my parents, José María Iriarte and Ana María Mugica, who have always supported my choice to become an anthropologist. Cecilia, my wife, and Iñaki and Maria Clara, have accompanied me throughout this long, fascinating and sometimes tiring process of collecting the field data, carrying out the laboratory analysis and putting it all together in writing. I could not have achieved this without their love and patience. Special thanks to Iñaki and Cecilia who encouraged me to develop the thesis of the book to new heights and gave me the support to meet their strong challenges. Although all these people aided in the successful completion of this book, I take full responsibility for all mistakes and errors that lie herein.

CHAPTER 1
A COUNTERFEIT PARADISE? THE MYTHOLOGY OF AMAZONIAN ECOLOGY

In the popular imagination, the Amazon forest is a virgin wilderness almost empty of people. It has traditionally been conceived as a deceitful Garden of Eden, whose infertile soils and scarce game prevented the development of intensive agriculture leading to complex societies. To some extent, Amazonia is a region that has been largely overlooked in human history (Barreto, 1998; Neves, 1998; Heckenberger and Neves 2009). However, a spate of recent discoveries and technological breakthroughs, such as lidar, which allows us to peer through the forest canopy, are overturning these long-held assumptions and creating an entirely new picture of Amazonian human history. In this book, I will present you with this untold story of Amazonia and show how the diversity of Amazonian people today is deeply rooted in prehistory. Today, Amazonia is facing a crisis and lessons from its indigenous and traditional people are needed more urgently than ever before. The extraordinary archaeology being discovered is not just a spectacle. It represents the history of a way of life that is rapidly disappearing – but on which the Amazonian forest as a major reservoir of biodiversity, and in turn all humanity, depends. This book connects the past to the present, and brings to light the critical role of today's indigenous and traditional lands and people in providing a barrier to deforestation under current climate and political pressures.

In this scene-setting chapter, I will start by explaining how the pristine myth originated with the travellers of the seventeenth and eighteenth centuries, who encountered somewhat empty landscapes after the population collapse that had followed the arrival of Europeans in the late fifteenth century. After laying out popular opinions of Amazonia as 'primaeval' or 'natural' refugium, untouched by humans until very recently, it will introduce the reader to long-lasting academic debates about the limitations and possibilities of tropical forests for the development of complex societies. This will be followed by a preamble to the latest archaeological evidence for human occupation and alteration of the rainforest environments from the time of the last Ice Age until the complex societies encountered by the first travellers to the Amazon River. The chapter briefly reviews previous work in Amazonian archaeology, history and ethnography, as well as the modern political ecology of Amazonia.

At the end of this chapter, the reader will learn about the most important recent findings about the deep time history of Amazonian people.

The creation of the pristine myth

Westerners' exploration of the Amazon can be divided into four main periods: travellers in the sixteenth century, missionaries in the seventeenth and eighteenth centuries, naturalists and scientists in the nineteenth century, and ethnographers in the twentieth century. All contributed to the ways in which we view the Amazon and Amazonian people today (Barreto and Machado, 2001).

In 1500, Vicente Yañez Pinzón explored the 170-kilometre mouth of the Amazon River and named it Santa Maria de la Mar Dulce. He sailed the river inland for approximately only twenty leagues. Later, in 1542, Francisco Orellana led an expedition from the west and discovered the Amazon. The river was named after the legendary female warriors known as the Amazons, from Greek mythology, famously described by Friar Gaspar de Carvajal (1984) during this expedition. A century later, Acuña 'confirmed' their existence and so the myth took root. Accounts of these early journeys along the major Amazonian rivers describe numerous complex and sedentary societies. These societies were part of extensive political territories engaged in large-scale organized warfare. Some occupied large continuous tracts of the Amazon River over dozens of kilometres, with populations ranging from 800 to 3,000. Some settlements were even as large as 10,000 people (Denevan, 1996). These chronicles speak of societies that were socially stratified units, with a central power ruling over several local groups. The hierarchies comprised regional and local chiefs, nobles, commoners and subordinate individuals, such as servants and captive slaves. The accounts also highlight the sophistication of Amazonian material culture, the efficiency of non-metal tools and the extent of indigenous knowledge of natural resources. Some sources even compare the local pottery to European artefacts, which throughout this book you will come to recognize is not unrealistic at all.

In the early 1600s, the arrival of Capuchin, Franciscan and Jesuit missionaries marked a significant turning point in the region's colonial history. The missionaries quickly spread from the river's mouth to the upper frontiers, with the aim of controlling Indian villages and preventing colonists from enslaving them. It is estimated that by 1740 around 50,000 Amazonian Indians were living in Jesuit and Franciscan missions. Missionaries were in a favourable position to gather valuable ethnographic and linguistic data about indigenous communities. By establishing peaceful relationships with the natives and living among them, they were able to interact with and learn from various groups, many of which, unfortunately, later disappeared. As a result, missionaries became the pioneers in compiling extensive information about the Amazon's indigenous peoples, which even today provides valuable insights into these groups' ways of life (e.g., Barreto and Machado, 2001; Eder, [1772] 1985).

In the mid-eighteenth century, expeditions to the Amazon were driven by a new purpose. Instead of conquest, discovery and conversion to Christianity, they were focused on rationally studying nature, following the values of the Enlightenment. The voyages of Humboldt and Darwin to South America reflect this new motivation among travellers visiting the region, in what is called the 'Age of Discovery'. The Amazon became a true paradise for botanists, zoologists, geologists and other natural scientists. During the eighteenth and nineteenth centuries, European colonization of the Amazon shifted its focus from searching for legendary cities of gold to exploring and utilizing the region's vast natural resources. These resources ultimately contributed to the economic growth of the newly colonized territory and the European empires that controlled it. Rubber exploitation, whose boom took place between 1850 and 1920, was one the major protagonists of this period (Hecht, 2013).

The 'Age of Discovery' ended with the modern anthropologists of the early twentieth century, such as Erland Nordenskiöld and Curt Nimuendajú. Carrying out both ethnographic and archaeological research in the Amazon, they were able to propose the most compelling theories for human cultural development in the region, and established the basis of modern anthropology (Nimuendajú, 2004; Nordenskiold, 1930). However, the image of native Amazonia has been over-simplified, fed by a steady stream of images in popular and scientific media: naked, painted and feather-bedecked bodies, with people living more or less 'at one' with nature in small, egalitarian villages amounting to little more than clearings in the forest. These stereotypes are deeply rooted in the Western imagination and appear time and time again in films, coffee-table books, magazines and on the internet. A substantial body of twentieth-century ethnographic documentation perpetuates the myth.

The notion of pristine rainforests has been challenged by increasing archaeological and ecological evidence for long-term human activities within even the most intact forests worldwide (Denevan, 1992; Roberts, 2019; Willis et al., 2004). Amazonia is no exception. Beginning in the 'Age of Discovery', the Amazon was viewed as a unique place where nature and humanity remained unchanged and pure, making it ideal for scientific experiments. Early European naturalists reported scattered indigenous populations living in huge and apparently virgin forests, an idea that has continued to fascinate the media, policymakers, development planners and even some scientists. This was the origin of the pristine environment myth, that is, the belief that the landscapes of the Americas were largely undisturbed until the arrival of Europeans, who proceeded to destroy the environment with their agriculture, mining, urbanism and industry. The myth is often linked to the idea of the noble savage, which suggests that indigenous populations have always lived in peaceful harmony with nature. A seminal article by Denevan (1992) debunked the idea of the pristine myth across the Americas and, more than thirty years of archaeological research later, we know that much of what has been traditionally regarded as 'empty wilderness' in the Amazon is a result of the drastic decrease in population caused by the first arrival of Europeans. The spread of diseases, slavery, missionization, resettlement and warfare led to the death and displacement of many native people within a century. Most students of Amazonian history now recognize these are landscapes with complex human histories, and that thousands of years of human activity have significantly altered forest composition. Meanwhile, indigenous Amazonian groups can no longer be typecast as small, isolated communities living in the forest's depths or dispersed along rivers. The perception of simple social structures and a low level of cultural achievement is largely the consequence of catastrophic population collapse and displacement experienced by indigenous groups since their first contact with Europeans. We are now able to identify the features of what can fairly be described as a tropical forest civilization that gave rise to diverse, sophisticated art styles.

The forest, with all its diversity, is still vital for the livelihood and economy of Amazonian peoples. Indications are that the Amazonian flora is, in part, a living heritage of its past inhabitants. Recent work, showcased in the following chapters, shows that native Amazonian societies did not merely passively adapt to the forest but had an active role in shaping it. What appears to be untouched wilderness is the result of thousands of years of intentional or unintentional human influence, from the time that people first arrived in the Amazon during the late Pleistocene.

Tropical wars: Debating the complexity of tropical societies

In this brief summary, I will only highlight major trends and will focus on the history of Brazilian Amazon archaeology (see summaries in Barreto, 1998; Neves, 1998). Some of the first interest in the past of Amazonia began with Brazilian naturalists, such as Alexandre Rodrigues Ferreira in the 1780s and Domingos Ferreira Penna, Ladislau Netto, João Barbosa Rodrigues and others a century later, who were the first to conduct investigations on the prehistory of Amazonia. These early pioneering works ended with Nordenskiöld's (1930) brief synthesis of Amazonian archaeology based on his and Nimuendajú's fieldwork, which can be considered as foreshadowing modern Amazonian anthropology.

During the 1940s, cultural ecology scholars in North America began to prioritize the study of how environmental factors influence social and cultural developments. Steward's work and the 'Handbook of South American Indians', were crucial in establishing ecologically-based models for Amazonian anthropology, and also had an important impact on the field of Amazonian archaeology (Steward, 1946). During that time, cultural ecology focused on systems theory, the ecosystem and adaptation, but did not give much consideration to human agency and cultural change (Balée, 2006).

The term 'tropical forest culture' was a category that encompassed the economic, social and cultural structures of indigenous populations living in the Amazon (Steward, 1946). The tropical forest culture was characterized by the cultivation of root crops, specifically bitter manioc, the use of efficient rivercraft, hammocks for beds and political decentralization, as well as a lack of an organized temple-cult religious system because of a perceived idea of local community autonomy (Steward, 1946). It was considered an evolutionary stage, comparable to Service's 'tribe' classification (Feinman and Neitzel, 1984). The typical tropical forest 'tribe' consisted of slash-and-burn horticulturalists organized in autonomous and egalitarian villages. Limited in size and permanence by both a simple technology and an unproductive environment, the villages were unable to produce the requisite economic surplus to allow the rise of the craft specialization, social stratification and political centralization that had developed in other areas of South America.

This model of the 'single-village-isolated-in-the-forest' (Viveiros de Castro, 1996) played a critical role in shaping how South American cultural history views Amazonia as a peripheral region. Steward (1946) proposed an Andean development centre with unlimited agricultural potential (a factor thought necessary for establishing large, sedentary populations), from which cultural traits spread to other parts of the continent. The theory proposes that cultural elements were adopted or lost in other areas because of historical or ecological circumstances. As a result, lowland South America was seen as marginal to the great Andean 'centre of inventiveness and social development' (e.g., Wüst and Barreto, 1999).

Steward's cultural history has greatly impacted archaeological interpretation, both in the academic world and the popular imagination, even though few people today would accept his theories. As Heckenberger and Neves (2009) point out, in the context of the global historical scheme, Amazonia was assessed on what it did not have, including traditional architecture made of stone, writing systems, an abundance of cereal crops and domesticated animals, such as ungulates.

Following in the steps of Steward, in her seminal book, *Amazonia: A Counterfeit Paradise*, Meggers (1996) argued that poor soils and the lack of animal protein prevented the development of intensive agriculture, and therefore the emergence of complex societies in Amazonia. In what Viveiro de Castro has dubbed as the 'Standard Model', the presuppositions are that game in Amazonia is scarce, patchy, arboreal and nocturnal, while soils are heavily leached and infertile, thus unsuitable for intensive agriculture. Within this paradigm, ethnographic groups have often been uncritically projected deep into the past and used as analogues to interpret the archaeological record. However, many of these groups were heavily impacted by the European Encounter. As a result, their numbers and the complexity of their political organization has been greatly reduced. The 'Standard Model' is based on selected examples of modern ethnography where the population rarely exceeds 0.3 persons per kilometre^2, consists of slash-and-burn horticulturalists who move settlement when soils and resources are depleted, and exhibit risk-reduction strategies, such as mandatory sharing of prey, long-distance trade, food taboos and population control. This broad picture also typically presents small groups who adapt passively to poor environments.

Meggers and Evans (1978) found that local cultural development in Amazonia was limited. When archaeological evidence surpassed their expectations, they attributed it to external migrations or influences, such as lost Japanese fishermen, brief intrusions from centres of 'high culture', such as the Andes, or European manipulation. The disappearance of cultures was attributed to 'degeneration' in the tropical forest. A classic example is Marajoara culture (Chapter 7), whose origins were to be sought in Valdivia culture on the coast of Ecuador.

In this context, the earliest available chronology elaborated specifically for the Amazon was presented by Meggers and Evans (1957). It involved the identification of four 'horizon styles' for the tropical forest: Zoned Hachured, Incised Rim, Polychrome and Incised Punctate. These horizons were defined based on decoration and on the types of temper found at the twenty-two ceramic complexes of the tropical forest area known at the time. Consistent with the peripheral perspective, all four horizons were ascribed an origin outside of Amazonia and were believed to be of very short durations (Meggers and Evans, 1957). Although later modified, mainly in terms of the timespans of the different horizons, now designated 'traditions', this scheme has been consistently employed by Meggers and her Brazilian collaborators over the years (e.g., Miller, 1992).

By the late 1960s, the PRONAPABA (National Program of Archaeological Investigations of the Amazon Basin) had been implemented. This was a joint research effort that brought together the Conselho Nacional de Desenvolvimento Científico e Tecnológico (CNPq), the Smithsonian Institution and eleven universities and museums from different states in Brazil. The main mission of the PRONAPABA was to establish a baseline chronological framework for the still largely unexplored prehistory of Brazil, which would eventually allow archaeologists to tackle more processual research questions, such as human-environment interactions, diffusion, migration and intergroup contacts, among other topics (Brochado et al., 1969). When evaluating the PRONAPABA, it must be remembered that at the time, exploring and studying Brazil's 8,500,000 kilometre^2 territory with only a small handful of archaeologists was an ambitious undertaking to say the least. As Brochado (1969) reminded readers, this was a mammoth task for the Brazilian archaeologists, who were fewer in number than the archaeologists employed in a single US county.

PRONAPABA represents what Willey and Sabloff (1974) have called the 'classificatory-descriptive' stage. Its methodology focused on obtaining representative ceramic samples from limited test units, in order to obtain maximum vertical depth and surface collections to define, describe and classify ceramics into phases. Ford's quantitative method for deriving cultural chronologies, seriation, became the tool used by Brazilian archaeologists to conduct a nationwide archaeological survey (Meggers and Evans, 1969). Along with radiocarbon dating, this allowed investigators to assess chronological relationships, organizing them into traditions, phases and subphases, which supposedly corresponded to distinct cultural units. Not much attention was paid to obtaining spatial horizontal relationships beyond individual features of the sites, such as single mounds, in order to infer site layouts, and landscape features were not studied in any depth. As a result, the well-planned and elaborated mounded architecture of many large Amazonian sites remained 'hidden in plain sight' (*sensu* Kehoe 1998).

Despite the caveats associated with the work of PRONAPABA, it still represents the first reconnaissance of a huge and archaeologically unknown region. It generated the first chronological schemes, it provided us with the first systematic description of sites and artefacts in the region, and it standardized both site nomenclature and ceramic terminology throughout the Brazilian Amazon, which facilitated comparison and communication.

But things were meant to change. The 'Standard Model' of Amazonia began to be challenged early in the 1960s. Robert Carneiro (1960) provided valuable information on the subsistence methods of indigenous peoples in Amazonia that contradicted the Standard Model. He argued that nomadism and low population levels were not because of ecological limiting factors, since, for example, the Kuikuru communities of the Upper Xingu River, which he studied, lived in the same interfluvial areas of Amazonia for almost 100 years, sustaining themselves through manioc cultivation and fishing.

In 1970, American archaeologist Donald Lathrap began to call attention to the importance of riverine adaptations in tropical forests. Lathrap proposed that ceramic techniques developed in the Central Amazon and then spread outwards through the network of rivers. For him, river floodplains, in contrast to hinterland interfluvial areas, were able to provide the basis for the development of complex societies because of their fertile agricultural soils and the year-round availability of animal protein from fish, mammals, reptiles and fowl (Lathrap, 1970). Such stable concentrations of resources favoured the demographic growth of sedentary populations, leading eventually to competition over resources with two possible outcomes: the colonization of other floodplain areas, or the occupation of the hinterland areas, which were poor in resources. In his so-called 'cardiac model', the *várzea* was considered the heart, and the Amazon tributaries were arteries that allowed people to expand and settle in the hinterland, leading eventually to the development of complex exchange networks, social interactions, warfare and alliances that facilitated the flow of goods, people and ideas.

This was also a time when scholars began to contemplate the idea that Amazonia was not just a recipient of complex cultures, but a centre of innovation. Lathrap (1970) put forward a theory that challenged conventional thinking, by proposing that the Amazon was not merely influenced by the advanced civilizations of the Andes but was actually the birthplace of these civilizations. Earlier, Tello similarly proposed that Amazonian thinking may have impacted Andean culture (1960), in particular at the Chavin de Huantar site with its characteristic Amazonian iconography (see also Lathrap 1977).

The 1980s signal a time when the first attempts to correlate climate and culture began. For example, drawing on refuge theory and the available palaeoecological records at this time, Meggers (1982) argued that the expansion of the Tupi-Guarani forest farmers out of SW Amazonia was a response to the onset of drier, climatic episodes around 2,000 years ago, which reduced the forest and forced Tupi-Guarani groups to migrate, leapfrogging to other forested regions. Later on, Meggers (1994) also argued that ENSO-related megadroughts in the lower Amazon may have caused discontinuities in local sequences at about 1,500, 1,000, 700 and 400 years before the present.

Greater expectations

Starting in the 1980s, Amazonian archaeology began to move away from a culture-historical perspective to embrace a more problem-oriented type of archaeology. It is now more than two decades since Neves (1999) proposed an 'emergency plan' that would shift paradigms from exploratory and inductive to a more problem-oriented and theory-based archaeology. This could only be achieved once a new generation of archaeologists had broken away from old epistemologies. As time has passed, his vision has increasingly materialized.

The work of Anna Roosevelt played a critical role in shifting paradigms, firstly by documenting the earliest hunter-gatherers in the tropical forest of Ice Age Amazonia, who were not big game hunters, but had a generalized economy (Roosevelt et al., 1996); secondly, by unearthing and dating the earliest ceramics discovered in the South American continent (Roosevelt et al., 1991); and thirdly, among other works, by proposing the existence of chiefdoms in the lower Tapajos (Roosevelt, 1999). Geophysics and large-scale excavations were beginning to reveal community organization at the larger site level, while the work of ethnobotanists, such as Posey (1984) and Balée (1989) had started to show that modern Amazonians were not adapting passively to the environment but actively modifying it. These were the initial steps of Historical Ecology, a research programme that returned humans and human agency to the centre of attention. More importantly, it began to show that the landscapes of today are legacies of past land use (Balée, 2006). During the 1990s and early 2000s, research into the Amazonian Dark Earths (ADEs), coupled with the Xingu Ethnoarchaeological Project (Heckenberger, 2005), the Central Amazon project (Neves, 2022), and the Geoglyph Project (Schaan 2012) gave rise to unprecedented international collaboration by large interdisciplinary teams. Starting in the early 2000s, several departments of history, including archaeology, were opened in Brazilian Amazon cities. The application of satellite remote sensing and lidar technology began to reveal the regional organization of ancient Amazon polities. The use of the palaeosciences (reviewed in Chapter 4) to answer anthropological questions is revealing the nature of landscapes and land use in pre-Columbian times. As a result of all this activity, the past two decades have seen the emergence of an image of Amazonia characterized by a growing emphasis on the complexity of indigenous social formations and the ecological diversity of the region.

Today, the discipline has become more self-reflective about its role in contemporary Amazonia. Many archaeological projects are now becoming more inclusive by involving native and traditional peoples in their research teams. Indigenous students participate in university-level programmes in archaeology. Indigenous people form part of Latin American governments and Brazil has recently created a Ministry of Indigenous People. This is a response both to a global trend towards inclusivity and to demands from the populations being studied. As we will see in the case studies of Chapter 10, these projects have established greater levels of dialogue and participation.

Setting the scene

This book tells the story of recent scientific findings, conclusions and debates about the history of humans in the largest tropical forest on Earth. Moving away from the perception of Amazonia as a pristine wilderness, research over the past decades has brought up fascinating insights and questions about the deep human past in the Amazon. This book tracks the timeline of human occupation in the region until the arrival of Europeans (Figure 1.1).

I use the term Amazonia instead of Amazon basin to refer to the tropical regions of South America that lie to the east of the Andes. Amazonia encompasses the Amazon basin proper, as well as the large regions adjacent to it, such as the Orinoco, Araguaia and São Francisco River basins. The justification for using the term Amazonia lies in the absence of major geographical barriers, the presence of numerous riverways that span

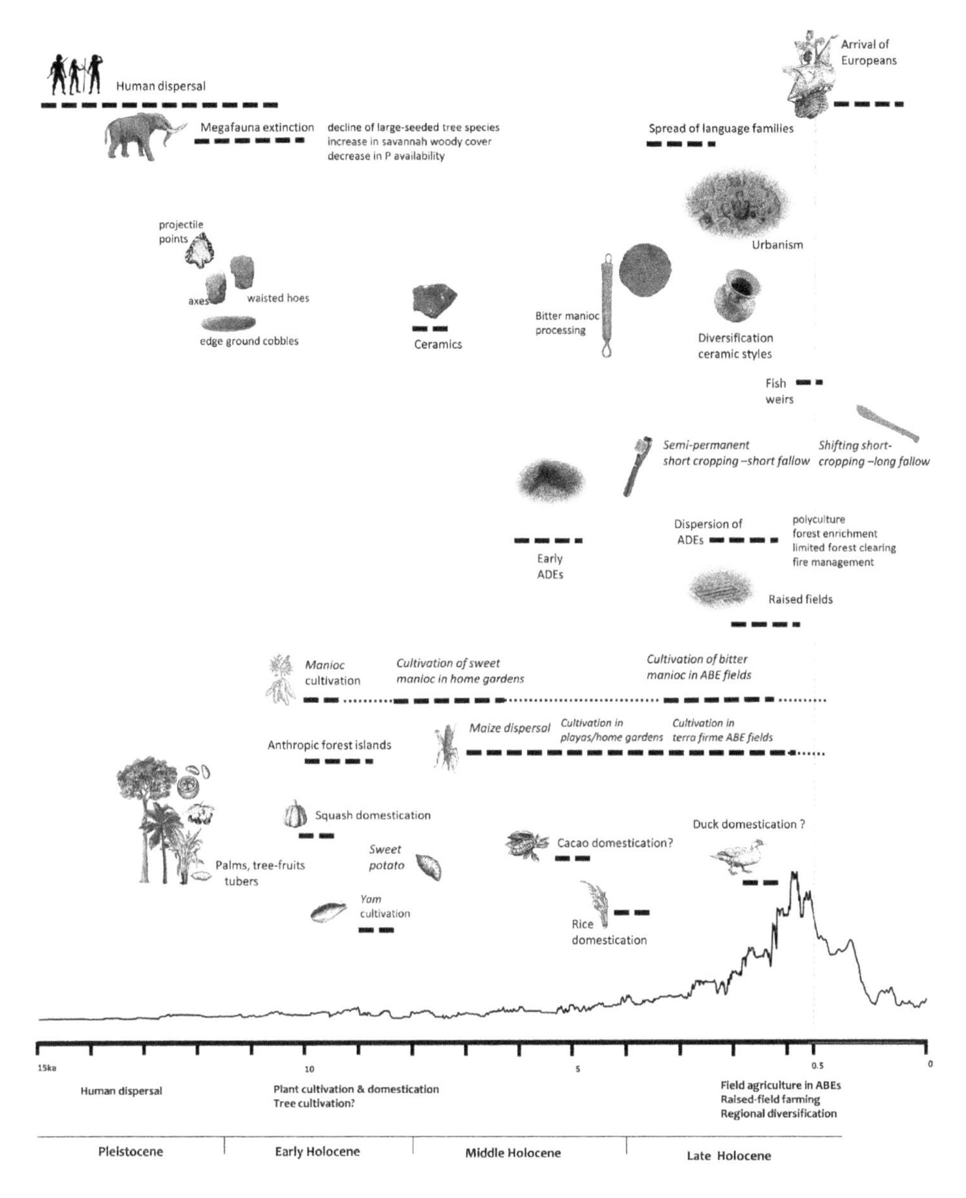

Figure 1.1 Schematic diagram of major developments in Amazonia since the time of human arrival. Graph in lower section represents the summed calibrated probability distributions (SPDs) of all radiocarbon dates for the Amazon basin.

this region and connect the Orinoco, Amazon and Rio de la Plata basins, and the fact that many language families span across Amazonia in what was space rich and intense interregional interactions.

In describing the general trends and major events, I have tried to include as much information as possible, although because of space restrictions, some regional variations have been omitted. This is the case, for example, of two important regions, such as the Orinoco Basin, and the Cerrados of Central Brazil. I refer the reader to the synthesis works of Gasson (2002) and Redmond and Spencer (2007) for the Orinoco and Prous (2019) for Central Brazil regions.

Because of my background and research experience, a significant portion of this book covers the topics of plant domestication, human-environment interactions and the techniques utilized to document them. The environment, chronology and ceramics phases, settlement patterns, material culture, and subsistence and mortuary practices for each region or archaeological culture are described. This is accompanied by a summary of the major environmental changes faced by early humans from their dispersal during colder and drier glacial conditions to the wetter and warmer climate of the Holocene.

A note on chronology. Dates from the late Pleistocene to the Common Era (CE) are given in ka, which stands for thousands of calibrated years before the present. Dates from 1 CE and onwards are given as CE, except for palaeoecological records, which are generally given in ka. To account for the uncertainty of calibrated radiocarbon dates, they are typically preceded by a tilde symbol (~), indicating an approximate date. To represent the chronological trends of the radiocarbon databases in the case studies, we used the summed calibrated probability distributions (SPDs) of radiocarbon dates for each particular region. This is a method commonly used as a proxy for human activity, based on the idea that more intense human occupation will leave behind a greater amount of datable materials (Rick, 1987). SPDs are created by calibrating each independent date in the sample and then combining the findings to create a single density distribution. Instead of utilizing single-point estimations, this method includes the whole range of probabilities associated with the calibrated dates. SPDs are far from perfect, but they are the best tool we have at the moment for assessing previous population dynamics in relative terms when an acceptable sample size and chronometric hygiene measures are utilized, as in these case studies. In this book, however, the summed probability densities are shown only for visual assessment of the distribution of dates associated with different archaeological traditions – with a cautionary note that, because of bias in research, these will not always correspond to population trends. Summed probability densities were built in the R statistical environment using the package rcarbon (Crema and Bevan, 2021) after calibrating the dates with the ShCal20 curve (Hogg et al., 2020).

I will conclude the chapter by summarizing some of the latest key discoveries about the history of the people of Amazonia:

- Despite the common conception of Amazonia as a ginormous homogeneous forest, the region actually consists of various types of rivers, soils, resources and vegetation formations. These include evergreen, seasonal, peatland and mangrove forests, along with forests dominated by certain plants, such as palms, bamboos and Brazil nut. Additionally, savannahs are also present in the region (Chapter 2).

- The diversity of Amazonian people is only rivalled by its biodiversity. Today, Amazonia is home to 3,000 distinct indigenous territories belonging to 200–385 ethnic groups representing 300 indigenous languages. Amazonia is a linguistic puzzle, where no single linguistic family (such as the Indo-European in Europe) dominates the region. Major linguistic groups include the Carib, Macro-Jê, Tupi-Guarani, Arawak, Tukoan and Panoan, while multi-lingual regional systems are common today and in the past. Amazonian animism does not separate nature from culture. Amazonian people perceive the body as constantly transforming and changing, and write history in the landscape through paintings, engravings, earthworks and a diversity of material culture (Chapter 2).
- Amazonia was peopled during the end of the last Ice Age by at least 13.1 ka by foragers with a expedient stone tool technology. They were not big-game hunters but had a generalized subsistence combining palms, tree fruits, and underground tubers with medium and small mammals, amphibians and fish. They had a unifacial lithic industry with few retouched formal artefacts, typically terminal or lateral scrapers, and rare evidence of bifacial artefact production. Current evidence shows that productive ecotones, in particular palm-dominated tropical forest-savannah-riverine mosaics, were preferred locations to settle, although people also successfully transited and settled in Andean and sub-Andean tropical forests, as well as savannahs, from the outset of their arrival. They produced 'art' from the time of their first occupation, painting their stories and myths on the walls of rock shelters – perhaps they painted the now-extinct large-bodied mammals they encountered on their arrival in South America (Chapter 3).
- From the outset, the early inhabitants of the Llanos de Mojos began to create a landscape that ultimately comprised several thousand forest islands within the treeless, seasonally flooded savannah, showing that – ever since their arrival in Amazonia – humans have markedly altered the landscape, with lasting repercussions for habitat heterogeneity and species conservation. It underscores the strong relationship between landscape and plant domestication that took place within Amazonian environments (Chapter 3).
- Amazonia is an early centre of plant cultivation and the birthplace of globally significant crops, such as manioc, yams, cacao and sweet potatoes, which were first domesticated there. The tropical montane forest of north-western South America in Colombia evidences the incipient cultivation of trees (*Persea*, *Caryocar* and *Virola*), palm and a variety of tubers (*Dioscorea* sp., *Calathea* sp. and *Maranta* cf. *arundinacea*), beginning ~11.5 ka. This plant evidence is supported by the appearance of a distinct plant processing tool kit, including hoes and hand axes, which were likely used for managing and cultivating

forest resources. In the mosaic of forest and savannahs of south-western Amazonia in the Llanos de Mojos, early Amazonians were cultivating squash (*Cucurbita* sp.) ~10.3k, manioc (*Manihot* sp.) ~10.4k, as well as a diversity of tubers (*Calathea*, *Marantaceae*, *Heliconia*, *Cyperaceae* and *Phenakospermum*) and palms (Chapter 4).

- Plant domestication in tropical South America, including Amazonia, is unique. Plant domestication is specific to tropical South America. It has diffuse, mosaic-like geographical patterns, goes hand in hand with landscape domestication, and includes a large variety of root and tree crops but only two grains (maize and rice). Even under intense management, plants that have been an important component of Amazonian diets since ancient times, such as palms, do not show morphogenetic alterations. Only one animal has been domesticated: the Muscovy duck. Muscovy duck (domesticated dog were brought by the first settlers). Plant domestication was not immediately followed by sedentary living or agricultural food-production systems (Chapter 4).
- During the middle Holocene, Amazonian people cultivated and likely domesticated cacao (*Theobroma cacao*) in the montane forests of the eastern slopes of the Ecuadorian Andes ~5 ka, and rice (*Oryza*) ~4 ka in the wetlands of the Guaporé-Itenéz River. The latter marks the third global event of rice domestication following China and Africa (see also debates about rice domestication in India, e.g., Bates 2022) (Chapter 5).
- Amazonia was an early centre of ceramic manufacture, with the first ceramics beginning to be manufactured about 8 ka at the shell-midden of Taperinha in the lower Amazon (Chapter 5).
- During the late Holocene, Amazonian people began to transform the landscape at a scale not seen before. Vast expanses of seasonally flooded savannahs were transformed into raised-field agricultural landscapes, while Amazonian anthrosols, the ADEs, spread across the basin both in riverine and interfluvial areas (Chapter 6).
- Polyculture agroforestry in ADEs through soil fertilization, closed-canopy forest enrichment, limited clearing for mixed cropping and low-severity fire management supported large populations and was resilient to climate change. ADE land use systems had an enduring legacy on persisting patches of highly fertile soil, and on the modern composition of the forest, including legacy plots where the richness and abundance of useful plants, such as palms, Brazil nut and cacao is higher than in non-ADE sites. The enrichment of the forest with plants of economic importance is not only evident in today's forest but is also shown in deep time pollen records. Polyculture agroforestry spread rapidly across the Amazon basin at the start of the second millennium CE, adopted by diverse cultures in varying cultural, bio-geographic and climatic regions (Chapter 6).
- Parallel to these major transformations, historical linguistics and archaeology hint at the spread of farmers and settled life associated with the ancestors of

major linguistic families, including the Arawak, Tupi and Carib across lowland tropical South America and beyond (Chapter 6).

- A period of regional florescence with distinct archaeological cultures emerged during the late Holocene, evidenced by a variety of earthen architecture (ditches, canals, landscape-scale fish weirs, reservoirs, causeways, raised enclosures, plazas, platform mounds and pyramids), sophisticated funerary practices and exquisite ceramics (Chapters 7 and 8).
- Amazonians are extremely skilled canoeists who use the rivers as natural arteries of communication. However, archaeology is revealing that people were also interconnected by land in interfluvial areas or in non-navigable rivers by a network of perfectly aligned radial and linear raised causeways and roads with earthen kerbs, as well as sunken roads (Chapters 7 and 8).
- Urban scale societies that were agricultural, hierarchical, organized in regional polities (more than 500 kilometres^2) and displaying large-scale civic-ceremonial architecture emerged in the montane forest of Ecuador (Upano) and the forest savannahs mosaics of the Llanos de Mojos (Casarabe). Unlike their Old World counterparts, characterized by compact, bounded and densely populated settlements, Casarabe and Upano urbanism is extensive, consisting of dispersed settlements incorporating large amounts of open space and water management networks (Chapter 8).
- Today's forests of Amazonia have a human footprint. Forest composition has been altered significantly over thousands of years of interaction with humans. At least eighty-five tree and palm species were cultivated and domesticated to some degree during pre-Columbian times. Edible trees are five times more likely to be Amazonian hyperdominants than non-edible trees, an example of the human effect on forest composition contribution of human to Amazonian hyperdominants (Chapters 2 and 10).
- The arrival of Europeans drastically impacted these societies whose population may have declined as much as 95 per cent according to some estimates (Chapter 9).
- Archaeology provides lessons for sustainable Amazonian futures. Archaeology has shown that the forest can be cultivated intensively with minimal deforestation, ancient controlled fires have been proven to prevent massive megafires, biochar studies rooted in ADE can help store carbon in soils, and working collaboratively with indigenous communities can benefit a better understanding of past, traditional communities and the conservation of the forest (Chapter 10).

In the next chapter, I will introduce you to the different environments, resources and people of the Amazon, as well as the various ways indigenous people have made a living there, before we delve into Amazonian human history starting in Chapter 3.

CHAPTER 2
BIOCULTURAL HOTSPOT: AMAZONIAN PEOPLES, LANDSCAPES AND CLIMATES

In this chapter, I introduce the reader to the range of human and ecological diversity in the Amazon. I begin with a brief description of the Amazonia climate. This is followed by an account of Amazonia's widely contrasting ecosystems and their ecological variations, from floodplains to upland forests, wetlands to savannahs. The unique characteristics of these ecosystems are described, and the limitations and opportunities for human resource use are presented. This is complemented by a summary description of their ingenious land-use systems grounded on their detailed knowledge of these environments (Denevan, 2001). Next, there is a description of Amazonia's indigenous and traditional (peasant) populations, who encompass a remarkable number of distinct languages, making Amazonia one of the most ethnically diverse regions of the planet, including 1.5 million people from about 385 ethnic groups, as well as Afro-descendants and other traditional people (e.g., Epps and Salanova, 2013; Quijano-Vallejos et al., 2020; Moran, 1993; Nichols, 1992). Some of the major language families and its geographic dispersion are described, as well as some common patterns of Amazonian ways of thinking about and acting in the world that have implications for how we interpret the archaeological record.

The river in the sky: Climate of Amazonia

Amazonia's size is reflected in the region's wide range of climates. Rainfall within the basin varies greatly in terms of total amount and seasonal distribution. It is heavier in areas influenced by the Andean mountain chain, where annual rainfall can reach 5,000 millimetres and there is almost no dry season. In contrast, other areas of Amazonia, such as the eastern Amazon of Brazil or parts of SW Amazonia, receive as little as 1,700 millimetres of rainfall per year, and have a four-month dry season, therefore supporting more open types of vegetation. Annual and daily temperature variability is low across the Amazon basin, with mean annual temperatures varying from 18–23°C.

Most of the tropical South American continent experiences a distinct seasonal cycle of precipitation related to two convective systems: the Intertropical Convergence Zone (ITCZ) and the South American Summer Monsoon (SASM), both of which are influenced by the disparity in thermal properties between the South American continental landmass and the surrounding oceans.

The ITCZ is characterized by a relatively narrow, longitudinally oriented tropical belt of low pressure, where moist trade winds converge over the equatorial oceans – the

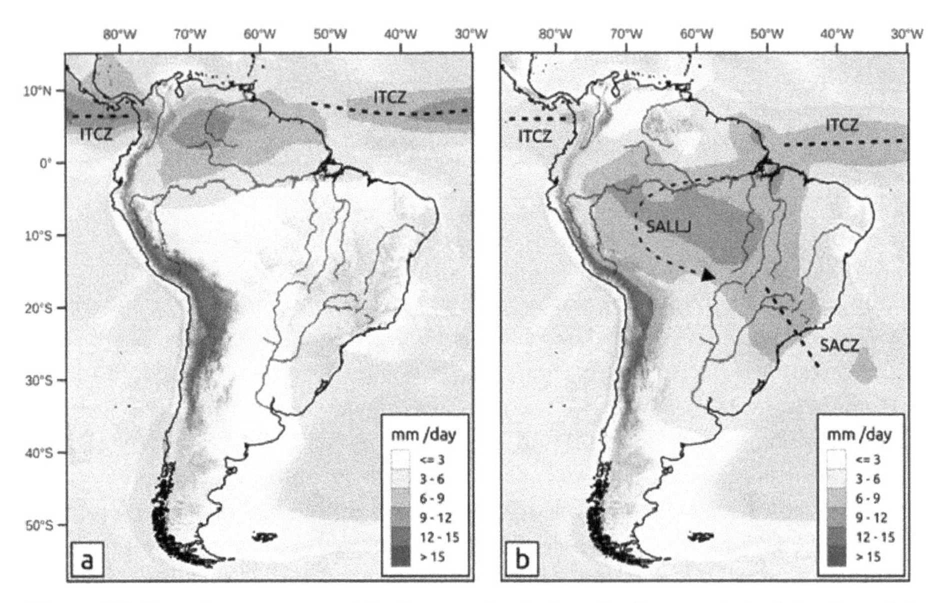

Figure 2.1 Long-term mean precipitation over South America for *a*. austral winter (June, July, August) and *b*. austral summer (December, January, February). Notice the position of the ITCZ, the SALLJ and the SACZ during the two seasons.

notorious 'doldrums' described by mariners passing through this area in historic times. The ITCZ is associated with convective clouds – unstable, low-pressure, rapidly rising air – that produce high precipitation. Shifts in the location of the ITCZ are the major influences on the seasonality of tropical rainfall. During austral winter (June, July, August), when the thermal equator (locations with highest mean annual temperatures) and ITCZ are located farther north to approximately 9°N, maximum precipitation over the continent occurs in northern South America, whilst central South America experiences its dry season (Figure 2.1a). During austral spring/summer (December, January, February), the thermal equator moves south to approximately 2°S and heats up the central South American land mass relative to the surrounding oceans. This continental heating causes areas of intense convection to form over central Brazil and southern Amazonia, which are fed with moist easterly trade winds blowing in from the Atlantic Ocean. The warmer continent compared to the Atlantic Ocean favours the entry of moisture into the continent, marking the onset of the SASM wet monsoonal season. As the moist easterly trade winds encounter the Andean mountain range, they 'bounce' and are diverted southward. This flow creates a feature known as the South American Low-Level Jet (SALLJ), associated with very strong low-level winds that are channelled southwards by the eastern Andes and the Brazilian highlands. The SALLJ helps to transport moisture from Amazonia into subtropical southeast Brazil (Smith and Mayle, 2018) (Figure 2.1b). The strengthening or weakening of the SALLJ has consequences for vegetation and people. As we will see in Chapter 7, the wetter climate of the late Holocene strengthened the SALLJ, which resulted in the replacement of areas of the savannah by

Figure 2.2 Clouds over the Tocantins River mouth, which were probably formed from water vapour released from trees and other plants throughout the day. Nasa Earth Observatory.

forest in the southern rim of Amazonia, which in turn created ecological opportunities for tropical forest farmers to expand south of Amazonia (Iriarte et al., 2017).

One of the important findings from research in the past decade has been the demonstration that half of the rainfall within the Amazon Basin is the result of internal recycling by the forests themselves (Pöschl et al., 2010). Amazonia has about 400 billion trees. A single large tree can release more than 1,500 litres of water as vapour. The vast quantities of water vapour pumped into the atmosphere daily by trees via transpiration (20 billion tons of water) contribute just as much as the moisture coming into the basin from oceanic evaporation, previously considered the dominant factor producing rainfall (Figure 2.2). Importantly, although much of this water falls locally as rain, some is carried across other parts of the continent by airflows, such as the SALLJ, which carries rainfall to the agricultural heartland of South America to the south. By one estimate, 70 per cent of Brazil's gross national product comes from areas that receive rainfall produced by the Amazon rainforest (Nobre 2014). The economic consequences of the Amazonian deforestation are simply obvious.

High convection over the SASM domain is also linked to the formation of the South Atlantic Convergence Zone (SACZ), an internal structure of the SASM characterized by a NW–SE band of convection that extends from the centre of the convection system to eastern Brazil. Like the ITCZ, the SACZ migrates, though in an SW–NE axis. The migration of the SACZ creates a rainfall dipole at the borders of the monsoon, resulting in a climatic antiphase between the western and eastern Amazon Basin. In contrast to the central and southern areas of tropical South America, the northeast of Brazil is conspicuously dry throughout most of the year (Smith and Mayle, 2018).

As we will see in the chapters to come, the climate of the Amazon has been anything but steady. Shifts in climate, along with human action, have produced major changes in the different environments of Amazonia through time.

The Amazon basin

The world's largest forest

Tropical forests form a green belt around the Earth. Even though they take up only about 14 per cent of the planet's total area, tropical forests store 68 per cent of the world's forest carbon and 50 per cent of its biodiversity. South American forests are the largest, comprising one-third of the total area, and the Amazon, lying at the heart of South America, is the largest tropical forest in the world. By any standard, the Amazon is awe-inspiring. The Amazon River originates from the melting of the Sajama ice cap in Bolivia at 6,400 metres above sea level (masl) and the Apacheta cliff in Peru, just about 150 kilometres from the Pacific Ocean. These sources release glacial seepage, which appears white and flows into a million small tributaries that eventually join larger rivers such as the Caquetá, Madre de Dios, Purus and Tapajós. When these tributaries meet, just south of the Equator, they form the Amazon proper, which reaches 15 kilometres across at its widest point.

The basin drains about seven million kilometres^2 of land. It is the size of the forty-eight contiguous US states. It encompasses about 40 per cent of the South American continent and includes portions of eight South American countries: Brazil, Bolivia, Peru, Ecuador, Colombia, Venezuela, Guyana and Suriname, along with French Guiana. The Amazon River flows for ~6,400 kilometres (slightly less than the Nile, 6,600 kilometres) from its headwaters in the high Andes. Some of the archaeological traditions that I will describe in this book, such as the Polychrome Amazonian ceramics, spread over vast areas comprising thousands of kilometres along the river.

The Amazon River crosses vast rainforests, meanders through the lowlands of Brazil, empties into a massive delta and then joins the Atlantic Ocean. The Amazon carries more water than any other river on Earth. The volume of water is five times greater than that of the Congo and twelve times that of the Mississippi River. During the high-water season, the river's mouth is ~450 kilometres wide, and every day up to 18 billion cubic metres of water flow into the Atlantic. That discharge, equivalent to 209,000 cubic metres of water per second (7.3 million cubic feet/sec), could fill more than 7.2 million Olympic swimming pools every second. It is calculated that 106 million cubic feet of suspended sediment are swept into the ocean daily. Silt deposited at the mouth of the Amazon has created Marajó island, a river island about the size of Switzerland and home to the Marajoara, one of the most sophisticated pre-Columbian cultures in South America.

The various names the Amazon River goes by can be perplexing to newcomers. Although the name Amazon is commonly used to refer to the entire river, it is only properly applied, in Peruvian and Brazilian nomenclature, to some sections of it. From its headwaters in the Andes, where it receives numerous tributaries, down to its confluence with the Ucayali River in Peru, the river is known as Marañón. From the Ucayali River in Peru to the Brazilian border, it is known as Amazonas. The river is known as Solimões from its source in Peru to its meeting with the Negro River in Brazil. Finally, from the Negro River to the Atlantic Ocean, it is known as Amazonas.

The tributaries of the Amazon River have played a major role in transport and trading networks, with more than 1,000 tributaries flowing into the Amazon from the Guiana Highlands, the Brazilian Highlands and the Andes. Six of these tributaries are more than 1,600 kilometres long, and include the Japurá (Caquetá in Colombia), Juruá, Madeira,

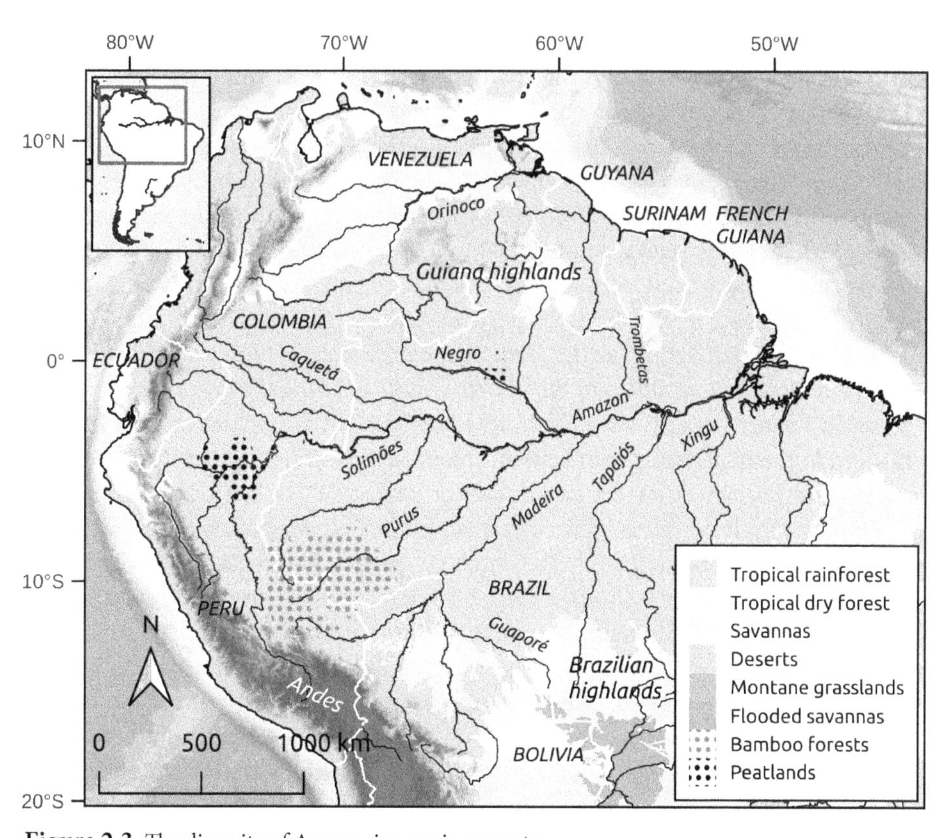

Figure 2.3 The diversity of Amazonian environments.

Negro, Purus and Xingu rivers. The Madeira River is more than 3,000 kilometres from source to mouth.

Amazonia is incredibly biodiverse. At least 30 per cent of all known plant and animal species live in the Amazon, making it the most diverse ecosystem on Earth. It is estimated that there are more than 40,000 plant species, 16,000 tree species, 3,000 fish species, 1,300 bird species, about 430 mammals, more than 1,000 amphibian species and more than 400 reptile species.

The tropical and subtropical lowlands of South America, which encompass a big chunk of the Amazon, are unique when compared with other tropical regions of the world. No major geographical barriers or deserts exist either between or around the tropical forests, as they do in Eurasia or Africa. Across lowland South America, the three major river basins of the Orinoco, Amazon and Rio de la Plata are all geographically integrated. It is unsurprising that many archaeological traditions, such as the Barrancoid, spread from the Caribbean to the Rio de la Plata, as noted early on by Nordenskiöld (1930).

The deep time history of the Amazonian forests

The Amazon and its forest have a long history. Below I only provide a very brief summary. Please refer to Hoorn and Wesselingh (2010), and Dick and Pennington (2019) for detailed reviews. The Amazon basin is a huge structural depression, a subsidence trough that has been filling with enormous amounts of sediment from the Cenozoic age (approximately 65 million years ago). This depression, which flares out to its greatest dimension in the Amazon's upper reaches, lies between two old and relatively low crystalline plateaus, the Guiana Highlands to the north and the Brazilian Highlands to the south. A huge freshwater sea occupied the Amazon basin during the Pliocene Epoch (5.3–2.6 million years ago). Sometime during the Pleistocene Epoch (about 2.6 m–11.7 ka), an outlet to the Atlantic was established, and the great river and its tributaries became deeply entrenched in the former Pliocene seafloor. The modern Amazon and its tributaries flow through a vast network of drowned valleys filled with alluvium. The steep-sided canyons eroded into the Pliocene surface during the lower sea levels, were gradually flooded because of the rise in sea level caused by the melting of the Pleistocene glaciers. In the upper basin – in eastern Colombia, Ecuador, Peru and Bolivia – recent Andean outwash has covered many of the older surfaces.

Tropical forests are some of the oldest land-based ecosystems on the planet, dating back 100 million years to the middle Cretaceous period. Amazonian forests also have a long and dynamic history. Middle Cretaceous Amazonian floras were dominated by non-angiosperm taxa. In contrast, by the Palaeocene, rainforests were dominated by angiosperms and were already populated by the plant families dominant in modern tropical Amazonian rainforests. The Neogene uplift of the Andes changed the drainage system from south–north to west–east, and from rivers predominantly born in the nutrient-depleted Precambrian cratons of South America to rivers coming from the Andes with high levels of nutrients. The cooling trend of the Neogene probably reduced the area available for rainforests (Dick and Pennington, 2019).

Amazonian forests, resources and land use

Describing the various environments and forests present in Amazonia can be quite challenging because of their diversity. One way to differentiate them is by looking at the contrast between *terra firme* upland interfluvial areas and *várzea* floodplains. *Terra firme* makes up about 98 per cent of the Amazon. These areas are older (>1.7 ka and 5.3 million years ago), generally have fewer resources and are less fertile. On the other hand, the *várzea* floodplains cover only 2 per cent of Amazonia, are younger (<11.7 ka), contain more resources and are more fertile. The Amazon *várzea* floodplains can be further distinguished by either white-water high-sediment-load rivers that mostly originate in the Andes, or black-water low-sediment-load rivers that originate in the Brazilian and Guianan Highlands. The *terra firme* uplands can be divided into various vegetation formations, including evergreen and seasonal forests, savannahs, and a diversity of bamboo, palm, liana and peat forests. In the following sections, I will discuss these ecosystems, their resources and the subsistence strategies used by modern indigenous people living in them.

Amazonian floodplains

White water várzeas The *várzea* forests grow alongside rivers that carry abundant sediment and nutrients from the Andes, resulting in waters of various shades of brown. Despite their brown appearance, these rivers are often called white-water rivers (ríos de agua blanca, rios de água branca). *Várzea* forests thrive in the fertile floodplains of white-water rivers, such as the Madeira and the Amazon, which have a constantly changing landscape of lakes, marshes, sandbars, abandoned channels and natural levees. River level fluctuations have a significant impact on the landscape. Large areas become dry from September–January, while from February–July they are covered by 10–20 metres of water. These forests are typically not as tall, diverse or old as those found in *terra firme* and are vulnerable to periodic floods.

Cultivation The soils of the *várzea* forests are probably some of the best in the world for agriculture, since they are replenished every year with sediments rich in nutrients originating in rivers of the Andes. As described by Denevan (2001), residents of the Amazon floodplain today utilize the fertile *várzea* regions and have identified a division of their resources based on both horizontal and vertical zones. Floodplains have many advantages. Agricultural patterns, including labour scheduling, amount of land cropped and crop type, are all linked to water-level variation. The soil texture and fertility vary greatly, allowing for the planting of various crops. For example, river beaches (*playas*) allow for flood-recessional agriculture of fast-growing crops, such as corn, beans, peanuts and squashes, representing a low investment and high yield. The yearly flooding of the *playas* helps control pests and weeds, which means less clearing of land is required and there are fewer crop losses. In addition, during the dry season, turtles lay eggs on the exposed playas, which provides Amazonian people with a vital seasonal source of fat and protein (see below).

Flood-recessional cultivation can also be an unpredictable enterprise. Floodplains are a rich habitat but are high-risk because of the irregularity and variability of flooding. Destructive floods can unexpectedly happen on the tributaries, even during low-water seasons. The rise and fall of the main Amazon River is more predictable, but occasionally extreme floods can still occur. These floods have the potential to fill the entire floodplain, overflow natural levees and damage all crops.

The natural levees, enriched yearly by alluvium, well-drained and covered with high forests, are also some of the most important agricultural areas. Today, the fine-tuning of planting is best exemplified by the cultivation of introduced Old World rice, which is characteristically planted (or transplanted) in progressive steps as the river level drops. Manioc and non-native bananas and plantains now dominate the higher levees, which are usually above flood levels. On the central Amazon, levees allow for plant growing periods of eight months or more.

Permanent tree crops are planted on the non-flooded river terraces, on the highest ground where flooding is rare or brief. In Chapter 6, we will learn that this is the place where we can find large areas of anthrosols (soils created by humans), also referred to as ADEs, which are extremely fertile.

Another characteristic vegetation formation of the *várzea* are the 'islands' of floating grasses, where *Paspalum* grasses dominate. These floating meadows filtrate water and are nurseries for fish. Along with them, large wild rice stands grow along the water's edge. It is unsurprising that native Amazonian people, who collected wild rice using canoes, gradually selected larger grains, leading to the domestication of rice in the middle Holocene (Hilbert et al., 2017) as will be described in Chapter 5.

Hunting and fishing The *várzea* has one of the major concentrations of animal protein for human populations. To date, 2,406 fish species have been identified (Jézéquel et al., 2020), with some scholars in the past estimating that the total number will exceed 3,000 (Goulding, 1980; Gragson, 1992). The *várzeas* are home to the Amazon's largest fish, known as *pirarucu* in Brazil and *paiche* in Peru (*Arapaima gigas*). The number of fish varieties by Amazonian groups varies from twenty (Waiwai groups) to 150 (the Machiguenga), while most groups still rely on 10–30 species (Gragson, 1992). Villages that rely on fishing for protein (such as the Shipibo of eastern Peru) can often grow large and remain completely sedentary because fish are much harder to deplete than game.

Through both historical and ethnographic evidence, it has been shown that indigenous populations have developed various techniques for capturing and storing aquatic resources, adapting to different geographic and seasonal conditions. These techniques include spearing, angling, netting, trapping and even poisoning. Tools such as bows and arrows, harpoons and fish traps are commonly used for both hunting and fishing from blind platforms and canoes (Figure 2.4).

The use of traps, dams and weirs has also been reported, suggesting the possibility of more permanent facilities. Poison obtained from both wild and cultivated plants is often used in shallow waters and small streams in the Amazon. Traps come in different shapes. Conical traps, known in Brazil as *covos* or *matapís*, made from different plants, have

Figure 2.4 Yaulapiti men fishing with bows and arrows from a canoe in the Upper Xingu. Fishing is the most important protein food source for riverine Amazonian people. Alamy.

likely been used since pre-Columbian times (see for example Noelli 1993 for the Tupi). The traps are placed on the banks of the river, on the upstream portion of rapids and falls. The wide mouth has a diameter of up to 2 metres and faces the direction of the water. The fish enter the mouth, go through the narrow neck and have difficulty escaping because of the sharp points aimed inward (Goulding, 1980). Rapids are preferred fishing locations since these is where traps are located, and during the dry season are abundant as pools where fish are trapped when water recedes. It is not uncommon to find large, multicomponent archaeological sites around them.

Another fishing technique involves building large traps or weirs known as *kakurís* to fence off sections of the river. Once the fish are caught within the enclosed area, various tools, such as bows and arrows (Figure 7.4), tridents, harpoons or nets are used to capture them. These big fish traps are especially helpful for maintaining large populations during high-water periods when fishing is less productive. They also serve as helpful storage tanks for the fisheries.

Given a knowledge of spawning and feeding behaviour, fish availability at any one time can be predicted. The fish can be isolated in shallow water and ponds, enabling mass capture to take place. Because of this predictability, Prestes-Carneiro et al. (2021) have contended that rather than the traditional comparison with hunting, the management and consumption of aquatic resources in Amazonia can more accurately be described as husbandry or farming. As we will see in Chapter 7, huge landscape-scale fish weirs were built in the Bolivian Amazon savannahs taking advantage of the spooning behaviour of some fishes that migrate into the savannahs during the floods.

The *várzea* is also characterized by the presence of large aquatic mammals, which provide a stable source of protein, as well as essential lipids and fat calories. The biomass and densities of aquatic mammals and reptiles are many times greater than those of the game available in upland forests. Manatees (*Trichechus inunguis*), capybaras (*Hydrochoerus hydrochaeris*), the world's largest living rodent and giant otters (*Pteronura brasiliensis*) are among them. A single manatee, for example, can produce up to 90 kilograms of meat (Linares, 1976), which is roughly the same as a tapir, the largest terrestrial animal in the forest. Just as fish could be easily trapped in remnant *várzea* lakes and other pools during low water levels, mammals congregating in groups near remnant stands of water could be easily hunted. It is clear that these animals once played important roles in human subsistence along some of Amazonia's major water courses.

Turtles and caimans also represent commonly captured game. In the case of turtles, techniques for their 'live' storage are commonly reported. Early chronicles describe how Amazonian people kept fish and turtles in corrals for food purposes. These structures were made of wooden sticks arranged in a geometric pattern to create an enclosure for the giant South American river turtles. Female turtles captured during their breeding season, on beaches in the dry season, were typically kept in these corrals for later consumption. The enclosures were often described as natural or artificial lakes located in domestic backyards, which were also used as water reservoirs. Reservoir and ponds associated to archaeological sites are typical of Santarem (Chapter 7) and the Casarabe (Chapter 8) cultures. Beyond turtle meat, turtle eggs were and still are a delicacy and a major source of protein and fat along the Amazonian rivers (Figure 2.5).

Techniques for the storage of aquatic resources were also observed. The Siona and Secoya, a Western Tukanoan group living at the Aguarico River, a tributary of the Napo River in Ecuador, smoked turtle eggs to keep them edible for months. Fish and meat could also be preserved in manatee fat or turtle oil, while dried fish was also used for trade. Aboriginal populations were also concerned with the preservation of fisheries. Even today the Tukano, for example, have restricted rules regarding the preservation of the riparian forest, which is an essential food source for aquatic animals (Dufour, 1990). Aquatic resources are considered to have been a major protein source for aboriginal Amazonians, with Carneiro (1970) pointing out that the abundance of aquatic resources encouraged a sedentary life, agricultural development, population growth and complex societies.

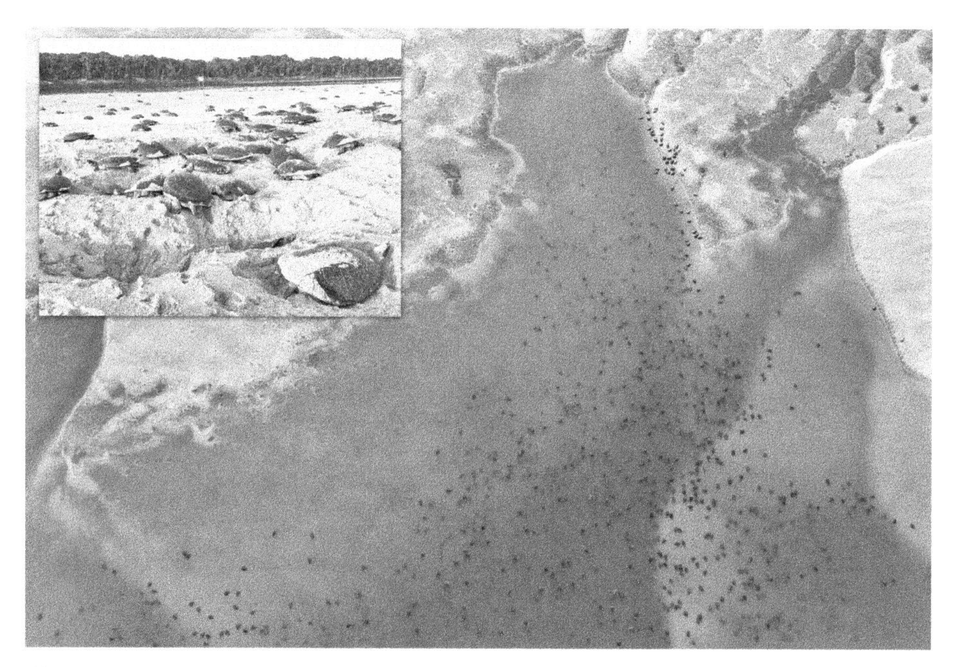

Figure 2.5 Hundreds of giant South American river turtles (*Podocnemis expansa*) gather to lay eggs on the sand beaches of the Guaporé-Itenéz River. They constitute a seasonally abundant source of protein. Courtesy of Christian Gutierrez, Wildlife Conservation Society.

First eyewitness chronicles Given this variety and abundance of resources, it is no surprise that the first eyewitness accounts of journeys along the major Amazonian rivers from the sixteenth to seventeenth centuries describe a plethora of complex, sedentary societies, which were part of vast political territories engaged in large-scale organized warfare (e.g., Medina, 1934; Myers, 1974; Porro, 1994). Some polities occupied long, continuous stretches of the Amazon River, spanning dozens of kilometres, with populations ranging from 800–3,000 people, and with some settlements housing as many as 10,000 people (Denevan, 1996). According to several sources, these 'provinces' were socially stratified units ruled over by a centralized power. Regional and local chiefs, nobles, commoners and subordinate individuals, such as servants and captive slaves were all part of such hierarchies (see summaries in Porro, 1994; Roosevelt, 1999).

Denevan (1976: 217–18) estimated that the lower floodplain had a population density of eight people per kilometre^2 in 1651. Adjusting this figure to take account of the estimated depopulation rate of the first century of contact, Denevan estimated a population of no less than twenty-eight people per kilometre^2 for the lower Amazon floodplain in 1500. Early historical accounts are confirmed by archaeology, which in the last thirty years has revealed large, regionally organized, complex societies living across the Amazonian floodplains (e.g., De Souza et al., 2019; Heckenberger and Neves, 2009; Prümers and Jaimes Betancourt, 2014; Roosevelt, 2013; Rostain and Jaimes

Bentancourt, 2017). This picture vastly differs from the small-scale societies described by anthropologists in the twentieth century, as we will see when we consider in detail the late Holocene pre-Columbian societies living in the Amazonian floodplains in Chapter 7. I now move to the other type of floodplain forest that grows along the blackwater *várzeas*.

Blackwater várzeas Forests found along rivers that rise in the ancient crystalline highlands, classified as either blackwater (Jari, Negro and Tocantins-Araguaia) or clearwater (Trombetas, Xingu and Tapajós), are generally referred to as *igapó*. The blackwater tributaries have higher levels of humic acids (which cause their dark colour) and originate in nutrient-poor, often sandy uplands. They carry little or no silt or dissolved solids. Clearwater tributaries have a higher mineral content and lower levels of humic acids. Blackwater ecosystems, such as those found in the Negro, Vaupés and Içana rivers in the north-west Amazon, represent the poorest and most limited areas of Amazonia. Because of the acidity of the soils and the water, above-ground biomass is smaller, fallen litter is low in nutrients and decomposition is slow.

Vegetation in blackwater habitats is diverse. However, one form of flora is more common in this area than elsewhere in Amazonia: campina, also known as caatinga amazônica. Caatinga grows in humid tropical climates with no dry season, as well as in locations dominated by podzolic soils or spodosols that are prone to waterlogging during and after heavy rains (Moran, 1993). Its vegetation is a dwarfed scrub forest that grows on hydromorphic, quartzy sands, reaching a height of 6–20 metres above ground level. Caatingas are found primarily in the Guianas and portions of the Negro River basin and its tributaries (most notably the Vaupés and the Içana). More minor spots can be found across the Amazon Basin, including Roraima and Serra do Cachimbo.

The stereotype of the Amazonia as an environment characterized by soils too poor and acid to sustain cultivation for more than a year or two, holds true for blackwater river watersheds. Blackwater river soils can vary significantly in growing conditions, but in their extreme forms, they are among the poorest in the world. In nutrient content, they are little different to rainwater. They occur in areas draining mostly white sand soils (spodosols) on which grows xeromorphic vegetation that contrasts both in height and biomass with other areas of Amazonian *terra firme*. The vegetation reminds one more of the scrub forests of the arid Brazilian northeast than an Amazonian landscape. Other kinds of vegetation grow in these basins as well, including tropical upland forests on oxisols occupying the higher ground. This tropical upland forest, however, is not as tall or productive as tropical upland forests elsewhere in Amazonia, where soils are less acidic, less prone to waterlogging and less depleted of nutrients (Moran, 1993). These blackwater habitats are one of the least known archaeologically. Despite that, where archaeological work has been carried out, evidence has been found for a human footprint on these forests with patches of Amazonian anthrosols identified (Franco-Moraes et al., 2019).

These descriptions of clearwater and blackwater rivers mainly apply to the section of the Amazon generally called the middle and lower Amazon. The upper headwaters of the Amazon and the estuary will be described in Chapter 7, along with the major archaeological cultures that developed in these regions during the late Holocene.

Amazonian interfluves

The *terra firme*, which covers more than 4 million kilometres^2, makes up 98 per cent of the Amazon Basin, and has a wide range of habitats. As archaeologists aim to study the diverse cultures across the basin, it is important to move beyond the *várzea-terra firme* redux and to differentiate Amazonia's individual ecosystems, each with its own unique characteristics. Before we describe these vegetation formations, let us begin by describing upland soils.

Upland soils

Despite the lush rainforest vegetation, much of the Amazonian region has notoriously infertile soils. Appearances are often deceptive and the early European settlers in the tropics were convinced that the dense vegetation was because of the rich soils. Hence, they cleared large forest areas to make way for croplands. The cleared land supported vigorous agricultural growth for one to four years before plant growth mysteriously declined to the point where copious amounts of fertiliser were required for any growth. Settlers were perplexed as to why their crops failed and how such poor soil could support the lush growth of tropical rainforests. The answer lies in the rainforest's rapid nutrient cycling. Unlike their temperate forest counterparts, where most nutrients exist in the soil, in most tropical forests, nutrients liberated by plant decomposition are mobilized not into mineral soil but directly back into the plants via interactions between fungi and mycorrhizae (major organic matter decomposers) that live on the above-ground root layer (see below).

Along the vast expanses of *terra firme*, the soils are typically deep, reddish, exhibit low pH, have a high proportion of exchangeable aluminium and contain low levels of critical soil nutrients, such as P, K, Ca, Mg, Su and Zn. These are the pre-Cambrian geological epoch's old soils, whose sediments have been weathered for hundreds of millions of years. No glaciers have eroded them, nor have volcanoes replenished them with ash – except for in the montane forest of the eastern slope of the Andes (see Chapter 8). These are the oxisols (also known as Ferrasols and Latosols), which are deep, generally well-drained, red or yellow in colour, and with excellent structure and little horizon differentiation. As vegetation dies, the nutrients are rapidly broken down and almost immediately returned to the system as living plants take them up. A unique relationship between the roots and the mycorrhizal fungi facilitates the uptake of nutrients by plant roots. The mycorrhizae attach to plant roots and are specialized to increase the efficiency of nutrient uptake from the soil. In return, plants provide the fungi with sugars and shelter among their roots. Studies have also shown that mycorrhizae can help a tree resist drought and disease.

Oxisols are most commonly found in areas geologically influenced by the Guiana and Brazilian shields, which date to the Archean and Paleozoic periods, and are composed of granite, gneiss and some sandstones. Ultisols are similar to oxisols but exhibit a noticeable increase in clay content with depth, which oxisols do not have. They are formed from

Tertiary alluvial materials (445–1,200 million years ago). Between oxisols and ultisols, there are patches of alfisols.

Because of their similar colour and structure, alfisols are easily confused with oxisols and ultisols. But they are not acidic, have little exchangeable aluminium, and are nutrient-rich. Geologically, they are derived from basaltic outcrops that are rich in bases and less weathered than the surrounding materials. Alfisols are also known as *terra roxa estruturada eutrofica*, luvisols and eutric nitosols. The Lower Xingu, Lower Tapajós and Lower Tocantins rivers have the highest concentrations of alfisols. As we will see later, particularly in Chapter 6, these poor soils were transformed by the Amazonian people to create the fertile anthrosols known as ADEs – constituting some of the most fertile soils on Earth. Following this brief digression to describe Amazonian upland soils, I now proceed with the description of Amazonian interfluvial forests and their resources. They range from the large expanses of evergreen forests, seasonal forests and savannahs, to more localized forests growing on pre-Cambrian shield rock outcrops, as well as forests dominated by specific plants (bamboo, palms, lianas, Brazil nut trees) or determined by hydrological conditions (peat and mangroves).

Evergreen forests

Tropical evergreen forests mostly cover the Amazon. These forests receive more than 3,000 millimetres of rain annually, with a fairly even monthly distribution of at least 100 millimetres. Evergreen forests make up at least two-thirds of the Amazonian forests, including the wettest areas on the eastern slopes of the Andes, the coastal strip of south-eastern Brazil, the Venezuelan Amazon and a significant portion of the Guianas (Moran, 1993). These are known as the most species-rich forest areas, some of which can reach up to 102 species per hectare (Gentry, 1988). Despite this huge species richness, current studies show that of the estimated 16,000 tree species in Amazonia, 222 cover 50 per cent of the land, the so-called hyperdominants, and that edible species are five times more likely to be hyperdominant than non-edible ones (see Chapter 4) (Levis et al., 2017; Ter Steege et al., 2013).

Seasonal forests

Interfluves are not only covered in evergreen and semi-evergreen forests. The Amazon is also home to seasonal forests. Seasonally dry tropical forest occurs when annual rainfall is less than 1,600 millimetres, and at least 5–6 months of the year receives less than 100 millimetres of rainfall (Gentry, 1995). Seasonally dry tropical forests grow on fertile soils, and have a smaller stature and lower basal area than tropical rainforests. The woody floras are mainly composed of the Leguminosae and Bignoniaceae families, the ground flora has few grasses, and its vegetation is mostly deciduous during the dry season. Before recent human intervention, it was estimated that more than 50 per cent of Central American and up to 25 per cent of South American forests were deciduous and semi-evergreen forests. The forests thrive on fertile soils, with moderate to high pH and nutrient levels but low levels of aluminium. The value of these soils for agriculture has led to the widespread destruction of much of the forest. Less than 2 per cent of seasonally dry forests on Mesoamerica's Pacific coast are still intact. In Amazonia, they are located mainly around the Amazon basin, but can also be found near the mouths of the Amazon's southern tributaries, such as the Tapajós and Xingu (see summary in Pennington et al., 2006).

Piperno and Pearsall (1998) presented a coherent argument for the significance of seasonal forests in relation to early human settlement and the origins of plant domestication based on the following tenets. Firstly, the wild ancestors of many important crop plants appear to have grown in these forests. Tuberous plants, for example, rich in edible starch for human consumption, appear to be much more common in the seasonal forest than elsewhere. The underground tuber is an organ that has evolved in part to store energy during the long, dry season. Secondly, soils are more fertile in seasonal forests. Thirdly, vegetation is less dense and, therefore easier to cut with stone axes. Fourthly, burning vegetation for field preparation is much simpler in a seasonal forest than in a permanently humid environment. This is because of the long and distinct dry season, the openness of the forest, and the fact that vegetation is lower and the forest is more simply structured. Finally, weeds and other agricultural pests are less of a problem in a drier climate, such as that of the seasonal forest.

Savannahs

The Amazon region includes savannahs that fit the criteria of a true savannah, characterized by a dry season of at least three months and a grass layer that can easily catch fire and cause outbreaks. During the rainy season, most savannahs experience some form of waterlogging. Many are hyper-seasonal, facing some form of water excess in the rainy season, primarily because of soil waterlogging caused either by poor drainage or by floods. These savannahs, such as the Llanos de Mojos, are extremely flat, with an average slope of 0.2 metres per kilometre. Surprisingly, as we shall see in Chapter 8, some of the most complex societies developed in these challenging environments, such as in the Llanos de Mojos, and reached low-density urban proportions. Many seasonally flooded savannahs across Amazonia were transformed into agricultural and aquacultural (landscape-scale fish weirs) landscapes (Chapter 7). Woodland savannahs, such as the one shown in Figure 2.6d of the Santa Ana region in the Llanos de Mojos are also common in some parts of Amazonia.

Other forests

Within these forests and savannahs that cover large areas of Amazonia, other forests grow within a particular rock, soil environment or hydrological conditions. Examples are the forests growing on the table-top hills of the pre-Cambrian shield (*tepuis*), the mangrove forests along the Atlantic coast and forests growing on impoverished soils of white sand formations. There are also peatlands. In addition, some *terra firme* forests,

Figure 2.6 Amazonian forests. *a*. Palm (*Attalea* sp.) forest on Triunfo ADE site (Itenéz Province, Bolivian Amazon). *b*. Bamboo (*Guadua* sp.) forest of Acre (Brazil). *c*. Brazil nut (*Bertholethia excelsia*) trees surviving on deforested pasture in Acre, Brazil. *d*. Cerrado (Santa Ana, Bolivia). *e*. cacao (*Theobroma cacao*) forest (Riberalta, Bolivia). *f*. Evergreen forest at Vila America overlooking the Tapajó River estuary in the background. *g*. Savannah palm forest (Brazil). *e*. courtesy Jennifer Watling; *g*. Wikicommons.

many of which are cultural forests, are dominated by plants of economic importance, such as bamboo, palms, Brazil nuts and lianas (Figure 2.6). We describe these vegetation formations succinctly below.

Tepuis The isolated, flat-topped rock outcrops, called *tepuis*, meaning 'house of the gods' in the native tongue of the Pemon indigenous people of the Venezuelan savannahs, are particularly visible throughout the Guiana Shield's chain of sandstone highlands, and on the tops of the numerous inselbergs of both the Brazilian and Guiana Shields. The *tepuis* are formed of the steep slopes and plateaus of the massive Palaeozoic sandstones overlying the Guiana Shield (Figure 3.4). Scrublands, meadows and open rock habitats featuring orchids, bromeliads and *Drosera* spp. dominate the higher part of *tepuis*, while palms dominate the slopes, piedmont and forests surrounding them. As we will see in Chapter 3, some of the first evidence of human habitation in the Amazon region is found in rock shelters on *tepuis*. The first humans to arrive in Amazonia appear to have used these rock walls as a canvas for their early works of art.

Mangroves Extensive tracts of mangrove forests run almost uninterrupted from the Brazilian island of São Luis to the Venezuelan Orinoco Delta. At the mouth of the Amazon, about 10,700 kilometres^2 of mangroves occur along 1,800 kilometres of the northern coast in the states of Amapá, Pará and Maranhão, Brazil, which can penetrate inland as far as 40 kilometres, gradually blending with flooded forests. This was, nevertheless, a very dynamic environment. According to a summary of pollen, carbon and nitrogen isotope records by Cohen et al. (2012), the Amazon mangrove belt is a result of rising sea levels after the last glacial period. From 8.8–2.3 ka, the marine influence was more extensive on the Amazon coast, while mangroves were replaced by freshwater vegetation near the Amazon in the late Holocene. The shell-middens of the Mina Tradition, who manufactured the first ceramics in the continent, developed in areas near the mangrove forests that were more prevalent during the early Holocene (see Chapter 5).

Peatlands The Amazon also contains large extensions of peat, that is, soil that contains at least 30 per cent of dead organic material, where a lack of oxygen in the waterlogged soil allows dead vegetation to accumulate without completely decomposing. Peatlands exist at the bottom of the Amazon basin, at elevations so low there is nowhere for the water to drain after the annual torrential rainfall. Current studies show that some of these peatlands, such as Peru's Pastaza-Marañon foreland basin, cover an area the size of Belgium and are at least 12,000 years old (Figure 2.3) (Wang et al., 2018). The mapping of peatlands in Amazonia is an ongoing process, with new areas being mapped continuously (e.g., Hastie et al., 2022). Alarmingly, the impact of climate change on Amazon peatlands could potentially change their role from being carbon sinks to becoming carbon sources. Archaeologically, peatlands are among the least studied regions in Amazonia.

Bamboo forests Notably, some interfluvial forests are dominated by plants of economic importance, such as bamboo, palms and Brazil nuts. Native Amazonians rely on woody bamboo for construction materials, as well as using it for making hunting and fishing arrows, and musical instruments, such as flutes. In the south-western Amazon, the woody bamboos *Guadua weberbaueri* and *G. sarcocarpa* dominate forests over a large area (161,500 kilometres^2), which coincides with the Fitzcarrald arch geomorphological formation – a broad NE–SE high dome against the Central Andes with a radial drainage network into the south-western Amazon (Figure 2.3, 2.6b) (Carvalho et al., 2013). In the south-eastern sector of Acre state, Brazil, one of the most fascinating ceremonial landscapes of Amazonia, was constructed more than 2,000 years ago. The landscape comprises more than 500 geometrically patterned earthworks, known as geoglyphs (each the size of Avebury henge). There has been a debate about whether bamboo forests have an anthropic nature. Palaeoecological data does not show a clear human footprint on these forests, which grew in the region at least six millennia before the arrival of the geoglyph builders (McMichael et al., 2014b; Watling et al., 2017). In other parts of Amazonia, the growth of bamboo forests appears to have resulted from human activities. Work in Maranhao by Balée (1989), shows that the Guajá Indians now inhabit bamboo forests that were previously occupied by the Guajajara of the Pindaré River region, which points to the role of humans in their spread. As we will see in the next chapter, debates about the nature and temporal depth of these cultural forests are issues that can be resolved with the palaeo sciences.

Figure 2.7 Palms in rock art. *a*. Desenhos site (Peruaçu, Brazil), possible *Mauritia flexuosa*. *b*. Chiribiquete, likely *Attalea* sp. *a*. courtesy of Renato Kipnis; *b*. courtesy of Fernando Montejo.

Palm forests Many forests dominated by palms occur across Amazonia. There is a wealth of ethnobotanical information showing how people today cultivate and manage palms (e.g., Balick 1984; Bernal et al., 2011). For example, during his ethnobotanical research with the Guajá, Tembé and Urub Ka'apor in the eastern parts of Pará and the north of Maranho, Balée (2013) measured forests of managed *babassu* (*Attalea phalerata*) that covered a total extent of up to 3 hectares. Similarly, as shown by Coimbra (1989), the Surui Indians of Rondônia's Aripuan Reservation use sandy, low-fertility soils that are never farmed to cultivate *babassu* palms (Coimbra Jr, 1989). Forests dominated by babassu are typical of ADEs in the Bolivian Amazon (Figure 2.6a), and tucumã (*Astrocaryum vulgare*) in the ADEs across the basin, whose origins are anthropogenic and pre-Columbian as shown by palaeoecology, closely integrated with archaeology (Iriarte et al., 2021; Maezumi et al., 2018; 2022). Palms that are well adapted to waterlogged conditions, such as *buruti* (*Mauritia flexuosa*) and *acai* (*Euterpe* spp.) dominate wetlands and estuaries. Palm dominated forests also occur over seasonally flooded savannahs (Figure 2.6g). Today, local populations manage or plant palms in these wetlands areas, but it is challenging to determine the extent of human involvement in their past growth since they are wetland obligates. Chapters 4 and 6 will delve into the use of multi-proxy analysis to compare fossil and modern records, an approach that, as we will see, can provide an insight into the lasting impact of past land use on current flora.

Brazil nut and cacao forests Forests dominated by Brazil nuts (*Bertholletia excelsa*) are also common in the Brazilian Amazon (Figure 2.6c). In many regions of the Bolivian Amazon, Brazil nut forests typically occupy Amazonian anthrosols (specifically ABE, see Chapter 6), and are usually accompanied by dense stands of cacao (*Theobroma cacao*) (Figure 2.6e). In some areas, where mapping studies have been carried out, such as in the Lower Tocantins, Brazil nut trees have been shown to cover approximately 8,000 kilometres^2. Significant areas have also been observed in Amapá, the Jari River basin and Rondônia. Kayapó Gorotire plant Brazil nut trees because they attract game and provide food for the human population (Anderson and Posey, 1989; Shepard and Ramirez, 2011). Brazil nut tree cultivation requires light, which means humans likely play a key role in spreading these forests across Amazonia (Caetano Andrade et al., 2019).

Liana forests Liana forests are another clear indicator of former human occupation. For those of us who walk the rainforest searching for archaeological sites, it is easy to identify areas of former habitation or cultivation because of the difficulty of walking through the thickets of vegetation, dominated by lianas, which characterize abandoned Amazonian anthrosols. The distinction is also easily visible in satellite photos (Robinson et al., 2020). Because of the high density of vines and lianas, liana forests have a smaller basal area than upland forests, with only 18–24 metres^2/hectare, as opposed to the 40 metres^2/hectare found in 'virgin' upland forests (Pires and Prance, 1985). Plants of economic utility are unusually concentrated in liana forests, as noted by Balée's (1989)

Figure 2.8 Slash and burn plot, French Guiana. Wayapi woman carrying a basket with manioc recently collected from this field. Alamy.

ethnobotanical inventories compiled among the Assurini and Arawate. These plants include food (*babaçu*, Theobroma, Brazil nuts), fruits attractive to game (*Eschweilera coriacea*, *Euterpe oleracea*), building materials (*Unonopsis guatterioides*, babaçu), implement materials and medicinal plants (Cenostigma, e.g., *Alexa imperatricis* for toothache).

Cultivation

Our knowledge of indigenous adaptations to the *terra firme* is based primarily on present-day observations. Today's indigenous agriculture is characterized by short cropping/long-fallow shifting cultivation, and low-protein crop staples (manioc, sweet potato, plantain), in association with small, temporary settlements (*c.* 10–100 people) and very low population densities (below 0.5/ kilometre^2) (Figure 2.8). As we will see in Chapters 7 and 8, this was very different in the past.

In the wettest areas of the Upper Amazon, a variation of slash-and-burn shifting cultivation is carried out. This is 'slash/mulch', also known as *tapado (covered)* or *tala y pudre (slash and rot)*. In this system, the vegetation cut for a clearing (slash) is not burned but instead is allowed to decompose (mulch). Although this is a slow process, resulting in less space available for crops, a larger portion of organic matter returns to the soil than with burning. The system protects the soil, reduces erosion, conserves moisture, reduces soil temperatures, and inhibits weed growth, weeds and pests; however, yields are lower. The system can be sustainable with periodic addition of new mulch from weeds and brush, with only short fallows. Most examples occur in very wet regions, where conditions during the dry period are too inadequate to allow for a good burn. Contemporary examples, both indigenous and traditional, occur in the Chocó of Pacific Colombia, Guanare in Venezuela, coastal Ecuador and some parts of Amazonia (e.g., Rival, 1998; Zurita-Benavides).

Hunting, fishing and gathering

Terra firme forests are home to various animals that dwell on the ground: rodents, such as capybaras (*Hydrochoerus hydrochaeris*), agoutis (*Dasyprocta* spp.) and pacas (*Cuniculus paca*); as well as coatis (a carnivorous raccoon-like animal) (*Nasua nasua*), armadillos (*Dasypodidae*) and rabbits (*Leporidae*). Most of these animals are solitary foragers or prefer small family groups to large gatherings. White-lipped peccaries (*Tayassuidae*), however, are known to travel in groups of more than 100 individuals. The brocket deer and the paca are nocturnal animals. The Amazon basin is believed to have the highest number of primate species in the New World. These primates, along with other tree-living species, make up more than half of the forest's mammal population (Eisenberg and Redford, 1989). The rock art adorning the walls of La Lindosa, in the Colombian Amazon, beautifully illustrates the region's diverse and captivating wildlife (Iriarte et al., 2022). As we will also see in the next section, Amazonian people have a particular way of interacting with animals that is completely foreign to most Westerners.

Regarding nutrition, hunting, fishing and collecting activities provide important sources of dietary protein, fat and other nutrients that are necessary supplements to the carbohydrates obtained from plants. Amazonians hunt a wide range of animals, but the most important are primates and rodents (Redford and Robinson, 1987). Large primates, particularly spider monkeys (*Ateles* spp.) and woolly monkeys (*Lagothrix* spp.), are some of the most highly valued animals among Amazonian groups. In general, individual hunting is most common because a group of hunters moving together in the forest tends to scare away the game. However, exceptions do occur. When hunting herd animals, such as the white-lipped peccary, having a large number of hunters may increase the chances of success. For arboreal game, the blowgun is one of the most effective hunting devices. To be effective against the tree-dwelling game, this weapon requires a potent poison, such as *curare*. *Curare* is a type of arrow poison from South America that comes from various substances, which are extracted from plants, such as Menispermaceae, Loganiaceae and *Anomospermum grandiflora.* It alters the structure or function of the nervous system and acts as a muscle relaxant, which causes a wounded animal to be paralyzed and fall easily from the trees. A glue-like toxic secretion released on the skin of a giant monkey frog (*Phyllomedusa bicolor*) can also be applied to blow darts, causing animals to be paralyzed and can even cause the death of small rodents (Figure 2.9).

Figure 2.9 Huaorani man using the blowgun to hunt woolly monkeys in the Ecuadorian Amazon. Alamy.

In horticultural societies, slash-and-burn plots play a major role in attracting game, most notably rodents, peccary and deer (Linares, 1976). This so-called 'gardening hunting' can account for a large proportion of the hunted animals. Tukanoan women, for example, plant extra sweet cassava for the small agouti rodent (*Dasyprocta punctada*) and only complain when 'he' appears to be eating more than 'his' share. During a three-month observation period in 1977 by Dufour (1990), this rodent accounted for more than 20 per cent of all animals killed, and women hunting in gardens with dogs were responsible for nearly half of all kills. Similarly, it has been observed that the Kayapo intentionally spread out their gardens to draw in the game throughout a wide region. Consequently, Posey (1985) proposed renaming old swiddens 'game-farm-orchards'. 'Garden hunting' is as much a matter of obtaining protein as of pest control (Shepard Jr et al., 2012).

One of the most effective fishing techniques in small *terra firme* streams is poisoning the waters with a vine called *barbasco*. This technique involves extracting vines' narcotic sap by pounding its cuttings in water (*Lonchocarpus utilis* and others' crushed roots, stems, and/or the leaves of various wild and cultivated plants). Large fish catches can be harvested from the poisoned waters of lagoons, dead arms of *igarapés* (small streams in Amazonia that are fed by rainwater and cut through the terra firme).

Collecting insects is also common. Ants (especially *Atta* spp.), termites, and larvae of both Coleoptera (especially Buprestidae, Curculionidae, and Scarabaeidae) and Lepidoptera are the most commonly collected and consumed insects. Tukanoans consume ants and termites at a slow but consistent rate. Nests are never destroyed, and some colonies in prime locations are actively guarded. Palm weevils (Curculionidae) are a managed resource: palms are cut with the expectation that weevils will invade and the larvae will be harvested later (see subsistence of tropical hunter-gatherers in the following chapter).

First eyewitness chronicles

The first European eyewitness accounts also describe how the complex societies of the floodplains spread throughout the mainland via elaborated road systems, with large interfluvial populations organized as interconnected polities and villages of 1,000 people not uncommon (Eder, [1772] 1985; Medina, 1934; Pires de Campos, 1862). Recent archaeological research, described in the coming chapters, backs up these accounts. It undermines the assumption that upland areas were marginal in relation to past human impact and the development of complex societies (de Souza et al., 2018; Franco-Moraes et al., 2019; Heckenberger et al., 2008; Paz-Rivera and Putz, 2009; Stenborg, 2016). Some interfluvial areas may have been low-density urban areas, similar to those found in other tropical regions (Heckenberger et al., 2008).

Amazon people: Cultures and languages

The diversity of Amazonian people rivals the diversity of Amazonian forests and environments described above. And the Amazon is not alone. The coincidence of biological and cultural diversity are most concentrated in tropical rainforests, particularly in megadiversity countries such as Brazil and Colombia, but also Mexico, Congo, Madagascar, Indonesia, and Papua New Guinea (e.g., Sponsel, 2021). Today's Amazonia population is a mosaic of indigenous and immigrant peoples from all of the constituent countries. It is difficult to get an accurate count of the Amazon basin's indigenous population. Still, estimates put the number at around 20 million living in eight different Amazonian countries and the Department of French Guiana (France). Several dozen groups also still live voluntarily in isolation, the 'uncontacted tribes', mainly in Brazil and Peru.

The Amazon is home to more than 3,000 distinct indigenous territories, which cover about one-third of the basin. When national parks and protected areas are included, roughly half of Amazonia is under some form of management or protection. Based on quantitative satellite data, Nepstad et al. (2006) concluded that deforestation and the occurrence of fires was significantly lower inside the perimeter of parks and demarcated indigenous lands. A fact that can be seen in Figure 10.2, showing how parks and indigenous reserves in the Amazon are critical to helping slow the pace of deforestation.

The rural peasantry of Amazonia, called *caboclos*, comprised of the descendants of native Indians, African slaves and Portuguese colonists, constitute a sizable portion of the Amazonian population today. They are now the principal inhabitants of *várzeas*. Even though caboclo communities rely on both traditional forest products and industrialized goods obtained from city markets, they retain some traditional knowledge that is instructive about the relationships between human societies and the tropical forest environment. The *colonos*, or colonists, are the newest arrivals in the Amazon rainforests. *Colonos* are subsistence farmers who have gone, and continue to go, to the Amazon as part of government-sponsored resettlement programmes. When most people arrive in the Amazon, they see the rainforest for the first time and, understandably, have little knowledge of how to make a living in it (Moran, 1993).

The number of ethnic groups in Amazonia is poorly quantified, but most scholars (e.g., Quijano-Vallejos et al., (2020) and UNICEF (2009)) agree on about 200–385 ethnic groups. A large number have vanished as a result of the arrival of Europeans. To give an example, half a century ago, Ribeiro (1970) estimated that eighty-eight ethnic groups disappeared in the first half of the twentieth century in the Brazilian Amazon. An estimated 1,500 languages were spoken in South America at the time of contact, 350 of which are still in use today.

Amazonia is one of the world's least known and least understood linguistic regions (Aikhenvald, 2012). Home to more than 300 indigenous languages, Amazonia has ten times the diversity of language families as Eurasia and Africa, and is only rivalled by New Guinea. It is often described as a linguistic puzzle, where no single linguistic family dominates the area at a large scale in the way Indo-European does in Europe, or Bantu in sub-Saharan Africa.

Despite the lack of geographical barriers, Amazonia has a large number of isolates (languages that cannot be classified into larger language families, such as the Basque in Europe) that are fairly locally contained. Beyond the isolates are four large, relatively

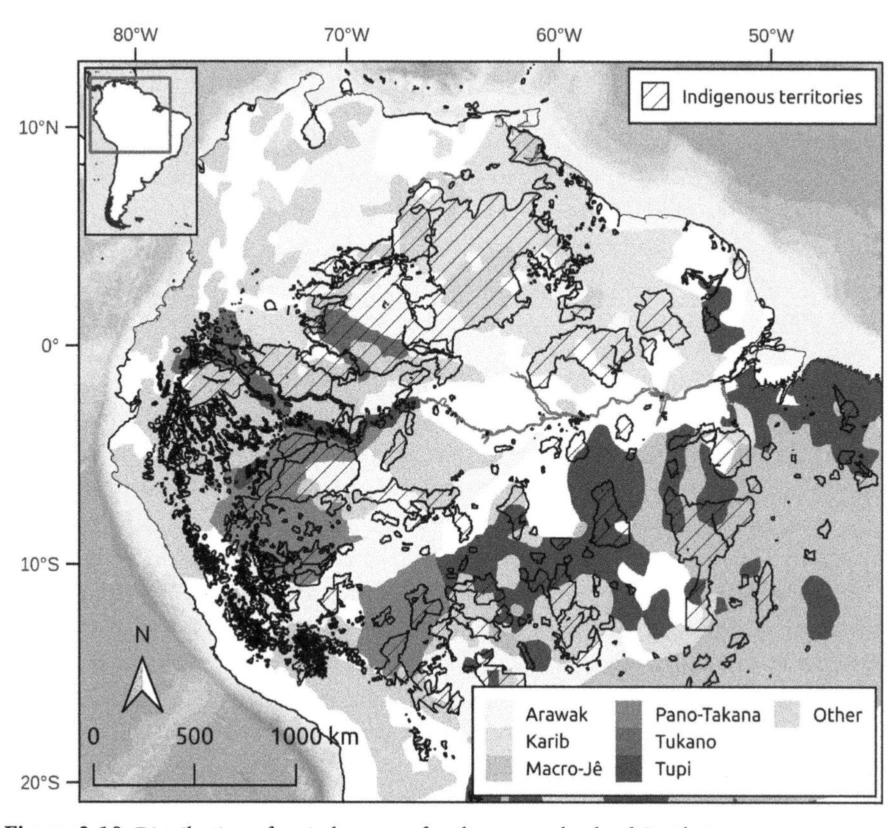

Figure 2.10 Distribution of main language families across lowland South America.

widespread, languages families: the Carib, Macro-Jê, Tupi-Guarani and Arawak. Tukanoan and Panoan are some exceptions to this pattern. Large language families are not contiguous, as shown in Figure 2.10. The Carib comprises about twenty-five languages spoken in South America, including Brazil, Suriname, French Guiana, Guyana, Colombia and Venezuela. The greatest linguistic diversity occurs in the Guiana highlands, which points to this region as the potential homeland. The Incise-Punctate Tradition (IPT), which flourished in the middle-lower Amazon about 900 CE, is usually associated with Carib-speaking people (Figure 7.1). The Macro-Jê languages are mostly found in central Brazil and are mainly represented by the Kayapó, Xavante and Timbira. They live in the Cerrado scrubland savannahs, conduct relay races while carrying heavy logs on their shoulders, their preferred weapon is a club, and they live in large circular villages. The Macro-Jê are associated with the Una Tradition. The Arawak and the Tupi-Guarani have broad distribution across the Amazon basin and beyond (Gregorio de Souza et al., 2020).

Ethnographers and archaeologists have postulated that some of these language families have specific and widely shared cultural characteristics, many of which appear to have archaeological correlates that allow us to trace them over time. Two of them, the Arawak and the Tupi, have been the most studied, and are briefly described below.

The Arawak: The lowland 'high culture'

Arawak is a geographically dispersed language family that spans lowland South America from Argentina to the Bahamas, and from the Amazon River's mouth to the foothills of the Andes (see Figure 2.10). Arawak societies can be found in many different ecosystems, including the lowland Amazonia, the Andes, the Caribbean, central Brazil's dry forests, the savannahs of Colombia, and Venezuela and Bolivia. Ethnographers have identified a number of cultural practices that, with a few variations, are unique to the Arawak people. These include socio-political alliances with ethnolinguistically distant peoples, a strong emphasis on religion, social hierarchy and descent, domesticated landscapes, central public spaces represented by circular plaza villages and towns, intensive agriculture and limited endo-warfare. The latter aspect contrasts with the cycles of vendetta and within-group warfare common among many lowland Amazonians. In multiple locations across the Amazon, Arawak identity appears to be based on control of fertile floodplains and riverine trade routes, which Hornborg (2005) argues must have played a crucial role in the emergence of regional exchange systems in pre-Columbian Amazonia. Based on these sophisticated cultural norms, Schmitd (1917) argues that the Arawak represent a lowland 'high culture'.

The connection of language and material culture, in particular ceramics, has a long history in Amazonian archaeology. Lathrap (1970) proposed a correlation between Barrancoid ceramics and groups speaking Arawakan languages. Heckenberger (2002) refined this hypothesis beyond ceramics, enlarging the number of Arawak archaeological correlates to include nucleated circular villages, concentric orientations and a settlement pattern clearly linked to the first Arawakan occupations in the Caribbean islands, as well as regional polities, connected by a network of river and terrestrial roads. In a process that Heckenberger (2002) has called the Arawakan diaspora, he proposes a process of Arawakan dispersion associated with early manioc agriculturalists at the start of the second millennium before the present. According to historical linguistics, proto-Arawakans began to diverge around 3 ka or earlier (Urban, 1992). The exact origin area is not known for certain, but Aikhenvald (2012) believes it may have been in the north-west Amazon, following the tendency for the greatest language diversity to occur in this geographical area. However, Lathrap (1970), and Walker and Riberio (2011) believe the origin area to have been western Amazonia. According to Heckenberger's (2002) reconstruction, the Arawak languages originated in the north-west Amazon, along the rivers between the Solimões River in Brazil and the middle Orinoco River in Venezuela. Arawak languages diverged as groups spread out before 3 ka, moving northward along the Orinoco drainage area and southward to the confluence of the Solimões and Negro rivers between 1000–500 CE. By 500 CE, speakers of Arawak languages were moving down the Amazon and upstream along the Amazon's major tributaries, such as the Ucayali in the Peruvian Amazon. Recently, de Souza (2020) has proposed that the Saladoid-Barrancoid material culture, which includes the Saladoid and Barrancoid series of the Orinoco, as well as the Pocó and Açutuba complexes of central Amazonia (Figure 7.1), spread from the Orinoco around 4.6 ka. It expanded throughout most of the Amazon by around 3.4–2.9 ka, except for the southern limits of the basin, which were settled around 1 ka. These Saladoid-Barrancoid occupations are associated with the initial formation of Amazonian anthrosols, marking the first settlement of areas where hunter-gatherer sites are scarce or absent, such as in the Central Amazon or the Upper Xingu (see Chapters 7 and 8). According to Souza and collaborators (2020), their dispersal may have been triggered by the successful development of agriculture following an interval of drought in the middle Holocene.

The Tupi

The Tupi (or Tupían) language family comprises more than forty languages, divided into ten subgroups. It was the *lingua franca*, the *Nheengatu* or *Lingua Geral* spoken across lowland South America during colonial times, a Tupi dialect with some Portuguese influence. During the first centuries of colonization in Brazil, this language was so popular that it was prohibited by an edict issued in 1757 by the governor of Grão Pará, Francisco Xavier de Mendonça Furtado.

The highest genetic diversity within the family is found in the south-western Amazon, with half of the subgroups restricted to the Brazilian state of Rondônia, the most probable homeland of the Tupi. The Tupi expansion has its material correlate in the appearance of polychrome and corrugated pottery outside of the Amazon (Figure 7.1), typically accompanied by secondary burials in urns, lip plugs and archaeological sites characterized by patches of anthrosols. This material culture package was conventionally called the 'Tupiguarani Tradition', in reference to the Tupi-Guarani languages. Originally, two ceramic styles were recognized, corresponding to the Tupinambá (Atlantic coast) and Guarani (Paraná Basin) branches. More recently, however, other regional styles have been identified. Because of the uncertainties in the regional subdivisions, and to avoid association with particular groups, we will refer to the whole archaeological complex as Tupi (Gregorio de Souza et al., 2021; Iriarte et al., 2017; Noelli, 1998).

As recently summarized in Souza et al. (2021), the first archaeological models for the Tupi-Guarani dispersal assumed an initial split in the central Amazon, with parallel expansion routes along the Atlantic coast and the Paraná Basin, corresponding to the two branches that effectively left the Amazon: the Tupinamba and Guarani, respectively. Later archaeological models shifted the hypothetical Tupi-Guarani homeland to the south-western Amazon, based on the linguistic evidence for the Tupi family as a whole. The Tupi-Guarani languages, however, have their highest diversity in the eastern Amazon. Archaeological models that incorporate this information suggest a southward migration of the Guarani along the Paraná basin headwaters, near central Brazil, or a return of that branch to the south-western Amazon before its southward displacement. According to glottochronological estimates, the Tupi started to diverge ~5 ka. The Tupi-Guarani subgroup is much shallower, with estimates of its initial split varying between ~2.5–1 ka.

The late Holocene expansion of the Tupi-Guarani languages from southern Amazonia to SE South America constitutes one of the largest expansions of any language family in the world, spanning ~4000 kilometres between latitudes 0°S and 35°S at approximately 2.5 ka. This topic has attracted a great deal of archaeological research over several decades. In

SE South America, historically recorded Tupi-Guarani groups were organized into regional chiefdoms, with war expeditions travelling hundreds of kilometres along major waterways to attack enemies, conquer territories, capture women and, in some cases, enslave the defeated. Unlike other Amazonian language expansions that seem to have spread through trade and a peaceful ethos (e.g., Arawak), historical Tupi-Guarani groups have long been perceived as bent on expansion and conquest. Almost all archaeological sites are found in forests near navigable rivers, where the Tupi-Guarani lived in large, palisaded villages. They practised agroforestry polyculture, complemented by fishing, hunting and gathering. Forest management was a key component of the Tupi-Guarani economy (Noelli, 1993). Their expansion brought about the widespread adoption of agriculture in SE South America, with a dozen varieties of manioc, maize, beans, sweet potato and yam. The cause of this huge human expansion remains a matter of debate in New World archaeology, bioarchaeology, genetics and linguistics. The explanation for the Tupi-Guarani dispersal from the Amazon has generally been linked to agriculture-driven population growth, coupled with strong territoriality, far-reaching political networks and an expansive warrior ideology. Lately, colleagues and I (2017), synthesizing and analysing the radiocarbon dates of about 200 Tupi sites and comparing them with more than seventy palaeoecological records of southern Amazonia, in what appears to be a clear example of ecological opportunism, proposed that the expansion of forests as a result of the more humid climate during the late Holocene, may have facilitated the spread of these tropical agriculturalists out of Amazonia. This is not to say, however, that the complex political organization of the Tupi-Guarani, along with their long-distance village network and warlike ethos, did not play a significant role. Still, current data suggest that climate change may have been the trigger for Tupi-Guarani expansion over the broad temporal (millennial) and spatial (subcontinental) scales of our study.

Multi-lingual regional interactions

Although anthropologists and archaeologists generally see the cultures they study as bounded entities, many researchers have also stressed that multilingual regional systems typically characterize Amazonia. This refers to regions where there is regular interaction, revolving around marriage patterns and trading relationships, among groups speaking a variety of distinct languages. One of the best regions for study is the Upper Negro River 'multilingual regional system', composed of the interfluvial Naduhupan and Kakua, along with the riverine East Tukanoan and Arawakan languages, as well as some riverine and some interfluvial groups. Some groups display intermarriage via linguistic exogamy (you need to find a partner from other linguistic groups) and frequent interaction in ritual activities. This is complemented by trade specializations and institutionalized exchange, where the Tuyuka provides canoes, the Tukano carved benches, the Baniwa manioc graters, the Naduhu baskets, hunted meat and forest products. Despite the diversity of languages, the region could be defined as a cultural area based on similar material culture (e.g., long houses), shared ritual practices, such as the Yurupari, and cosmology and ethnoastronomy (Epps and Salanova, 2013).

Another example is the Upper Xingu in the southern rim of Amazonia (see Chapter 8), home to a wide variety of people and languages. There are more than half a dozen languages spoken here, from the Carib, Arawak, Jê and Tupi families, plus the isolated Trumai language. As with the Upper Negro River, the speakers of these languages interact with one another frequently, especially during rituals and ceremonies, and have specialized in providing different goods for trade: the Wauja (Arawak) provide pottery, the Carib groups shell necklaces and beads, the Mehinaku (Arawak) and Aweti (Tupi) produce salt from plants, the Kamayura (Tupi) craft bows, while the Trumai (Tupi) fashion stone axes.

Finally, there is the Guaporé-Mamoré region, which spans northern Bolivia and western Brazil, and exhibits more than fifty languages, including Arawak, Macro-Jê, Chapacuran, Tupi, Nambikwara, Panoan and Tacanan families, in addition to numerous other isolates. Despite this linguistic diversity, the people who speak these languages share many cultural similarities that can be described as a regional 'cultural complex', and which have been shaped by extensive interethnic contact, intermarriage and exchange. The presence of territorial subgroups named after plants and animals, items of material culture, such as the *marico* (a carrying net made of palm fibres), a head ball game (a game that resembles football, but players crawling along the ground are only permitted to use their heads to push the ball forward), the absence of bitter manioc consumption, common elements of body ornamentation, roundhouse construction and mythological themes are among these cultural similarities. Similar regional multilinguistic cultural areas occur in the southern Guianas and the Caquetá-Putumayo areas. As we will see in the chapters to follow, many researchers propose that these multi-lingual regional systems go back to pre-Columbian times and are apparent in the hybrid nature of many archaeological traditions. For example, Hornborg (2005) and Eriksen (2011) have postulated that the emergence of these ancient pan-Amazonian exchange systems was built on a set of key transportation river routes that united various areas from very early times from about 4,000 years ago.

Seeing through Amazonian eyes

Amazonian animism Amazonia remains one of the few regions of the globe in which the survival of many indigenous groups allows the interpretation of the past to be informed by present observations and working along indigenous people. Therefore, it is a productive exercise to attempt to extract some common patterns of Amazonian worldviews. It is extremely difficult to find pan-Amazonian cultural distinctiveness in this region of such cultural diversity. Some authors, however, have noted characteristics that appear to occur, with variations throughout most of Amazonia. How native Amazonians interact with the natural world is one of them. To indigenous Amazonians 'nature' and 'culture' are not separate. Everything that grows, moves or evolves is equal to a human, with a soul and a social life. Each living being's physical body can be imagined as an 'outer cover', hiding its human form. Only other members of the same species or special beings, such as shamans who cross species boundaries, can see through this external covering. According to this Amazonian way of seeing and living, the world is inhabited by various types of beings, including humans and nonhumans, who perceive reality from different points of view. These entities, such as spirits, animals, certain plants and even objects, are considered to have consciousness and, like humans, the ability to reflect. This is called Amerindian perspectivism, a theory developed by anthropologist Viveiros de Castro (1996) and others, based on ethnographies of the Amazon.

Animals are often key actors in cultural contexts. Sometimes they are seen as the ancestors of humans, and on other occasions as the bringers of knowledge about how tools and utensils were first acquired and used. In the distant past, it is believed all beings shared a common humanity. However, over time, separation occurred, and different groups developed unique physical attributes while still maintaining human cultural behaviour. As a result, animals and other beings are considered 'ex-humans', who still perceive themselves as humans. They exhibit anthropomorphic behaviour and act like humans in their own world, where physical features such as fur, feathers, claws and beaks are viewed as cultural tools or body adornments. This particular worldview is important for archaeological interpretations, because myths, cosmological order and beliefs about the roles played by

Figure 2.11 In Amazon rivers, petroglyphs are a common way of writing in the landscape. Engraved designs can be found on thousands of rapids and rock outcrops throughout its tributaries. According to the Yukuna, an Arawak community living by the lower Caquetá and Apaporis rivers, the petroglyphs were carved on the rapids '... when the stone was soft, when Yuruparí came and met with the fish drinking yajé; the fish painted this all over the river' (Von Hildebrand, 1975: 309). Courtesy Fernando Urbina.

animals and people find visible expression as symbols and motifs in body and ceramic paintings, and in rock art. We will analyse in more detail these aspects when we describe the material culture of archaeological traditions in the following chapters.

The body as a canvas The Amazonian idea of the individual self and body is also very different from Western thinking. For Amazonians, a person is not a whole and indivisible self, but they are constantly changing. Across the lowlands of South America, this concept can be seen at work in the spiritual transformation of a human into another species through rituals and the use of psychoactive plants. To some extent, in lowland South America, the body can be seen as a 'canvas' upon which an individual's social identity is transformed and constructed. Individuals' social identities in Amazonian societies are formed over the course of their lives as they mature and move through different age groups, acquiring new social duties and obligations at each stage. These stages in a person's life are symbolized and visibly marked by body decorating, and wearing appropriate ornaments, such as ear spools, pendants and necklaces, to indicate newly attained status (Barreto, 2017; Gomes, 2001). The deployment of body paint to effect these changes in identity and social role often works in tandem with ceremonies involving masks. In this sense, body and facial painting, ear and lip plug use, scarification, tattooing and head hair shaving are physical modifications that accompany changes in

Figure 2.12 As you gaze up at the night sky over the Guaporé-Itenéz River in the southern hemisphere, you will be amazed by the abundance of stars. Most cultures around the world identify patterns in the stars, although the shapes and meaning of these constellations differs from group to group. The Milky Way's curvy path is particularly striking, and is viewed by several Amazonian communities as a celestial river representing the giant anaconda. Courtesy Mark Robinson.

social position, privileges and obligations. As we will see in the Santarém and Marajoara cultures, many of these traits become apparent in ceramic figurines.

A range of ethnographic studies have shown that the themes and motifs reproduced in the ceramics, and in the material culture of pre-literate societies in general, have a rich mythic content. The decorative motifs on ceramics, vessels and other objects were not intended merely as a passive portrayal of a pantheon of mythical creatures. They encapsulate scenes, episodes and stories from oral traditions, and leave a vivid and visible record of this animate world. The depiction of these creatures and scenes has an intimate and specific relationship with the way in which the myths themselves are ordered. Lévi-Strauss (1978) demonstrated how myths share a similar structure, and that myth narratives are often circular in the sense that episodes are metaphorically related to each other. There are recurrent elements within myths, and the end of the story may be connected to the beginning. Likewise, there are often several versions of the same myth, which although differing in detail, retain a broadly similar structure. Lévi-Strauss (1978) concluded that the structure of a myth or set of myths may be as important as its content. For the Marajoara culture (Chapter 7), Schaan (2012a) has suggested that the structure and organization of the iconography on the vessels may well reflect fundamental aspects of such myths and stories.

As Cristiana Barreto (2017) reminds us, we need to be aware of two aspects of Amazonian perspectivism when analysing representations of the body in Amazonian materials. First, the unstable and transformational nature of the body means that materialization in clay or stone of a particular body form may reveal the intention to reverse or prevent the dangers of body transformation. Second, the external and visible appearance of bodies does not necessarily correspond to the inner essence of beings represented by ceramic or stone figurines, but instead may depict transitory conditions.

Writing in the landscape In concluding this section on Amazonian seeing and acting in the world, I would like to draw attention to how the people of the Amazon region document their stories on the land. According to Fernando Santos Granero (1998), the Yanesha people, along with many other Amazonian societies, have a unique way of documenting their history. They use the landscape as a form of 'writing', which Granero refers to as 'topographic writing'. This method involves identifying specific elements of the terrain that hold historical significance through myth and ritual, which are known as 'topograms'. When combined in various ways, these topograms create 'topographs', which tell longer stories. This mnemonic device helps the Yanesha people remember not only the mythical consecration of their traditional land, but also its despoliation and desecration in recent times.

I end this chapter with a clarification about the use of the terms iconography and art in this book. Iconography comes from the Greek 'Eykon', meaning image, and 'graphic', meaning description or script. I use iconography in this book as a way of visualizing language that uses images to represent a particular topic. This is the case with the iconographic language of Marajoara ceramics (Figure 7.21) (Schaan, 2012a). Similarly, we should bear in mind that these are societies without a written language, where customs and traditions are passed orally and with material artefacts, such as ceramic or rock art. Within this concept, the concept of art as employed here includes but also goes beyond making ornamental or pretty things. In particular, for Amazonian indigenous people, art is a language, it conveys a series of messages that represent their culture, their world view and also everyday life. Each culture has its way of representing and passing these messages from generation to generation. As used here, following Schaan (2012a) and Barreto (2017), art, which comes from the Latin 'ars' meaning technique or ability, is used as the human activity linked to manifestations of an aesthetic or communicative nature, carried out employing a wide variety of languages. The creative process is based on perception, with the intention of provoking emotions or expressing ideas.

In the next chapter, we start our journey through Amazonian human history, beginning with the arrival of the first people to Amazonia at the end of the last Ice Age.

CHAPTER 3
INTO THE UNKNOWN: PEOPLING AMAZONIA

Migration to the last continental *terra incognita*

Understanding the human journey of global dispersal is to understand the history of modern humanity and the development of the diverse cultural and physical characteristics of humans around the world. Modern humans evolved in Africa about 300,000 years ago. Approximately 70,000–60,000 years ago they began migrating across the six continents. They moved into Asia, dispersed in Australia about 50,000 years ago, and entered the Americas, the last continental *terra incognita* (other than Antarctica), between 25,000–15,000 years ago (e.g, Boëda et al., 2014; Braje et al., 2017; Pigati et al., 2023; Sutter, 2021).

Exactly how many groups, and when and how they entered the Americas, is a matter of lively debate. Forty years ago, researchers thought that the peopling of the Americas was rather straightforward. People migrated from Asia to the Americas between 15,000–14,000 years ago when glaciers began melting and an 'ice-free corridor' between these continental ice sheets provided a route for these first Americans to spread southward. According to this 'Clovis First Hypothesis', people rapidly spread over the Americas all the way to the southern tip of South America and on their way hunted down the large Ice Age mammals to extinction (Martin and Klein, 1989). Clovis people (named after the characteristic projectile points found in the 1930s at a site in Clovis, New Mexico) were big game hunters, who roamed the open plains of North America, and possessed distinctive long, narrow and fluted points tailored to fit on the ends of spears and penetrate the bodies of the large Ice Age mammals, such as mastodons, mammoths and bison. Clovis was a very uniform, short-lived cultural tradition, lasting from 13.3–12.8ka, which spread all over North America. However, new archaeological discoveries, fresh reconstruction of ancient environments, more precise techniques to date archaeological sites and the employment of ancient DNA on human skeletons are dramatically changing our understanding of the early peopling of the Americas. The new picture shows that the initial occupation of the Americas is more complex and diverse than previously conceived, and that several groups of people arrived in the Americas at least a few millennia before Clovis (Figure 3.1).

A major challenge to the Clovis First Paradigm was the discovery of the Monte Verde site by archaeologist Tom Dillehay (1997). This site is in the cool temperate rainforest of southern Chile, 16,000 kilometres from the Bering Strait, and dates to around 18.5–14.5 ka (Dillehay et al., 2015). It is located in a small creek called Chinchihuapi, where, soon after a band of hunter-gatherers abandoned camp, a bog was formed, enabling unusual preservation of organic remains. Dillehay's team unearthed the log foundations of a settlement consisting of ten to twelve connected dwellings. Several dozen plant species were recovered, including nuts, berries and fruits, and even algae from the Pacific Ocean, as far away as 30 kilometres. The site contained a prolific assemblage of stone tools, including 'willow-leaf-shaped' projectile points, bola or sling stones, and scrapers on wooden shafts, along with wood and bone tools – the latter fabricated from the remains of as many as seven individual mastodons. The site firmly established the occupation of South America before Clovis by foragers who were not big game hunters, but had a generalized subsistence (Dillehay and Rossen, 2002).

The study of genetics is also emerging as a significant player in resolving this matter (Nielsen et al, 2017). It is helping to answer important questions, such as where the people who settled Amazonia came from. By examining the DNA of people both alive and dead it is allowing the epic migration across the Americas to be charted. Genetic studies with available data show that Native Americans originated from Asian populations and over time became genetically distinct from them. Based on the time that it would have taken to accumulate these differences, geneticists calculate that Native Americans' ancestors split from people living in Siberia about 25ka. These populations later moved across Beringia, the 1,600 kilometre land bridge connecting Siberia and Alaska, created as a result of the lower sea levels of the last Ice Age. On the other side of Beringia, their movement was blocked by massive ice sheets. Therefore, it is only when land corridors opened that they crossed into the Pacific Northwest, between 17–14 ka. To account for this 10,000-year gap, in what is called the 'Beringian Standstill Hypothesis', geneticists argue that these populations must have settled and diversified in Beringia for this period, building up genetic diversity before entering the New World (Tamm et al, 2007). Once considered a barren flyover country covered by treeless tundra steppe not propitious for large human populations, new palaeoecological evidence suggests the contrary. It shows that Beringia was dotted with oases of brushy shrubs and even trees, such as spruce, birch, willow and alder, which may have provided fuel for fires, raw materials for shelter and cover for animals such as hare, birds, elk and moose (Willerslev et al, 2014). Substantial archaeological evidence supporting this hypothesis has not been forthcoming, since Beringia is now largely submerged. But on the basis of the existing evidence, these authors (Tamm et al, 2007) suggest that humans who reached the regions south of the glaciers sometime between 19–16ka must have made the journey south by another route, most likely moving south along the Pacific coast and exploiting the rich marine resources of the so-called 'Kelp Belt Highway'. This would appear to have been the route taken by the settlers of Monte Verde (Braje et al, 2017).

Later in time, once the ice sheets that spread over much of what is today Canada receded, these ancestral Native Americans were able to move south. They then split into two genetically distinct groups. The so-called Northern Native Americans (B lineage) moved to the east, with some of their descendants settling in what is today southern Ontario. The other branch, the Southern Native Americans (A lineage), rapidly moved south about 14ka, becoming the principal ancestors of today's indigenous Central and South Americans. It is this branch that was likely one of the migration waves that arrived in South America and the Amazon basin at least 13,000 years ago (Moreno-Mayar et al., 2018; Posth et al., 2018).

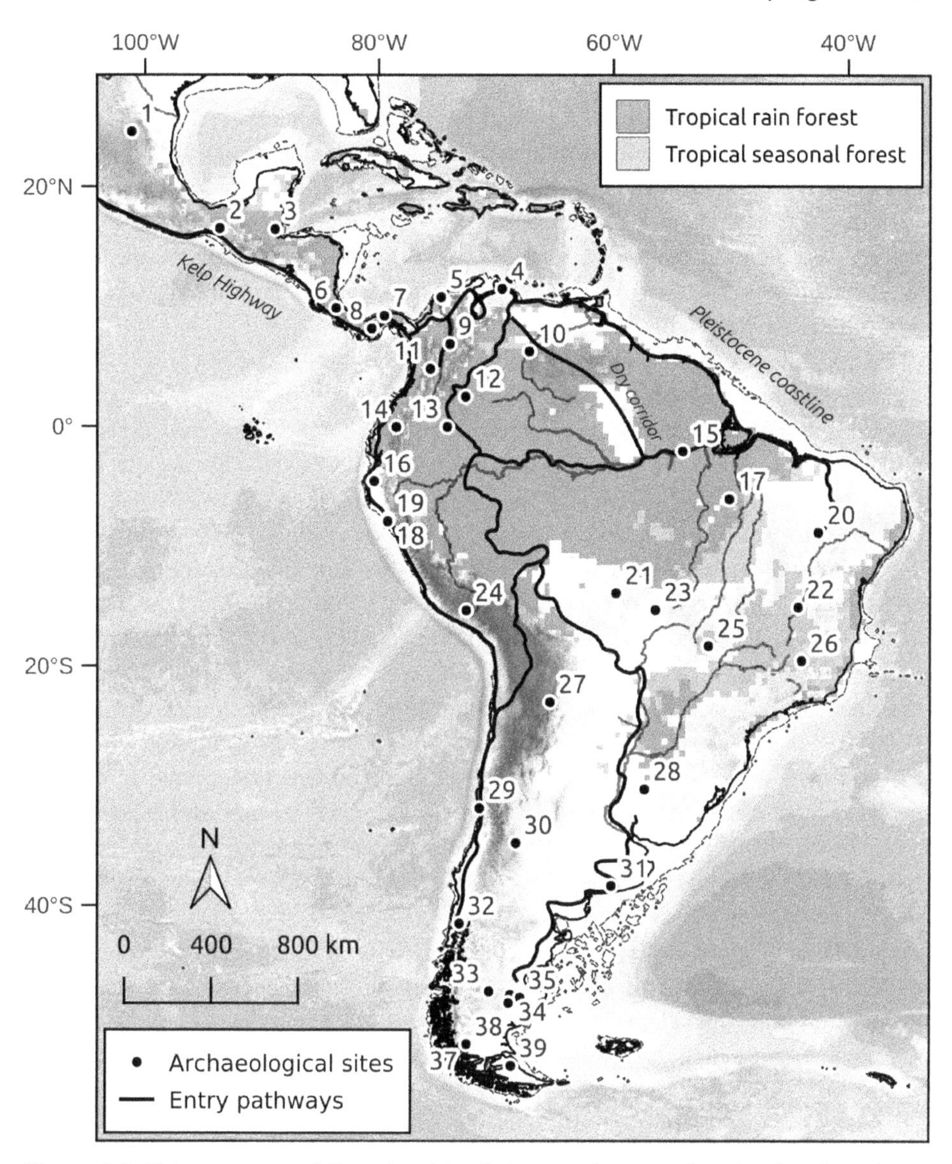

Figure 3.1 Pleistocene map of Central and South America showing selected archaeological sites, sea levels and potential routes of entry into Amazonia. Low sea levels exposed dry land off the Atlantic and Pacific Ocean during the last Ice Age. 1. Chiquihuite. 2. Los Grifos. 3. Mayahak Cab Pek. 4. Taima Taima. 5. San Isidro. 6. Turrialba. 7. Madden Lake. 8. Cueva de los Vampiros. 9. Middle Magdalena. 10. Cerro Gavilán. 11. Middle Cauca. 12. Lindosa. 13. Peña Roja. 14. El Inga. 15. Pedra Pintada. 16. Quebrada Jaguay. 17. Grutra do Gavião. 18. Paijan. 19. Huaca Prieta. 20. Pedra Furada/Serra da Capivara. 21. Abrigo do Sol. 22. Lapa do Boquete. 23. Santa Elina. 24. Cuncaicha. 25. Itaparica (Serranópolis). 26. Lapa Vermelha/Lagoa Santa. 27. Inca Cueva. 28. Pay Paso. 29. Quebrada Santa Julia. 30. Gruta del Indio. 31. Arroyo Seco 2. 32. Monte Verde. 33.Cueva de las Manos. 34. Los Toldos. 35. Piedra Museo. 36. Cerro Tres Tetas. 37. Cueva del Milodon. 38. Cueva del Medio. 39. Tres Arroyos.

Arriving to Amazonia

The peopling of South America is a momentous event in our human history. It took place during one of the most significant climatic, environmental and subsistence regime shifts in human history, which overlaps with the extinction of the large Ice Age mammals, the beginning of plant domestication and the emergence of today's remarkable diverse South American indigenous groups (Dillehay, 2000). So, how did these people entering South America via the Darien Gap move into Amazonia and how did they adapt to the new conditions they found there?

Although Amazonia occupies 40 per cent of South America, the peopling of the Amazon has until recently received little consideration. This has to do with an array of factors. The dense forest creates logistical difficulties for fieldwork and impedes the initial identification of early sites, while the acidic and clayed soils negatively affect the preservation of organic remains. The young nature of Amazonian archaeology, and the research focus on more recent ceramic traditions to the expense of early human activity in the region, are also factors to take into account. Importantly, there are also issues relating to how researchers in the past have conceptualized hunter-gatherer lifeways in tropical forests. Traditionally, the early settlers of the Americas have been portrayed as highly specialized mobile hunter-gatherers exploiting coastal resources and large game in temperate environments (Lynch, 1990; Sauer, 1944). Scholars reasoned that in contrast to more open landscapes, humans might have found rainforests difficult to navigate, with less food available to catch or hunt. In the 1980s some researchers postulated that life as a hunter-gatherer in the tropical forest was impossible without the cultivation of the starchy roots that provide the necessary calories for human populations to survive (Headland and Bailey, 1991). They argued that the scarcity of animals that might provide the necessary fats and proteins, and the dearth of starchy plants, converted the forests into green deserts and discouraged foragers from settling them without exploiting additional environments and resources. But subsequent research has shown that tropical game (including fish) are fatty and that many plants that are abundant in the forests, including palms and root tubers, are full of carbohydrates. Furthermore, modern ethnographic and archaeobotanical studies show that hunter-gatherers across the globe do not passively adapt to tropical forests, but are often 'niche-constructors', modifying the rainforest as they go about their daily business. Such modifications include the management of forest composition, the use of fire, the cultivation of edible plants, the detoxification of particular plants to make them edible, and the hunting of arboreal and terrestrial tropical game (see summary in Roberts, 2019).

Importantly, it should not be forgotten that rainforests are not an alien environment for our species. From the Miocene (an epoch of the Tertiary period from 23.3–5.2 million years ago) onwards, they were the backdrop to the ongoing evolution of the great apes, and provided the cradle for the emergence of early hominids, who retained arboreal physiological adaptations at least into the late Pleistocene. There now exists growing evidence, from the late Pleistocene onwards, for the intensification of tropical forest occupations, aided by tools, by *Homo sapiens*. The human manipulation of forest ecosystems is evident in SE Asia from at least 50–45 ka, Near Oceania from 45 ka and now from at least 13 ka in South America (Roberts, 2019). The picture arising from tropical South America reviewed below reveals that early settlers did not avoid tropical rainforests, nor were they passive consumers of their resources. The evidence hints at early cultivation of annual crops and the management of trees of economic importance (Iriarte et al., 2020a).

So, when did the first humans enter the Amazon? When did the ethnic diversity that we appreciate today begin? The groups that spread into the Amazon Basin were foragers who likely journeyed into NW South America via the Darien Gap, the narrow bottleneck representing the gateway to South America, reaching eastern Amazonia by 13.1 ka (Ranere et al., 2002; Roosevelt et al., 1996). The earliest evidence comes from the Caverna da Pedra Pintada site located on the Paituna hills overlooking the Amazon River near the town of Monte Alegre in the Lower Amazon, a site adorned with paintings (Pereira and Moraes, 2019; Roosevelt et al., 1996). Our recent excavations in three rock shelters in the Colombian Amazon have shown that the NW sector of Amazonia was occupied at least 12.6 ka (Morcote-Ríos et al., 2021).

Making a living in the rainforest

So what type of diet did these early migrants have? And can it tell us something about the environment they lived? The study of discarded plant remains from archaeological sites is providing a greater appreciation of the role of plants in the diets of early settlers in the tropics and elsewhere in South America (Dillehay and Rossen, 2002; Iriarte et al., 2020a; Piperno and Pearsall, 1998). As we will see in the next chapter, the systematic recovery of plant remains from excavations and the development of new methods, such as the study of phytoliths, the examination of starch grains and charred seeds, have played a key role in unlocking our understanding of the plant component of the diet of early Amazonians.

The groundbreaking excavations by Roosevelt and collaborators (1996) at Caverna da Pedra Pintada dated by fifty-six radiocarbon evidencing the arrival of humans to lower Amazon ~13.1 ka showed that unlike their contemporaneous North American Clovis counterparts, the early residents of this Amazonian cave had a very broad diet consisting of fruits, nuts, palms, small game from the tropical forest, and fish and turtles from the Amazon River – which is located 10 kilometres from the rock shelter. Lithics include formal tools, including triangular, stemmed bifacial projectile points along with unifacial gravers and scrapers made of chalcedony and quartz.

The majority of these food items are typical of closed-canopy forests. This shows that these early Americans making the Amazon their home were not big-game hunters, but had a broad-spectrum diet. The lower components of Caverna da Pedra Pintada show consumption of several plants, including a leguminous tree called *jutai* (*Hymenaea* sp.), the seeds of which are used to this day to make a sort of flour. Tree fruits, including *Sacoglottis guianensis* (Humiriaceae), *Talisia esculenta* (Sapindaceae), *Mouriri apiranga* (Melastomataceae), *Coccoloba pixuna* (Polygonaceae) and *muruci* (*Byrsonima crispa*,

Malpighiaceae), as well as Brazil nuts (*Bertholletia excelsa*, Lecythidaceae), were also consumed. All these continue to be used by indigenous groups today. In addition to tree fruits and nuts, three common varieties of palms, including *sacuri* (*Attalea microcarpa*), *tucumã* (*Astrocaryum vulgare*) and *curuá* (*Astrocaryum spectabilis*) were present at Caverna da Pedra Pintada.

In the Colombian Amazon, along the Caquetá River, the site of Peña Roja dated between 11.1–9.2 ka also show insights into the plant component of the diet of the first people to arrive to Amazonia. The botanical remains include a variety of palms: *Astrocaryum aculeatum*, *A. chambira*, *A. jauari*, *Bactris* sp., *Euterpe precatoria*, *Oenocarpus bacaba*, *O. bataua*, *O. minor*, *Mauritia flexuosa*, along with *Anaueria brasiliensis*, *Parkia multijuga*, *Inga* spp., *Passiflora quadrangularis*, *Brosimum guianense*, *Sacoglottis* spp. and *Caryocar* spp. Phytoliths from *Cucurbita* spp. squash, bottle gourd (*Lagenaria siceraria*) and lerén (*Calathea* sp.), along with starch grains from *Xanthosoma* spp. were also evidenced (Mora, 2003; Piperno and Pearsall, 1998).

Palms deserve special mention. Ethnoarchaeological work shows that palms are a key resource of hunter-gatherers across greater Amazonia today (Politis, 2009) and were likely a key plant resource for the early migrants of the late Pleistocene tropical 'moving south' in the tropical forests (Robinson et al., 2021). They are predominant in early records across lowland Amazonia, and changes in vegetation composition to include a greater proportion of palm is closely associated with humans (Morcote-Rios and Bernal, 2001; Robinson et al., 2021). Today, the human-made ADEs can be easily identified from the palm groves that grow on them (Chapter 6). As reviewed in Chapter 2, traditional communities make innumerable uses of palms (e.g., Balick, 1984; Bernal et al., 2011). Palm fruits are nutrient-rich (oil and proteins), non-poisonous and available for a large part of the year, while palm starch can be extracted from their trunk fibres (see summary in Meggers, 2001; Bernal et al., 2007). Palm can also be a host for an additional, much-valued source of protein: by cutting palms and leaving them to rot, Amazonians convert them into a hotbed for the much appreciated edible weevils. The Joti of the Venezuelan highlands, for example, exercise controlled supply of this protein-rich food source by deliberately felling palm trees (López-Zent and Zent, 2004). Other groups, such as the Nukak and Joti, make deep cuts in the palm trunk, and the Paraguayan Ache cut it into smaller pieces (Hill et al., 1984), since some weevils are specifically attracted to exposed inner palm tissue. Palm leaves have been used throughout history for the thatching of homes and temporary campsites, and their fibres are extracted for making various implements. Palm leaves are even used as canoe sails to navigate rivers. The trunks serve as posts or walls in buildings, and are used in the manufacture of baskets, blowguns, darts, bows and harpoons for hunting and fishing (Figure 3.2) (See Chapter 4).

Some of the finest evidence for the adaptation to life in the tropical forest also comes from the inter-Andean montane forests of the Cauca River. Here, plant remains show evidence of incipient tree, palm and tuber cultivation, beginning around 11.5 ka. Starch granules recovered from plant processing tools indicate the cultivation of local root crops, such as yams (*Dioscorea* sp.), arrowroot (*Calathea* sp.) and leren (*Maranta* cf. *arundinacea*), as well as *Phaseolus* sp. beans. These root crops and vegetables are

Figure 3.2 Importance of palm use among current hunter-gatherers in Amazonia. *a.* Nukak carrying recently collected *Attalea* sp. fruits to the camp in a backpack. *b.* Nukak camp using *Oenocarpus* leaves to build roof shelters. *c.* Awa women removing palm fruits from *Oenocarpus* sp. bunch. *d.* Hoti using *Attalea* leaves to build a roof shelter. *e.* Abandoned Nukak camp with *Oenocarpus* palms sprouting from discarded seeds. *a–d.* courtesy of Gustavo Politis.

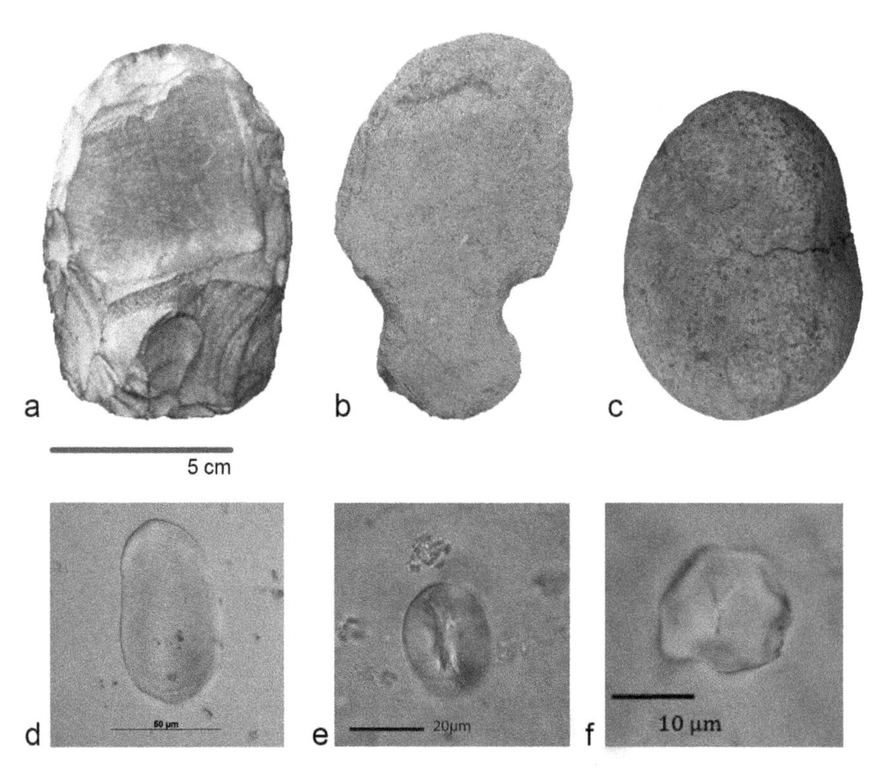

Figure 3.3 Notched axes, waisted hoes and starch grains from the middle Cauca Valley, Colombia. *a.* Axe, Site 21, 7.5–6.5 ka (Porce River). *b.* Hoe, El Jazmin site, 10.1–7.1 ka (middle Cauca River). *c.* Handstone, La Pochola site, 6.7–5.9 ka (middle Cauca River). *d. Canna* spp. starch, Tabladito site, 11.0 ka (Musinga River). *e.* Fabaceae-type starch, La Pochola site, 6.9–6.7 ka (middle Cauca River). *f.* Maize (*Zea mays*) starch, La Pochola site, 6.9–6.7 ka (middle Cauca River). Courtesy Javier Aceituno.

accompanied from about 10 ka by tree fruits, including soursop (*Annona* sp.), mora (*Rubus* sp.), *pequi* (*Caryocar* sp.), *Virola* and avocado (*Persea*) (Aceituno and Loaiza, 2018). Characteristic of these Andean montane forests is the ubiquitous presence of notched axes and waisted hoes, which were likely used for tree-felling, and possibly for the tillage of soft Andean soils, digging roots or felling palms – either for their starch or weevil nurturing (Figure 3.3).

Along the Cerrados in the southern rim of the Amazon, similar evidence indicating a broad-spectrum diet of tree and palm fruits, along with small animals and fish, is recorded from sites dating to the early Holocene, 13–11 ka, belonging to the Itaparica Tradition (Schmitz et al., 2004) and Gruta do Gavião ~11.6–8.5 ka (Magalhães et al., 2019). Itaparica sites are mostly located on painted rock shelters and exhibit characteristic large unifacial scrapers of quartzite (likely for woodworking), along with bifacial chalcedony projectile points.

In terms of technology, in contrast to the sites of early settlers in North America, many of which exhibit bifacial technologies associated with 'big-game hunting', most early sites in tropical South America from around 13 ka exhibit expedient unifacial technologies associated with broad-spectrum economies, where plants likely played a major role (Dillehay, 2000). Many early sites, such as Taima-Taima, Paiján, sites in the middle Magdalena River and Caverna de Pedra Pintada concurrently used unifacial, bifacial and flake tools in association with a variety of ground stones (manos, grinding stones, axes, waisted hoes) attesting to the diversity of their subsistence economies (Dillehay, 2000). In south-western Amazonia, the earliest evidence comes from the Abrigo do Sol rock shelter in the Guaporé-Itenéz River Basin, on the border of the Brazilian Shield. Early work by Miller (1987) at this site on 7-metre-deep layers dating between 14–6 ka and purportedly associated with megafauna, contain expedient chert and quartz flakes. Resuming work on this site is of utmost importance to confirm these early dates. The Santa Elina rock shelter contexts, located nearby but beyond the Parecis range, which provided dates dating back to the late Pleistocene, around 22 ka, also possess expedient unifacial technologies (Vialou et al., 2017). Collectively, these sites illustrate the variety of adaptations to the diverse array of environments the early settlers encountered in the Amazon rainforest and its periphery.

Amazonia during the last Ice Age

What type of environments did these early settlers meet under the colder and drier conditions of the late Pleistocene? Although much of North America was covered by glaciers and dominated by tundra environments, in Central and South America, glaciers were restricted to relatively small portions at very high altitudes (the high Andes) and the very tip of the southern cone of South America. Therefore, when early humans crossed the Darien Gap, it constituted a virtually unprecedented migration of modern humans across and into richly diverse, empty landscapes devoid of hominins. These landscapes comprised savannahs, a diversity of tropical forests (montane, seasonal and humid tropical forests), and coastal environments (mangroves, deserts). In this region, in what is actually Colombia, the altitudinal range equates to a temperature span of nearly 30°C, resulting in a change in vegetation from diverse tropical rainforest to high altitude alpine tundra. As will be seen below, the early settlers also encountered very different animals, many of which subsequently became extinct during the late Pleistocene/early Holocene transition.

People arrived in Amazonia under very different climatic conditions of the last Ice Age. In general, across the Neotropics, temperatures were at least 5°C lower and precipitation was reduced by about 30–50 per cent (Piperno and Pearsall, 1998). The Late Glacial Maximum is likely to have resulted in coasts 130 metres below present-day mean sea level, exposing roughly 200 kilometres of the equatorial Atlantic marine shelf (Figure 3.1) (Peltier and Fairbanks, 2006). The Amazon River would have cut its way through this exposed landmass, eventually emptying into the Atlantic through a massive delta (Irion, 1984). If these early migrants followed and lived near the coasts, their places are now submerged.

The vegetation these Ice Age climates supported, and the origin of the exceptional biodiversity of Amazonia, described in Chapter 2, have been matters of considerable debate. Drawing on refugia theory, and a few vegetation reconstructions based on pollen from the southern rim of the Amazon, some authors (Simpson and Haffer, 1978) argue that the Amazon forest experienced a long, dry spell, which caused tropical forests to shrink into patches of forest separated by dry savannah that served as refuges for plants and animals. The theory goes that pockets of endemicity (plant and animals restricted to a certain location) in some regions of Amazonia were produced in these refugia. Species that ended up in more than one refugial pocket remained separate, thus allowing for the development of new native species. This, in turn, promoted biodiversity in the long term. When wetter conditions returned, the Amazonian forests expanded, excluding savannah and forming the modern biodiversity pattern. However, palaeoecological and molecular evidence has increasingly led to the questioning of this paradigm. Notably, pollen evidence from Amazon river sediments deposited in the ocean floor of the Amazon deep-sea fan, which provides a 50,000-year-old history of the Amazon vegetation, indicates that the lowland tropical forest areas were not replaced by savannah during glacial periods (Haberle and Maslin, 1999). Furthermore, the Ice Age pollen deposits from lake bottoms in several regions across central and western Amazonia, examined by palaeoecologists Paul Colinvaux and Mark Bush and their groups (Bush and Oliveira, 2006), indicate that forest not savannah was present in glacial times. Recent paleoclimate data (Wang et al., 2013) suggest that the so-called Dry Corridor of the Amazon, (Figure 3.1) an arch that runs from the Guianas to the lower Amazon and receives less than 2,000 millimetres/year of precipitation, may have been dry tropical forest rather than savannah. Despite a significant drop in precipitation levels, the Amazonian landscape remained forested. This was possible because the lower temperatures helped to reduce the rate of evaporation from the forests, and thus offset the loss of rainfall. As Bush (2017) proposes, cooling was actually responsible for saving the Amazonian forests. Other areas such as south-western Amazonia (Mayle et al., 2000) were mosaics of savannahs and seasonal forests. Charred seeds recovered from the earliest occupation of Caverna de Pedra Pintada and Serrania de la Lindosa suggest that the sites were surrounded by tropical forests. On the whole, current evidence indicates that these early Amazonians encountered a tropical rainforest and not a tropical savannah, with pockets of tropical forest refugia.

The Sistine Chapel of the Ancients

Some of the latest evidence for the peopling of Amazonia comes from the savannah-forest boundary in the Serrania de la Lindosa, Colombia (Figure 3.4). The 2016 pacification process has allowed us to start a new archaeological project in a region that was until recently one of the strongholds of the FARC guerrilla. The region is famous for its spectacular rock. Our project LASTJOURNEY has dug three rock-shelters, with early human occupation of the region dating to 12.6 ka (Figure 3.4–7). Plant remains from our archaeological excavations show the consumption of a diversity of palms,

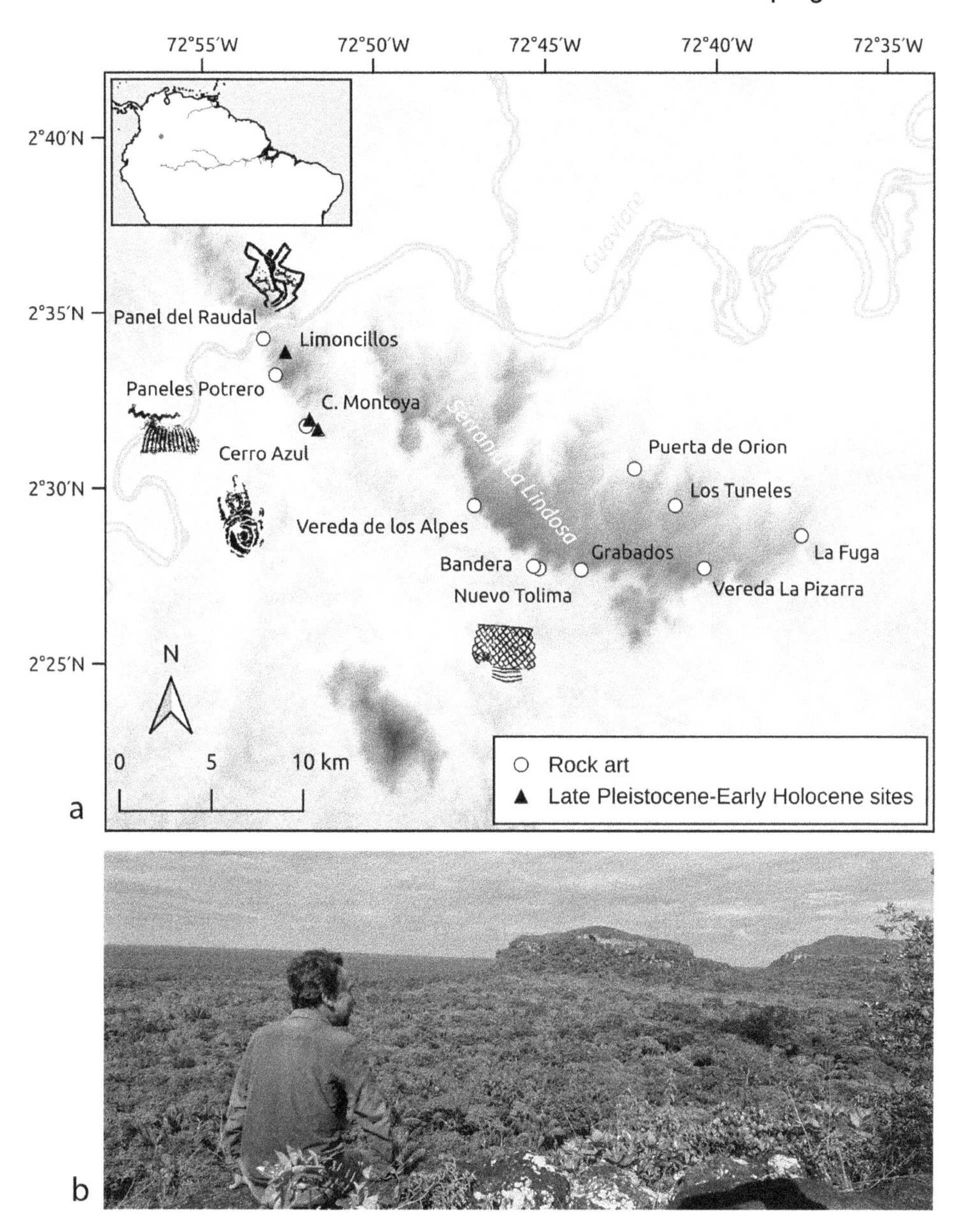

Figure 3.4 *a*. Map of archaeological sites and major rock art panels of La Lindosa. *b*. Panoramic view of the La Lindosa rainforest.

including *Astrocaryum chambira*, *A.* sp., *Attalea racemosa*, *A. maripa*, *Euterpe precatoria*, *Mauritia flexuosa*, *Oenocarpus bataua*, *Syagrus orinocensis*, *Socratea exhorriza* and *Bactris* sp., from the time of the initial occupation of these sites (Morcote-Ríos et al., 2021). The menu of the early inhabitants of the La Lindosa was complemented by a diversity of small animals. Fish included *cachama* (*Piaractus* sp.) and *piranha* (*Pygocentrus* sp.), while small mammals, such as the rodents *paca* (*Cuniculus paca*) and *capybara*

Figure 3.5 La Lindosa Principal rock art panel showing a diversity of animals, plants, humans, handprints and geometric designs. Such paintings provide unique, invaluable, generalized information on ancient lifeways, as well as insights into ancient collective rituals, as exemplified by the individuals dancing across the panel.

(*Hydrochoerus hydrochaeris*), as well as armadillo (*Dasypus* sp.), were also consumed. Reptiles included turtles, iguanas, snakes, caiman and crocodiles. Remarkably, the animal remains of La Lindosa lack medium-sized and large mammals, such as peccaries (*Tayassuidae*), tapirs (*Tapiridae*), primates and carnivores, indicating that this was a site for processing small animals. If the ancient occupants did hunt larger animals, these were processed at a different site. Intriguingly, as will be seen below, these large animals not eaten at Cerro Azul nonetheless had a dominant role in the rock art paintings (Iriarte et al., 2022; Morcote-Ríos et al., 2021).

The diversity of Amazonian plants and animals is depicted with incredible naturalism on the walls of La Lindosa. Its rock walls, with their thousands of documented paintings, represent one of the earliest and richest rock art sites in South America, along with the spectacular rock art of nearby Chiribiquete National Park (Castaño Uribe, 2019). These sites consist of sandstone rock shelters with ochre paintings of animals, plants, human figures, abstract designs and handprints (stencils are absent). Unlike the Upper Palaeolithic artists of Europe, who chose to paint in deep, dark caves (could also be the only place where their art is still preserved today), these early Amazonians painted in open rock shelters, protected from direct rain but exposed to sunlight. The rock walls are vertical, up to 10 metres high. Many contain 'sub-chambers', where today paintings can only be viewed either by an experienced climber with appropriate gear, or with the advantage of drone technology. However, these early artists possibly constructed wooden scaffolding, as it appears to be depicted in some of the paintings. The earliest level of Cerro Azul excavations contain grooved ochre tablets used as painting materials.

Fragments of rocks with paintings fallen from the wall have been recovered from archaeological layers dating to 10.2 ka. The paintings were made using mineral pigments, in particular ochre, which gives them their characteristic reddish-terracotta colour. They were usually made on freshly exfoliated sandstone walls that provided 'smooth canvases'.

The animal paintings consist of naturalistic outlines and/or infilled designs depicting wild animals (Figure 3.5). Their realism allows for identification into zoological groupings, including fish, turtles, caimans, rays, *capibaras*, deer, porcupines, felines, possibly canines, monkeys, and aquatic and predatory birds that could resemble harpy eagles and king vultures. The animals are usually represented in profile, although some of them, such as the reptiles, are characteristically shown as if seen from above. Animals are represented individually, with their offspring, or in packs. They are usually shown running (deer), leaping or climbing trees (monkeys), or standing. Some of them are represented doing acrobatics and there are scenes of movement created by showing the same animal in a different position of its acrobatic act. Some figurative elements and particular scenes predominate, pointing to the fact that these ancient artists shared graphic codes. Many of the paintings depict hunting and ritual scenes, showing humans interacting with plants, forest and savannah animals. Between the most common plants, large fruits hanging from trees are depicted. The trees could be calabash, bottle gourd or even cacao. Some of the depictions of palms show enough detailed characteristics to allow them to be tentatively assigned to a particular species, such as probably *Attalea* sp., likely *Attalea orinocensis*, which is very common in the region (Figure 2.7b) (Iriarte et al., 2022).

The first humans to arrive in NW South America were confronted with a greater diversity of large mammals, now extinct. South America was teeming with large animals that coexisted with Ice Age hunter-gatherers, including several species of elephant-like creatures called gomphotheres, including the mastodon, ground sloths, saber-toothed tigers, the rhino-like toxodons and the glyptodonts, armoured armadillo-like creatures the size of a Fiat 500, to mention a few. Despite the fact that South America experienced less dramatic climatic changes at the end of the last Ice Age compared to other continents, the proportion of megafauna extinction in South America was far greater, totalling 83 per cent of animals with a body mass >44 kilograms (53 genera) – compared with a loss of 35 per cent in Eurasia. All fifteen megaherbivores (> 1 ton) were lost and even most herbivores (>500 kilograms) became extinct, with just some species of tapir (*Tapirus* spp.) surviving to the present day (Barnosky and Lindsey, 2010). The extinction of these major ecosystem engineers would have had fundamental impacts, including a decline in the volume of large-seeded plant species, which the megafauna would have helped to disperse, such as squashes, cacao and avocado. Changes in land cover would also have occurred, for example an increase in savannah tree cover, as well as a decrease in Phosphorus availability (Doughty et al., 2016; Doughty et al., 2013). Many of these now-extinct animals, including horses, the *Palaeolama* camelid, giant sloths and possibly a mastodon, appear to be vividly depicted in the rock art of the Colombian Amazon, as far back as 12.6 ka (Figure 3.6) (Iriarte et al., 2022a and b).

As with the 30,000-year-old depictions of now-extinct bison and woolly rhinoceros in European Upper Palaeolithic caves, the work of the early Amazonian artists at La

Lindosa likely represent some of the earliest artistic expressions of native Amazonians, as well as recording their interaction with Ice Age megafauna (Iriarte et al., 2022b). The paintings include images that appear to depict giant sloths, mastodon, camelids, horses and three-toed ungulates with trunks that bear some resemblance to *Xenorhinotherium* or *Macrauchenia*. The overall shape of the animal depicted in Figure 3.6a, as well as the large head, thorax and prominent claws, allows us to consider that it could be a giant sloth. The Figure 3.6b drawing, exhibiting a trunk and the characteristic protuberance in the back of the head, reminds us of a mastodon. Figure 3.6c with the distinctive small head, long neck and the characteristic tail of a camelid, likely represents a *Palaeolama*. It also possesses another characteristic attribute of wild South American camelids, in that the hind legs are longer than the front ones. Lastly, it is markedly distinct to all the deer that are profusely painted in La Lindosa.

The horses represented in Figure 3.6d–e exhibit the large, heavy head characteristic of the American Ice Age horses. In some of them, the horsehair is clearly discernible, while others show the characteristic 'galloping stallion pose'. Unlike other researchers (Urbina and Peña, 2016), who interpret them as European – Old World – horses, we tend to favour the hypothesis that these are Pleistocene horses. This interpretation is based on their anatomical features, as well as the fact that in the majority of indigenous post-Columbian pictographs Old World horses are shown with riders – the aspect that most caught the attention and curiosity of Native Americans when they saw horses for the first time (e.g., Martínez, 2009). In general, Old World horses drawn in post-Columbian times do not exhibit the heavy head associated with Pleistocene horses.

Some of the purported megafauna representations are accompanied by an assemblage of human figures of diminutive size in comparison (Figure 3.6a). Many of these large animals are on the upper part of the panels. Despite the presence of these paintings, the faunal remains of La Lindosa and Caverna de Pedra Pintada did not include any megafauna bones. However, the association of humans and megafauna has been recorded in other areas of tropical South America, such as Tibitó in the Bogotá highland plateau (Correal-Urrego, 1982), and the arid savannahs of coastal Venezuela (Bryan et al., 1978). At Caverna da Pedra Pintada, the lower occupational levels contain many pigments in the form of hematite or iron oxide fragments, which were likely used for powdered pigment production and form the mineral base of paint. These fragments have similar iron and titanium ratios as the paintings, which led Roosevelt (2002) to suggest that the paintings are from the late Pleistocene age.

As summarized in Iriarte et al. (2022b: Figure 1), many early sites in the Americas are in painted rock shelters. What do these paintings represent at La Lindosa? Looking at today's indigenous groups gives us a hint of the past. As we have seen in Chapter 2, for native Amazonians, the natural world has a social domain (Descola, 1996; Viveiros de Castro, 1996). Humans and non-humans differ only in their 'outer appearance': they all have a soul, spirit or 'mental consciousness'. The non-humans have their rules, and communicate with humans, so that humans and non-humans engage in different ways, some cooperative and some hostile. Communication is subject to rituals performed by medicine men, or 'shamans', who use hallucinogenic drugs or fasting to enter the other

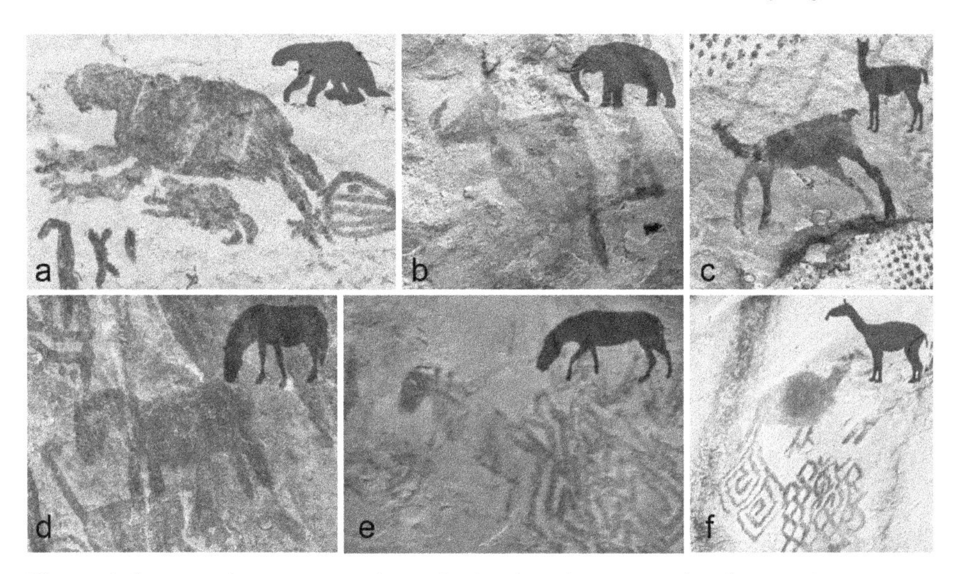

Figure 3.6 Potential Ice-Age megafauna displayed in the pictographs of La Lindosa. *a*. Giant sloth (Megatheriidae, *Eremotherium*?). *b*. Mastodon (Gomphotheriidae). *c*. Camelid (*Palaeolama*?). *d–e*. Horses (Equidae, *Hippidion*?). *f*. Long-neck, three-toed ungulate with trunk (*Xenorhinotherium? Macrauchenia*?). The black silhouettes in the top left corner of each figure represent the potential megafauna depicted in the paintings. These large mammals of the last Ice Age have been extinct for more than 10,000 years.

world and carry out negotiations with the non-humans. The seminal study of the Desana people by Reichel Dolmatoff (1971) is one of the most relevant works in understanding the meaning of the paintings. According to the beliefs of the Desana, all game animals inhabit certain rocky hills, such as those of the La Lindosa, in the depths of the forest. These are places where the animal-spirits, imagined in human form, live, reproduce and are periodically released by the Owner of the Animals, to be hunters' prey. Fish, it is believed, live the same way at the bottom of deep, dark wells in rivers or lakes. In the shaman's mind, the rock crystal enables him not only to travel to these places and meet with the Owner of the Animals, but also to observe the animals, recognize their different kinds, count them and thus make an inventory of food resources, in order to achieve the balance agreed between humans and non-human beings. In the La Lindosa and Chiribiquete rock art, humans appear in scenes alongside animals. There are some zoo-anthropomorphic beings, part human, part animal; and in many scenes humans appear to be raising their hands toward animals in scenes that could be interpreted as worshipping the animals. Without committing a major leap of interpretation, it would not be too far-fetched to say that the rock art of La Lindosa and Chiribiquete represents the enduring rituals around the relationship between humans and their non-human counterparts, such as animals and plants (Figure 3.7).

The plausible 13,000 years of stories in the La Lindosa wall could well record the origins of an Amazonian way of viewing and living in the world. This may well be the

Figure 3.7 Ancestral understandings of the paintings. *a*. The paintings, according to Ulderico Matapi of the Uchia ethnic group, represent images of the beginning, of the creation of the world. Each image represents shamanic knowledge, which is only available to those who have been initiated. The knowledge contained in the graphisms allows the territory to be inhabited. *b*. The animals painted on the walls, according to Ismael Sierra of the Tukano ethnic group, belong to the spirit worlds. The animals live on the 'other side', and the rocks have entrance portals that only shamans can pass through. The ancestors carved geometrical motifs into the rock, which are now repeated in indigenous handicrafts. When mankind did not yet exist, the paintings were inhabited by spiritual beings, it was like a *maloca* (house) full of life, where animals swarmed.

beginning of a very Amazonian tradition of 'writing in the landscape', a way of embedding history and cosmological conceptions in the landscape (see Chapter 2).

Intriguing forest islands dotting the savannahs

Recent evidence from the Llanos de Mojos in the Bolivian Amazon also sheds light on the lifeways of these early Amazonians. Using a range of satellite image resources, including Google Earth, Lombardo and collaborators (2020) reported more than 6,600 forest islands in this region (Figure 3.8). By painstakingly drilling by hand auger cores from eighty-two of these sites, this team found that sixty show the telltale signs of human occupation: charcoal, burnt earth and coprostanol (a chemical signature of human faeces). Using radiocarbon dating of charcoal from thirty-one of these sites, Lombardo et al. (2020) revealed human occupation of the region dating as far back as 10.9 ka – just as the last Ice Age came to an end.

Crucially, the recovery of phytoliths – tiny mineral particles that form inside plants, their shape determined by the plant on which they form – allowed our team (Lombardo

Figure 3.8 The Llanos de Mojos landscape dotted with human-made forest islands. Courtesy Umberto Lombardo.

et al, 2020) to identify the consumption of root plants, including *Manihot*, *Calathea*, Marantaceae, *Heliconia*, Cyperaceae and *Phenakospermum* (Figure 3.9). Roots likely provided a considerable part of the calories consumed by these early Amazonians. These plant underground organs are pre-adapted and abundant in savannahs with long, dry seasons (Piperno and Pearsall, 1998), and are also concentrated in wetlands (Dillehay and Rossen, 2002). They produce carbohydrate-rich foods that, with the exception of some varieties of manioc (McKey et al, 2010a), are easy to process and cook – all of which are consumed by indigenous groups today. It has long been hypothesized that the rich, disturbed soils of home garden areas acted as laboratories, where people were able to bring plants from the forest and experiment with them in perfect conditions (e.g., Lathrap, 1970; Arroyo-Kalin, 2012). It is likely that these forest islands where these 'home gardens' were, is where these plants were initially cultivated.

What is also becoming increasingly clear from this research is that the human footprint in Amazonia is not restricted to large-scale transformations by farming groups in the late Holocene (Chapter 6). From the outset of their dispersion, these foragers had a larger impact on their environment than previously thought. This early record from the Llanos de Mojos shows that along with the beginnings of plant cultivation, the early settlers transformed this region of south-western Amazonia into an archipelago of fertile forest islands, dotting the grassy savannah. These artificial forest islands likely had lasting repercussions for habitat heterogeneity. Their presence indicates that the practices recorded ethnographically by the Kayapó, of creating resource-rich forest islands (Hecht, 2009), may well go back to the very start of the Holocene. Called 'apêtê', these forest islands created in the Brazilian Cerrado tropical savannahs by the Kayapó consist of mounds prepared with crumbled termite and ant nests, mulched out and planted with

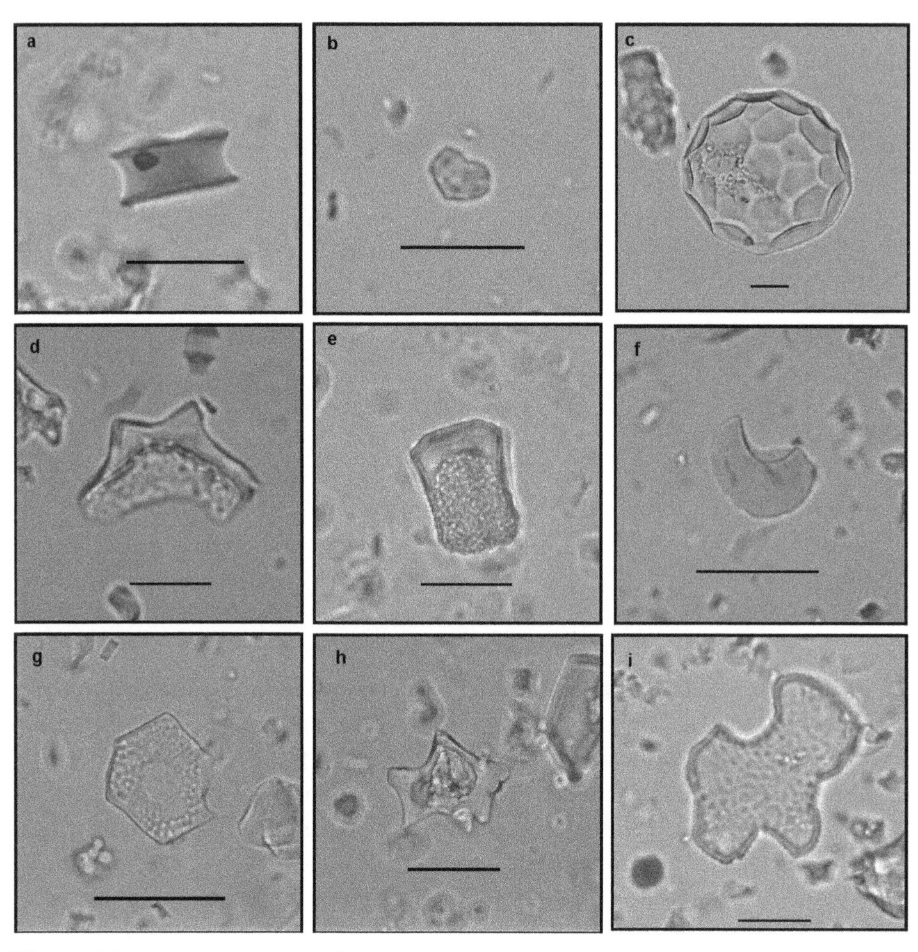

Figure 3.9 Photomicrographs of phytolith morphotypes recovered from Isla del Tesoro, La Chacra and Isla Manechi forest island in the Llanos de Mojos. *a.* Wavy-top rondel from the cob of maize (*Z. mays*). *b.* Heart-shaped phytolith from the secretory cells of manioc (*Manihot*). *c.* Scalloped sphere from the rind of squash (*Cucurbita* sp.). *d.* Double-peaked glume from the seed of rice (*Oryza* sp.). *e.* Flat domed cylinder from the rhizome of *Calathea* sp. *f.* Short trough body from the rhizome of *Heliconia* sp. *g.* Stippled polygonal body from the seed of a member of the Cyperaceae. *h.* Phytolith with nodular projections and a pointed apex, from the seed of Marantaceae. *i.* Stippled plate from the fruit of a hackberry (*Celtis* sp.) Scale bars, 20 μm. Courtesy Umberto Lombardo.

useful plants. This initiates a process of forest succession, with forest islands expanding into the savannah, creating zones of different shade, light and humidity, where a diversity of plants could flourish. Through these practices, communities increased resource abundance and heterogeneity for both humans and animals, underscoring the strong relationship between plant and landscape domestication and the significant human footprint on Amazonian environments.

Similarly, ethnoarchaeology among the Nukak foragers of the Colombian Amazon provides a glimpse of how the transformation of the forest may have begun. Ethnoarchaeology – ethnography carried out by archaeologists looking at material correlates of human behaviour – can illuminate how these processes took place. This does not mean that these societies are our 'contemporary ancestors' or are 'frozen in time'. Looking at ethnographic examples with an archaeologist's eyes can provide us with analogies to inform our thinking when interpreting the past. For example, the ethnoarchaeological work of Politis (2009) shows how the accidental but repeated discarding of unshelled seeds/nuts by the Nukak (Figure 3.2e) on the rich, organic soils of the frequently-visited camps, creates groves of edible fruit-bearing trees, which, in turn, progressively alters the forest composition. As the work of this author demonstrates, the Nukak create 'wild orchards' with selected species of economic importance, including *seje* (*Oenocarpus bataua*, *Oenocarpus bacaba*), *cumare* (*Astrocaryum aculeatum*) and *platanillo* (*Phenakospermum guyannense*). Similar practices in which humans become a plant dispersal factor have been recorded for the Kayapó and Ka'apor in Brazil (Posey and Balée, 1989) and the Waorani in Ecuador (Rival, 1998). The age of these practices is unknown, but the dominance of tree and palm fruits from the earliest levels of La Lindosa, Caverna de Pedra Pintada and Peña Roja suggest that these patterns are ancient. And they must have had an early impact on forest composition. As Politis reasoned in relation to today's Nukak, if we take into account that the surface area of residential camps ranges from 32–179 metres^2, the fact that they have a high mobility occupying 70–80 camps a year, then they create about 0.6 hectares of wild orchards per band per year. Similarly, the use of fire was likely common in seasonal forests, savannahs and forest-savannah ecotones. The presence of axes in the early records of the Cauca River Basin attests to the ability of these early settlers to fell trees, which likely contributed to the disturbance and clearance of these montane forests.

All these new research initiatives to understand early Amazonians confirms that the spread of early Americans through the South American continent was more complex than accepted theories would indicate. They show that the Amazon was no barrier to human occupation. Not only did early settlers adapt to the Amazon from the outset, but they also began to modify it, thus setting into motion the long history of the complex societies that evolved during the late Holocene (Chapters 6–8).

Similarly, the research challenges the widely held assumption, based on our knowledge of Clovis people, that the earliest Americans were primarily specialized big-game hunters who lived in open, temperate country and could not have sustained a culture in the humid tropics, where large animals were scarce. Unlike the northern Clovis counterparts, they did not possess a curated bifacial technology. Except for the Caverna da Pedra Pintada assemblage, the lithic technology of early Amazonian was unifacial in which projectile points are exceptions in the broader artefact assemblages (Bueno, 2010; Rodet et al. 2023). For example, a bare of ten projectile points have been collected from surficial context across the lower Amazon (Hilbert, 1998).

The belief now is that productive ecotones, in particular palm-dominated tropical forest-savannah-riverine mosaics, were, on the contrary, attractive to early foragers for the establishment of temporary or semi-permanent camps. The research strongly suggests that areas of forest-savannah, such as the Llanos de Mojos, and localities with palm-dominated forests, such as Monte Alegre and La Lindosa, were, in the minds of these first Amazonians, ideal settings. These groups were foragers who were likely egalitarian, mobile and organized in small bands, and their social organization is expected to be non-complex. However, their material culture and conceptual culture, as seen in the rock paintings, was elaborate.

As we will see in the next chapter, early Amazonians not only began to domesticate landscapes but from the outset of human dispersal were also ingenuous plant breeders who began to domesticate a diversity of globally important crops. We will also discuss the two major centres of plant domestication in lowland South America: the montane Andean forests of Colombia and the tropical savannahs of the Llanos de Mojos in Bolivia, and learn how Amazonian plant domestication and food production is unique, and therefore, as Arroyo-Kalin (2010:474) points out 'sits uncomfortably' in traditional Eurasian narratives of Neolithic Revolution and agriculture.

CHAPTER 4
TRANSFORMING THE GARDEN OF EDEN: CREATING NEW PLANTS AND LANDSCAPES

This chapter opens with a brief introduction to the abundance and diversity of useful and edible plants constituting the raw materials for plant management. This is followed by some key definitions about plant and landscape domestication, as well as how I used the terms 'horticulture' and 'agriculture'. After that, I introduce the reader to the latest methodological developments that are allowing us to document plant domestication and its ancient human impact, as well as its legacy for today's Amazonian landscapes. Following this, I will delve into the ingenuity of native Amazonian plant breeders in cultivating and domesticating a diversity of globally important plants. Current genetic and archaeological evidence shows two major centres of plant domestication for Amazonia (defined in this book as the tropical regions of South America that lie to the east of the Andes), where plant selection began during the late Pleistocene–early Holocene transition. One is the sub-Andean montane forest of Colombia, where important tubers, such as sweet potato, yams, arrowroot and leren were cultivated from as early as ~9.6 ka (Aceituno and Loaiza, 2018). The other centre encompasses the shrub savannahs and seasonal tropical forest environments of Llanos de Mojos in SW Amazonia, where manioc appear to have been brought under cultivation ~10.3 ka. This latest research by Lombardo and collaborators (2020) at Llanos de Mojos defines SW Amazonia as the fifth centre of early Holocene plant domestication in the world, adding to two in the Old World (Near East and China) and two in the New World (south-western Mexico and north-western South America) (Larson et al., 2014). I end the chapter with a reflection on how plant and landscape domestication in Amazonia and the Neotropics differs from the way these processes took place in other regions of the world.

A cornucopia of edible and useful plants

Tropical South America is home to an extraordinary variety of edible plants. Amazonia alone hosts an estimated 20,000, of which 2,000 are economically important, while thirty provide most of the world's food. The Amazon is the birthplace of many staple crops now eaten all over the world. These include manioc (*Manihot esculenta*), sweet potato (*Ipomoea batatas*), yam (*Dioscorea trifida*), cocoyam (*Xanthosoma sagittifolium*), peach palm (*Bactris gasipaes*), chilli peppers (*Capsicum* spp.) including *murupi* pepper (*Capsicum chinense*), squash (*Cucurbita* spp.), pineapple (*Ananas comosus*), papaya (*Carica papaya*), peanut (*Arachis hypogea*), cashew (*Anacardium occidentale*), *guava*

(*Psidium guajava*), *biribiri* (*Averrhoa bilimbi*), tobacco (*Nicotiana tabacum*), *annatto* (*Bixa orellana*), *bacuri* (*Platonia insignis*), *cupuaçu* (*Theobroma grandiflorum*), *mapati* (*Pourouma cecropiifolia*) and *cubiu* (*Solanum sessiliflorum*) (Clement, 1999b; Clement et al., 2016; Iriarte, 2007; Piperno and Pearsall, 1998; Shepard Jr et al., 2020) (Figure 4.1). Furthermore, the Neotropics including Amazonia provide more than 50 per cent of crop plants cultivated in the Americas (Clement, 1999a; Piperno and Pearsall, 1998), while indigenous societies of the tropical forest 'domesticated a larger assemblage of root and tuber crops than anyone else on earth' (e.g., Harlan, 1995). Ethnobotanical works provide an idea of the number and variety of annual and perennial crops cultivated by indigenous Amazonians (see summary in Cunha, 2019). Some groups, such as the Amuesha of Peru, plant up to 204 varieties of manioc (Emperaire, 2001; Salick et al., 1997), while Brieger (1958) recorded dozens of varieties of maize being planted in lowland South America. Because annual crops disappear after human abandonment (Clement, 1999a; b), it is likely that many varieties existed in the time before indigenous populations were decimated following the arrival of Europeans to the region. Tree, palm fruit and Brazil nut management is also important to Amazonian traditional economies. Sixty-eight per cent of the 138 cultivated and domesticated food crop species cultivated by Amazonian

Figure 4.1 Fruits of the Amazonian forests for sale at a neighbourhood fair in Belém do Pará. *a. goaiaba* (*Psidium guajava*, Myrtaceae). *b. pupunha* (*Bactris gasipaes*, Arecaceae). *c. uxi* (*Eudopleura uchi*, Humiriaceae). *d.* Biribá (*Annona mucosa*, Annonacea). *e. pequi* (*Caryocar brasilensis*, Caryocaceae). *f. anana* (*Ananas comosus*, Bromiliaceae). *g. avocado* (*Persea Americana*, Lauraceae). *h. cupuaçu* (*Theobroma grandiflora*, Malvaceae). *i.* Brazil nut (*Bertholethia excelsa*, Lecythidaceae). Photo courtesy of Daiana Alves.

peoples at the time of first European contact were perennial and woody crops, as documented by Clement (1999b), the majority being tree fruits and nuts. Most were native species, but many came from other parts of South America and Mesoamerica.

Besides this vast array of edible plants, the Amazon is also known as a 'healing forest' because of its abundance of medicinal plants. This has resulted in an extensive pharmacopoeia used traditionally to heal physical and psychological ailments. This topic is too vast to be fully described within the given space limitations of this book (see for example, Duke and Vasquez, 1994 and Schultes and Raffauf, 1990 for a summary of them).

Domesticating plants, domesticating landscapes

Plant domestication and the beginnings of agriculture are turning points in human history (Larson et al., 2014; Smith, 1998). Plant domestication is understood as the human creation of a new plant form, one that is distinguishably and observably different, that is, expresses morpho-genetic changes from its wild ancestors and extant wild relatives. Domesticated plants in their most extreme form are those that would no longer exist if human manipulation were discontinued.

In evolutionary terms, plant domestication and the emergence of agriculture are extremely recent. Modern humans evolved in Africa ~300–200 ka, and agriculture began only around 10 ka. For approximately 95 per cent of our prehistory as modern humans, people relied on foraging, hunting, fishing and collecting wild plant foods provided by nature. Only in the remaining 5 per cent of the time have we engaged in plant domestication. However, as we have seen, foragers engage in various forms of landscape domestication (see below).

Plant domestication happened independently in various parts of the world. It involved different people at different times and entailed a diversity of plants. According to Harris (2007), plant domestication is a continuum of human investment in selection and environmental manipulation; thus, strict definitions are constructs that imperfectly reflect reality. This is especially true in the tropics, as I will discuss below. During the process of plant domestication, people selected plants with larger seeds (maize) or tubers (manioc), or those that were less bitter (*Cucurbita* squashes), or that were easier to harvest by keeping the seeds in the pod when ripe (*Phaseolus* beans). Plant domestication had far-reaching consequences. Ten thousand years ago, before the advent of plant domestication, the estimated global population was only 4–10 million, whereas today the planet has more than 7.7 billion people. Population density also increased greatly following the adoption of agriculture. Among today's hunter-gatherer groups there is a density of 0.1 persons per kilometre^2; this rises to 1,000 persons per kilometre^2 among Asian rice paddy agriculturalists. For some scholars, such as Smith and Zeder (2013), plant domestication marks the onset of the Anthropocene and the beginning of artifactual landscapes: a time when the landscape began to be completely shaped by humans. According to these authors, plant domestication represents a turning point, with environment becoming more dependent on human activity. The domestication of plants also marks the emergence of new technologies to prepare the land: stone axes to open forested areas; hoes for digging and moving the soil; new harvesting tools, such as sickle blades; and new tools for processing and preparing meals, such as plant grinding tools and ceramic containers. It is also important to remember that domestication is not a thing of the past. Plant domestication is an ongoing process, amplified in recent times by genetic engineering.

In this book, following Piperno and Pearsall (1998), I use simple definitions and focus on practices that can be documented in the archaeological and palaeoecological records. The presence of small-scale plantings, in residential home gardens, is loosely defined as horticulture, with gardens typically including a variety of plants, ranging from the morphologically wild to the clearly domesticated. As defined here, horticultural systems likely characterized Amazonian people during the early and middle Holocene. A move towards agriculture is reflected in the occurrence of fields dedicated to long-term cultivation, in and around larger and more permanent settlements. This defining moment, when people begin to invest in long-term physical and chemical improvements to the soil, with the aim of intensifying cultivation and productivity at specific sites, marks the beginning of agriculture in some areas of Amazonia, with the advent of Amazonian anthrosols and raised field agricultural landscapes (see Chapter 6).

As well as individual plants, in time people domesticate entire landscapes. According to Clement (1999a: 190), the domestication of the landscape refers to the 'conscious process by which human manipulation of the landscape results in changes in landscape ecology and the demographics of its plant and animal populations, resulting in a landscape more productive and congenial for humans'.

Before we turn to the description of the centres of plant domestication in Amazonia, in the following section I will present the latest methodological advances and integrative methodologies that are helping to document plant domestication and investigate pre-Columbian land use in Amazonia.

Sources of evidence and methodological advances

Amazonia is huge and is roughly the size of the continental US. It contains a great diversity of peoples living among heterogeneous ecosystems and a variety of cultivated landscapes (Chapter 2). It has a long history of human occupation starting from at least 13,000 years ago (Chapter 3). Understanding plant and landscape domestication, and the nature and extent of past human impact and its modern legacy, is not an easy task. It has been made more difficult by the isolation of different academic disciplines. But by bringing the natural sciences and humanities together, and embracing the full breadth of Amazonian scholarship, we can start to reach an understanding of these important topics (Figures 4.2–4.3) (Clement et al., 2015; Iriarte et al., 2020a; McMichael et al., 2023; Mayle and Iriarte, 2014).

Over the past three decades, a combination of archaeological and archaeobotanical projects in previously unexplored Amazonian regions has radically altered our understanding

Figure 4.2 Interdisciplinary work. *a*. S. Maezumi examines and records the colour of a sediment core retrieved from Lago Caranã in the vicinity of Santarém, where she has conducted pollen and charcoal analysis. A catamaran was created by tying two small boats together and placing a wooden platform between them that has a hole for pushing down the piston corer used to extract the sediment core. *b*. U. Lombardo uses a motor-assisted corer to extract a sediment core from the 'Isla del Tesoro' forest island in Beni, Bolivia. *c*. J. Watling collects sediment samples from modern reference soil in Acre, Brazil, for phytolith, charcoal and stable carbon isotope analysis. *d*. A. Damasceno takes soil samples from a test pit in the vicinity of Jaco Sá geometric ditch enclosure. *e*. G. Morcote Ríos recovers light buoyant charred seed from the flotation machine in the Colombian Amazon. *f*. D. Alves digs an Amazonian anthrosol in Santarém. *g*. F. Cruz labels a recently collected speleothem. *h*. M. Robinson attaches a lidar sensor to a helicopter to conduct a lidar mapping session on the Casarabe culture in Trinidad, Bolivia. *i*. E. Almeida and I. Brasil da Silva carrying out botanical inventories in the FLONA Tapajós around Santarém city. *b*. courtesy of Umberto Lombardo; *d*. courtesy of Francisco Cruz.

of the timing, geographical origins and diversity of plant domestication, and food-producing systems in Amazonia and beyond (Carson et al., 2014; Iriarte and Dickau, 2012; Iriarte et al., 2004; Kistler et al., 2018; Maezumi et al., 2018a, 2022; Piperno et al., 2009; Robinson et al., 2018; Watling et al., 2017). Also of relevance has been the use of molecular data, the systematic application of microfossil botanical techniques, and related palaeoecological research pioneered in the Neotropics by Pearsall (1995) and Piperno (1984). The historical ecology programme (e.g., Balée, 2006; Balée and Erickson, 2006; Walker, 2020a) has played a vital role in this research, by bringing humans back to the centre of the debate.

Our sources of information are proxies, that is, materials, such as phytoliths, starch grains, pollen grains and charred seeds that have survived from the past, trapped within sediments. Since they reflect the environment in which they were deposited, they can be used to reconstruct ancient environments and economies. Additionally, as we will see below, there is much to be learned from contemporary traditional communities via ethnography, ethnobotany and ethnoarchaeology. In this section, it is impossible to cover all the methodologies and proxies used to study plant domestication, agricultural development and past human impact on Amazonia, so only the most recent and relevant methodologies will be highlighted, along with their advantages and limitations (see Iriarte et al., 2020a; Mayle and Iriarte, 2014; McMichael et al., 2023; Montoya et al., 2020).

Plant remains

The study of the plant component of pre-Columbian subsistence and economy in Amazonia is at an early stage. Until recently, only a few projects systematically applied archaeobotanical recovery techniques, and thus, there is a paucity of primary data. However, progress has been rapid in the past few decades. Reference collections of macro- (e.g., Morcote-Rios and Bernal, 2001) and micro-botanical remains (e.g., Piperno and McMichael, 2023; Watling et al., 2020) are being built, and the recovery of plant remains is becoming a systematic practice in archaeological projects.

Starch grains and phytoliths are proving useful in identifying seed and root crops, and the nature of different environments. Phytoliths are microscopic silica structures (measuring between 4–200 microns) that form in the roots, stems and reproductive parts of plants. They can only be seen under high magnification using biological microscopes. These structures, also called 'plant rock', are composed of opaline silica, a non-crystalline form of silicon dioxide. Because of their durability, they are considered one of the most resilient fossil plants. They survive in tropical soils, whereas other plant remains do not. Because they are deposited *in situ*, they can be used to document crop cultivation in agricultural landscapes, such as raised fields and Amazonian anthrosols (Chapter 7). A large number of plants indicative of particular environments, such as wild kinds of rice (wetlands), *Heliconia* (disturbed environments) and *Phragmites* reed (brackish water), as well as many important crops, including, maize, squash and rice, can be identified using phytoliths. As a result of ongoing refinements in the identification of the micro-morphological features of phytoliths and their three-dimensional morphology, archaeobotanists are able to distinguish phytolith morphotypes to an ever-greater degree of taxonomic resolution. Some palm (Arecaceae) phytoliths can now be distinguished to the genus level, thanks to the identification of micro-morphological features. Examples are *Geonoma*'s unique conical variant with basal projections morphotype, and *Euterpe*'s large symmetric globular echinates with short bold projections morphotype (Dickau et al., 2013; Huisman et al., 2018; Morcote-Ríos et al., 2016; Witteveen et al., 2022). These developments apply not only to the identification of individual plants but also to the analysis of soil phytolith assemblages, used to identify the nature of neotropical ecosystems (Dickau et al., 2013; Watling et al., 2016). More recently, much-needed work has started on understanding the phytolith signature of indigenous land use systems (Watling et al., 2023; Witteveen et al. 2023; but see also Piperno, 1984).

Starch grains are microscopic starch granules, representing the energy storage mechanism of plants. They are usually located in a plant's roots and seeds. Until recently, it was not possible to document root and tuber crop domestication unless the sites investigated were in arid environments, such as on the Peruvian coast and in the Tehuacán Valley, where conditions permitted the survival of these soft underground plant organs. These regions were outside the original areas of domestication of the major crops for which they yielded evidence (e.g., manioc, sweet potato, squashes, cotton, chilli peppers). But these data lacunae are being filled, thanks to the refinement of microfossil botanical techniques. Starch grain research now provides robust information on the domestication and spread of root crops and various important seed crops in tropical regions of the Americas, as well as in the Old World tropics (e.g., Denham, 2018; Ezell et al., 2006; Pearsall et al., 2004; Perry et al., 2007; Piperno, 2006; Piperno et al., 2000). Additionally, the study of starch grain residues from plant processing tools, such as grinding stones and chipped stone, is helping to illuminate the function of these tools, enabling a revision of traditional interpretations based on ethnographic analogy and other, less direct, forms of evidence (e.g., Perry, 2004). Many tuber crops, such as sweet potato and yams, do not produce diagnostic phytoliths, but they do produce diagnostic starch grains, which can be recovered from tool residues or ceramic containers (e.g., Dickau et al., 2007; Piperno et al., 2009). Back in the 1960s, a revolution occurred when flotation was systematically applied to recovered charred seeds in the Near East. Arguably the 1990s saw a similar turning point, when microbotanical techniques began to be applied to Neotropical contexts (Pearsall, 2015; Piperno and Pearsall, 1998).

Macrobotanical remains are large plant remains, visible to the naked eye, which can be seen under low magnification using stereoscopes. They are preserved in a charred condition (fungi and bacteria do not eat charcoal), and because they are lighter, they float in water, and in turn, buoyancy makes them more efficiently recoverable through a flotation system. Palms, tree fruits and nuts, such as the Brazil nut and *pequi* (*Caryocar* sp.), are now being systematically recovered from archaeological sites across Amazonia using flotation (e.g., Furquim et al., 2021; Morcote-Rios et al., 2021; Shock et al., 2014; Watling et al., 2018). Direct AMS dating of macrobotanical remains and, more recently, phytoliths retrieved both from archaeological and palaeoecological contexts, is starting to provide more precise chronologies of plant domestication and environmental history (e.g., Piperno and Flannery, 2001).

Most importantly, using both macro- and micro-botanical analysis allows for more comprehensive plant consumption inventories (Dickau et al., 2012; Furquim et al., 2021; Herrera et al., 1992; Watling et al., 2018). As we will see in the archaeobotanical analysis of the Casarabe culture in Chapter 8, cotton and peanut, which do not produce diagnostic phytoliths, were documented via the flotation of charred macro-remains. By contrast, yams and manioc, whose uncharred soft root tissues do not survive in tropical soils, were documented by retrieving them from plant processing tools in the form of phytoliths and starch grains (Dickau et al., 2012).

Although plant assemblages recovered in archaeological sites can provide relevant information on the surrounding ancient environments, they cannot be considered perfect representations of it. They can tell us, for example, that early sites in the Amazon, such as Caverna da Pedra Pintada in the lower Amazon or Lindosa in the Colombian Amazon, were surrounded by tropical forests; but they cannot be used to reconstruct the environment as if they were 'naturally-deposited' pollen records perfectly reflecting the regional vegetation.

The past is a foreign landscape

Amazonian palaeoecology, like archaeobotany, is a relatively new discipline that began in the late 1960s. The primary aim was to reconstruct natural vegetation histories through pollen analysis of long-term sedimentary sequences (e.g., lake and bog cores), with a focus on glacial cycles (Colinvaux, 2008). However, palaeoecologists are increasingly aware that today's forests do not represent pristine baselines, and that ecosystem trajectories have been profoundly affected since humans arrived in Amazonia. There is a growing recognition of the need to integrate on-site archaeological data with off-site palaeoecological and paleoclimate records, resulting in novel insights into our understanding of land use systems in Amazonia, such as Amazonian anthrosols and raised field systems (e.g., Iriarte et al., 2012; Maezumi et al., 2022; McMichael et al., 2012; Whitney et al., 2014), which will be presented in detail in the chapters to follow.

Pollen is a key proxy for reconstructing ancient Amazonian landscapes (Bennett and Willis, 2001). Pollen is produced by all seed-bearing plants, Angiosperms (flowering plants) and Gymnosperms (cone-bearing plants), in order to reproduce. Because pollen contains the male gametes of the plant, it generally needs to travel and disperse from the anthers of one plant to the stigma of another. Much of it is dispersed by wind and animals, eventually reaching the bottom of lakes, where the anaerobic conditions favour its preservation. Palaeoecological records accumulate gradually, over thousands of years. Lake sediment cores are an environmental archive (Figure 4.6). They typically provide continuous, uninterrupted time series of vegetation records, from the sub-centennial to the multi-millennial level. They offer a longer temporal perspective, supplementing the modern data gathered from ethnobotany, floristic studies and ecology. Environmental archives often have the additional advantage of providing uninterrupted records, which are not always present in the archaeological data. In many areas where archaeological investigations have been limited, palaeoecology takes precedence over archaeology to indicate human presence. Because palaeoecological records often predate human occupations, they can also provide ecological baselines against which to compare pre- and post-human environmental impacts. Early appearances of pollen from crops such as maize can tell us that humans have cultivated a specific area even when the archaeological sites have yet to be discovered. This is the case, for example, with the Ring Ditches of Bolivia (Chapter 7), where maize pollen goes back to 5,700 years ago, but only sites pertaining to the late Holocene have been discovered (Carson et al., 2016). Unfortunately, lakes are rare in Amazonia. However, in their absence, soil-depth phytolith and stable carbon isotope transects provide an alternative method for reconstructing regional vegetation and fire histories (e.g., de Freitas et al., 2001; McMichael et al., 2012; Robinson et al., 2018; Watling et al., 2017).

The long-term nature of palaeoecological records can help resolve long-standing controversies about the past human footprint on modern vegetation formations. It is only by comparing palaeo records with modern floristic inventories that we can start to disentangle recent from pre-Colombian influences on the flora. For example, it has been proposed that many palm forests in Amazonia are the result of recent historical land use (Heijink et al., 2020; McMichael et al., 2017). However, although historical land uses may have dramatically altered the landscape in certain regions of Amazonia (Heijink et al., 2023), and cannot be ignored, numerous palaeoecological records show that increases in economically important plants began during pre-Columbian times. Examples include the increase in palms detected when human activities intensified during the late Holocene in Acre's geoglyph region (Watling et al., 2017) and along the Gran Sabana (Rull and Montoya, 2014), as well as the 1.5 ka increase in *Attalea* palms in the Versalles lake (Maezumi et al., 2022) to give some examples. Palaeoecological analysis has also been very useful in documenting early forest cultivation, which unlike raised fields, irrigation canals and agricultural terraces, leaves no visible imprint on the landscape (Pearsall, 2007).

Many methodological advancements are helping to improve palaeoecological reconstructions, while pollen taxonomic resolution of important ecological taxa is being refined continually (e.g., Burn and Mayle, 2008). These efforts are being aided by the creation of a searchable Neotropical pollen database (Bush and Weng, 2007) and the consolidation of a Latin American Pollen Database (Flantua et al., 2015b). It has become easier to detect and differentiate between various types of palms in pollen records. An increase in *Mauritia/Mauritiella* palm pollen has been argued to be evidence of more intensive land use (Rull and Montoya, 2014), while, in contrast, the decrease or disappearance of other palms used as construction materials, such as *Iriartea deltoidea*, has been argued to be evidence of more intensive land use (Bush and McMichael, 2016).

Technologically simple but ingenious methodologies are being designed to deal with the challenge of flat landscapes, shallow lakes and abundant crop pollen. Crop pollen is large, heavy and poorly dispersed. Maize pollen, for example, typically disperses only 70 metres from the plant. Therefore, if crops were cultivated around a lake, the crop's pollen is usually deposited around the lake margins, which makes it unlikely that it will be recovered from the centre of large lakes. The following actions are helping to improve the situation: i) coring lake margins close to archaeological sites (e.g., Maezumi et al.,

2022; Piperno et al., 2007); ii) using particular-sized sieves, to concentrate large, heavy crop pollen, which has significantly increased the diversity and volume of crop pollen recovered from lake records (Whitney et al., 2012); and iii) carrying out extended counting (looking at more slides of the same sample). However, we need to be aware that some important pollen taxa, such as *Theobroma cacao*, which has a highly specialized pollination mechanism (Ceratopogonidae midges), are difficult to detect in pollen sedimentary records even with extended counting (Carson et al., 2016).

The complementary nature of phytolith and pollen analyses has proven especially advantageous in relation to taxonomic resolution and spatial scale. Although phytoliths have better taxonomic resolution than pollen for many grasses and herbs, pollen analysis has a better taxonomic resolution for woody taxa (but see recent improvements Piperno and McMichael, 2023). Lake pollen records, for example, can capture regional signals (>10 metres^2), whereas phytoliths from soil-depth profiles typically provide local spatial scale (1 metres^2). Using these proxies together provides more floristic detail and spatial resolution than using either proxy alone (e.g., Iriarte et al., 2004; Piperno and Jones, 2003). In addition, combining pollen data with more localized proxies, such as soil carbon isotopes, has been effective in distinguishing human influence on broad vegetation change from naturally occurring events, such as shifts in the climate (Robinson et al., 2018; 2020).

Charcoal is a key proxy to reconstruct fire histories (e.g., Maezumi et al., 2018). More recently, the application of FTIR spectroscopy, which examines the chemical properties of charcoal fragments, can provide valuable information about the temperature of a fire and the type of plants that were burned. This technique is capable of distinguishing between woody and grassy materials that were burned, as shown by studies conducted by Gosling et al., (2019) and Maezumi et al. (2021). Diatoms are not discussed in detail here, but they offer valuable insights into changes in hydrology, water quality, human activity and climate, as well as human-induced vegetation changes in lake sediment records (e.g. Bush, 2016; Duncan et al., 2021). Likewise, lake sediment stable isotopes and chemical element analysis, which are not covered in this review, can provide important information on pre-Columbian human activity (Hodell et al., 2005).

Environmental ancient DNA from sediment cores can be used in addition to pollen to determine the composition of both terrestrial and aquatic local plant communities (see Pedersen et al., 2015). Finally, improved statistical methods, such as Bayesian age-depth modelling, are providing more precise chronologies of plant domestication and environmental histories (Blaauw and Christen, 2013). Last but not least, dendrochronology is an emerging tool in the tookit of Amazonian paleoecology. A study led by Caetano Andrade et al. (2019) has shown how patterns in the establishment and growth of living Brazil nut trees in Central Amazonia reflect more than 400 years of changes in human occupation, politics and socio-economic activities in the region.

Genes

Molecular research is another resource for Amazonian and other Neotropical researchers seeking to understand plant domestication and management (Clement and Junqueira,

2010; Pickersgill, 2007; Sanjur et al., 2002). Endless debates over which plant was the wild ancestor of a given domesticated plant based on morphological traits are now largely over, thanks to molecular data that can help fingerprint the wild progenitors of domesticated plants and pinpoint their current and – by inference – ancient geographical distributions. Molecular data can also tell us whether a crop was domesticated only once or several times. For example, current data indicate that some crops, such as maize (Matsuoka et al., 2002), manioc (Olsen and Schaal, 2001) and sweet potato (Mu et al., 2018), were probably domesticated only once. Conversely, other major crop plants were most likely domesticated multiple times in different parts of the Americas, including, for example, *Cucurbita pepo* (Sanjur et al., 2002) and common beans (*Phaseolus vulgaris*) (Sonnante et al., 1994). Some important root crops, such as arrowroot, cocoyam and sagu, have yet to be studied, while others, such as *Ipomoea*, are currently being researched (Mu et al., 2018).

Modern genetic data can also provide us with 'molecular clocks', which can indicate the relative timing of plant domestication (Matsuoka et al., 2002; Olsen and Schaal, 2001). Additionally, genetic analysis reveals the specific loci responsible for domesticated traits in plants, such as lignification in domesticated squash rinds (Piperno et al., 2002) or the branching architecture of maize tassel and ear (Sigmon and Vollbrecht, 2010).

Establishing the phenotypic and genetic characterization of these ancient and modern Amazonian plants as they changed from wild to domesticated is a huge task. This is especially true for many Amazonian tree crops, whose initial classification into domestication categories, based on the works of Balée (1989), Cavalcante (1991), Frikel (1978) and Levi-Strauss (1952) was mainly based on qualitative observations. However, progress is being made. Research by Moreira et al. (2015) demonstrated the selection of annato (*Bixa orellana*) for increased pigment yields and fruit dehiscence, while Smith and Fausto (2016) identified selection for larger pulp thickness and the absence of spines in *pequi* (*Caryocar brasiliensis*) varieties among the Kuikuro of the Upper Xingu. Finally, genetic biogeography is another important and powerful tool. Genetic studies on Brazil nuts, for example, support rapid and recent irradiation from an ancestral population, based on the lack of sequence diversity and the absence of geographical structuring within population variability (Shepard and Ramirez, 2011; Thomas et al., 2015). This likely took place in northern/eastern Amazonia during the first millennium CE.

Carbon and nitrogen isotopes

Stable carbon and nitrogen isotope analysis of bone collagen and apatite is a well-established method for obtaining dietary information from human and faunal remains. It has been used to reconstruct pre-Columbian subsistence economies across much of South America (e.g., Colonese et al., 2020; Hermenegildo et al., 2017; Müller et al., 2022; van der Merwe et al., 1981).

The following summary, based on the work of Colonese et al. (2020) and Muller et al. (2022), explains how carbon and nitrogen isotope analysis functions in the Amazon tropics. Plants that utilize two different primary photosynthetic pathways, C3 and C4, drive stable carbon isotope ($\delta^{13}C$) variability in tropical terrestrial ecosystems. When compared to wild C4 grasses or domesticates, such as maize, strong discrimination against $\delta^{13}C$ during CO_2 fixation in C3 plants leads to lower $\delta^{13}C$ values in the great majority of trees and shrubs that dominate tropical forest settings, as well as in domesticates, such as manioc. $\delta^{13}C$ values for C4 plants range from about −9 to −17 per cent (global mean −12 per cent), while $\delta^{13}C$ values for C3 plants range from about −24 to −36 per cent (global mean −26.5 per cent). With 1–2 per cent trophic level impacts, these variations are mirrored in the tissues of consumers who consume these plants. The 'canopy effect', which results in plants living beneath a dense canopy having a lower $\delta^{13}C$ than those living in more open situations, causes additional variety within a C3-dominated context.

In terrestrial ecosystems, $\delta^{15}N$ varies with trophic level, with ~2–6 per cent trophic shifts recorded in terrestrial and aquatic systems. The extended length of marine food chains results in unusually high $\delta^{15}N$ levels in marine species. Freshwater species have high $\delta^{15}N$ levels for the same reason. However, because of distinct carbon sources in these ecosystems, freshwater $\delta^{13}C$ does not follow the same co-varying trend with $\delta^{15}N$ towards higher readings as seen in marine food chains, and highly variable $\delta^{13}C$ has been observed in freshwater settings around the world.

Because of these principles and distinctions, stable isotope analysis is a highly effective tool for addressing a variety of important questions concerning past human diets. Although thresholds of 100 per cent C3 consumption, 100 per cent C4 consumption or 'canopy consumption' have been established, environmental factors that can lead to both $\delta^{13}C$ and $\delta^{15}N$ variability, because of soil dynamics and climatic effects (e.g. rainfall), mean that baseline data from associated animal remains in archaeological sites is essential. The isotopic values of protein in the diet are predominantly determined by $\delta^{13}C$ and $\delta^{15}N$ analyses of human bone collagen, with a much smaller contribution from lipid and carbohydrate sources. This suggests that high-protein diets, such as fish and meat, will have a significant impact on the $\delta^{13}C$ and $\delta^{15}N$ values of bone collagen. In contrast, $\delta^{13}C$ measurements of tooth enamel bioapatite ($\delta^{13}C$ ap) reflect the 'whole-diet' throughout the enamel formation phase, which varies depending on the species and tooth studied. Depending on the element examined, these tissues will also represent different dietary eras. Femur bones are said to reflect the last ten years of life.

In Amazonia, this technique is in its early stages. Contextual isotopic baselines for robust quantitative and qualitative reconstructions for the Neotropics are being compiled, which is critical given that freshwater fish and C3 plants may have similar δ13C and, in some cases, δ15N values depending on species and environments (e.g., Martinelli et al., 2007). Similarly, the majority of domesticated annual crops (manioc, sweet potato, yams, beans and peanuts, among others) have a C3 photosynthetic pathway and, in general, their stable carbon isotope composition (δ13C values) cannot be distinguished from other C3 plants, whether wild, managed or domesticated. As a result, obtaining bone collagen and apatite δ13C values consistent with C3 plants does not necessarily imply that people ate mostly wild C3 plants. Conversely, the absence of a C4 signature that can only be produced by maize does not imply the absence of other C3 annual crops in pre-Columbian diets. However, carbon and nitrogen stable isotopes can provide us with a clear indication of when maize became a staple crop. For example, a recent study from fifty-two radiocarbon-dated human remains from rock shelters in Belize's Maya Mountains, spanning the last 10 ka, sheds light on the role of maize in this region. The study found no clear evidence of maize consumption before 4.7 ka. Between 4.7–4.0 ka, evidence for substantial maize consumption (30 per cent of total diet) appears in some individuals, whereas isotopic evidence shows that maize became a staple (>70 per cent of total diet) after 4.0 ka (Kennett et al., 2020). Carbon and nitrogen isotope studies in Amazonia revealed that, while certain societies, such as the Casarabe culture, rely on maize as a staple crop (Prümers and Betancourt 2014), others, such as those in the Amazon's mouth, rely less on it (Hermenegildo et al., 2017). The next chapters present more comprehensive results for carbon and nitrogen isotopes in the different regions of Amazonia where these analyses have been carried out.

Ancient climates

The collection of new, localized, high-resolution ancient climate records is beginning to reveal the heterogeneity of climate change across Amazonia's various regions. For example, new records show antiphasing between SW Amazonia and NE Brazil, that is, when is it wetter in SW Amazonia it is drier in NE Brazil and vice versa (Deininger et al., 2019). By analysing the chemical composition of stalagmites, palaeoclimatologists can track the history of rainfall in the region where the stalagmites are growing. For example, the relative abundance of oxygen isotopes (expressed by $\delta^{18}0$) in the calcium carbonate layers that make up the stalagmites, is proportional to that of the rainwater that carries calcium and carbonate ions dissolved from the limestone rock of caves. The rainwater $\delta^{18}0$ itself depended on the balance between rainfall and evaporation, so that, for example, higher values indicate reduced precipitation.

Because of the availability of these new palaeoclimate records, we can now conduct integrative studies comparing archaeological, palaeoecological and palaeoclimatological data to assess the relationship between climate change, distinct subsistence strategies and cultural transformations in Amazonia (De Souza et al., 2019). Examples include a study of the relative roles of climate and human activity in the expansion of the *Araucaria* forest in SE Brazil over the last millennium (Robinson et al., 2018), and an investigation into the role of the drier middle Holocene climate in the decline of radiocarbon dates across the basin (Riris and Arroyo-Kalin, 2019). Last but not least, local palaeoclimate sequences are particularly useful in disentangling natural and human-induced changes in vegetation. For example, the increase in fires during the wetter climate of the late Holocene is almost certainly because of human activity, rather than climate change.

Ethnography, ethnobotany and historical accounts

The disciplines of ethnography and ethnobotany, combined with historical accounts, have documented the diversity and nuances of traditional land use systems, such as agroforestry, flood-recessional agriculture, slash and burn, slash and mulch, and ADE cultivation (see summaries in Denevan, 2001; Levis et al., 2018). They have given insights into the diversity of annual crops and the importance of many non-domesticated (or partially domesticated) plant species for lowland South American livelihoods today (e.g., Balée, 2013; Cassino et al., 2019; Clement, 1999b). Modern ethnography has also revealed how the domestication process in native Amazonian societies is linked to cosmological

Figure 4.3 Interdisciplinary fieldwork and teaching of ethnobotany. *a.* Gustavo Politis carrying out ethnoarchaeological work among the Hoti in the Sierra de Maigualida, Venezuela. *b.* Local resident of the FLONA Tapajós shows Carolina Levis how to use and manage *piquiá* trees (*Caryocar villosum*). *c.* Wao man tells ethnobotanist W. Balée about the plant materials used in making the traditional Waorani blowpipe and darts in the Ecuadorian Amazon. *d.* J. Iriarte and students learn from the Tranchichi Embera about the uses of tropical plants along the Rio Chagres in Panama. *a.* courtesy of Gustavo Politis; *b.* courtesy of Carolina Levis; *c.* courtesy of William Balée.

and ontological processes, and has explored the role of non-human agents (Fausto and Neves, 2018; Shepard Jr et al., 2020). Knowing more about how indigenous epistemologies have guided indigenous domestication practice can provide insights into the social processes that likely occurred over the past ten millennia, as Amazonian people began to domesticate and manage hundreds of plants (Rival and McKey, 2008).

However, making extrapolations from modern ethnography to the past is not straightforward, since the arrival of Europeans beginning in 1492 AD had a profound impact on Native American populations, as we will see in Chapter 9. A further constraint on the use of modern ethnography is that there may be no modern analogues to compare past land use systems with. Many land use systems, such as the vast expanses of raised fields and landscape-scale fish weirs in the Llanos de Mojos, were abandoned after 1492 CE, and today's residents have no social memory of them. Despite their scarcity, ambiguity and potential exaggeration, the early chronicles provide one of our best opportunities to learn about pre-Columbian land use systems. To determine their accuracy, it is important to compare them with the archaeological evidence. Sometimes, looking at modern-day Africa can provide insight into how landscape-scale fish weirs functioned in the past (McKey et al., 2016).

Floristic inventories

Floristic inventories, along with interviews, have brought to light the variety of crops grown in home gardens, nearby swiddens and managed forests. As we will see in Chapter 6, this work has been particularly productive in showing the distinct vegetation communities growing on Amazonian anthrosols.

These local floristic inventories and basin-wide analyses suggest that modern tree communities in Amazonia are structured to a significant extent by a long history of plant domestication by Amazonian peoples. For example, Levis et al. (2017), using 1,170 forest plots of the Amazon Tree Diversity Network, overlaid a map of the 3,000 known archaeological sites in Amazonia with maps showing the distributions and abundances of eighty-five woody species and the distribution of pre-Columbian peoples. By combining these data with the distribution of archaeological sites, this team was able to look at how pre-Columbian peoples might have influenced the diversity and distribution of trees in the Amazon. Interestingly, they found that the relative abundance and richness of these cultivated and domesticated species increased in forests on and around archaeological sites (Figure 4.4). Furthermore, Ter Steege et al. (2013; 2020) have estimated that there are approximately 390 billion trees in the Amazon, consisting of around 16,000 species. Of these, almost 50 per cent of the total number of trees are made up of just 227 hyperdominant species. Research by Levis et al. (2017) discovered that domesticated species were five times more likely than non-domesticated species to be hyperdominant, pointing to a large human footprint in today's forests (see also Coelho et al., 2021). As we will see in Chapter 6, the comparison of local floristic inventories on Amazonian anthrosols with the deep-time palaeoecological records from the same region, also reveals the lasting repercussions of ancient land use in today's forests

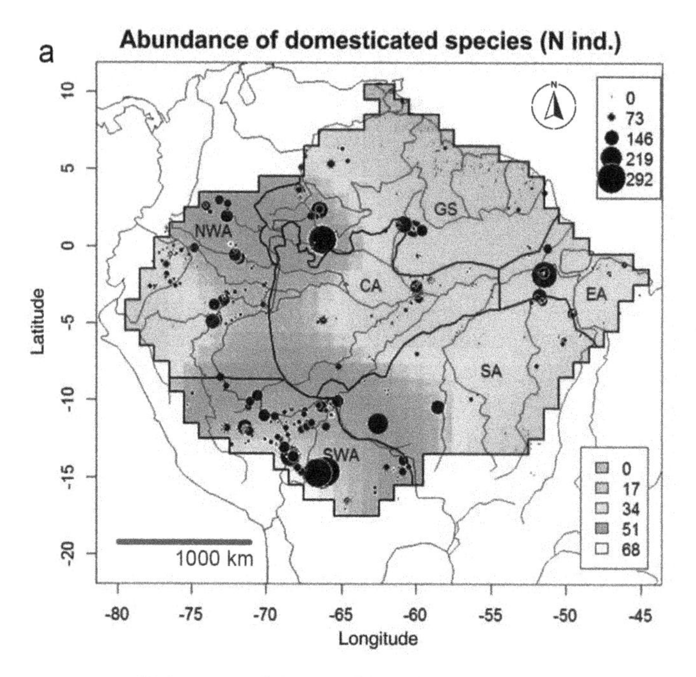

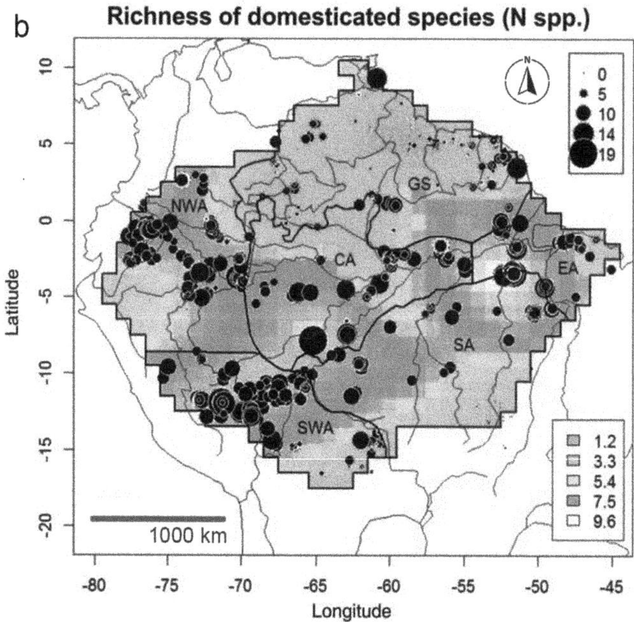

Figure 4.4 Domesticated forests. *a.* Spatial variation of the total number of individuals of domesticated species (abundance) per hectare. *b.* Total number of domesticated species (richness) per plot in six geological regions of Amazonia (NWA, north-western Amazonia; SWA, south-western Amazonia; SA, southern Amazonia; CA, central Amazonia; GS, Guiana Shield; and EA, eastern Amazonia). Black circles show the observed values of absolute abundance ranging from 0 to 292 individuals of domesticated species per 1 hectare, and the observed values of absolute richness ranging from 0 to 19 domesticated species per plot. The filled-in background shows the interpolation of the observed values (in per cent) in each plot modelled as a function of latitude and longitude on a 1°-grid cell scale by use of loess spatial interpolation. Modified from Levis et al. (2017: Figure 2).

(Figure 6.4c). In recent work by Peripato et al. (2023), we have discovered another twenty-four earthworks across Amazonia by scanning lidar transects across Amazonia that were originally obtained to estimate aboveground biomass of forests. Based on existing and this new data, we modelled the distribution and abundance of large-scale earthworks across Amazonia and predicted that between 10,000–24,000 earthworks remain to be discovered mostly in south-eastern Amazonia. More telling, this study also identified fifty-three domesticated tree species significantly associated with earthwork occurrence probability, which reinforces the thesis that past management practices have important lasting repercussions in today's forests proposed by Levis et al. (2017). Finally, hotspots of domesticated plants documented in floristic inventories in archaeologically unexplored places can signpost to prospective archaeological research locations and help document cultural forests as a key bio-cultural heritage for conservation efforts.

A best practice integrative methodology

To understand pre-Columbian land uses, their environmental impacts and their modern legacy, environmental archaeologists have designed a multi-disciplinary approach tied to careful site selection (Figure 4.5). To overcome the limitations of utilizing singular proxies, multiple archaeobotanical and palaeoecological methodologies are employed on different spatial scales by integrating both on-site and off-site proxies. Archaeological on-site phytolith and micro-charcoal data, with palaeoecological and paleoclimate off-site pollen, charcoal and speleothem records, are integrated to obtain continuous, uninterrupted multi-millennial vegetation and climate baselines at a regional level, in addition to *in situ* direct evidence of cultivation at a local scale. The approach aims to combine the best available taxonomic resolution and spatial scale, resulting in the highest possible floristic detail and spatial resolution. The wider use of microscopic archaeobotanical remains has revealed many plants that are often invisible in the macro-botanical record, and vice versa. In contrast to studies that concentrate on either the fossil record (archaeology/paleoecology) or the modern record (floristic inventories/ethnobotany), this approach stresses the importance of comparing the fossil archaeological, archaeobotanical, palaeoecological and palaeoclimate records with modern floristic inventories, to properly assess the legacy of past land use in today's forests, as illustrated in Figure 4.5. Whenever possible, pollen, phytoliths and charcoal stratigraphic diagrams are now generally accompanied by the cultural stratigraphies and regional settlement patterns that allow for a close inspection of human-environment interactions at different spatial scales.

All these proxies are now allowing us to chart with greater precision the deep history of humans and landscapes in Amazonia. As we will see in the concluding chapter, this history needs to be taken into consideration in any attempts to restore or rehabilitate these landscapes for biodiversity conservation. The paleo sciences provide us with baselines, tell us how resilient or fragile environments were in the past and inform conservation efforts on what we want to restore. As a result of these advances, our understanding of pre-Columbian landscape, and plant domestication and human impact

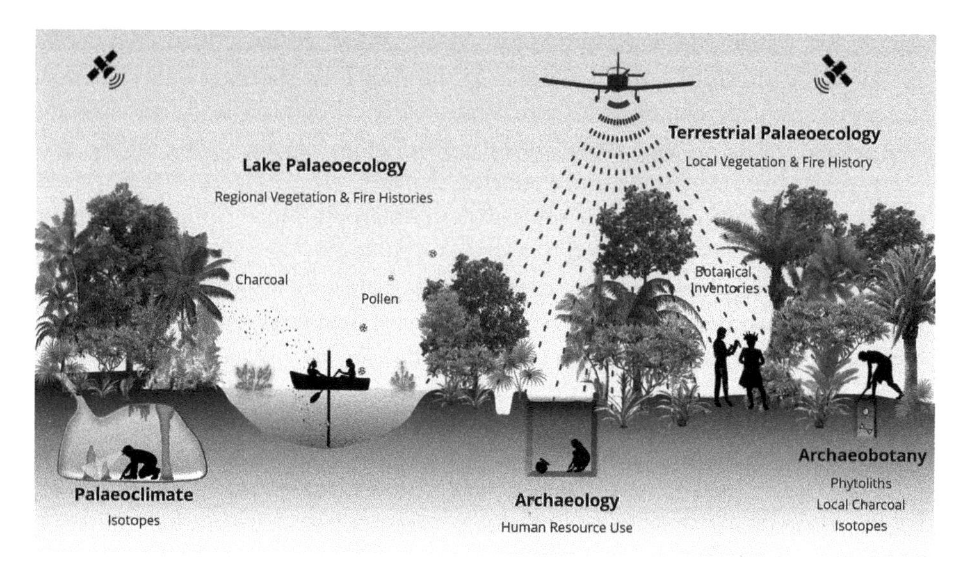

Figure 4.5 Integrative methodology. Schematic diagram of the integration of the multiple techniques. Modified from Iriarte et al. (2020: Figure 2).

on the Amazon has both increased and changed significantly. The new data are revising our perceptions of the geographical origins of plant domestication, early dispersal of crops, as well as chronology, and the diversity of indigenous food-producing economies in the Americas.

Centres of plant domestication in Amazonia

Based on genetic, biogeographic and archaeological evidence, two major centres of plant domestication have been proposed in Amazonia, where selection began in the late Pleistocene and early Holocene: SW and NW Amazonia (Figure 4.6) (Piperno, 2011). Before we delve into the description of these plant domestication centres, let's briefly review the history of the studies of plant domestication in the Neotropics, including Amazonia.

A little bit of history

Historically, the initial work on the transition to agriculture in the Americas was biased toward those geographical areas exhibiting good preservation of desiccated and charred macrobotanical remains, such as the western desert coast of South America (Towle, 1961) and the dry highland caves of central Mexico and Peru. The results of these investigations suggested that plant domestication began independently only in two regions, Mexico and Peru. When and where the numerous indigenous American root and tuber crops had been originally brought under cultivation and domesticated was little understood, as was the role of the Neotropics, and other areas beyond Mexico and Peru, in the development and spread of food production. Decades ago, however, Sauer (1952) postulated the importance of seasonal tropical forests and the role of underground plant organs in early agriculture. Later, Lathrap (1970) proposed a leading role for lowland vegeculture, with manioc as the founder crop that motivated the development and spread of food production throughout South and Central America. Lathrap (1970) also envisioned how house gardens must have played crucial roles as experimental plots during the early stages of Neotropical crop domestication. Sauer and Lathrap's views were influential and widely discussed, but empirical evidence to support them was rare. At that time, few archaeological projects had been carried out in the lowland tropical forest, with only a small number of these including the systematic application of archaeobotanical recovery techniques. In any case, macrobotanical remains were usually poorly preserved in early sites of interest to document plant domestication.

But as seen in this chapter and the following to come, investigations into plant domestication and the dispersal of cultigens in the Americas has been revitalized. This is because of several factors. Firstly, major technical methodological breakthroughs and their incorporation as standard components of archaeological excavation and data analysis reviewed in the previous section. Secondly, new archaeological projects are being carried out in previously unexplored regions where genetics and botany points to locations of plant domestication (e.g., Piperno et al., 2009; Lombardo et al., 2020). And thirdly, the elaboration of new models to conceptualize and form hypotheses concerning early plant domestication. The groundbreaking work of Piperno and Pearsall (1998), a large majority of their own work, summarizes all these advances. As we will see below, in the past two decades, further research in this field has been inspired by their work, including the work in north-western and south-western Amazonia described below.

North-western South America

The montane and lowland tropical forest of Colombia, as well as the seasonal forest of southern Ecuador and Peru, provide some of the earliest evidence of plant cultivation and domestication in Amazonia. This region represents a major early centre, with evidence for the domestication of squashes (*Cucurbita ecuadorensis*) (Piperno and Stothert, 2003) and *C. moschata*, yams (*Dioscorea*), sweet potato (Mu et al, 2018), arrowroot (*Maranta arundinacea*), leren (*Calathea allouia*), cocoyam (*Xanthossoma safitifolium*) and cacao (Clement et al., 2010; Iriarte, 2007; Piperno, 2011; Zarrillo et al., 2018). Archaeobotanical records from north-western South America evidence incipient tree, palm and tuber cultivation, beginning ~11.5 ka in the montane forests of Colombia, including the tuber crops *Dioscorea* sp., *Calathea* sp. and *Maranta* cf. *arundinacea*, along with the tree fruits *Persea*, *Caryocar* and *Virola* (Aceituno and Loaiza, 2018; Piperno, 2011), and a variety of palms. In addition, the presence of pollen associated with human disturbance (*Plantago*, Asteraceae) suggests the clearance of small patches of forest. The middle Cauca region is one of the regions where some of the more intensive archaeology and archaeobotany of plant cultivation and domestication in the South American tropics has been conducted. Starch grains indicate the cultivation of local root crops, such as *Dioscorea* sp. and *Calathea* sp. by ~9.6 ka, as well as *Phaseolus* sp. beans. *Manihot esculenta* was present by ~8.4 ka, while *Ipomoea* sp. is first recorded ~7.7 ka (Aceituno and Loaiza, 2018). These root crops and vegetables are accompanied in the record by the presence of tree fruits, including soursop (*Annona* sp.), mora (*Rubus* sp.) and avocado (*Persea americana*) (Aceituno and Loaiza, 2018). Forest clearing began around 7 ka, concurrent with this early food production. The presence of notched axes and waisted hoes, which were likely used for tree-felling and possibly for soil tillage and digging roots, endorse pollen records, indicating that these plants were cultivated in open spaces within a wet and cool montane forest (Figure 3.3) (Aceituno and Loaiza, 2018).

As described in the previous chapter, archaeobotanical records for the Colombian Amazon are also informative. Recent excavations in the Guaviare forest-savannah ecotone show the presence of the palms *Astrocaryum chambira*, *A.* sp., *Attalea racemosa*, *A. maripa*, *Euterpe precatoria*, *Mauritia flexuosa*, *Oenocarpus bataua*, *Syagrus orinocensis*, *Socratea exorrhiza* and *Bactris* sp. from ~12.6 ka, in addition to *Brosimum lactescens* (Morcote-Ríos et al., 2021; Morcote-Ríos et al., 2014; Robinson et al., 2021). Evidence for the early consumption of palms is parallel to that attested by the archaeobotanical data from Peña Roja (Mora, 2003), which similarly contained domesticated plants, including squash (*Cucurbita* sp), bottle gourd (*Lagenaria siceraria*) and leren (Piperno and Pearsall, 1998). As Aceituno and collaborators (2018) remind us, along with the presence of specialized artefacts, such as axes, what makes Peña Roja unique is the record of non-Amazonian cultivars during the early Holocene. This shows us that from very early on there was a circulation of plants throughout Amazonia.

The seasonal forests of southern Ecuador and northern Peru are other key areas of plant domestication. In southern Ecuador ~10 ka, phytolith evidence documents the domestication of local species of squash, *Cucurbita ecuadorensis*, at the Las Vegas site (Piperno and Stothert, 2003), along with bottle gourd and *Calathea* sp. rhizomes, accompanied by typical early Holocene plant-grinding implements called 'edge ground' cobbles. The early Holocene residents of the Las Vegas site had a broad-spectrum subsistence, exploiting a mosaic of productive terrestrial, estuarine and mangrove environments (Piperno and Pearsall, 1998). Further south, in the Zaña Valley, on the north coast of Peru, macro- and microfossils – the latter from the calculus of human teeth – document the presence of squash, peanuts, beans and the tree crop pacay (*Inga feuillei*) around 10–7.8 ka (Dillehay et al., 2007; Piperno and Dillehay, 2008). Archaeological surveys in this region document a shift in settlement patterns towards the utilization of small but fertile alluvial patches. In the Nanchoc region, the evidence suggests that effective food production systems, contributing significant dietary inputs, were present from the early Holocene. In the Casma valley, the Huaca Prieta record documents the presence of palms (Arecaceae), *Cucurbita* sp. (squash), *Persea* sp. (avocado), *Phaseolus lunatus* (lima beans), *Schinus molle* (Peruvian peppertree), *Prosopis* sp. (algarrobo) and *Capsicum* sp. (chilli) among others, between ~14.5–7.5 ka (Dillehay, 2017).

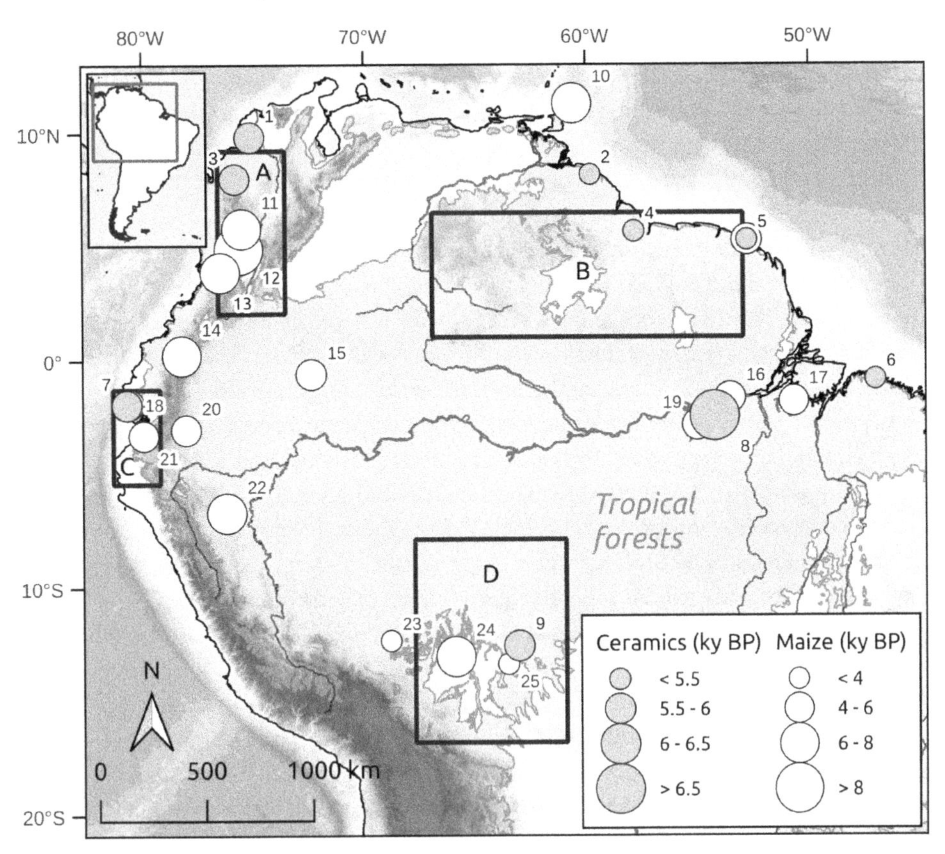

Figure 4.6 Map showing early and mid-Holocene centres of plant domestication, locations of cacao and Amazonian rice domestication, early arrival and W–E dispersal of maize and the earliest occurrence of ceramics in tropical South America. 1. San Jacinto. 2. Alaka. 3. Puerto Hormiga. 4. Dubulay. 5. Eva 2. 6. Mina. 7. Valdivia. 8. Taperinha. 9. Monte Castelo. 10. St. John (Site SPA–11). 11. El Jazmín. 12. La Pochola. 13. Hacienda el Dorado. 14. Lake San Pablo. 15. Abeja. 16. Lake Geral. 17. Tucumã. 18. Loma Alta. 19. Lake Caranã. 20. Lake Ayauchi. 21. La Emerenciana. 22. Lake Sauce. 23. Lake Gentry. 24. Lake Rogaguado. 25. Laguna de la Luna.

South-western Amazonia

South-western Amazonia is the other major centre for early plant cultivation and domestication in Amazonia. Supporting evidence is growing. The plant assemblage in this region includes *Manihot esculenta* subsp. *flabellifolia*, the wild ancestor of manioc (Olsen and Schaal, 2001); *Cucurbita maxima* subsp. *andreana*, the wild ancestor of squash (*Cucurbita maxima* subsp. *Maxima*) (Sanjur et al, 2002); *Canavalia piperi*, the wild ancestor of jack bean (*Canavalia plagiosperma*) (Piperno and Pearsall, 1998); and *Capsicum baccatum* var. *baccatum*, the wild ancestor of chilli peppers (*Capsicum baccatum* var.*pendulum*) (Scaldaferro et al., 2018). This is also the region where the domestication of peach palm (*Bactris gasipaes*), the only neotropical palm with domesticated populations, has been proposed to take place (Clement et al., 2016).

Additionally, the region is purportedly the cradle of the domestication of important stimulants, such as coca (*Erythroxylum coca*) (Plowman, 1984), which was being chewed by people at least 8 ka in northern Peru (Dillehay et al, 2010) and tobacco (*Nicotiana tabacum*) (Gerstel and Sisson, 1995), as well as dyes, such as annato (*Bixa orellana*) (Clement et al., 2016).

As summarized in the previous chapter, recent work in Llanos de Mojos (Lombardo et al., 2020) has documented squash cultivation (*Cucurbita* sp.) at about 10.3 ka, and *Manihot* sp. at about 10.4 ka. This early use of *Manihot* coincides with the estimated time for the molecular divergence of the domesticated species from its wild ancestor, and with the current biogeography of the closest wild ancestor of manioc (Olsen and Schaal, 2001; Rival and McKey, 2008). Importantly, this is when these first cultivators started to develop a landscape, which eventually included 4,700 human-made forest islands surrounded by a savannah that was periodically flooded. *Manihot*'s early use and potential selection in this environment is hardly surprising. Manioc's wild ancestors are adapted to forest-savannah ecotones and thrive in ecological successions that are frequently interrupted by disturbances, such as fire. Their tuberous roots store underground reserves, facilitating rapid regrowth; they exhibit plasticity in growth form according to the openness of the environment, and they regenerate quickly from a soil bank (Rival and McKey, 2008). The disturbed environments created by the forest islands must have created perfect conditions for manioc's early ancestors to thrive. Since its wild ancestors do not readily sprout from stems, the timing and specific processes of how the reproductive biology of manioc changed from sexual reproduction to vegetative propagation (under cultivation) are matters to be resolved (Rival and McKey, 2008). The presence of domesticated *Cucurbita* sp. begins at around 10.3 ka, representing the oldest evidence for *Cucurbita* sp. in Amazonia. Further studies that analyse larger sample sizes are required to determine whether the domesticated squash cultivated in the early Holocene epoch was adopted in the Llanos de Mojos from other regions, or was domesticated *in situ*. The dates from Llanos de Mojos are broadly contemporaneous with the earliest evidence of *Cucurbita* sp. in Huaca Prieta ~10.5–9 ka, and in the Nanchoc region ~11–9.8 ka (Dillehay, 2017) and *C. ecuadorensis* ~ 10 ka in Ecuador (Piperno and Stothert, 2003). The evidence indicates that the consumption of Cucurbits was widespread in tropical South America from the start of the Holocene. Also in SW Amazonia, there is early Holocene evidence of plant consumption at the Teotônio site, an open-air site located on a 40-metre-high bluff on the south bank of the Madeira River. Here, there is evidence for the consumption of the tree fruits guava (*Psidium guajava*), *pequiá* (*Caryocar* sp.), Brazil nuts and leren (*Calathea* sp.), starting ~9 ka (Watling et al., 2018).

Sui generis **domestication in the tropics?**

As initially proposed by Sauer (1952), plant domestication and agriculture in tropical South America show distinct aspects that differentiate them from Eurasian contexts. Similar to the picture emerging in New Guinea and Africa (Denham, 2018; Harris, 2007), the available data suggest that more diffuse spatial patterns characterized the domestication of plants in the Neotropics than in Eurasian regions. Endorsing previous views (Bray, 2000; Harlan, 1995; Piperno and Pearsall, 1998), current archaeological, genetic and biogeographical evidence shows no single centre of domestication or agricultural origin in the Americas. On the contrary, independent origins in Central and SA are now apparent, while multiple origins within lowland South America are likely (Clement et al., 2015; Piperno, 2011). The available data from the Neotropics suggest a mosaic-like pattern of domestication, diffuse in space, with multiple areas of early, independent agricultural innovation involving different plants. It is also becoming clear that crop plants in the same genus, such as *Cucurbita* squashes, were sometimes concurrently brought under domestication in several different regions, such as highland Mexico (Smith, 1997), tropical southern Mexico (Sanjur et al, 2002), south-western Ecuador (Piperno and Stothert, 2003) and possibly the Llanos de Mojos (Lombardo et al., 2020), among other areas (Sanjur et al., 2002). The data from Amazonia summarized above corroborates previous assumptions indicating that in the Neotropics, plant domestication started in shrub savannahs and in seasonal tropical forest environments (Piperno and Pearsall, 1998), but also underscores the role of tropical montane forests as key environments during this process.

Regarding their impact on the environment, it is during these initial phases that early Amazonian foragers may have started to create groves of edible fruit-bearing trees. A practice similar to the recurrent discard of seeds/nuts at frequently visited locales recorded ethnographically for the Nukak described in the previous chapter (Politis, 2009). These groups were likely taking advantage of naturally disturbed areas, such as tree falls, landslides or lightning strikes, similar to today's Hoti practices in Venezuelan Guayana (López-Zent and Zent, 2004). The use of fire was likely common in seasonal forests, savannahs and forest-savannah ecotones. The presence of axes in the early records of the Cauca River Basin attests to the ability of people to fell trees, which likely contributed to the disturbance and clearance of these montane forests (see Levis et al., 2018 for a summary of how indigenous and traditional Amazonian people have managed forest resources to promote useful plant species).

Establishing the extent to which these subtle changes resulted in enduring anthropogenic settings requires further interdisciplinary work. However, the evidence from Llanos de Mojos suggests a strong relationship between landscape and plant domestication in the Americas, long argued for Amazonia by Clement (1999a). The study by Lombardo et al. (2020) reviewed in the previous chapter, which documented thousands of anthropic keystone structures, represented by forest islands that likely had lasting repercussions for habitat heterogeneity, shows that the human footprint in Amazonia is not restricted to large-scale transformations by farming groups in the late Holocene epoch. Similar practices recorded ethnographically by the Kayapó, of creating resource-rich forest islands (Hecht, 2009; Posey, 1985), may well go back to the very start of the Holocene.

In addition, unlike Eurasian plant domestication, which was traditionally focused on relatively few cereals, a number of different plants are known to have been brought under domestication in the Americas. These include a variety of root crops (e.g., manioc, sweet potato, yams), beans and pulses, squashes, vegetables, tree crops and condiments. Some of them, such as the majority of palms, do not show morphogenetic changes even under intensive management. The lowland South American crop plant complex (Pearsall, 2008) consists of a large and diverse assemblage of tree fruits, nuts and palms. Only one palm was domesticated, peach palm (*Bactris gasipaes*), with the selection of varieties with varying starch and oil content used for food (Clemente et al., 2017). It includes only two demonstrably domesticated grass grains: maize and rice (*Oryza* sp.) (Hilbert et al., 2017). Of the eighty-three crops native to Amazonia and adjacent areas inventoried by Clement (1999b), 68 per cent are trees and woody perennials with some degree of domestication. Along with these plants that show some evidence of domestication, there are an estimated 3,000–5,000 non-domesticated plant species used by humans in the Amazon (Borem et al., 2012).

The data summarized in Chapter 3 and this chapter show that the peopling of the Amazon forest was based on a reliance on palm, tree fruits and underground tubers. Palms, an essential resource for tropical forest residents, providing food (palm fruits) and construction materials (thatch, fibres and wood), also appear to have played a major role in the diet of these early colonizers. They are predominant in early archaeobotanical records across lowland Amazonia, and changes in vegetation composition to include greater proportions of palm is closely associated with humans from their first appearance (Morcote-Rios and Bernal, 2001). The diets of these early settlers and first cultivators were certainly complemented by other faunal and terrestrial resources (Capriles et al., 2019; Morcote-Ríos et al, 2021; Roosevelt et al., 1996). Intriguingly, many of the earliest plants consumed by people in the tropics later became Amazonian hyperdominants (Levis et al., 2017). Unsurprisingly, phytoliths derived from plants that produce underground storage organs – including *Manihot*, *Calathea*, Marantaceae, *Heliconia*, Cyperaceae and *Phenakospermum* – constitute an important part of the total phytolith assemblages from the earliest records of NW SA and SW Amazonia. Root plants are pre-adapted and abundant in savannahs with long, dry seasons (Piperno and Pearsall, 1998) and are concentrated in wetlands (Dillehay and Rossen, 2002). They produce carbohydrate-rich foods, which, except for some varieties of manioc (McKey et al., 2010a), are easy to process and cook. Indigenous groups consume them (Hanelt et al., 2001) today and they probably provided a considerable proportion of the calories consumed by the first inhabitants of the Llanos de Mojos. Many, such as *Dioscorea* yams and *Ipomoea* tubers, are amenable to vegetative propagation within gardens, or in their 'natural' habitats via 'paracultivation' (sensu Dounias, 2001). Our data are consistent with the hypothesis that plants that produce underground storage organs were a fundamental part of the diet of human populations as they colonized new territories globally (Aceituno and Loaiza, 2018; Jones, 2009; Piperno and Pearsall, 1998). Brazil nut was also part of the diet of Amazonian people since their early arrival to the basin (Roosevelt et al., 1996).

Although forest people have interacted with and managed aquatic and terrestrial environments in Amazonia throughout history, few animals in lowland South America, particularly Amazonia, have been domesticated. The Muscovy duck (*Cairina moschata*) is the only case of classical animal domestication that could have occurred in the tropical lowlands of South America apparently during the late Holocene (Stahl, 2008; von den Driesch and Hutterer, 2011) (see Casarabe culture Chapter 8). Neves (2013) has argued that domestication of animals did not occur in the Amazon region because of their abundance, especially along alluvial settings. In other words, there has been little selective pressure for animal domestication, given the wide availability of fish and aquatic mammals. Besides, there are few potentially 'domesticable' animals in terrestrial settings. Most terrestrial mammals are solitary and nocturnal, and a large part of animal biomass in the rainforest does not live on the ground but in the canopy. The strongest candidate for a domesticable land mammal is the peccary, which lives in packs. Its behaviour, however, is too unpredictable and aggressive to allow for domestication. The few animals domesticated in Amazonia have parallels in other tropical regions of the world (see Roberts, 2019).

As summarized above, plant domestication in tropical South America, including Amazonia, is unique. It exhibits diffuse, mosaic-like geographical patterns, goes hand in hand with landscape domestication and includes a wide diversity of root and tree crops, but just two cereals (maize and rice). Plants that were a significant component of Amazonian diets since early times, such as palms, do not show morphogenetic changes even under intensive management. Only one animal shows evidence of classical domestication, the Muscovy duck. The development of sedentary life or agricultural food-production systems did not immediately follow plant domestication.

Given all that, is the process of plant domestication in Amazonia unique? As reviewed by Denham and Vrydaghs (2007), debate continues around the definition of plant domestication and agriculture and its archaeological/palaeoecological correlates (e.g., Harris, 2007; Smith, 2001; Terrell et al., 2003). The need to study plant domestication and agriculture 'on its own terms' in different locations and environments around the globe has long been recognized (e.g., Harris, 2007). The evidence from lowland South America presents a very different scenario from that of the Near East, for example, where plant domestication was quickly followed by the establishment of a sedentary and urban life. Researchers working in non-Eurasian regions, particularly the tropics, have become increasingly aware of the fundamental differences in the origins of plant domestication and the origins of agriculture in different parts of the world, and the methods we should employ for its study. These issues have been re-affirmed for the Neotropics by the seminal works of Piperno and Pearsall (1998), and Clement (1999a). However, a tendency has persisted to evaluate plant domestication and agriculture across the globe using concepts, lines of evidence and methods derived from Eurasian research. The contributors to 'Rethinking Agriculture' (Denham et al., 2007) compared the nature of plant domestication and spread of agriculture in tropical regions of the world against the Eurasian model, which is characterized by clear morphogenetic changes in plants or animals, environmental transformations resulting from forest clearance for agriculture, and packages of associated cultural, political and social traits (see also Denham, 2018; Whitehouse and Kirleis, 2014). The fact that Eurasian processes of 'becoming agricultural' and the definition of agriculture itself are not necessarily transferable to Amazonia, has been restated in different works since then (Arroyo-Kalin, 2010; Cunha, 2019; Fausto and Neves, 2018; Moraes, 2015; Neves, 2007; 2013; Neves and Heckenberger, 2019; Shepard Jr et al., 2020). Based on these epistemological issues in the domestication discourse, Amazonian scholars recommend replacing the concept of domestication with alternative concepts, such as antidomestication, familiarizing predation, co-domestication and mutual-domestication, among others (Cunha, 2019; Fausto and Neves, 2018). This debate will undoubtedly be enriched now that archaeobotanical and palaeoecological techniques, as well as molecular biology, are being employed in archaeological projects.

In the next chapter, we look at the developments that took place during the middle Holocene across Amazonia.

CHAPTER 5
FROM EARLY TO MIDDLE HOLOCENE

In this chapter, I focus on the middle Holocene, a period that is usually defined between 8.2–4.2 ka (Walker et al., 2012). Many important processes took place during this time, including the development of the first ADEs, and the spread of fluvial and marine shell middens across the Amazon basin, which are, in turn, linked to the appearance of ceramic technology. To these can be added the domestication of cacao and rice, the spread of manioc and sweet potato, and the arrival and dispersal of maize from Central America (Figure 4.1). The middle Holocene is also a time when the economic, social and political changes that became widespread during the late Holocene were just beginning to occur. Examples are the domestication of bitter manioc, the spread of fruit trees and their domestication to different degrees, the development of long-distance trade networks across the Amazon and the dispersal of major language families.

Despite all these processes taking place, many authors have noted that certain regions of Amazonia that show initial late Pleistocene–early Holocene occupations exhibit a gap of occupation during parts of the middle Holocene. This is the case, for example, in the Central Amazon (Neves, 2007), the Amazon (Gomes, 2011) and in Central Brazil (Araujo et al., 2005). In the Central Amazon, as Eduardo Neves (2013:40) has noted: '. . . evidence of human occupation from 5700 to 500 BCE is absent, despite the identification of more than 100 archaeological sites in a 900 kilometre^2 research area.' A recent analysis of archaeological radiocarbon data (Riris and Arroyo-Kalin, 2019) suggests a decline in population throughout South America, including Amazonia, after 8.6 ka. As we will see below, this population decrease is coeval with the onset of more arid conditions and marked precipitation variability across South America (Deininger et al., 2019).

The absence of archaeological evidence in many regions of Amazonia – this so-called 'Archaic Gap' – could well be related to the lack of archaeological work in these regions. It could also be explained in part by geomorphic processes, such as the late Holocene river dynamics that could have buried archaeological sites under alluvium (deposit of sediment left by flowing floodwater) (Lombardo et al., 2019), and the possibility that rising sea levels may have covered low-lying archaeological sites situated on floodplains. In some areas, however, recent research has started to fill the gaps (e.g., Lombardo et al., 2013b; Pugliese et al., 2018). In this chapter, I will dedicate special sections to the most important processes that took place during this period. Before that, I will describe the changing climate during the middle Holocene.

The drier mid-Holocene climate

During the middle Holocene, Amazonia experienced a drier climate. Observable shifts in austral summer insolation because of the Earth's precessional cycle, are generally believed to be responsible for these millennia-scale precipitation changes. Lower austral summer insolation levels caused a northward shift in the mean position of the ITCZ during the middle Holocene (Haug et al., 2001), and a decrease in the intensity of the SASM (Cruz et al., 2005). This drier climate is well evidenced by Lake Titicaca on the Bolivian altiplano (largely fed by Amazonian rain), where water levels were 100 metres lower than present levels at ~6 ka (Baker et al., 2001). Enriched $\delta^{18}0$ values from the Huaguapo speleothem and Lake Junin, which indicate reduced convective activity and lower moisture levels (Kanner et al., 2013), also point to a drier climate. These Andean records show that modern precipitation levels were not reached until ~4–3 ka.

As the synthesis of palaeoenvironmental records from Smith and Mayle (2018) shows, the Amazon forests were affected differently by these middle Holocene drier conditions, with the magnitude of the impact inversely correlated with mean annual precipitation, length and severity of the dry season, and proximity to ecotones. Parts of Amazonia that rely on the SASM, which was weaker during the middle Holocene, were particularly affected, such as SW Amazonia. As the pollen records from Laguna Bella Vista and Laguna Chaplin in the Noel Kempff National Park show, areas that are today covered by evergreen forest were dominated by a dry forest/savannah mosaic during the drier conditions of the middle Holocene. Similar evidence comes from stable carbon isotope analysis from a 200-kilometre soil test pit transect between the cities of Porto Velho and Humaita in Brazil (600 kilometres north of Noel Kempff). The results of this analysis indicate an expansion of savannahs in this region during this time (de Freitas et al., 2001). In the southern rim of the Amazon, the Carajas pollen record similarly shows a replacement of forest by savannah (Absy, 1979).

Other regions, such as the tropical forests of central, western and eastern Amazonia, remained largely intact throughout the middle Holocene. Even if there was a slight decrease in precipitation during this period, it appears that it was not enough to trigger a biome turnover. It would take a significant decrease in precipitation levels to trigger widespread forest die-back or biome turnover in what is currently one of the wettest parts of tropical South America, with annual precipitation >3000 millimetres. This is the case, for example, with Lake Parker and Lake Gentry (Peruvian Amazon), which have experienced little change over the past 6–7 ka. However, other records, such as those from Lake Pata (Brazilian Amazon) and Lake Maxus-4 (Ecuadorian Amazon), exhibit floristic changes during the middle Holocene, despite the fact that they occur in the wettest part of the Amazon basin. Lake Pata exhibits a distinct pollen assemblage zone, dated to *c.* 6–7 ka, which is characterized by peaks in the herbs *Borreria* and grasses (Poaceae) and the *Mauritia* palm, as well as the almost complete disappearance of Moraceae and Urticaceae pollen – ubiquitous wind-pollinated families, which are the ultimate indicators of close-canopy forest (Bush et al., 2004). This pollen assemblage suggests a transition from a closed-canopy forest to forest/woodland open enough for herbaceous understorey plants to thrive, consistent with the reduced precipitation of the middle Holocene. However, as Smith and Mayle (2018) warn, the very low sedimentation rate at Lake Pata means that the duration and timing of this middle Holocene vegetation zone is uncertain. In the Ecuadorian Maxus-4 pollen core, the pioneering weed tree *Cecropia*, an indicator of disturbance, dominates the assemblage (*c.* 60 per cent). This could be because of the episodic droughts under a drier climate causing increased gap formation, thus favouring such pioneer species (Weng et al., 2002). Alternatively, it could be a result of human disturbance (Smith and Mayle, 2018). Interestingly, a cluster of five pollen records in eastern Amazonia (Sarucuri, Santa Maria, Comprida, Geral and Tapajós) all show signs of forest disturbance during this period, evidenced by substantial peaks in pollen (30–40 per cent) of the weed tree *Cecropia* (Bush et al., 2007; Irion et al., 2006). This coincides with a period when current archaeological evidence shows a hiatus in the occupation of the region (see Chapter 7). More work, in the form of systematic archaeological surveys targeting middle Holocene sites, is needed in the region to untangle the natural and human agency on these changes.

The middle Holocene is also a time when sea levels rose and the extensive *várzea* floodplains that exist today began to form (e.g., Latrubesse and Franzinelli, 2005). Present-day sea levels were likely attained by 7.7–6.9 ka, with maximum Holocene transgression levels occurring around 5.7–5.1 ka (e.g., Angulo et al., 2006). This rise in sea level would have caused the Atlantic tidal zone to penetrate further inland, partially damming the flow of the large rivers draining into the lower reaches of the Amazon, and creating estuaries, such as the one we see today at the mouth of the Tapajós River (Figure 7.16).

Those who inhabited middle Holocene Amazonia certainly lived amidst a dynamic landscape. Inexorably rising sea levels, and, as a consequence, river levels, must have had a visible impact on familiar floodplain terrain within a generation, the topography being much reduced and water level rises measurable in multiple centimetres a year. Groups must have had to move frequently to higher ground in the face of rising sea levels at the mouth of the Amazon and rising river levels in interior Amazonia. Unfortunately, many key sites of this period are likely under water.

The shell mound pottery archaic: A window into the mid-Holocene

Shell middens are one of the most common types of sites dating from the middle Holocene in the Amazon (Figure 4.1). They provide us with a glimpse into the lives of the people who occupied the area at the time. The term 'shell midden' is usually used for a pile of shell unintentionally created by the discard of shells. The term 'shell mound', however, denotes the deliberate intention of depositing shells and other materials to create a structure, usually evidenced by construction events. Shell middens and shell mounds exhibit regional-specific characteristics in terms of material culture, construction history and their uses, emphasizing their cultural context diversity. Some of these sites have extensive histories of occupation, such as the Llanos de Mojos 'forest islands', which were inhabited between 10.6–4.0 ka, and the Monte Castelo shell mound in the Guaporé-Itenéz River, which dates back to the early Holocene (Capriles et al., 2019; Lombardo et al., 2020; Lombardo et al., 2013b; Pugliese et al., 2018). In the lower Amazon, shell mounds can be particularly large, ranging from 5–20 hectare in area and from 5–20 metres deep. Some contain long, uninterrupted stratigraphic sequences, which may indicate large and rather permanent settlements (Roosevelt, 1991).

Shell middens are also associated with the earliest ceramics in Amazonia and the Americas, and characterize a period dubbed the shell midden pottery archaic. Unlike the shell middens of the Atlantic coast of South America, commonly known as *sambaquies*, shell middens of Amazonia are associated with very early ceramics.

In South America, all centres of early ceramic production were in the tropical lowlands (Figure 4.1). The Lower Amazon region, in particular where the Tapajós River flows into the Amazon, has yielded the earliest dates for ceramic production in the Americas. Findings from the Taperinha shell midden, first excavated by geologist Charles Hartt in the 1870s, have been especially illuminating in this regard. Located about 50 kilometres downstream from Santarém city on the Amazon's left margin, the shell midden covers several hectares and is primarily composed of freshwater pearly mussels (*Castalia ambigua*, *Paxyodon ponderosus* and *Triplodon corrugatus*). It reaches a height of 6 metres. Excavations at the site by Roosevelt and collaborators (1991) revealed forty-eight strata of shells, charcoal, animal bones, rocks, pottery fragments and a few human bones, within a matrix composed of very little sediment. Eleven radiocarbon dates, ranging from 8.0–7.2 ka, were obtained from a variety of materials collected in the deepest levels. Ceramics from the basal levels of Taperinha consist of brownish-red simple bowl with direct rims tempered with sand. Decorated sherds are rare (3 per cent of the sample) and are restricted to incised rims. Lithic materials consist of hammerstones, chipped stone tools and groundstone tools. An awl made of bone, scrapers of mollusc and turtle shell, and a pendant made of marine mammal bone are also examples of the material culture unearthed at Taperinha. Food remains show intensive fishing and collection of fluvial resources, primarily freshwater shellfish, but also turtles and fish, the latter mainly catfish and characins. Across the river at the Caverna da Pedra Pintada site, the basal ceramics date back to ~8 ka (Roosevelt, 1995), making them the continent's earliest ceramics so far.

Taperinha is not an isolated occurrence. More than forty of these shell midden sites have been recorded in the estuary of the Amazon along the Atlantic coast, some 500 kilometres downstream from Taperinha. These littoral shell middens (as opposed to fluvial shell middens) have been dated to 5.7–3.3 ka (Simões and Correa, 1971). They are typically found on riverbanks, in bays and on islands, and are almost always surrounded by mangroves. They occupy small areas, ranging from 0.1–2 hectares in size, with depths reaching up to 4 metres. They are composed predominantly of marine *Anomalocardia brasiliana* shells, followed by *Crassostrea* sp. and *Mytella* sp. The additional presence of large quantities of crustacean shells and fish bones led Simões (1971) to suggest that the groups of people living there had a diet predominantly consisting of estuarine and marine aquatic resources. Recent work by Hilbert et al. (2023) has documented the earliest arrival of maize and squash to Marajó island at ~4.0 ka. The evidence comes from the Tucumã shell midden, located on the western sector of an island exhibiting Mina

Phase ceramics. The phytolith record from Tucumã additionally records the presence of other plants of economic importance, including *Bactris*/*Astrocaryum*, *Euterpe* sp., Attaleinae and *Mauritia* sp. palms, hackberries (*Celtis* sp.), as well as soursop (Annonaceae), tree fruits and wild rice (*Oryza* sp.), indicating that these groups cultivated and consumed a variety of plants. Applying state-of-the-art methodologies could offer valuable insights into the dietary habits of these groups. For example, recent analysis of phytolith and starch grains from plant processing tools and human dental calculus, as well as isotope evidence on human bones from some shell-mound along the southern Atlantic coast of South America is revealing the important role that carbohydrates from plant resources played in the diet of the Sambaqui people, previously considered to be mainly fishermen (e.g., Pezo-Franco et al., 2018). The application of new techniques for this old problem will certainly bring new insights. The spread of middle Holocene shell middens follows north along the Atlantic towards the Guianas coast, where we will find the settlements of the Alaka culture in Guyana dating between 6.8–3.4 ka (Daggers et al., 2018; Meggers, 2007; Williams, 1992).

The term 'Mina Phase' has been applied to the ceramics discovered in the shell middens. 'Mina' is the Portuguese word for 'mine', referring to the fact that these sites are mines for the extraction of shells used in the manufacture of lime. The ceramics are characteristically small, simple, tempered with sand and ground shells or *caraipé* (see below). They have characteristically open shapes, a simple outline and flat base, and are predominantly without surface decoration, or else with incisions and applied slip in very small quantities (Figure 5.1).

Figure 5.1 Mina ceramics sherds from the Uruá site. Notice white dots represent the shell temper. MCTI/Museu Paraense Emílio Goeldi, Reserva Técnica Mário Ferreira Simões, photos by Brenda Bandeira. Courtesy Daiana Alves.

Before we further describe ceramics in this book, it may be helpful to provide some additional information about the nature of Amazonian ceramic paste – the characteristics of the clay from which the vessel is made. Amazonian ceramics makers use different methods to improve their quality. One way is by adding various elements to the paste, or else leaving them in the clay to prevent cracks and breaks during burning, increasing resistance to impact and improving thermal capacity for cooking. The most common tempering agents are minerals, such as sand, crushed stone and quartz grains, but also crushed shells (as in the Mina ceramics), ground ceramics, *caraipé* and *cauxi*. *Caraipé* is made from the ash of the bark and inner parts of *Licania* plants (specifically *Licania scabra* sp.), and is added to ceramic paste in varying amounts and sizes to create the final product. *Cauxi* is a freshwater sponge (Demospongiae, *Drulia* sp or *Parmula batesii* sp.) that thrives in clean, oxygen-rich water free of small, suspended particles. During dry seasons when water levels are low, *cauxi* can be easily collected from tree trunks or branches on the rivers' banks.

The early dates of the lower Amazon ceramics show that eastern Amazonia is the most ancient centre for the invention of pottery in the Americas. Ceramics here are 1,000–1,500 years older than those from the sites of western Amazonia, such as Valdivia on the Ecuadorian coast (Meggers et al., 1965), Monsú (Dolmatoff, 1985) and San Jacinto in northern Colombia (Oyuela-Caycedo and Bonzani, 2005). Collectively, current data counter the idea of Amazonia as a periphery where ceramics were introduced. Indeed, it is necessary to reverse the diffusion route, acknowledging the possibility that ceramics began in Amazonia and spread to the rest of the continent. As Neves (2013) has stressed, the invention of ceramics did not immediately lead to sedentary agricultural societies. There appears to be a gap of more than 3,000 years between the dates for early pottery production and the establishment of sedentary societies.

Plant cultivation, domestication and spread across the basin

Despite the decline in populations shown in radiocarbon databases, and the apparent gap in some regions of Amazonia, the progressive application of archaeobotanical and palaeoecological analyses has documented the domestication of native crops and the dispersal of exotic ones during the middle Holocene. Modern and ancient DNA, along with microbotanical analysis, have evidenced the use of cacao in the Ecuadorian Amazon from about 5.3 ka (Zarrillo et al., 2018), at Santa Ana La Florida. Maize, which was domesticated in the Balsas River basin, Mexico, ~8.7 ka, from *Zea mays* sp. *parviglumis* (Piperno et al., 2009), arrived in lowland South America at the start of the middle Holocene epoch in a partially domesticated state. It is also during the middle Holocene that manioc likely spread from SW Amazonia to other regions of Amazonia and beyond (Arroyo-Kalin, 2012). A similar scenario of spread during the middle Holocene can be detected for sweet potato, from the earliest dates in the middle Cauca Valley ~7.7 ka (Aceituno and Loaiza, 2018) to its arrival in the Caribbean and coastal French Guiana ⊠6.6 ka (Pagán-Jiménez et al., 2015) and the Ecuadorian Upper Amazon ~5.6 ka (Zarrillo et al., 2018). SW Amazonia is also where wild varieties of peanuts (*Arachis hypogaea*) occur today. Early archaeobotanical evidence has not been forthcoming for this period, but Favero and Valls (2009) propose a date of ~7–6 ka for the start of peanut domestication. The middle Holocene also sees the first appearance of Amazonian anthrosols in the Upper Madeira region ~6 ka (Miller, 1992; Watling et al., 2018), while in the middle Caquetá River region, small-scale but permanent communities appear to have been growing maize and manioc on Amazonian anthrosols ~5.5 ka (Mora et al., 1991). The middle Holocene is possibly when the dispersal of other important native crops, such as Brazil nut (Shepard and Ramirez, 2011), occurred across the basin. Watling et al. (2018) suggest that ADE formation at the Teotônio site ~6 ka allowed for the adoption of and experimentation with exotic crops, such as *Cucurbita* squash and *Phaseolus* beans. Recent genetic analysis of modern varieties of cupuaçu (*Theobrama grandiflorum*) suggest a first phase of domestication ~8.0–5.0 ka (Colli-Silva et al., 2023).

New evidence is also emerging in the northern rim of the Amazon. At the Eva site in French Guiana, maize, sweet potato, *Zamia* sp., *Canavalia* sp. and *Capsicum* sp., were being grown between 6.0–3.9 ka, according to research by Pagan-Jiménez et al. (2015). In coastal Guyana, the analysis by Daggers et al. (2018) of bone stable carbon and nitrogen isotopes from eighty-one individuals from shell mounds dating to ~7.5–2.6 ka show values indicative of the use of C3 plants in an open canopy environment.

Manioc

From its potential early cultivation in the Llanos de Mojos around 10 ka, manioc appears to have spread to northern Peru (8.5 ka), Colombia (7 ka) and Panamá (7.6 ka) (Piperno, 2011), suggesting that the exchange of cultivars between Amazonia and the Andes began in the early Holocene. There are two major groups of manioc varieties: sweet varieties have low amounts of toxic substances (cyanogenic glycosides) and may be consumed with minimum processing, while bitter varieties have a high degree of toxicity and must be detoxified before consumption (McKey and Beckerman, 1993). Arroyo-Kalin (2010) has eloquently argued that during the early and middle Holocene, sweet manioc, along with maize, was likely grown in refuse middens and house gardens in the periphery of the Amazon basin, while the cultivation of bitter manioc evolved as the result of the agricultural intensification in fields that took place during the late Holocene, with the regional spread of ADE into the centre of the basin. Recent genetic analysis, suggesting that sweet varieties of manioc originated during the initial domestication in SW Amazonia, followed by bitter varieties, lends support to Arroyo-Kalin's model (Santos Mühlen et al., 2013). More research is needed to uncover the history of this important crop.

Maize winding journey: Down and up the Darien Gap

By the time the European colonization of the Americas got underway in the fifteenth century, maize had already established itself as the dominant food crop throughout much of the continent, comprising hundreds of landraces (distinct populations of traditional varieties with limited geographic distribution) varying in size, shape and colour, from the tiny Argentine popcorn type to the huge Cuzco Gigante with its large starchy kernels. Contact between Europeans and Native Americans in the fifteenth and sixteenth centuries paved the way for the global spread of this productive crop. Experimentation worldwide has led to a staggering array of morphological diversity and adaptations to various geographical and climatic conditions, adding to the thousands of landraces developed by indigenous cultivators in the Americas. Unfortunately, western societies today, because of the action of colonization and agro-industry, have lost the original, wonderful diversity of corn flavours, and are familiar only with the so-called sweetcorn.

Domesticated maize (*Zea mays* ssp. *mays*) took the first steps toward domestication from wild Balsas teosinte (*Z. mays* spp. *parviglumis*) around 8.7 ka, in the lowland seasonal tropical forest of SW Mexico, one of the major centres of plant domestication in the Americas (Piperno et al., 2009). From there, it spread through Central America, traversing Panama by 7.5 ka. It is likely that, after that, it initially diffused into northern South America through the drier inter-Andean valleys and the lower elevations to the east of the Andes (Piperno and Pearsall, 1998). Maize pollen shows a temporal gradient of dispersal that begins in western Amazonia at ~6.9 ka and reaches the eastern Amazon at ~4.3 ka (Hilbert et al., 2017, 2023; Maezumi et al., 2018a) (Figure 4.1). In northwest South America, the earliest reliable dates come from the middle Caquetá River at the Abejas site ~5.5 ka (Mora et al., 1991). In other parts of Amazonia, the earliest dates come from the Llanos de Mojos, documented at 6.9 ka at Isla del Tesoro (Lombardo et al., 2020) and 6.5 ka at Lake Rogaguado (Brugger et al., 2016), with similar dates for the Ecuadorian Amazon at 6.3 ka at Lake Sauce (Bush et al., 2016), and 6 ka at Lake Ayuach (Bush et al., 1989).

Some surprising new details about the domestication of maize have emerged from recent research. Archaeogenomic evidence suggests that maize was only partially domesticated in Mexico 5.3 ka, with a mix of wild-type and maize-like alleles at loci involved in the domestication syndrome. By this time, for instance, the domestic-type teosinte glume architecture 1 (tga1) gene variant responsible for eliminating the tough teosinte fruit case, for example, was already present, while other loci associated with changes in seed dispersal and starch production during domestication still carried wild-type variants (Vallebueno-Estrada et al., 2016).

Interestingly, this partially domesticated maize was grown in Mexico well after maize had become established in South America, prompting researchers to wonder how it was that maize in South America eventually acquired all its fixed domestication traits. To answer this question, a team led by Logan Kistler (2018) sequenced indigenous maize landraces, and maize and teosinte genomes, as well as maize archaeological samples. The results indicate that maize first arrived in South America as a partially domesticated plant, where the domestication syndrome became independently fixed and improved varieties developed without interference from the wild ancestor teosinte. That is, native South Americans continued to 'tame' the partially domesticated plant. This is not surprising at all, considering how versatile maize is as a food crop and how plant domestication is an ongoing process. This new discovery would explain the variety of distinct maize races found in the early context of Huaca Prieta on the north coast of Peru, dating back to around 6.2 ka (Grobman et al., 2012).

The history of crop movements is intricate and has revealed evidence of people and plants, such as cacao and manioc, travelling between Central and South America for thousands of years. Continued research by Kistler and collaborators (2020), evidences the introduction of newly developed maize varieties from South America to Central America around 4.0 ka, resulting in more productive crops. Unsurprisingly, this coincides with the time that people in Central America began to rely on maize as their staple crop (Kennett et al., 2020).

The latest ancient DNA evidence from human remains shows that crops and people migrated from the south to the north. The genomes of skeletons dating from 9.6–3.7 ka from two caves in Belize were significantly different from those of earlier individuals, and shared ancestry with Chibchan populations from southern Central America and northern South America, pointing to a migration of people from South to Central America. This southern genetic population's arrival coincides with the first evidence in Mesoamerica of a number of South American crop plants, including chilli peppers, manioc and domesticated maize, suggesting that these plants and the technologies used to cultivate them were brought by these southern folks (Kennett et al., 2022).

Related to more recent times, the work of Kistler et al. (2018) indicates that another wave of South American maize cultivation spread eastward around 1,000 years ago, from the foothills of the Andes Mountains to near the Atlantic coast. Researchers propose that this could be related to the emergence and spread of circular mound villages across the southern rim of the Amazon, which took place at this time (see Chapter 7). As we will see in the next chapter, current evidence also indicates that maize became more predominant with the spread of anthrosols across the basin.

Cacao: An early South American indulgence

Our addiction to chocolate is much older than we previously thought. It may also have a different origin. Biologists, plant breeders and archaeobotanists have long wondered when and how cacao (*Theobroma cacao*), originally from South America, was domesticated. Cacao was extremely important to ancient Mesoamerican civilizations, such as the Maya and Aztecs, who valued chocolate so much that they used it in religious rites and as currency. Until recently, the earliest archaeological evidence of using processed cacao seeds to produce drinks for use in rituals, based on ancient texts and ethnohistorical accounts, goes back to Mesoamerica, ~3.9 ka (e.g., Coe and Coe, 2013). Archaeologists have long assumed that Mesoamericans were not only the first to use cacao, but also the first to cultivate it.

But recent studies are changing this perspective. Molecular biologists, analysing 200 varieties of *Teobroma cacao*, have found that the greatest diversity occurs in the humid montane forest of the Upper Ecuadorian Amazon region of north-west South America (twenty-two species of *Theobroma* and seventeen species of its wild genus *Herrania*), pointing to this region as the original home of all wild cocoa trees (e.g., Motamayor et al., 2008). The evidence suggests that this is where people first had the opportunity to use and cultivate the plant. By using three state-of-the-art independent proxies – starch grains, absorbed organic residues and ancient DNA – Zarillo and collaborators (2018), working at the site of Santa Ana de la Florida, a site related to the Mayo-Chinchipe ceramic tradition, have been able to document the consumption and possible domestication of cacao at around 5.3 ka, about 1,700 years before its appearance in Mesoamerica.

Ethnographic and ethnohistoric sources document a plethora of uses for both *Theobroma* and *Herrania* in South America. These include the use of the seeds as medicine and food, the pulp as a juice or fermented alcoholic beverage, and the bark and leaves for medicinal extractions and infusions. Ancient ceramic vessels from Ecuador and the north coast of Peru also contain iconographic representations of cacao pods and *T. cacao* was cultivated on Ecuador's Pacific Coast before the arrival of the Spanish. However, despite all these reports pointing to the importance of South America, no direct archaeological evidence for the use of cacao in South America before the arrival of the Spanish has been uncovered until recently (Zarrillo et al., 2018).

The Santa Ana La Florida (SALF) site, located at 1,000 metres above sea level in the montane forest of Ecuador, was discovered and excavated as recently as 2002 by Ecuadorian and French archaeologists. It is the oldest village site of the Mayo-Chinchipe culture, which occupied this region from about 5.5 ka (Valdez, 2021). This team exposed the remains of approximately twenty domestic buildings arranged around a central public sunken plaza, which served as the local ceremonial centre in this small 1 hectare village. Close to the village, a round structure on top of an artificial platform, with a wall arranged in a spiral, contains tombs exhibiting elaborate funerary offerings, including the Americas' earliest examples of stirrup-spout bottles (Figure 5.2). The team sampled a variety of artefacts from tombs, middens, sunken plaza floors and a ceremonial hearth surrounded by turquoise beads. The representation of *Spondyllus* shells in the ceramics, as well as *Strombus* shell fragments, shows contact with groups of the Ecuadorian coast. Ceramic vessels show individuals whose puffy cheeks indicate they are chewing coca. It is worth noting that the earliest evidence of coca processing dates back to 8 ka in the Nanchoc valley of northern Peru (Dillehay et al., 2010).Theobromine, a biochemical compound present in mature *T. cacao* seeds but absent in other *Theobroma* and *Herrania* wild species, was also detected in dozens of ceramics and lithics at the site. The analysis of residue from ceramics found in a variety of contexts, including ritual vessels (elaborately adorned from mortuary offerings in the tombs of presumably high-status individuals) and unadorned vessels from domestic settings, suggests that cacao plants were used from at least 5.3–2.1 ka as an important source of food, drink and medicine, as well as being used as stimulants and in ceremonies at the site. The evidence comes from charred cooking residues consisting of starch grains only found in *Theobroma cacao* (Figure 5.2d–e). The organic residue adhering to the wall of pots was also directly dated, giving similar dates. Ancient DNA extracted from the pottery also matched sequences from modern cocoa trees.

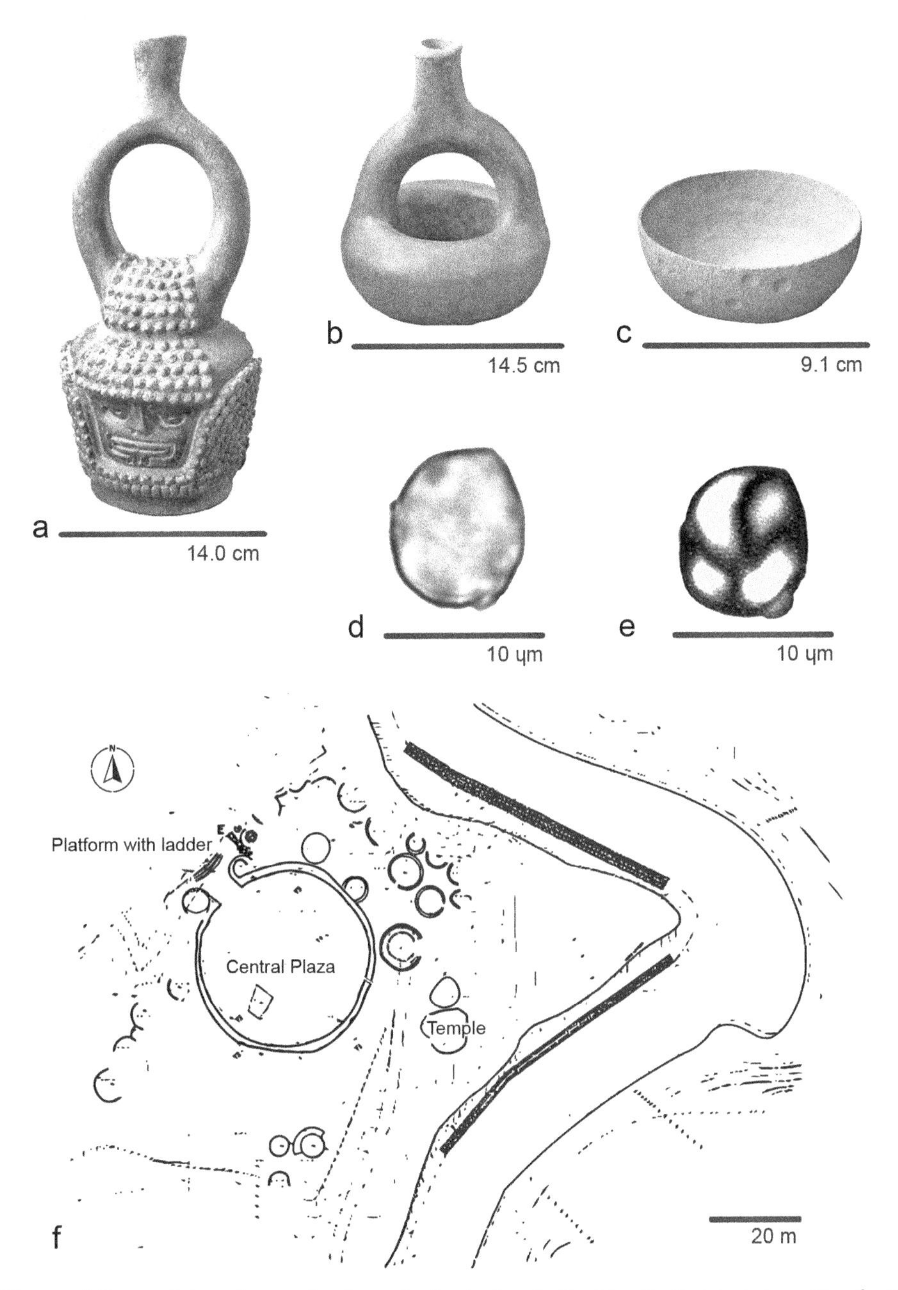

Figure 5.2 *a–c.* Selected ceramics from the Santa Ana la Florida site that tested positive for *T. cacao* and *Theobroma* spp. by DNA, starch grains and theobromine analyses. *d–e.* Starch grains of *T. cacao*. *f.* Site plan of SFL. *a–e.* courtesy Sonia Zarillo; *f.* modified from Valdez (2021).

Whether wild cacao was being used and cultivated, or whether the cacao was domesticated, remains a point of contention. Researcher Cornejo and co-workers (2018) place the genetic fingerprint of cocoa domestication at around 3.6 ka in Central America. However, they have found no such evidence in samples from the Upper Amazon region, arguing that the cacao consumed in Santa Ana La Florida was wild. The 'tasty' debate continues.

Rice so nice it was domesticated thrice

I have titled this section by paraphrasing Normille's (2017) piece, to present a surprising development that has recently emerged in the Amazon region. Current evidence shows that rice was domesticated in three different independent regions. The first occurrence was during the early Holocene in the Yangtze River, China (*Oryza sativa*) (Callaway, 2014). The second was approximately 2,000 years ago in West Africa (*Oryza glaberrima*) (Linares, 2002). And, more recently, Hilbert et al. (2017) have documented the third global event of rice domestication, in the wetlands of the Guaporé River in SW Amazonia (see also discussion of rice domestication in India, e.g., Bates 2022).

Before Old World species were introduced in the eighteenth century, wild rice was already a seasonal staple for indigenous subsistence in the Americas. Ethnologists in the early twentieth century recognized the Upper Great Lakes Native American tribes' dependence on *Zizania* wild rice, designating the region as a unique 'wild rice culture area'. From the sixteenth to the nineteenth centuries, there is a wealth of historical and ethnographic accounts that provides extensive information on how indigenous groups in South America consumed wild rice species. Wild rice grew extensively in various regions, such as the Amazon, La Plata and Orinoco basins. These regions made up a significant part of South America's seasonally flooded lowlands accounting for 10 per cent of South America's total lowland area (Hilbert et al., 2017).

Historical accounts report that Native South Americans harvested wild rice by using wooden poles to beat mature inflorescences into their canoes, similar to the traditional North American method. The importance of wild rice in culinary practices is also alluded to in these early chronicles, which mention, for example, that rice was mixed with maize to make bread, or describes its consumption as a fermented brew similar to wine (Hilbert et al., 2017). Wild rice, known locally as *arroz-de-pato* (duck rice) or *arroz-do-brejo* (swamp rice), is still consumed by riverine communities throughout the Amazon as a valuable source of carbohydrates when other food resources are scarce. Until recently, communities along the Guaporé-Itenéz River, such as Costa Marquez and Santo Antônio, still gather and consume wild rice, which was managed by these communities until the first half of the twentieth century. Native Guató communities in the Pantanal also consume the wild native species *O. glumaepatula* and *O. latifolia* by sun-drying the grains, peeling and then boiling them (e.g., Bortolotto et al., 2015).

Despite the occasional mention of rice's potential role in pre-Columbian diets, the domestication of rice remained unexplored until recently. It is yet another topic where microbotanical remains have proven extremely informative. The evidence comes from

Figure 5.3 Wild rice growing in the vicinity of Monte Castelo shell mound. Wild rice is a tall grass (reaching up to 4 metres), with large seeds forming spikelets. Courtesy Eduardo Neves.

the Monte Castelo shell mound, which is part of a larger collection of coastal and freshwater shell mounds that date back around 10 ka, providing us with a window into early to middle Holocene Amazonian lifeways. The shell mound lies in a large ecotonal zone between the Amazonian rainforest to the north, the Brazilian savannah (cerrado) biome and semideciduous dry forests to the south and the seasonally flooded forest-savannah mosaics of the Llanos de Mojos to the west. Current vegetation around the site is a seasonally flooded savannah, with gallery forest and palm-dominated savannahs. Wild rice is abundant across the seasonally flooded savannahs of this region (Figure 5.3).

The Monte Castelo shell mound and others in its vicinity are artificial structures, part of a larger collection of similar mounds. Found mostly in the Llanos de Mojos region (Lombardo et al., 2020; Lombardo et al., 2013b), the mounds provide evidence for early plant cultivation and landscape domestication. Monte Castelo stands 6.3 metres high, it has a diameter of 160 metres and dates back to 9.4 ka. Between June and November, the wetlands surrounding Monte Castelo mostly dry up. But during the flood season, the site becomes an island, entirely surrounded by water (Figure 5.3).

The first Monte Castelo excavation by Eurico Miller in 1984 revealed a 7-metre-deep stratigraphy spanning a long period of occupation from 9.1–6.7 ka (Miller, 2013). The stratigraphy indicated a series of construction events, evidenced by unburned entire *Pomacea* shell layers and occupation floors marked by crushed shell lenses, primary burials and human-created dark soils. Based on stratigraphy, artefact content and sixteen radiocarbon dates, Miller defined three major occupation phases. These included the Cupim phase (7.0–6.9 metres; 9.1–7.8 ka), the Sinimbu phase (6.7–2.75 metres ; 7.7–4.8 ka) and the Sinimbu-Bacabal transitional stratum (2.75–2.20 metres; 4.8–4.4 ka) (Miller, 2013). The Laboratory of Tropical Archaeology of the University of São Paulo expanded the earlier excavation at Monte Castelo, defining twenty-one layers named A–U from the surface to the base as follows: Cupim strata, U–S, 6.0 ka; Sinambu strata, R–J, 5.8–5.2 ka; I–E, 5.2–5.0 ka; Sinimbu-Babacal transition, D–B, 4.3–2.0 ka; and A, 0.7 ka (Furquim et al., 2021).

Analysing the phytoliths from Monte Castelo, Lautaro Hilbert and collaborators (2017) were able to document that the *Oryza* sp. husk phytoliths, called *Oryza* double-peak glume phytoliths, significantly increase in size during the middle Holocene levels dating to around 4.0 ka in layer D. As we saw in Chapter 3, selective exploitation causes a gradual increase in plant size from wild to domesticate. As the plant becomes larger, so do the phytoliths. For example, larger fruits and seeds of maize, squash and bananas often yield considerably larger phytoliths. Therefore, the increase in *Oryza* phytoliths likely reflects the progressive selection of larger wild rice seeds by the pre-Columbian residents of the Monte Castelo shell mound. Cultivation was not alien to them, since phytolith data also show that they were already engaged in the cultivation of maize (*Zea mays*) and squash (*Cucurbita* sp.) (Figure 5.4).

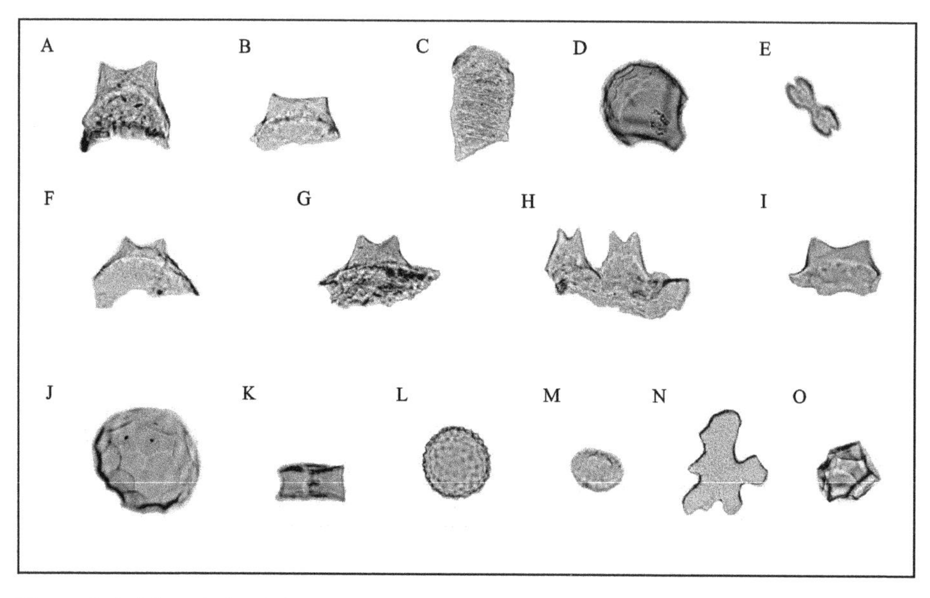

Figure 5.4 Selected phytoliths from Monte Castelo layers. *a–e. Oryza* sp. phytolith morphotypes recovered in the Monte Castelo shell mound: double-peaked glume (*a.* layer A; *b.* layer J); deeply serrated body (*c.* layer C); cuneiform keystone bulliform (*d.* layer D 1, 3–1.4 metres); scooped bilobate (*e.* layer E). *f–i.* Double-peaked glume phytoliths from modern wild rice species native to the study area: *O. alta* (*f.* PRI–1); *O. latifolia* (*g.* Arg–5); *O. grandiglumis* (*h.* SO–23); *O. glumaepatula* (*i.* SO–17). *j–n.* Crops and other native edible plants recovered in the Monte Castelo shell mound: scalloped sphere from the rind of squash (*j. Cucurbita* sp., layer F); wavy-top rondel from the cob of maize (*k. Zea mays*, layer C); large globular echinate from Arecaceae (*l.* layer J); conical to hat-shaped phytolith from Arecaceae (*m.* layer H); spherical facetate from Annonaceae (*n.* layer C). Scale bar, 20 μm. Courtesy Lautaro Hilbert.

Interestingly, phytoliths from rice seed husks (glumes) and leaves could be distinguished. It is likely that leaf and stem phytoliths (called bulliform and scooped bilobates) would be found in the place of harvest, at the lake edge, where they would have been discarded, with seed phytoliths (double-peaked and deeply serrated glume phytoliths) more abundant at residential sites where only the grain was brought for consumption. The analysis shows that over time, more husk phytoliths than leaf phytoliths were recovered at the site, implying that Monte Castelo residents became more efficient harvesters, bringing more grain and fewer leaves and stems to the site.

The analysis of macrobotanical remains, phytoliths and starch grains by Furquim et al. (2021) has shown a diversity of plants cultivated and consumed at the site, including the palms *moriche* (*Mauritia flexuosa*), *tucumã* (*Astrocaryum* sp.) and *Bactris*, as well as Anacardiaceae, soursop (*Annona* sp.), fig (*Ficus* sp.), nance (*Byrsonima* sp.) fruits and Brazil nuts. The analysis of starches of ceramic residues from D contexts reveals the consumption of tubers, including yams (*Dioscorea trifida*) and sweet potato (*Ipomoea batatas*), while *Heliconia* sp. and Zingiberales phytoliths were also identified. According to these authors (Furquim et al., 2021), there is a trend towards increasingly diverse diets, with people no longer relying on a single staple but rather a broad-spectrum food procurement. Phytolith analysis from this study confirms that *Cucurbita* phytoliths (scalloped spheres) appear at about 5.8 ka. Rice domestication also coincides with the arrival of the new Bacabal phase (4.0–2.0 ka), a distinct type of ceramics with incised zone-hatched designs (Pugliese et al., 2018). Collectively, this is yet another example of how combining different plant proxies provides more robust results.

This story of rice domestication has yet another intriguing twist that relates to climate change. The beginning of rice domestication coincides with a rapid increase in precipitation in the Amazon, as we will see in more detail in the next chapter. Palaeoclimate records from southern Amazonia and adjacent regions influenced by the SALLJ show a consistent long-term trend of increasing precipitation beginning during the middle Holocene (6.0 ka), with a rapid rise of up to 4.0 ka, and then continuing to rise slightly until the present. This increased precipitation would have likely increased the spatial extent of wetlands across the basin, potentially lengthening the flooding season. Wild rice is a particularly important resource during the rainy season, when flooding disperses resources in riverine and wetland areas, making them scarcer. Increased precipitation, therefore, would have likely made wild rice a critical seasonal resource, leading people to focus on its manipulation, eventually leading to its domestication.

Faunal data, particularly the fish assemblage, provide additional support for this correlation. Fish bones make up the majority (about 80 per cent) of the vertebrate fauna recovered at Monte Castelo, followed in minor quantities by aquatic turtles, caimans, snakes, lizards, amphibians, cervids, small rodents and armadillos (Prestes-Carneiro et al., 2020). Changes in fish bone assemblages appear to closely follow changes in climate. From 6–4 ka, the assemblages consistently show the presence of species that can withstand droughts, such as swamp-eels, armoured catfish, lungfish and tiger fish. This trend corresponds with paleoenvironmental findings that suggest low precipitation levels and extended dry seasons, during the early to middle Holocene. Approximately 4 ka, the archaeological record shows the appearance of various fish species (characids and cichlids) from flooded forests. This suggests that the inhabitants of Monte Castelo may have expanded their fishing practices to include the flooded forest landscape (*igapós*). The inclusion of fish from the flooded forest in the diet of Monte Castelo residents during the late Holocene is likely correlated with the increasing precipitation trend during this period. In addition, the presence of fish species from both dry and flood seasons implies a prolonged occupation, which is supported by the discovery of cultivated squash, maize and rice at the site.

What happened to this domesticated rice? We believe that the population decimation that occurred with the arrival of Europeans on the American continent in 1492, along with the impact on cultural practices, caused the domesticated traits to gradually fade away. This is not an unusual process. The extinction of domesticated varieties has occurred for other indigenously domesticated species in both South and North America. For example, the 'extinct cultigen' marsh elder (*Iva annua*), a member of the Asteraceae family valued for its achene oil content, was originally domesticated in south-eastern North America before being abandoned with the introduction of maize (e.g., Smith, 2001).

To conclude this chapter, let's briefly summarize some of the major developments during this period. The middle Holocene is characterized by the appearance of shell middens in riverine settings, indicating a focus in the exploitation of aquatic resources. Pottery cultures emerged in various regions of the Amazon more than 3,000 years before their appearance in the Andes, calling into question the idea of Amazonia as a periphery where ceramics were introduced. Several important crops, such as cacao, rice and cupuaçu were domesticated, while others, such as the exotic maize and manioc, dispersed across the basin, likely planted in home gardens. Evidence from the tropical montane forest of Ecuador suggests early contacts between Amazonia and the Pacific coast, while new findings on the history of maize show that cultivars and people may have travelled up and down the Darien Gap.

This chapter highlights that while some parts of Amazonia may have a gap of human occupation and a decrease in radiocarbon dates during the middle Holocene, many processes and changes occurred across the basin. We must be careful when extrapolating the absence of human occupation or the decline of carbon dates in some regions of Amazonia to the entire basin.

In the next chapter, we will discover how several of these processes that were 'brewing' during the middle Holocene materialized during the Late Holocene. The upcoming chapter will mainly discuss two primary types of land use in Amazonia, namely Amazonian anthrosols and raised fields. The chapter delves into a crucial turning point in Amazonian history when societies started to alter the landscape on a much larger scale than ever before.

CHAPTER 6
THE EMERGENCE OF TROPICAL FOREST AGRICULTURES: THE AMAZONIAN ANTHROPOCENE

Tipping points

During the late Holocene, starting around four millennia ago, Amazonian farmers began to transform the landscape at a scale not seen before across lowland South America (Figure 6.1). The food production impulses prevalent throughout the middle Holocene reached new heights during the late Holocene. As described in previous and succeeding chapters, Amazonian people have been incredibly skilled at not only domesticating single plant species but also entire landscapes. These are processes that go hand in hand, as we have seen from the creation of early Holocene forest islands in the Llanos de Mojos. The presumed incapacity of the soil to ensure permanent agricultural production (sustain large populations) has been proved wrong since Amazonians found ways to overcome the soil's limitations and develop adequate strategies for sustainable food production. The construction of raised and drained fields, water management canals, artificial ponds, landscape-scale fish-weirs and the formation of human-modified soils or 'anthrosols', are clear examples of the creation of *landesque capital*, a huge multi-generational investment in infrastructure and landscape modification that likely required the sophisticated organization of large groups of people during the late prehistory of the Amazon. This defining moment, with the development of Amazonian anthrosols and raised fields landscapes, when people begin to invest in long-term physical and chemical improvements to the soil with the goal of intensifying cultivation and productivity at specific sites, marks the beginning of agriculture in some areas of Amazonia.

As we will see at the end of this chapter, these major landscape transformations appear to be generally correlated with the spread of farmers associated with the ancestors of major language families, including the Arawak, Tupi and Caribs, as well as several other smaller groups, such as the Pano and Tukano (Epps and Salanova, 2013; Eriksen, 2011; Gregorio de Souza et al., 2020; Heckenberger, 2002; Hornborg et al., 2014; Noelli, 1998), and with their ceramic traditions associated with the beginning of sedentary life. As these farming populations spread, they accrued crop genetic resources, creating centres of crop genetic diversity, evidencing the transformation and diversification of plant resources (Clement, 1999a; b; Clement et al., 2015).

Acknowledging that ADEs correspond to many different archaeological traditions, which will be described in the following chapters, this chapter begins by summarizing the last two decades of soil science, ethnobotanical and ethnoarchaeological work on ADEs (Glaser and Woods, 2004; Hecht, 2003; Lehmann et al., 2004; Schmitd and

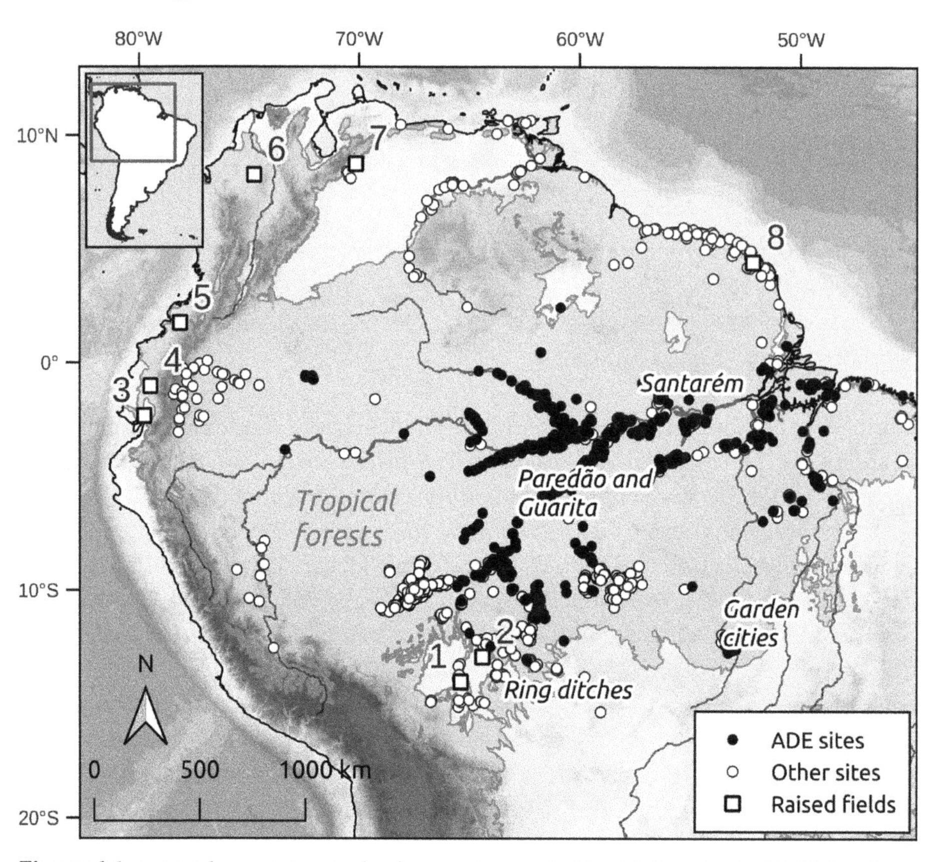

Figure 6.1 Late Holocene intensive land-use systems including ADEs and raised fields locations. 1. Llanos de Mojos. 2. Baures. 3. Guayas River. 4. Daule River. 5. Tolima-Toluca. 6. San Jorge River. 7. Llanos de Barinas. 8. Guiana coast.

Heckenberger, 2009; Woods et al., 2009). Despite major advances in understanding the formation of ADEs, until recently, we knew very little about the land-use systems that ADEs supported. I will describe how recent research has shown how through soil fertilization using 'cool burning' (smouldering fires with little oxygen) and organic additions, closed-canopy forest enrichment, limited clearing for crop cultivation and low-severity fire management, long-term food security and nutritional diversity was attained by Amazonians who lived on ADEs (summarized in Iriarte et al., 2020a). Notably, the comparison of fossil and modern botanical records shows how these millennial-scale polyculture agroforestry systems have an enduring legacy in the continuing presence of patches of highly fertile soil and in the modern composition of the forest, including legacy plots of palms, Brazil nut and cacao, among other tree crops (e.g., Almeida de Oliveira et al., 2020; Maezumi et al., 2018a). These systems provide evidence of successful, sustainable subsistence strategies and highlight a rich cultural-ecological heritage. Furthermore, ADE land use appears to have been resilient to climate change (De Souza et al., 2019). As I will argue in the final chapter, our understanding of the ADE land use system provides scientifically grounded data that can address the modern challenges faced by the rainforest and its marginalized indigenous inhabitants, who still harbour and utilize much of this ecological knowledge accumulated over millennia. ADE land use provides examples of intensification without large-scale removal of the forest canopy, and within controlled, low-severity fires that could be important clues for sustainable Amazonian futures. After describing ADEs, we will turn our attention to how Amazonian farmers transformed the seasonally flooded tropical savannahs of tropical South America into productive raised-field agricultural landscapes. The chapter concludes with a brief review of the spread of farming and languages, as well as a comparison of climate change and cultural developments on the eve of the 1492 CE conquest. This concluding section argues that societies with more intensive, specialized land-use systems were more vulnerable to transient climate change than land-use systems on ADEs, which relied primarily on more diversified polyculture agroforestry. I begin the chapter by describing the late Holocene climate shift to wetter conditions.

The wetter conditions of the late Holocene

During the late Holocene, there were significant changes in the climate of the Amazon basin. As we discussed in Chapter 2, the majority of rainfall in the southern hemisphere tropics of South America is seasonal and monsoonal. The SALLJ carries moisture from deep convection in the Amazon basin towards the Andes foothills during the austral summer. It then follows a diagonal path along the eastern flank of the Bolivian Andes towards southern Brazil, where it exits the continent at the South Atlantic convergence zone (Figure 2.1). All palaeoclimate records in the regions influenced by the South American Monsoon System demonstrate a consistent long-term trend of increasing precipitation. As reviewed by Iriarte et al. (2017), palaeoclimate records in the regions influenced by the SALLJ – Lake Titicaca (the Altiplano) (Baker et al., 2001), Laguna La Gaiba (the central lowlands) (Whitney and Mayle, 2012) and Botuverá cave (southern Brazil) (Cruz et al., 2005) indicate a consistent and gradual increase in precipitation from the middle Holocene period (~ 6.0 ka). This trend continued to rise rapidly up to 4.0 ka, and has since slightly increased towards the present day. The trend has been attributed to a progressive strengthening of the monsoon over this period as orbital forcing (precession cycle), which leads to more sunlight during austral summer and a decrease in the length and intensity of the dry season (Berger and Loutre, 1991). This wetter trend of the middle to late Holocene had an impact on the vegetation. Synthesis of palaeovegetation records (Flantua et al., 2015a; Iriarte et al., 2017) shows that, despite some variability, forest cover increased consistently between 5–1 ka at the expense of areas that were dominated by savannahs or savannah/forest mosaics during the drier middle Holocene. This trend is evidenced by the expansion of the southern Amazon rainforest margin, the seasonally dry tropical forest margins in the Chiquitanía region of lowland Bolivia and the southern margin of the *Cerrado* (savannah) biome, and the gallery forests in the central Brazilian savannahs (see summary in Iriarte et al., 2017). A more detailed description and analysis of the timing and diverse nature of these late Holocene climate and vegetation changes will be provided below, when we revisit the archaeological cultures that flourished during this time period.

Amazonian Dark Earths

Soils all throughout the world have been deliberately transformed by humans for cultivation, which has made them darker, loamier and richer in specific nutrients. In this section, I explore how Amazonian people produced rich agricultural soil by adding charcoal, manure and animal bones to the otherwise nutrient-poor soil of the world's greatest rainforest. Initially studied by Dutch soil scientists (Sombroek, 1966), the highly modified anthrosols, traditionally known as *Terras Pretas do Indio*, literally 'the dark earth of the Indians', and more recently as ADEs, are among the most compelling examples of how humans have transformed tropical environments in the Americas (e.g., Denevan, 2001, 2004; Heckenberger and Neves, 2009; Schaan, 2012b). The anthrosols result from subsistence intensification, likely linked to the growth of Amerindian populations during the late Holocene. Current research shows that ADEs are unique to Amazonia in the Americas. The Maya created anthropogenic forests and anthropogenic soils akin to ADE soils, but nowhere to the extent of the Amazon (Graham et al., 2017).

Although we generally refer to ADEs as a single type of anthrosol, soil scientists, geographers and archaeologists have long recognized two types of Amazonian anthrosols: Terras Pretas or ADEs, and *Terras Mulatas* or Amazonian Brown Earths (hereafter ABEs). Because ADEs have been studied more thoroughly than ABEs, the summary presented below focuses primarily on ADE studies. However, as we will see below, ABEs are critical to understanding this land use system.

ADEs are known for their black colour (Munsell colours 7.5YR 2/1–3/2; 10YR 2/1–2/2) (Kern et al., 2017: 695), given by their high content of charcoal and organic matter, elevated pH values and higher concentrations of plant available P, Ca, K and Mg, which together with low exchangeable aluminium, make them extremely fertile. These properties make ADEs able to maintain nutrient levels over hundreds of years in Amazonia, where typical Amazonian *terra firme* soils are generally heavily leached and infertile (Clement et al., 2004; Denevan, 2004; Teixeira et al., 2010; Woods et al., 2009). Charcoal is responsible for maintaining high pH levels, reducing leaching by increasing cation exchange capacity and stabilizing chemical elements to improve soil fertility (Glaser et al., 2002). They have also demonstrated a high potential for carbon sequestration, an aspect to which we will return in Chapter 10.

ADEs are widely distributed in Amazonia. They are typically found in strategically advantageous non-floodable (*terra firme*) locations in the landscape, such as river bluffs or plateaus overlooking rivers and streams (German, 2003; Heckenberger et al., 2008; Schaan, 2012b; Stenborg et al., 2012). Along the main channel of the Amazon River, they are usually found on high terraces close to the river channel (Denevan, 1996). They bear

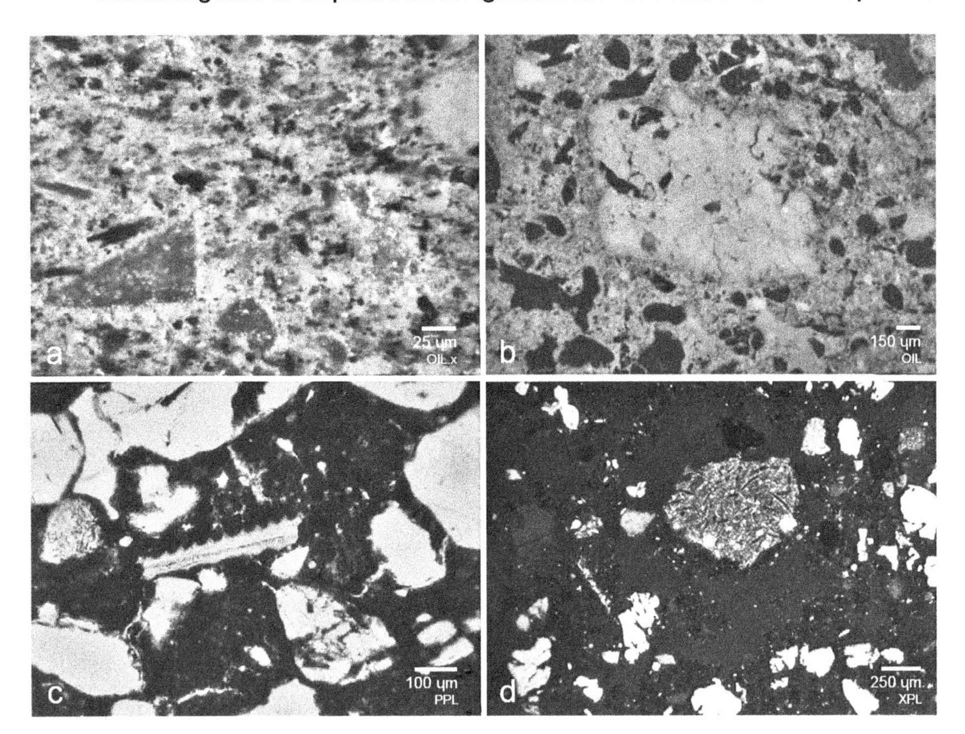

Figure 6.2 The ingredients of ADEs. Soil micromorphology slides showing: *a.* microscopic charcoal, *b.* microscopic fragments of pottery and rubified clay, the latter probably originating in clay ovens, *c.* microscopic fragment of fish bone, *d.* fragments of spicule-tempered (*cauxi*) pottery. Courtesy Manuel Arroyo-Kalin.

witness to the numerous and complex Amerindian societies, which once occupied the main channel of the Amazon, as described by the early European accounts, and who have now perished or been reduced to small autonomous communities. Predictive modelling by McMichael et al. (2014a) estimated that ADEs may have covered as much as 3.2 per cent (*c.* 154,063 kilometres^2) of the Amazon basin. This 'forecast' was mostly based on the ADE data available at the time, which was largely restricted to main rivers where archaeological surveys had been carried out. Mounting evidence of ADE sites in interfluvial areas across the basin (de Souza et al., 2018; Franco-Moraes et al., 2019; Gonda, 2018; Heckenberger et al., 2008; Paz–Rivera and Putz, 2009; Schaan, 2012b) also indicates that ADE sites cover a much larger extension than previously estimated (Figure 6.1). However, in some areas of Greater Amazonia, such as the 'geoglyph' region, Orinoco drainage sectors and French Guiana, ADEs appear to have never formed at all, or else been very confined.

Depth of ADEs suggests that they were formed over long periods. For ADEs to form, the rate of organic matter deposition must be greater than the rate of loss. Estimates range from 0.002–0.004 centimetre/year to 1 centimetre/year (see review in Erickson, 2004). Some of the earliest evidence of ADEs comes from the Teotonio site in SW

Amazonia, dating back to 5.5 k (Watling et al., 2018). Nevertheless, the widespread formation of ADEs dates to the late pre-colonial period of Amazonia, generally dating to 1,000–2,000 years before the advent of Europeans to the region (Arroyo-Kalin, 2010), implying that their formation occurred simultaneously across this vast region. In the Central Amazon, the spread of ADEs is associated with the Pocó-Açutuba Tradition, purported to belong to Arawak groups starting 2,000 years ago (Neves et al., 2014). However, as we will see in the next chapter, ADE sites during the late Holocene are associated with a variety of ceramic traditions, such as the Polychrome Tradition, Incised Rim Tradition and Incised Punctate Tradition.

Among archaeologists and geographers, the general view is that *Terra Preta* ADEs are cultural deposits formed by the decomposition of waste items near habitation sites, such as plant and animal food wastes, plant materials used for construction, fish bone fragments and human faeces (Bozarth et al., 2009; Glaser and Birk, 2012). As a result of the midden refuse accumulation from long-term habitation sites, they are typically loaded with ceramics and other cultural artefacts/ecofacts (e.g., Erickson, 2004). Ethnoarchaeology among the Kuikuro of the Upper Xingu provides us with clues on how these Amazonian anthrosols were formed. In this region, near residential areas, you will find a dark soil the

Figure 6.3 Amazonian Dark Earth profile from the Couro Velho site. This ADE site belongs to one of the least archaeologically studied regions of Central Amazonia, the interfluves of the Purus-Madeira rivers along the trans-Amazon BR 319 road. Phytolith and charcoal analysis shows polyculture agroforestry practices since the late Holocene in this region (Gonda 2018).

Kuikuro call *eegepe* (dark earth). Kuikuro farmers intentionally spread organic ash, charcoal and cassava waste in *ilũbepe* fields along with specialized soil-management activities, such as controlled burning of vegetation cover to create the fertile dark earth, *eegepe*, for later cultivation (Schmidt and Heckeberger, 2009; Schmidt et al., 2023).

ADEs are some of the most fertile soils on the planet (e.g., Lehmann et al., 2003) based on their high nutrient availability and levels of organic matter. Soil science tells us that pyrogenic carbon (black carbon, charcoal) is the key to unlocking the mystery of their prolonged fertility. Pyrogenic carbon contributes to a stable soil organic matter stock and high nutrient retention capacity. As a result, nutrients persist in the soil for centuries, even under the intensive leaching (removal of soil material in solution from one soil horizon to another) characteristic of tropical soils. Charcoal concentration in ADEs is typically four times that of neighbouring soils, but it can be as much as seventy times higher in the first 0.3 metres of soil profiles (Glaser and Birk, 2012). As we will see in the following sections, in contrast to raised-field soils that were formerly rich in nutrients to enable maize growth but are now depleted of them (McKey et al., 2010b; Rodrigues et al., 2020), ADEs are still exceedingly productive.

Research conducted in traditional and indigenous communities shows that ADEs are used to plant nutrient-demanding crops because of their fertility and resilience. For example, in the lower Tapajós and Central Amazon, ADEs are commonly used to plant crops, such as maize, beans (*Phaseolus* spp.) and squash (*Cucurbita* spp) (German, 2003; Hiraoka et al., 2004; Woods and McCann, 1999). Traditional communities in less commercially oriented areas, such as the middle Madeira River, use ADEs to farm many varieties of manioc, which grows productively (Fraser et al., 2012). Maize thrives on the ADE's fertile and non-acidic soils, frequently intercropping with other crops, such as squash and beans. The Kuikuro indigenous community of the Upper Xingu grows manioc in highland *terra firme* soils, while maize, papaya (*Carica papaya*) and tobacco (*Nicotiana tabacum*) are grown in ADEs established around modern and abandoned communities (Schmidt and Heckenberger, 2009). The modern Araweté people of the Xingu River prefer to cultivate maize on the nutrient-rich ADEs, which they claim 'makes the corn thrive' and/or 'makes the corn happy' (Balée 2013: 44). The same preference has been observed for the enawene-nawe of Mato Grosso (Santos, 2006).

ADEs can potentially deliver large yields of both maize and manioc compared to post-Columbian slash-and-burn agriculture in natural soils. For example, it was found that in ADEs, maize yields can be sixty-five times higher than on the notoriously nutrient-poor Amazonian Oxisols. Data from multiple measurements on two ADE sites in central Amazonia show an average yield of 3.925 t hectare^{-1} at Apui and a range between 3.6–6 t hectare^{-1} at the Caldeirão research station (Wenceslau Teixeira, Pers. Comm. 2010). On the negative side, experiments show that weeds grow five times faster in ADEs than in non-anthropic soils (Major et al., 2005). Therefore, although they are exceptionally productive, they do require a lot of maintenance. This is corroborated by ethnographic evidence from Carneiro (1960), who showed that the Kuikuro Indians in the upper Xingu River abandon their fields not because of declining soil fertility, but because of a lack of labour to clear invading weeds. The high labour investment involved in ABEs was also noted by Denevan (2004), who maintained that the cultivation of ABEs must have required high labour inputs, in particular for controlling weeds, which are more aggressive in areas of intensive cultivation than in clearings from mature fallows or primary forest. Based on observations of ADE farmers today in Brazil, who rotate crops with a few years of bush fallow to reduce the labour cost of weeding, Denevan (2004) suggests that ABEs were cultivated semi-permanently rather than permanently.

Several studies have also shown that particular vegetation grows on ADEs (Clement et al., 2004). For example, ADE forests have a distinct species composition, exhibiting greater richness and a higher abundance of domesticated and edible plants (used as food resources) than surrounding forests (Junqueira et al., 2011). They have also found that increased fertility associated with ADEs improves conditions for the establishment and growth of exotic species that are generally more nutrient demanding than native Amazonian species (de Souza et al., 2017). Furthermore, the more complex the ADE archaeological context (for example, multi-component sites), the greater the floristic composition of cultivated useful plants in modern home gardens (Lins et al., 2015), pointing to the lasting repercussions of past land use.

The size of ADE sites varies. Although the majority of ADE sites recorded cover less than two hectares (Kern et al., 2003), some are several hundred hectares in size. The Santarém site in the lower Amazon, for example, may have covered more than 500 hectares (Roosevelt, 1999), whereas the Açutuba site in the lower Negro River extended over 3 kilometres of river bluff and covered 30 hectares (Heckenberger et al., 1999). ADEs typically develop on Ferralsols and Acrisols, but can also occur when other soil types, such as Arensols, Podzols, Luvisols, Nitisols and Cambisols, are present (Kern et al., 2003). Their thickness and composition are also variable, both within and between sites. They can range in depth from very shallow (0.15 metres) to quite deep (up to 4 metres). ADEs located along or near large rivers are typically larger, deeper and more concentrated than they are elsewhere. This disparity appears to be related to more intensive habitation along larger rivers. As for why ADEs can be so different, this could be attributed to differences in the composition of the refuse deposited, or to the intensity, duration, nature and distribution of human activities (Kern et al., 2017).

The extensive and lighter soils that usually surround patches of ADEs or ABEs are critical to understanding land use on these Amazonian anthrosols. Patches of ABEs are frequently found surrounding ADEs, although the separation between them is more of a transitional gradation than an exact cut-off point (Fraser et al., 2011). ABEs are generally more extensive, lighter in colour (dark brown to brown or brownish-grey), shallower and with a high organic matter and charcoal content in the A-horizon. Because archaeological features and remains are rare or absent in ABEs, they are rarely recognized as archaeological sites and have received far less attention than ADEs.

Woods and McCann's (1999) studies of ABEs around Santarém revealed that they have slightly higher total carbon but lower P and Ca values, implying that mulch was intentionally burned on these soils. Micromorphology work on ABEs by Arroyo-Kalin (2010) in the Central Amazon shows evidence of a clear truncation between the lower part of a well-preserved buried A horizon and its underlying B horizon, indicating some sort of scraping, raking and churning activity. The high magnetic susceptibility of ABEs shows that soil iron was magnetized through *in situ* heating, which suggests soil management techniques involving the burning of organic debris at or near the soil surface (Arroyo-Kalin, 2010). On the same lines, Costa et al. (2013) discovered evidence of organic matter burning, changes in minerals (maghemite to goethite) and pottery re-firing at ABE sites of the lower Amazon. 'Cool burning', where charcoal was left relatively intact rather than being reduced to ashes, which degrade over time, appears to have been a critical feature in ABE formation. This incomplete burning, or 'slash and char', contrasts with the current prevalent practice of slash and burn, in which combustion is hot and complete after a lengthy period of drying out (Denevan, 2004). As seen above, the key to the long-term fertility of ABEs is their high concentration of pyrogenic carbon.

Little research has been undertaken into the spatial extent of ABEs. Like ADEs, ABEs appear to be a pan-Amazonian phenomenon, with sites reported from the middle Caquetá River in the Colombian Amazon to the mouth of the Amazon River (Kern et al., 2017). Studies show that ABEs can range in size from being three times as large as the related ADE (e.g., Triunfo site in SW Amazonia) to being ten times as large (e.g., Juruti area near Santarém) (Costa et al., 2013). So far, the largest ABEs have been reported in the Belterra plateau in the vicinity of Santarém, where they were estimated to be 1,000 hectares in extent (Bozarth et al., 2009). Other areas are characterized by smaller ABEs, such as in the middle Madeira, where they are typically 10 hectares in size (Fraser et al., 2009), as well as in the Colombian Amazon (Herrera et al., 1992).

Like many other students of anthropogenic soils of Amazonia (Arroyo-Kalin, 2010; Denevan, 1996; Denevan, 2001; Herrera et al., 1992; Sombroek, 1966; Woods et al., 2009), I have argued that ABEs are intentionally prepared cultivation fields (Iriarte et al., 2020a). Current data points to the fact that ABE anthrosols were fields where spatially intensive (high labour input/unit area) cultivation, relying on organic amendments and likely requiring soil preparation and maintenance, took place. ABEs implied intentional, deliberate, possibly labour-intensive movement of organic matter from domestic contexts to fields, the cutting and removal of trees with stone axes, and systematic burning as part of semi-permanent agricultural activities (Denevan, 2001; Kern et al., 2017; Mora et al., 1991; Myers, 2004; Sombroek, 1966; Woods and McCann, 1999). As Carneiro (1960) and Denevan (2001) remind us, stone axes are not as effective as metal axes and machetes. Despite this, palaeoecological data reveal that indigenous Amazonians were able to cultivate annual crops by creating open patches of land. They would do this communally by taking advantage of tree falls, patches of more open forests, controlled fire and tree girdling (the removal of bark from around the entire circumference of large trees). ABEs also represent an investment in the land as well as in the labour required to cultivate trees needing management practices (e.g., weeding, clearing of undergrowth) with long productive cycles. For example, Brazil nuts and *pequi* only start producing after several years, sometimes decades, but can subsequently remain productive for centuries (e.g., Junqueira et al., 2011). This happened not only in Amazonia; Robinson et al. (2018), for example, have documented the afforestation of entire landscapes in south-eastern Brazil with forests of *Araucaria*, which only become productive after 17–21 years.

ABEs as permanent fields with large investments of labour are difficult to imagine in the ethnographic present, but not in pre-Columbian Amazonia before the decimation of agricultural populations. The labour-demanding but high-yielding ADE agroecosystems that integrated annual and perennial crops, along with faunal resources, were able to sustain the large populations that developed during the late Holocene, and were observed by the first Europeans in the Amazon. As spatially intensive and highly fertile settings, ABEs should be regarded as tangible evidence of increased productivity per unit of land. They represent an investment in *landesque* capital that could be regarded as a technology of soil enhancement to increase productivity in upland settings. They indicate both the cultivation of root and seed annual crops, ready for harvesting several months after planting, and managed agroforestry, which requires a long-term investment of labour. The functional integration of ABE cultivation and duck husbandry as 'pest control' is an intriguing possibility, at least for the central and southern rim of the Amazon, where it has been historically and archaeologically documented. Additionally, the plots in different stages of succession that likely happen in ABEs must have also served to attract a large number of game.

Land use on ADEs

As we have seen above, and will explore further in the following chapters, much has been learnt over the past twenty years about the genesis and archaeology of ADE soils, and their current use and potential. However, until recently, we understood very little about the land use practices on these Amazonian anthrosols. In particular, we had a limited knowledge of the types of crops grown on Amazonian anthrosols. Key unanswered questions were: what annual and perennial crops were planted and consumed in these anthrosols? What was the extent of forest clearing associated with them? Were ADE residents enriching the forest with edible plants? Were they practising agroforestry? What was the role of fire in these agro-ecosystems? These are questions that can only be resolved by employing a multi-proxy approach and closely integrating archaeology with the palaeosciences.

Polyculture The analysis of charred plant remains from ADE excavations and phytoliths from test pit transects, along with pollen and charcoal from lake cores, indicates that ADE farmers across the Amazon basin planted a mix of annual and perennial crops (polyculture), including maize, manioc, sweet potato, yams, squash, bottle gourd, arrowroot and leren (Caromano, 2010; Gonda, 2018; Iriarte et al., 2020a; Maezumi et al., 2018a; Robinson et al., 2020). Pollen data from ADEs in the Colombian Amazon indicate the presence of a diversity of plant resources from about 790 CE, including tuber crops, such as sweet potato and manioc, maize, fruit trees such as cashew nut (*Anacardium occidentalis*) and maraca (*Theobroma bicolour*), and palms, including *Astrocaryum*, *Euterpe*, *Geonoma* and *Iriartea*, along with spices, such as chilli peppers (*Capsicum chinensis*) (Herrera et al., 1992).

Land cover Pollen cores from lakes and phytolith from test pit transects, have revealed that ADE farming did not result in large-scale deforestation but rather maintained the canopy cover. Stable carbon isotopes from soils in the Bolivian Amazon (Robinson et al., 2020) show that a canopy cover was maintained at ADE sites throughout their history. These records also show constantly high levels of tree taxa and low levels of herbs. Overall, this points to a land use system characterized by a mosaic of patches in different stages of succession, forming a complex landscape that likely transitioned from forest to field and back to forest again. In Chapter 10, I will detail one of these records from the Bolivian Amazon, which provides us with one of the most important historical lessons for sustainable Amazonian futures.

Agroforestry Crucially, pollen and phytolith profiles from sites, such as Lake Caranã in the lower Amazon and the Versalles lake in the Bolivian Amazon, reveal an increase in the abundance of economically important plants as ADEs developed (Iriarte et al., 2020a). They show that ADE residents enriched the forest with plants of economic importance, that is, they practised 'agroforestry', including palms (e.g., *Bactris*, *Mauritia*, *Attalea*), Brazil nuts and *pequi* (Maezumi et al., 2018a). The following chapter will describe similar crops recovered from ADEs in the Central Amazon. Because a large portion of perennial tree fruits and palms are not amenable to an increase in fruit size, even under intensive management, it might be argued that Amazonian farmers increased the density of trees on their land to attain higher yields, by cultivating ABE soils that were favourable to them. Similar patterns have been found in pollen records from the wet forests of W Amazonia in Peru on ADE sites (Kelly et al., 2018), in the phytolith records from interfluvial areas (McMichael et al., 2012) and in combined archaeobotanical and zooarchaeological data from the late Holocene western coastal Ecuador Jama-Coque II cultures, which all suggest agroforestry land use combining annual crops with perennial tree crops and useful forest taxa (Stahl and Pearsall, 2012).

Fires Clearance and burning also seem to have played a role in the establishment of ADEs. As summarized in Iriarte et al. (2020a), the analysis of charcoal from soil pits shows a general increase in charcoal counts over time, with drastic charcoal increases at the onset of anthropogenic soil development. Similarly, the lake charcoal records show charcoal peaks correlated with the development of ADEs followed by stagnation (Caranã) or decline (Versalles). These charcoal records suggest that controlled in-field burning was likely practised in these fields to clear weeds, thereby releasing nutrients and contributing to anthropogenic pedogenesis once ADEs were established. The practice of controlled in-field burning also meant that the impact of late dry season wildfires was minimized. In the final chapter, where I describe the charcoal record from Caranã Lake, I will go into greater detail on this topic and its implications for policymakers.

The findings briefly described above from the lower, central and SW Amazonia, however, differ from those in other regions of tropical South and Central America. For example, the pollen records from the Meidote phase of the Abeja site (1.6–0.8 ka), Middle Caquetá River, Colombian Amazon, show high forest disturbance frequencies, suggesting

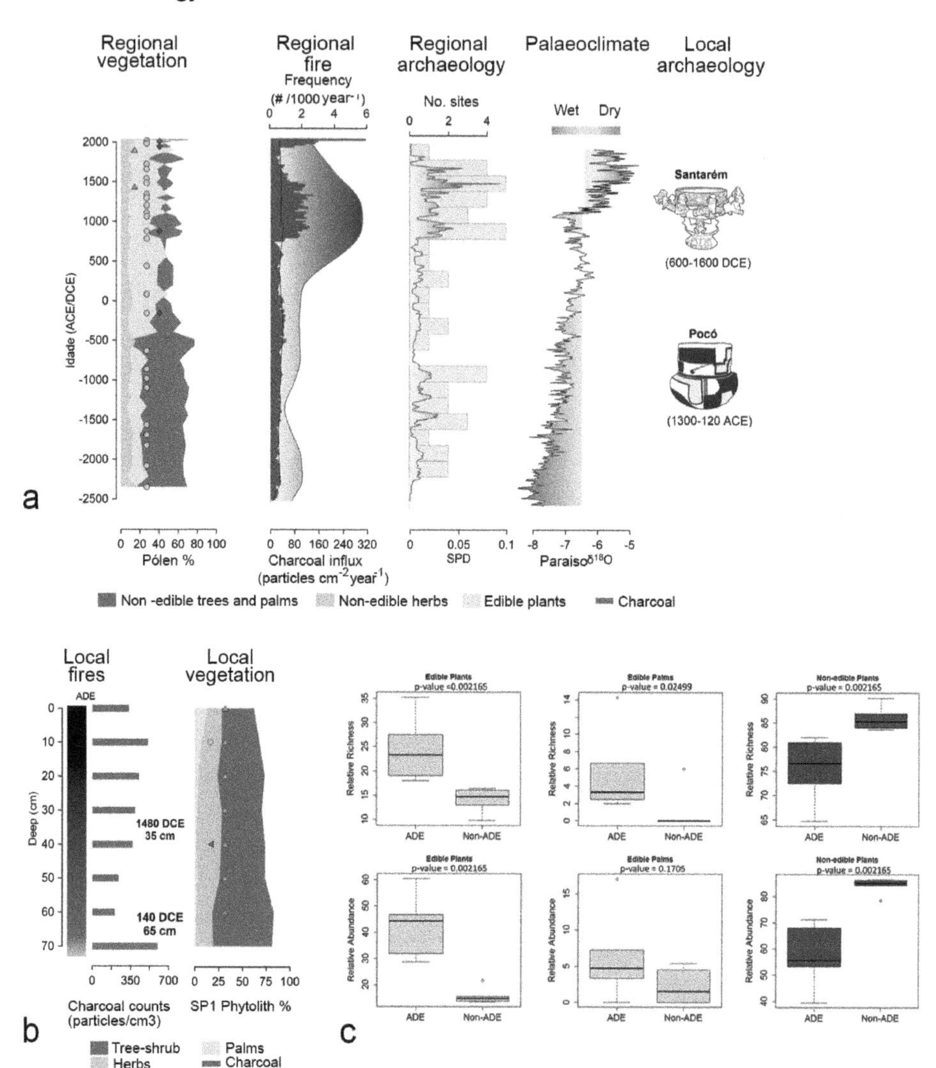

Figure 6.4 *a.* Pollen and charcoal data from Caranã Lake (Santarém) sediment core along with SPD values from the region's archaeology, palaeoprecipitation data ($\delta^{18}O$) from Paraíso Cave (Wang et al., 2017) and local archaeological ceramic phases. *b.* Charcoal and phytolith data from a soil profile located at the Serra de Maguari 1 ADE site (modified from Maezumi et al., 2018b). *c.* modern vegetation surveys from the three ADE and three non-ADE sites showing the lasting repercussions of past land use in today's flora.

that the area around the site was widely cleared for agriculture (Mora et al., 1991). We need to take into account that these data are not coming from an environmental archive that reflects the regional vegetation history, but from the soil profile of an archaeological site. Therefore, they need to be taken with caution. Records from the Maya lowlands also differ with the Amazonian records presented above, with evidence of increased forest burning and clearing, maize cultivation and erosion at the start of the middle Holocene ~4.5–4.0

ka (Pohl et al., 1996; Wahl et al., 2006). Amazonian records also contrast with and differ significantly from those of the Mediterranean and temperate regions of Europe, where agricultural expansion was accompanied by deforestation (Roberts et al., 2018).

Raised-field agriculture

Along with ADEs, the late Holocene across tropical South America witnessed another major landscape transformation. Large tracts of previously uncultivated seasonally flooded savannas, mostly on the periphery of Amazonian rainforests, were reclaimed as agricultural landscapes through the construction of systems of raised or drained fields (Denevan, 2001; Iriarte and Dickau, 2012; Lombardo et al., 2011; Rodrigues et al., 2018; Rostain, 2012b).

Raised or drained fields were a cultivation strategy used in seasonally flooded savannahs. It created patches of raised soils above water that provided cultivation platforms with better drainage and aeration, moisture retention during dry seasons, and increased fertility through the incorporation of wetland organic sediments and nitrogen fixation. Additionally, this method possibly facilitated weed collection and clearing, as well as the potential for fish farming in canals (see for example Denevan, 2001; Renard et al., 2011).

Figure 6.5 Map of raised fields in the Santa Ana de Yacuma region. Satellite map courtesy of Umberto Lombardo.

Raised fields cover vast swathes of South America's floodplain savannahs, from the Llanos de Mojos and the Mompos depression where the Magdalena flows into the sea, to the coast of the Guianas (see Figure 7.25). Similar to ADEs, they are associated with different cultural traditions. In some regions, such as the Llanos de Mojos, a seasonally flooded savannah the size of the UK was transformed into raised field systems.

New technologies are allowing us to better document their extent. For example, in his pioneering studies, Denevan (1966) calculated a minimum of 20,235 hectares for Mojos, Bolivia, based on aerial photographs. New techniques available for the identification of raised fields, combining high-resolution satellite imagery and GIS, indicate that the density of raised fields appears to have been more considerable than previously assumed. For example, in a sector of the Santa Ana de Yacuma region in north-western Beni alone, Lombardo (2010) estimated the presence of 51,500 hectares of platform-type upland fields.

There are a variety of raised fields in the Americas. They can be up to 350 metres long, 20 metres wide and over a metre high, and were built in a variety of shapes (Denevan, 2001: 211), possibly related to the way pre-Columbian farmers managed water under different conditions. This is the case on the coast of French Guiana where a great diversity of raised fields are found, including: a) small round mounds (~1–1.5 metres diameter), known in Spanish as 'montones', which are very numerous and completely cover some plots of floodable savannahs; b) larger, medium-sized, circular raised fields, with a diameter of up to 5 metres, which are found on the coast of French Guiana; and c) elongate fields (1 metre high, 1–5 metres wide and 30–50 metres long), known as ridged fields or 'camellones' in Spanish, which are usually located in the deepest wetland areas, such as in the lower Mana River (Figure 10.4d) (Rostain, 2012b).

In most regions where raised or drained fields occur, there is no historical information illustrating this agricultural practice, possibly because many of them had already been abandoned as a product of the Columbian Encounter. However, some early European chronicles illustrate the practice of wetland agriculture, as in the case of the Otomaco Indians in Venezuela or the Tainos in Hispaniola, who constructed small mounds of earth for cultivation using wooden shovels similar to a purported Arauquinoid digging shovel found in Surinam, dating from ~1240 CE (Rostain, 2012b; Versteeg, 2003).

Some of these raised field systems appear to have been in operation for hundreds, if not thousands, of years. Unfortunately, direct dating of raised fields is one of the most significant challenges facing the archaeology of wetland agriculture, although progress has been made (e.g., McKey et al., 2010b; Parsons and Shlemon, 1987; Rodrigues et al., 2018).

Modern construction and cultivation experiments, as well as rehabilitation of raised fields, shows that raised fields are highly productive (at least in the short term), with yields of 2–5.8 t hectare^{-1} of maize and up to 21 t hectare^{-1} of manioc (see summary in Iriarte et al., 2010).

What was planted on them? A review of palaeoecological and archaeobotanical data of raised fields across South America by Iriarte and Dickau (2012) shows that a wide variety of plants were cultivated on the raised and drained agricultural fields and associated habitation sites. These include maize, tubers and roots, vegetables such as squash and peanuts, industrial crops such as cotton, dyes such as indigo and annatto, and even stimulant and hallucinogenic herbs such as *coca*, *yerba mate* and *yopo*. Despite this diversity, the data indicate that maize was undoubtedly the most ubiquitous and probably one of the most important crops planted in the raised and drained fields. These results are similar to those found in archaeobotanical studies in Central American wetland agriculture, which also indicate that maize appears to have been the predominant crop (Whitmore and Turner, 2001). Interdisciplinary work in French Guiana led by Doyle McKey has been particularly enlightening on the history and land use system of raised fields. It shows that the raised-field landscape that we see today was co-constructed by human and ecosystem engineers. On the one hand, farmers created physical and biogeochemical heterogeneity in flat, marshy environments by constructing raised fields. On the other, when these fields were later abandoned, the mosaic of well-drained islands in the flooded matrix set in motion self-organizing processes, driven by ecosystem engineers (ants, termites, earthworms and woody plants), which occur preferentially on abandoned raised fields. Engineer organisms transport materials to abandoned raised fields, and modify the structure and composition of their soils, reducing soil erosion (McKey et al., 2010b).

One of the major challenges has been to identify which crops were grown in raised fields. Phytoliths, which are deposited *in situ* and are resistant to decay in these open air, acidic and wet sites, along with the analysis of the stable carbon isotopes in the soils, and pollen grains from lake cores, provided the answer. Phytoliths from the raised field profiles at the K8, Bois Diable, Pilliwa and Savanne de Gran Macua sites were analysed (Figure 10.5d). The upper levels of the profiles represent the establishment of raised fields, and the associated phytolith assemblages contain the crops and vegetation that grew during the fallows and were adapted to the relatively dry environments created by the raised platforms on the raised fields. The combined phytolith and carbon isotope analyses evidence the reclamation of these seasonally flooded savannahs into agricultural landscapes. In the upper, raised-field strata, they show the transformation of a relatively homogeneous wetland vegetation, comprised of a mixture of C4 and C3 plants, mainly including Cyperaceae, Marantaceae and *Heliconia* herbs, Panicoid and Oryzoideae grasses, into agricultural raised fields dominated by C4 plants, including maize and other Panicoid grasses.

Phytolith analysis from raised fields in French Guiana documented both the diagnostic wavy-top rondels produced in the glumes of maize cobs and cross-shaped leaf phytolith assemblages were detected in every type of raised field analysed. Phytoliths of squash (*Cucurbita*) were also found in Piliwa, and preliminary starch grain residue analysis from the contemporary Arauquinoid site of Sable Blanc evidenced the consumption of maize and manioc (McKey et al., 2010b).

As we will see in Chapter 10, our work (Iriarte et al., 2012) also shows that pre-Columbian raised field farmers practised fire-free savannah management, which calls into question the widely held assumption that pre-Columbian Amazonian farmers pervasively used fire to manage and alter ecosystems, and offers fresh perspectives on savannah land use and conservation. A section of the next chapter describes the Arauquinoid Tradition that created these raised-field agricultural systems along the coast of the Guianas and Chapter 10 describes the fire-free practices of raised-field farmers and its implications for sustainable Amazonian futures.

Population increase, spread of agriculture and language expansions

To end this chapter, I would like to draw attention to the relationship between the population expansion indicated by the increased number of sites, the spread of agriculture and language expansions. It is evident that during the late Holocene period, certain societies in the Amazon region significantly altered the landscape through the practice of ADE farming and the conversion of large areas of seasonal savannahs into raised-field agricultural landscapes. This scale of transformation was unprecedented. The rather simultaneous and broad spread of ADEs suggests that around BCE 500 something new began in terms of occupational intensity across much of the region. Radiocarbon databases also show population growth trends that are most likely related to the increased carrying capacity brought about by intensive cultivation on ADEs (Figure 1.1) (Arroyo-Kalin and Riris, 2021). ADEs and raised-field farming likely constituted the economic basis for population expansion and social complexity. The larger regional populations currently being documented by archaeology across Amazonia, many of whom relied on polyculture agroforestry systems supported by intensive cultivation in Amazonian anthrosols, fall well within the range of medium-sized pre-Columbian polities elsewhere in the Americas, as well as the range of medium-sized pre-modern urbanized forested landscapes in other regions, which we will explore in Chapters 7 and 8. These developments are also purportedly characterized by an increase in local and regional interaction via trade, exchange, feasting, warfare and alliances (Heckenberger, 2002; Heckenberger and Neves, 2009; Lathrap, 1970). As these farming populations spread, they accrued crop genetic resources, likely creating centres of crop genetic diversity, evidencing the transformation and diversification of plant resources (Clement et al., 2015).

The evidence synthesized in this and the forthcoming chapters does not support suggestions that late Holocene agricultural systems were characterized by opportunistic agroforestry (Fausto and Neves, 2018; Neves, 2007) akin to those reported in historic or modern ethnographic settings.

The overall land use pattern on ADE and ABE soils during the late Holocene does suggest a similar signature of polyculture agroforestry for ADE systems across Amazonia, regardless of the regional cultural, bio-geographic and climatic variations in site location indicating the spread of a successful agro-ecosystem that was adopted in various regions by a diversity of cultures.

As argued in Chapters 4 and 5, plant domestication and the development of agriculture in Amazonia needs to be studied 'on its own terms'. The development of agriculture in Amazonia took a different path from the Eurasian experience. Regardless, all evidence points to the fact that some late Holocene agricultural systems, such as Amazonian anthrosols, were intensive across Amazonia. The lines of evidence presented in this chapter, along with the first eyewitness accounts along the Amazon and its upland forests, show that in many regions Amazonian societies became numerous and socially complex, investing in the landscape and practising intensive systems of land use.

Parallel to these major transformations and a changing climate, historical linguistics shows the dispersal of traditions and language families associated with plant cultivation and forest management in the South American tropical lowlands (Gregorio de Souza et al., 2020; Heckenberger, 2002; Iriarte et al., 2017; Neves, 2013). To what extent these major landscape transformations are correlated with the spread of farmers associated with the ancestors of major linguistic families, including the Arawak, Tupi, Caribs, as well as several other smaller groups, such as the Pano and Tukano, and with ceramic traditions associated with the beginning of sedentary life, is a topic heavily debated in archaeology.

Direct connections between material culture, language and ethnicity in Amazonia are not without problems (see Neves, 2013). Nevertheless, persistent associations of ceramic styles, settlement patterns and site architecture have been shown to pervade the Amazonian past, with strong links to historically recorded populations. For example, as seen in Chapter 2, the spread of the Saladoid-Barrancoid culture has been hypothesized for some time to reflect the expansion of Arawak languages; the Incised-Punctate expansion has been suggested to coincide with the spread of languages of the Carib family; and the Tupiguarani archaeological tradition, one of the most widespread in South America, shares the exact name given to the Tupiguarani language family given its historical overlap with the area occupied by its speakers.

Along these lines, Souza et al. (2020) has coherently argued that the territorial extent of archaeological cultures related to the spread of ceramics and farming mirrors the distribution of the largest language families in South America, suggesting that culture and language spread was a consequence of population growth and expansion from centres of domestication. Furthermore, Souza et al. (2020) argue that the concurrence of precipitation increase, forest expansion and population dispersal suggest that the establishment of modern climatic conditions and the geographical extent of current biomes favoured the expansion of forest agriculturists and their languages across the tropical lowlands of South America. In most of the regions where these 'archaeological phenomena' settled, those archaeological cultures introduced the cultivation of domesticated plants (e.g., Admiraal et al., 2023), marked the transition to more permanent settlements and diffused practices of landscape modification, including the formation of ADEs. In summary, they argue for a spread and economic model conventionally called 'polyculture agroforestry', combining extensive cultivation of domesticated plants with the management of useful and semi-domesticated species in enriched forests. As research progresses on this fascinating subject, we will have more certainty about these population movements and their relationship to ceramic traditions.

The role of maize and manioc in late pre-Columbian times

For several decades, the nature of Amazonian pre-Columbian agricultural systems has sparked considerable debate, specifically as to whether one or more cultigens, maize or manioc were able to provide a stable agricultural base for sedentism and population growth in pre-Columbian Amazonia (Carneiro, 1998; Gross, 1975; Meggers, 1996; Roosevelt, 1987b).

To what extent some of these crops became a staple in the diet of specific population groups is a difficult question to answer with the data at hand. Unfortunately, the presence of microfossils in soil profiles and lake sediments does not tell us accurately what proportion of people's total diet these crops constituted. And, only a few sites in Amazonia preserve human skeletal remains for stable carbon and nitrogen isotope studies, which also have its limitations to document the degree of maize consumption (see Chapter 4).

Despite these shortcomings, several lines of evidence point to an increase in maize consumption during the late Holocene in some regions of Amazonia. Significantly, maize either appears or becomes more dominant only after the development of Amazonian anthrosols. This implies that the development of ABEs may have allowed for the expansion of the cultivation of this productive crop beyond fertile lake or river margins (Maezumi et al., 2018; 2022). The isotopic composition of a small sample of human bones from some regions of the Amazon, including the middle Orinoco River ~400 CE (van der Merwe et al., 1981), the Upper Ucayali (Roosevelt, 1989) and the Llanos de Mojos (Prümers and Jaimes Betancourt, 2014), evidence of an increasingly maize-based diet. In the central Amazon, carbon and nitrogen stable isotopes from a small sample of human bones associated with the formation of ADEs suggest a 'maize-existing but not maize-reliant diet' (Arroyo-Kalin, 2010). The lower Amazon paints a different picture. Stable carbon and nitrogen analyses of twenty-one individuals from twelve ADE sites in the Lower Xingu region, dated between 0.4–1.7 ka, shows a clear spectrum of variation in human diets. These range from reliance on closed canopy terrestrial plants, animals and different types of aquatic resources to a clear input of $\delta^{13}C$ resources, which are likely representative of additional C4 resource use, such as maize. Isotopic analyses from skeletal remains pertaining to the Maracá tradition from the mouth of the Amazon, dating to ~0.5 ka, indicate that these populations had diets based on the exploitation of fish and a wide range of C3 plant resources, with maize not a significant component (Hermenegildo et al., 2017). The Marajoara cultural tradition (400–1300 CE) does not appear to be based on a maize economy, although paradoxically isotope data from skeletons dated to the last centuries before European colonization show a strong C4 signature (Roosevelt, 1991). Collectively for this latter region, despite the fact that maize has been present in the region since 4.3 ka, it does not appear to have been the staple crop, as stable isotope averages from Marajó (−19.0 ± 1.1), Maracá (−16.7 ± 1) and São Luis Island (−17.0 ± 0.9) indicate. It should be noted that some individuals exhibited a strong C4 maize signal, which calls for further investigation. The presence of maize in the archaeobotanical evidence in eastern Amazonia is congruent with early historical accounts describing maize as the staple food for the populations living in the confluence of the Tapajós and Amazon rivers during early post-Columbian times (Heriarte, 1874 [1662]).

A compilation of palaeoecological and archaeobotanical data from raised fields across South America's seasonally flooded tropical savannahs shows that maize was an important crop in late Holocene raised-field agricultural systems (Iriarte and Dickau, 2012). In some regions, changes in diet, as evidenced by human bone isotopes, appear to be reflected in material culture changes. The *budares*, flat pans traditionally used to cook bitter manioc tortillas, are replaced by *manos* and *metates*, employed to process maize grain, in the middle Orinoco River ~2.7 k (Roosevelt, 1987a), the Caribbean littoral of western Venezuela ~3–2 k (Rouse and Cruxent, 1963) and at Caverna da Pedra Pintada ~3–2 k (Roosevelt et al., 1996).

Collectively, the data indicate that maize likely played a supplemental role during its adoption and dispersal during the middle Holocene, possibly becoming a more important part of the diet with the development of ADE polyculture agroforestry. This would be consistent with Roosevelt's (1987b) contention that the introduction of maize as a storable protein supply ~2 ka prompted the emergence of socio-political complexity in the Central and Lower Amazon. This, in turn, increased the carrying capacity of the land to sustain growing populations, as indicated in the evidence supplied by radiocarbon databases (Figure 1.1) (Arroyo-Kalin and Riris, 2020). As can be seen from the summary of data above, the picture is complex and varied, and current data do not show maize consumption as a staple in other regions where complex societies developed, such as Marajó.

Now, we turn to manioc, which is arguably the most important root crop in the tropics (Scott et al., 2020), dubbed by Oliver (2001) as the 'super-crop'. It has the highest starch content of all Amazonian tuber crops (Piperno and Pearsall 1998: 120). It is easy to cultivate via vegetative propagation, by simply cutting and replanting stems. Manioc can be grown in a wide range of environmental conditions, including less than optimal soils, but it is also extremely productive in highly fertile ADEs (Fraser et al., 2012). Bitter varieties are pest resistant. Manioc can be pound or grated. It can be stored in the ground for up to six months, while the different forms of flour can be stored for more than a year (see summary in Oliver 2001: 77–81).

Available data to weigh the role of manioc in late Pre-Columbian diets is very scant. However, several lines of evidence point to its importance in late Holocene Amazonian economies, including the presence of manioc phytoliths and pollen in ADEs and lakes, the appearance of bitter manioc-processing material and the existence of hundreds of varieties of manioc developed by Amazonian farmers since its initial cultivation in the very early Holocene. Manioc may have played an important role in pre-Columbian land use systems that featured polyculture agroforestry with the use of stone axes. Its cultivation was possibly somewhat distinct from the slash-and-burn techniques used in post-Columbian cultures, which were characterized by the use of metal axes. However, it is not certain that manioc was less common in pre-Columbian Amazonian diets, as some authors have recently claimed (Fausto and Neves, 2018; Shepard Jr et al., 2020). Until we have more sophisticated techniques to document the importance of manioc in late Holocene Amazonian societies, claims that manioc was not an important crop should be treated with caution. Similarly, there is uncertainty about the extent to which bitter manioc replaced sweet manioc during the middle to late Holocene (Arroyo-Kalin, 2010), and whether manioc gradually replaced other tubers in pre-Columbian times (Piperno and Pearsall, 1998). All of these are complex issues that need further research.

In the upcoming chapter, I will delve into the period of regional fluorescence during the late Holocene in Amazonia. I will describe the explosion of regional cultures expressing socio-political complexity, complex terraforming projects, sophisticated ceramics and integration into regional systems across the basin from the Upper Amazon to Marajó island.

CHAPTER 7
REGIONAL FLORESCENCE DURING THE LATE HOLOCENE

Accompanying the spread of ADE and raised-field farming described in the previous chapter, the late Holocene witnessed the beginning of the Formative period. This period was characterized by population growth, an explosion of regional cultures expressing socio-political complexity and integration into regional systems, and the development of low-density urban societies (Chapter 8). Such cultures created sophisticated ceramics and polished stone prestige artefacts, and built monumental structures on a scale previously unseen and huge infrastructure, including complex networks of roads, anthrosols and raised-fields landscapes, reservoirs and landscape-scale fish weirs (e.g., Clement et al., 2015; Erickson, 2000; Heckenberger and Neves, 2009; Schaan, 2012b).

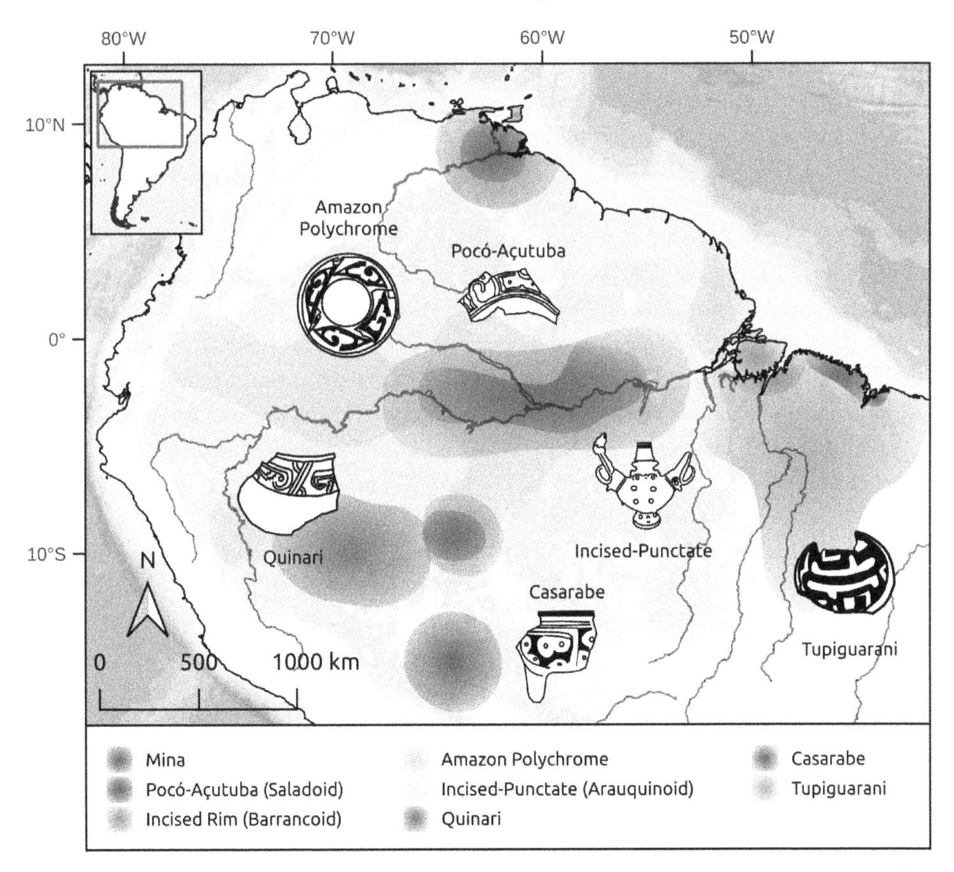

Figure 7.1 Major ceramic traditions: their geographical distribution and chronology. Modified from Barreto et al. (2016: 53).

During this period, Amazonia saw the emergence and spread of major ceramic traditions, each displaying significant regional variations.

In this chapter, I will briefly overview the archaeological evidence for the diversity of complex cultures that flourished in the Amazon basin during the late Holocene period, specifically within the past 2,000 years. I will start by discussing the Upper Peruvian Amazon, the middle Caquetá River, followed by SW Amazonia, the central Amazon. and finally the late Holocene cultures of the lower Amazon and the Guiana coast. This is a long and descriptive chapter, which reveals the many fascinating details of these late Holocene complex cultures across Amazonia. Much of the research in Amazonian archaeology has focused on the ceramic cultures of the late Holocene period, and this emphasis is reflected in the length of this chapter. Before delving into a summary of the archaeological cultures that thrived in the late Holocene, I would like to touch on the technology that is helping to uncover the details of site layouts and regional organization of these fascinating societies.

'Our lasers in the sky': Revelations beneath the canopy

Lidar technology has been key to our understanding of socio-environmental landscapes, especially in tropical regions covered by forest, where it has revealed the existence, extent and organization of pre-Columbian tropical cities and their associated landscape engineering (Figure 7.2). Although the technology is very complex, the underlying concept is actually quite straightforward. A lidar sensor (usually called an airborne laser scanner) is mounted to an aircraft (drone, plane or helicopter), which flies at a specific altitude and airspeed, and follows a predetermined flight path over the area to be scanned. The lidar sensor sends out laser beams, which bounce back to the sensor at different times, depending on the elevation of the terrain. The time the laser pulse takes to return to the sensor determines the elevation of each individual data point. Some hit the canopy, while others penetrate the canopy and hit the ground. The data generated from the lidar sensor, known as the point cloud, is downloaded and calibrated, and a 3D model is created. This is known as a digital terrain model, or DTM. A vegetation removal algorithm is used to remove vegetation from the model, which helps to create a DTM of the ground beneath the canopy. The data can then be processed and visualized to identify any changes in the terrain, some of which may correspond to archaeological structures, which archaeologists later analyse.

The ability to reveal archaeological landscapes beneath the dense rainforest canopy has revolutionized our understanding of monumental tropical cities, such as Angkor (e.g., Evans et al., 2013) and the lowland Maya (e.g., Beach et al., 2019). It has recently started to be employed in the tropical forests of South America with similar results (e.g., Iriarte et al., 2020b; Osorio et al., 2023; Peripato et al., 2023; Prümers et al., 2022; Prümers and Jaimes Betancourt, 2014; Rostain et al., 2023; Sánchez-Polo and Litben, 2023). It offers a cost-effective alternative to a full coverage survey, which is generally time-consuming, expensive and often impossible in remote tropical regions. By way of an

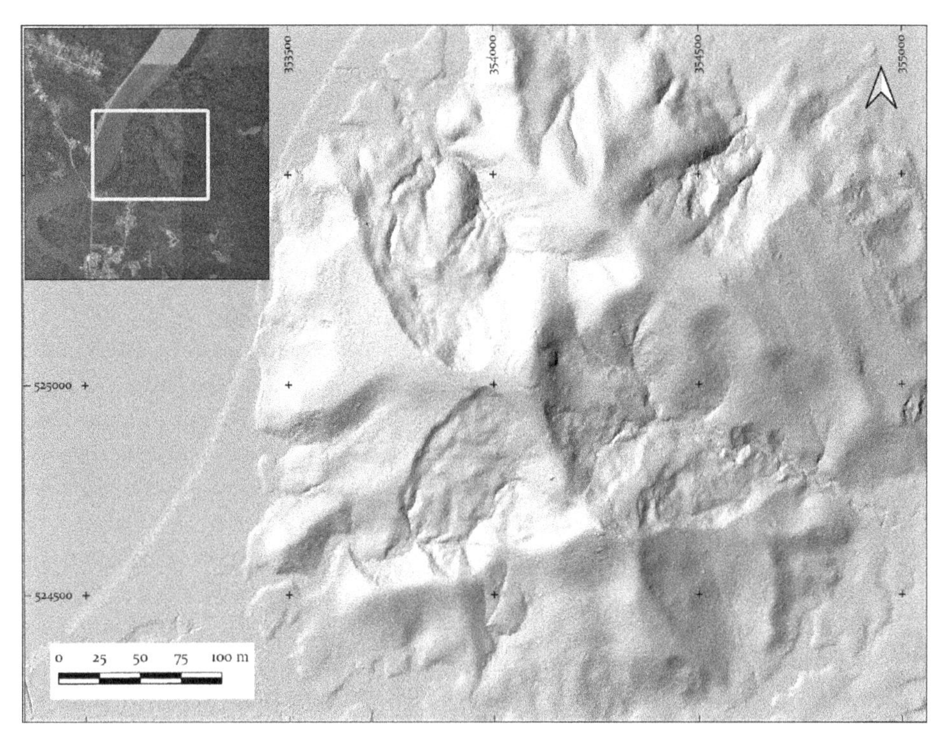

Figure 7.2 Lidar mapping is revolutionizing Amazonian archaeology with its ability to peer through the forest canopy. This lidar image shows a double-ditched *montagne couronnée* (crowned mountain) at the summit of Montagne Anglaise situated on the right bank of the Mahury River, French Guiana. Courtesy Martinj van del Bel.

example, the German-Bolivian team who mapped the Loma Salvatierra mound in Llanos de Mojos, with a theodolite and a huge team of field assistants, took three full field seasons to complete the work: the equivalent of one pass of the lidar sensor over the site with an aircraft. In the sections below, and in the next chapter, I will describe case studies showing how lidar has significantly contributed to our understanding of Amazonian cultures.

Amazonian Regions I: The Upper Peruvian Amazon and the Middle Caquetá River

The Upper Amazon region is situated at the intersection of two significant cultural hubs in South America: the Andean mountains and the Amazon rainforest. Archaeological and ethnohistorical research has demonstrated that these areas were not isolated from one another, but that there was considerable economic interaction between the Upper Amazon, the Andean highlands and the Pacific coast. The scale of interaction was not limited to commercial networks. Inhabitants of this region also exchanged technological knowledge, ideologies, and cosmological principles and ideas (e.g., Burger, 1995; Lathrap, 1970; Rostain, 2012a). This area has historically been viewed as both a barrier and a means of transportation and communication. It has often been considered a transitional zone between the highlands and the tropical lowlands, rather than being recognized for its unique cultural developments. The Upper Amazon was also critical in the proposition that Andean civilization had Amazonian origins through the works of Tello (1960) and Lathrap (1970). Julio C. Tello asserted that the Chavin civilization originated in tropical forest societies. This was a groundbreaking idea since there had been very little archaeological exploration in the Amazonia region up to that point.

Traditionally, archaeologists have applied the same environmentally deterministic models across Amazonia, seeing the topography and vegetation of the eastern slopes as hindrances to agriculture and large populations (Steward, 1946). Despite its importance, this area has not been studied as extensively as the nearby highlands and coastal valleys, and there are significant gaps in the archaeological coverage of the region. This picture is changing rapidly. As we have seen in Chapter 5, and will see below and in Chapter 8, the region was a hub of significant cultural developments that occurred in tandem with and independently from contemporaneous occurrences in neighbouring coastal, highland and tropical lowland settings.

Archaeological research indicates that the region of the Upper Amazon was settled by at least circa 12.2–11.9 ka, as evidenced by discoveries of points and other lithic artefacts from the basal layers of Manachaqui Cave in Peru (Church, 2021). Developments during the middle Holocene have already been described, using the Santa Ana La Florida site as a case study. These developments are contemporary, with many of the better-known instances of public architecture from coastal highland Peru and Ecuador dating to the third and second millennia BCE (Burger, 1995; Lathrap et al., 1977).

Below, the late Holocene cultures of the Lower Ucayali River are briefly described.

The Ucayali

Like the Upano River in Ecuador (Chapter 8), the Ucayali River was the primary trade artery in prehistory linking central Andean imperial centres of Wari on the Apurimac River, and later, Cuzco on the Urubamba with the tropical lowlands (Eriksen, 2011). In the late pre-Columbian period, this region was culturally vibrant. Various goods, information, ideas and customs were transported along the river through trading alliances between the Arawak, Panoan and Tupian peoples. These alliances facilitated exchange relations over vast distances, extending to regions such as the Ecuadorian and Colombian piedmonts and the Tapajós and Madeira rivers of the Central Amazon (Taylor, 1999). The Ucayali River was divided among various tribal groups, with the Panoan Piros controlling the upper reaches, the Panoan Conibos on the middle section and the Tupian Cocama on the lower part of the river (Santos-Granero, 1992).

The Lower Ucayali region, which was once home to one of Peru's largest tropical forest groups, the Cocama people, is the most studied. Juan Salinas de Loyola, in 1557, journeyed about 1,000 kilometres to the confluence of the Urubamba and Tambo rivers, and made a notable description of this group. He described chiefs dressed as lords and obeyed by their people. The people wore high-quality cotton clothes and adorned themselves with gold and silver jewellery, such as breastplates, bracelets, nose and ear pieces, and headdresses made of silver and feathers. Their settlements were located on the elevated riverbanks and consisted of 100, 300 and 400 houses. The Cocama polity ruled over a river area that spanned about 300 kilometres (Myers, 1974). They were in charge of the trade of precious metals, copper, salt, tobacco and animal products between the Andes and the nearby tropical lowlands. They produced polychrome ceramics, canoes, calabashes and cotton fabric (Eriksen, 2011). Like most complex societies living along the main channels of the Amazon River, the Cocama suffered greatly and quickly from Old World diseases, inter-ethnic conflict and displacement.

Not much archaeological work has been done in the region since Lathrap's (1970) seminal work in the 1960s, and his chronology remains the most widely used until new archaeological programmes refine it. This brief overview of the chronology below is based on the work of Lathrap (1970), his students and a recent summary by Coomes and colleagues (2021). The earliest period dating to BCE 2000 belongs to the Tutishcainyo Tradition, which, according to Lathrap, practised agriculture based on manioc and used stone axes, and experimented with the cultivation of maize – no archaeobotany was carried out for this period. The Shakimu Tradition succeeded the Tutishcainyo Tradition dating to BCE 900–200. Lathrap proposed that this tradition had a Chavín style influence – the Andean Early Horizon that expanded over much of the Andean area. After that, around BCE 200, the Hupa Iya ceramic tradition appears, which Lathrap suggests is an intrusion from Barrancoid people. The relatively brief occupation by the Barrancoid people ended with the arrival of the Panoans around 300 CE. The Panoan-Pacacocha ceramic tradition consisted of rather simple pottery, mainly smooth-surfaced vessels with zoomorphic *adornos*. The Panoans also introduced the practice of secondary burials in pottery urns, which were often found beneath their *malocas* (multi-family houses). Trade flourished with the highland Wari empire along the Apurimac, Ene, Tambo and Ucayali rivers, as shown by copper artefacts unearthed at excavated sites. Around 100 CE, the Yarinacocha style is interpreted as yet another displacement, interpreted by Lathrap (1970) as the return of culturally degraded descendants of the Late Shakimu peoples who had been moved away from the floodplain by the Hupaiya invaders two or three centuries earlier. Another ceramic tradition, Cumancaya, emerged from the Pacacocha heritage by introducing Quechua speakers from the north, incorporating Guaran traits from the south and Ecuadorean influences. Ceramics are often decorated with red zones delimited by incised lines, corrugated design and a wide range of vessel shapes. Cumancaya ceramics relate to current Shipibo, Conibo and Piro pottery. T-shaped stone axes, as well as copper ornaments and tools, are common during this period.

During the year 1,000 CE, the Tupí Omagua and Cocama peoples brought a new cultural pattern and material culture to the Upper Amazon region. This quickly spread upriver with the Cocama people, reaching Imiríacocha in the Central Ucayali. The newcomers brought with them a distinctive ceramic tradition, Polychrome (Miracanguera subtradition). These are the populations that were devastated by the European Encounter. The post-Colombian period is followed by missionization. The polychrome decoration of recent Panoan pottery can be traced to their close coexistence with the Cocama at mission settlements during the seventeenth to nineteenth centuries. This is certainly a region that deserves future archaeological attention.

The Napo River, located in Ecuador, to the north of the upper Peruvian Amazon, is yet another region of western Amazonia that remains largely unexplored. However, new research work is being carried out to fill the knowledge gaps in this area. To learn more about the archaeology of the region, you can refer to the summary provided by Arroyo-Kalin and Panduro (2019) (Figure 7.3).

The Caquetá

Another region of NW Amazonia where substantial work has been carried out is the middle Caquetá River, Araracuara, Colombian Amazon. The Caquetá River is a significant contributor to the Amazon River, originating in the Colombian Andes. As it meanders

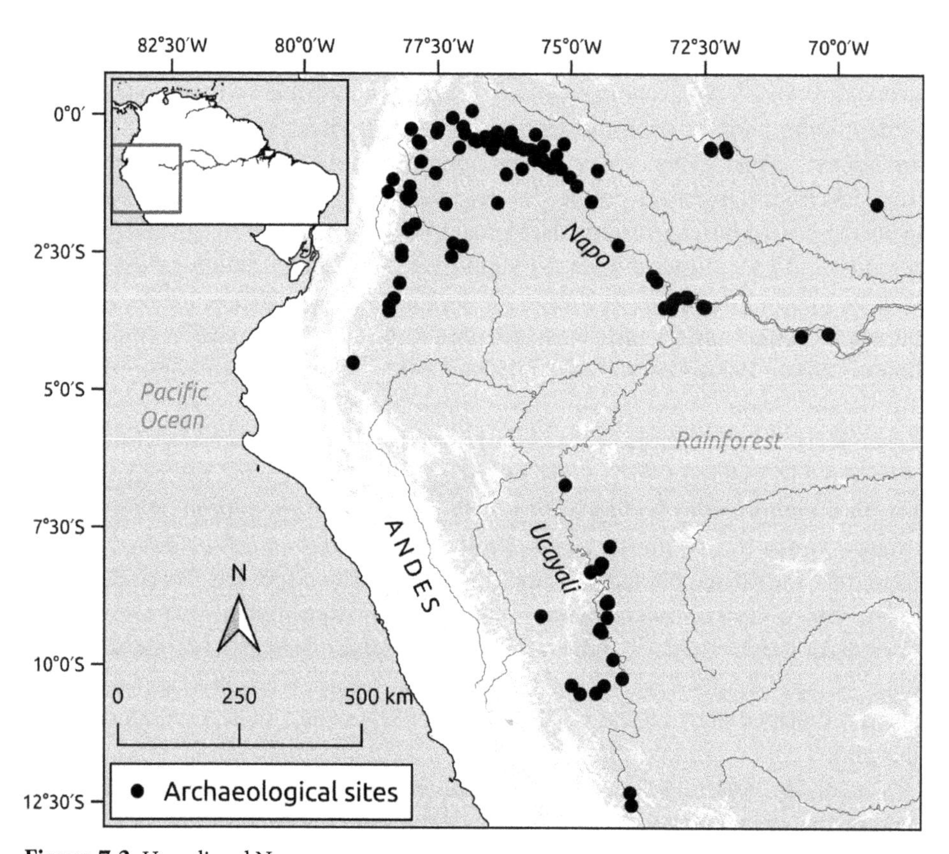

Figure 7.3 Ucayali and Napo.

through the lowland rainforest landscape, the river encounters rocky plateaus and hills, which are part of the pre-Cambrian Guiana Shield. The encounter with these rock outcrops creates endless rapids, many of which are a significant barrier for navigation, including canyons (Figure 7.3). These geographical features are well-known for their abundance of petroglyphs, figurative and geometric designs carved into river rocks using a technique of repeated pecking with another stone until an indentation is created. The waters of the river cover most of the petroglyphs for most of the year. Fernando Urbina (1991) recorded more than 2,000 engravings upstream of Araracuara. He found out that a good number of these engravings depict anthropomorphic figures that are associated with serpent-like figures. The anaconda is a formidable animal, a top predator in the water world. It can grow to more than 10 metres long and weigh more than 300 kilograms. Linked in Amazonian cultures with waterways and the underworld, the anaconda is central to many myths, mostly related to shamanic practices around the creation of the universe, in which the anaconda generally represents the ancestral creator. Urbina (1991) proposes that these snake images relate to myths about the origin of the canoe anaconda, which is important to the eastern Tukano groups living in the region. According to this myth, the primordial snake-canoe anaconda glided down the big river, populating the river bars with human communities as it went. For Amazonian people, rivers are used as a metaphor for this gigantic, wandering creature.

Araracuara is the region where one of the earliest occupations of Amazonia has been recorded at the Peña Roja site between ~11.1–9.2 ka (Mora, 2003). The only evidence for a middle Holocene occupation of the region comes from the Abeja site, a multi-component site situated on a plateau that is 140 metres above the Caquetá River. Here, at 0.85–1 metres, pollen of manioc and maize was retrieved from sediment cores corresponding to the Tubaboniba phase (Mora et al., 1991), along with maize phytoliths and abundant charcoal fragments (Piperno and Pearsall, 1998). No artefactual evidence has been recovered from these layers. For these researchers, the Tubaboniba phase indicates the presence of incipiently agricultural groups towards the end of the middle Holocene. The late Holocene occupation of the site is known as the Méidote phase. Based on a programme of intensive augering, Mora et al. (1991) have identified living areas with individual house structures and probable locations of former gardens and fields. This site component dates back to between ~385–1,175 CE, covers an area of 6 hectares and features a 0.4 metre deep ADE soil. Pollen analysis showed that people consumed maize, manioc, cacao, chilli peppers and avocado. Cotton was also present. Charred seeds and pollen from the excavation show the presence of maize, manioc, chilli peppers (*Capsicum chinenses*), cacao (*Theobroma bicolor*), chonta (*Bactris gasipaes*), a diversity of palms (*Attalea*, *Oenocarpus* sp., *Lepidocaruym* sp.), as well as Sapotaceae and Anonaceae tree fruits (Herrera et al., 1992; Mora et al., 1991). Phytolith analysis has identified maize, manioc and *Cucurbita* squash, along with a diversity of palms. The pollen record from excavation profiles shows high frequencies of forest disturbance, suggesting that the area was significantly cleared for cultivation and settlement purposes. The site was abandoned ~1,175 CE and tree pollen became the dominant feature in the pollen record.

Lithics include edge ground cobbles, manos, hammers, and triangular hoes with a sharp end and triangular section. Ceramic materials include domestic vessels and bowls with extended lips decorated with *appliqué* technique and red paint, as well as ceramic supports and pots with everted or externally reinforced rims, generally using sand, caraipé and ash as a tempering agent (Arroyo-Kalin et al., 2019).

More recently, excavations at the La Pedrera location by Morcote Rios and collaborators (2013) have documented an area of 3–5 hectares with Amazonian anthrosols with a depth of 0.7–1.2 metres. In this location, the upper part of the site named Curure, bears abundant fish, turtle and rodent bone remains. Charred seeds of *moriche* (*Mauritia flexuosa*), *açai* (*Euterpe precatoria*), *seje* (*Oenocarpus bataua*), *milpesitos* (*Oeonocarpus bacaba*), *chambira* (*Astrocaryum chambira*), *palma real* (*Attalea maripa*), *puy* (*Lepidocaryum tenue*) and species of the *Bactris* genus were identified. Phytoliths from manioc, maize and *Cucurbita* squash, as well as a diversity of tree fruits, including *Annona* sp., along with herbs and *Licania* sp. – the raw material for *cariapé* temper – have also been documented.

The upper, more recent levels of these sites are associated with a distinct version of the Amazonian Polychrome Tradition (APT) pertaining to the Nofurei phase (Figure 7.5) (Arroyo-Kalin et al., 2019). As elsewhere in the Amazon, early eyewitness accounts and scientific explorers (Martius, 1867) before the rubber exploitation process (late-nineteenth century) describe the Caquetá River as a densely inhabited region. By the beginning of the twentieth century, the few available reports depict relatively small and dispersed communities heavily impacted by the arrival of Europeans.

Figure 7.4 Araracuara Canyon, middle Caquetá River. Courtesy Fernando Urbina.

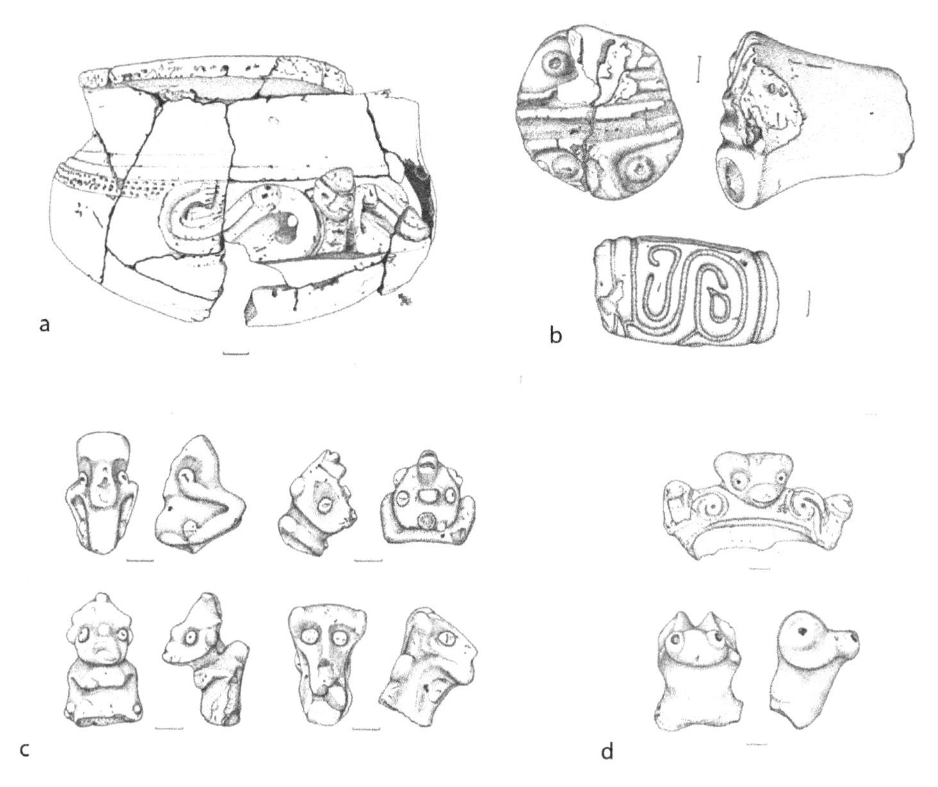

Figure 7.5 Ceramics from the Nofurei phase, Curure site, La Pedrera, middle Caquetá River. *a.* Ceramic vessel from Cut 3d. *b.* Stamp, Cut 2. *c* and *d.* Zoomorphic and anthropomorphic appendages. Courtesy Gaspar Morcote Ríos.

Amazonian Regions II: SW Amazonia and the southern rim of the Amazon

The 'Geoglyphs': Ceremonial landscapes of Acre

No other region in Amazonia evokes such a sense of awe and mystery as the vast, geometrically-patterned ditched enclosures discovered in the upland forest state of Acre, Brazil (Figure 7.6). Known as 'geoglyphs', these structures have inspired archaeologists and captured the public imagination over the past two decades (Mann, 2005: 63) This is the region where Chico Mendes, the rubber tapper and land rights leader, pioneered the world's first tropical forest conservation initiative advanced by forest peoples, leading to the creation of Extractive Reserves (RESEXs), which include protected areas that are inhabited and managed by local people (Fearnside, 1989). Before the onset of large-scale deforestation to create pasture for cattle in the 1980s, Acre state was completely blanketed by *terra firme* rainforest. This forest was assumed by most tropical ecologists to be pristine, but deforestation has revealed a massive ceremonial landscape of more than 500 geoglyphs, which combine square, circular and hexagonal earthworks enclosing 1–3 hectares (approximately one to four football fields).

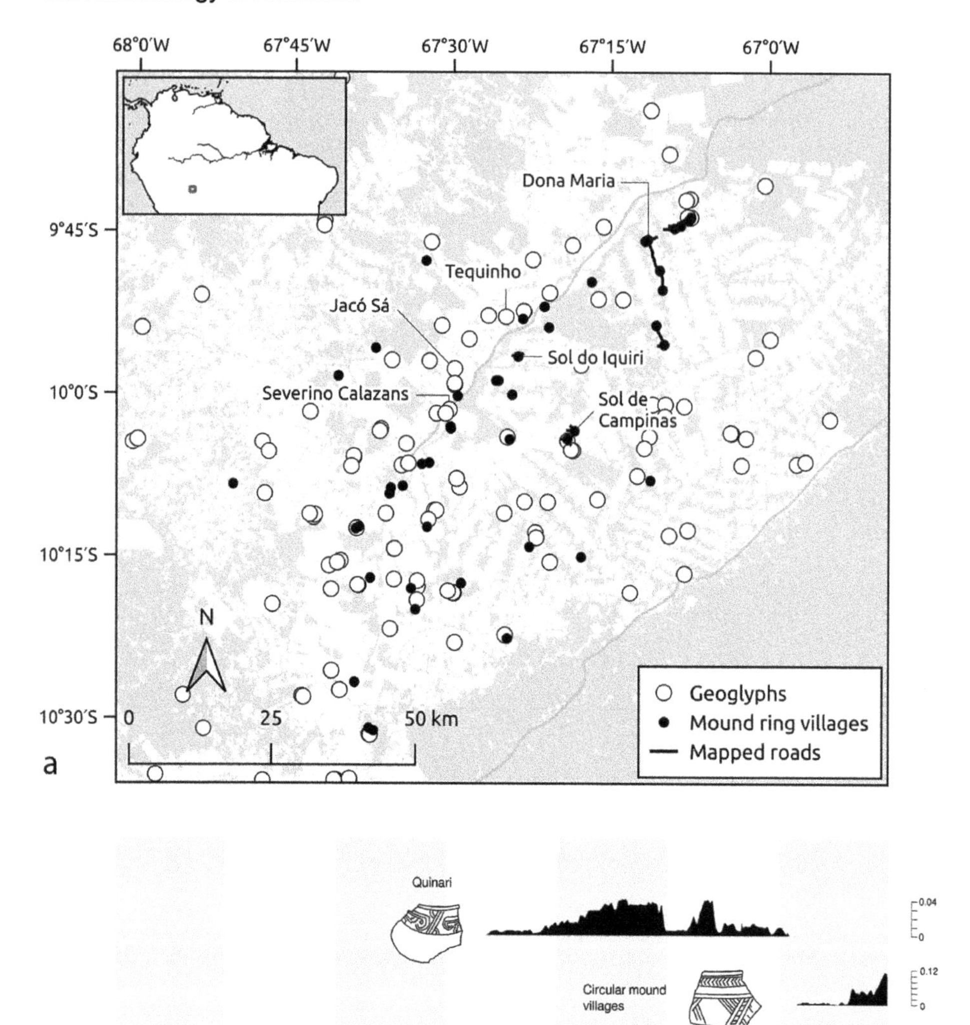

Figure 7.6 The geoglyph region of south-eastern Acre state, Brazil. *a*. Site distribution map of geoglyphs and circular mound villages in south-eastern Acre. *b*. SPDs of radiocarbon dates along with major ceramic phases for the region.

Geoglyphs were first identified and excavated in the mid-1960s by Ondemar Dias (1988). But it was not until the 1980s, when palaeontologist Alceu Ranzi was surprised by some intriguing geometric marks in the earth while flying over the area, that the true nature and spatial extent of these earthworks began to be revealed. For the first time, the magnitude of the achievement of these ancient Acreans was acknowledged. In early 2002, Ranzi teamed up with Denise Schaan and Martti Pärssinen to start the first systematic long-term archaeological project in the region, which entailed the training of the first professional archaeologists from Acre (see Schaan, 2012b; and Ranzi and Pärssinen 2021 for a detailed account of the history of the archaeology of the region). Relatively rapid advances in archaeological work since that time have begun to document a diversity of earthen architecture that is coming into focus as work progresses (e.g., Parssinen, 2021; Pärssinen et al., 2009; Ranzi and Pärssinen, 2021; Ranzi, 2011; Riris, 2020; Saunaluoma, 2010; Saunaluoma and Schaan, 2012; Schaan et al., 2007; Schaan et al., 2012).

The 'Geoglyph' or Aquiry tradition (Ranzi and Pärssinen 2021) appeared around 1 CE and lasted until about 1,000 CE, when it was superseded by the circular mound villages (next section). Aquiry possibly derives from the word for caiman '(k)aikyry' from the Apurinã (Arawakan), Rivers of the Caimans, which today is known as Acre River. Current work shows that these geometrically patterned ditch enclosures are restricted to the south-eastern sector of Acre state, Brazil, along the upper Purus River, where because of deforestation, most can be identified with satellite images. South-eastern Acre is one of the driest sectors of Amazonia (Chapter 2). Most of the state of Acre is covered by forms of open forest that allow greater light penetration to the understorey and the growth of bamboo, palms and understorey herbs (Silveira et al., 2008). The forests of Acre are unique in Amazonia, being dominated by bamboo and palms, and with a preponderance of Brazil nut trees. Seen from above, the terrain resembles an eroded washboard, with gently undulating, closely and regularly spaced hills, which only become steeper upstream from the major rivers. They are located in the easternmost expression of the Fitzcarrald arch (see Chapter 2). The southeastern sector of Acre state, where the majority of geometric ditched enclosures and mound villages have been documented, exhibits extensive plateaus compared to other portions of Acre state, such as the Cazumba-Iracema Extractive Reserve, where lidar has revealed a dissected landscape lacking earthen architecture (Iriarte et al., 2020b). Geoglyphs are generally located on the edges of plateaus, 180–230 metres above sea level, with good views of the surroundings, and between 1.5–8 kilometres away from navigable river courses.

The geoglyphs are geometrically perfect and symmetrical ditched enclosures, delimited by contiguous ditches and banks. In shape, they are either square or circular, but also include other forms, such as hexagons and octagons (Figure 7.7). The ditches are on average 11 metres wide and up to 4 metres deep, with external embankments up to 2 metres high. The enclosures generally surround an area of 1–3 hectares, although larger sites exist. The banks are built on the outer side of the enclosure, suggesting that these were not defensive structures (Figure 7.8). If you want to create a defensible site with a ditch, you will pile up the back dirt of the ditch excavation on the interior of the structure, so you can build a palisade on top of it, which in turn would create a very steep wall if a potential attacker were to climb from the bottom of the ditch. It appears, therefore, that geoglyphs were built not as defensive features but to demarcate the space so that certain people were included or excluded. If movement was constrained, it was likely by custom and convention, not by a physical barrier.

Noted for their symmetry, the architecture of geoglyph sites can be complex, juxtaposing square and circular ditches, walled enclosures, mounds and causeways, which likely reflects a long history of construction and remodelling. The uniform and consistent standard of earthwork engineering speaks to strong material and symbolic interaction within the region of south-eastern Acre. Circular and rectangular forms predominate. Circular enclosures

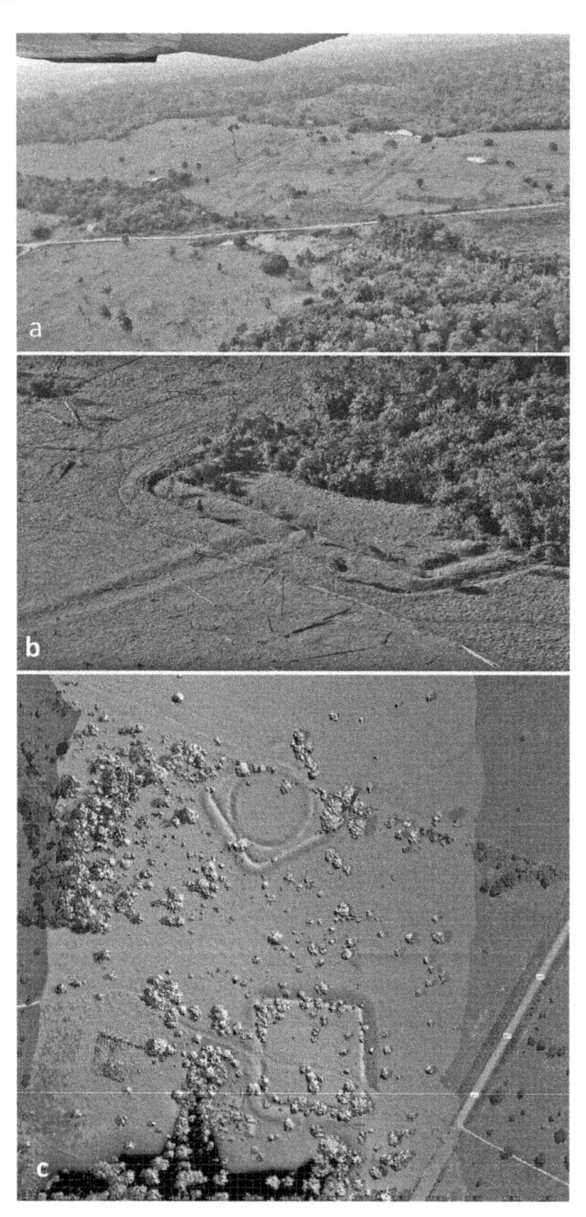

Figure 7.7 The geometric ditch enclosures, which were part of a larger sacred landscape consisting of avenues, annex enclosures and walls, showcase the impressive complexity of these earthworks. *a.* The complexity of the geometric enclosures is revealed in this aerial view of Tequinho showing concentric square-shaped ditches, linear wall enclosures, the main entry avenue with raised curbs (1.5 kilometres long, 40 metres wide) and other tree linear roads point in the cardinal directions among other features. *b.* Aerial view of JK site partially covered by vegetation showing a double-ditch enclosure and a huge, banked avenue entering the site from the north. *c.* Combining geometric forms is not unusual for these geometric enclosures. This lidar map of Jaco Sá shows a rectangular enclosure along with a circular enclosure surrounded by a quadrangle. *b.* Projeto Geoglifos CNPq courtesy of Antonia Damasceno.

Figure 7.8 Quadrangular ditched enclosure with circle inside of the Jaco Sá site. Notice that the higher bank (dashed white line) is on the outer side of the enclosure indicating that these sites serve no defensive function.

dominate in the southern part, while quadrangular forms are more common in the north. Complex forms are common in the central sector of the geoglyph region. Avenues, delineated by low banks, frequently connect the separate enclosures and link them to a network of streams carved in the upland soils. The earthwork systems also include low-relief rectangular enclosures, called annexes, attached to the geoglyphs. Lidar imaging has shown that these are more common than previously thought. Excavation of these annex enclosures is needed before we can begin to understand their function at these sites.

Despite their potential for accommodating a vast number of people, it appears that the enclosures were not home to large resident populations. This is evidenced by a lack of artefacts in the centre of the enclosures, suggesting they were used as public areas for gatherings and festivities, as is customary among modern indigenous communities in Amazonia. The location of settlement sites related to the geoglyphs remains a mystery. This could be because of a lack of regional systematic survey, or the fact that the habitation sites are difficult to identify because they are not associated with easily visible ADEs, or because the geoglyph builders may have lived in dispersed hamlets across the landscape, which are harder to spot.

Geoglyph excavations have often revealed ceramic deposits in those parts of the ditch closest to the enclosure's entrance, and in special features, such as the small artificial mound inside the enclosure. The low density of ceramics and the lack of ADE soils associated with the enclosures, along with the presence of these alleged votive deposits inside the ditches, supports the interpretation that geoglyphs were public spaces for gatherings, rather than sites of permanent habitation.

The ceramics associated with the period of geoglyph construction have been classified in the Quinari Tradition (Figure 7.1). Quinari ceramics are tempered with *caraipé* and charcoal. Most of the potsherds recovered from excavations are fragmented, plain and eroded, with white and red slips. Vessels are cylindrical or globular, and may display angular shoulders. The most distinctive type of Quinari ceramics is anthropomorphic jars representing human faces. However, their direct association with the geoglyphs is uncertain, since these distinctive ceramics do not come from excavations. Other decorated vessels are incised with angular, parallel, curved and spiral lines, forming concentric and interlocked designs (Saunaluoma, 2016). Recently, 38,000 ceramic sherds, mostly consisting of high-quality drinking and serving vessels, have been recovered from the excavation of a mound situated in the northern entrance of the Tequinho site. Pärssinnen (2021), the excavator, has interpreted this sector of the site as some kind of redistribution point where food and beverages were deposited and served during different ceremonies. According to Pärssinnen (2021), the fact that Tequinho ceramics show affiliations with different Amazonian ceramic horizons (western Amazonia, Saladoid-Barrancoid Horizon, Tupi-Guarani) indicates that the ditched enclosures were multi-ethnic, bringing together groups from greater Amazonia (Pärssinen, 2021).

Plants recovered at geoglyph sites include maize and squash crops but also include a diversity of tree and palm fruits, including Brazil nuts, *pupunha* (*Bactris gasipaes*), hog plum (*Spondias mombin*) and rubber tree (*Hevea brasiliensis*), suggesting that the geoglyph builders likely practised a form of polyculture agroforestry (Pärssinen et al., 2020; Watling et al., 2015). As of now, no anthrosols have been found in this area.

We also know what the landscape was like during geoglyph construction. Like most of Amazonia, Acre has no lakes that could allow us to reconstruct the environment using lake palaeoecology. Therefore, Jennifer Watling, Frank Mayle and I decided to carry out transects of soil pits across an 8 kilometre transect starting at the centre of the Jaco Sá geoglyph. Our purpose was to study the phytoliths extracted from the soil and use the data to reconstruct the vegetation and fire history of the region. The results indicated that the region was always covered by forests containing bamboo. The work led by Watling and collaborators (2017) showed that geoglyphs were built on bamboo-dominated forests, as had been predicted by comparing the distribution of modern bamboo (*Guadua* sp.) forests with the distribution of archaeological sites in the region (McMichael et al., 2014b). The record clearly picks up a signal showing an increase in fires around 4.0 ka. This was a time when the weather was becoming wetter, which suggests that the increase in fires was human-induced and not caused by a drier climate. These burnings were followed by increased palms associated with geoglyph construction, indicating that this was a forest enriched with palms by people. These records indicate that the region was never an open environment. The phytolith records also show that today's clearance activities are on a much greater scale than pre-Columbian times – fire frequencies are much higher, and the vegetation more open than at any other time in the records. Ironically, a region that was covered by cultural forests of bamboo, palms and Brazil nut trees is now largely covered by 2-metre tall African grasses *(Brachiaria* spp.), which are grazed by Eurasian megafauna, the Nelore cows.

So, what can we say about these fascinating structures? We know that these are well-planned, huge ceremonial sites that likely required an advanced system of social order to plan, build and maintain. Judging from the labour involved in constructing some of the largest geoglyphs, the size of participating communities was likely well beyond the local scale. For example, building a circular enclosure with a diameter of 100 metres, and a ditch 10 metres wide and 3 metres deep, would entail the removal of 3,000 metres^3 of soil. Assuming that a person can remove 1 metre^3 per day using digging sticks and baskets, it would be necessary to have 3,000 persons per day to do the job, or 100 persons working for thirty days. Because workers generally have families, and need food and shelter, a larger population was probably involved in such activities, and for longer periods of time (Schaan, 2012b). Palaeoecology tells us that the region was forested, so to the effort of digging the ditches, we need to add the effort of cutting the forest. However, as described in Chapter 2, the vegetation of this sector of Amazonia is dominated by bamboo stands. Bamboo is easier to cut than trees. Besides, the geoglyph's builders may have taken advantage of the fact that the stands of bamboo reproduce every fifteen years when they have massive die-off events. As a result, large patches of land would have become periodically naturally cleared, providing space to build these monuments.

The perfection of their geometry has fascinated archaeologists and raised questions about how they were built. The circles were probably drawn using a human compass: two people holding either end of a stick, one person remaining still while the other drew a circle around them.

Although current evidence shows that the geoglyphs were likely ceremonial in purpose, it is not known exactly what they represent. What kind of ceremonies could have taken place within? When considering these issues, we should not forget that these are societies without a written language, where myths, traditions and customs are passed down and recreated through rituals in specific ceremonies (see Chapter 2). For these societies, iconography inserted into the landscape is both a form of writing and also emerges as an agent, affecting people through visual and corporal practices. South-east Acre appears to be a prime example of how ancient history and socio-cosmology are deeply 'written' onto the landscape in the form of geometric earthworks carved out of the soil. The uniform and consistent standard of earthwork engineering speaks to us of strong material and symbolic interaction within the region of southeastern Acre. These were likely ceremonial places: liminal, transitional spaces separated from everyday life by the demarcating elements of the ritual architecture. These were places where the society, or a restricted part of it, likely interacted with the world of creation, where mythical stories were told, where initiated shamans possibly took hallucinogenic drugs and dances were performed. As Virtanen and Saunaluoma (2017) remind us, in Amazonian animist ontologies, some animals, plants and natural phenomena have living souls, and consequently, they possess characteristics of humans. Geometric designs may be a way of manifesting the physical forms of these non-human beings. Therefore, geometric images bring nonhuman beings into existence and make them visible. For example, for many Amazonian indigenous peoples, the circle is often associated with the design on a jaguar's pelt, or the eyes of certain birds, such as the harpy eagle. It has thus come to symbolize various qualities: the physical strength of the top predator, for example, or the ability to see far and wide. The circle is also linked to fertility and life, for example to seeds, as well as to the sun, moon and sky. For societies that live by a cyclical rhythm, with day followed by night, followed by day, it also represents the continuous circle of time. The four cardinal points represent the forces that maintain and reproduce life and the openness in all directions.

Most of the geoglyphs are away from the main rivers. They contain ancient roads delineated by low earthen banks that traverse the landscape, connect geoglyphs, lead to streams or end up in the landscape without getting to any standing architecture or visible landscape feature. These suggest that movement was constrained and processions of people likely took place on them. Intriguingly, at some sites ceramics were only found accumulated in sectors of the ditches closest to the entrance of the enclosure. It is not difficult to imagine people entering the structure in a ritual procession following the ancient roads coming from the east, the rising sun, and depositing carefully made ceramics as offerings to deities. The avenues suggest that movement was constrained. The potential scale of the meetings could have been huge, based on the size of the enclosures. Thousands of people may theoretically have gathered inside the largest enclosures and as Pärssinen (2021) proposes, the ditched enclosures may well represent, at some point, spaces of multi-ethnic gatherings. In summary, the spaces enclosed by the geoglyph earthworks seem to have been spaces for prescribed behaviour, where possibly people adhered to a precise protocol and consented to expected conduct. Leading avenues were processional ways, and the entryways were portals that delimited changes in space and behaviour. Future work in the region will certainly reveal more fascinating facts about this unique culture.

Interconnected 'suns': The Circular Mound Villages of Acre

The recently discovered mound villages showcase the early stage of archaeological research in the vast region of SW Amazonia. Based on the legacy of the geoglyphs, the circular mound villages emerged as a distinct archaeological tradition around 1000 CE. Over the following centuries, until around 1700 CE, they became one of the most widespread traditions along the southern rim of the Amazon basin.

Mound circular villages consist of circular, rectangular or elliptical arrangements of mounds surrounding a central plaza, from which roads radiate out in a pattern. The tradition spread from the Tapajós headwaters to the eastern and southern sectors of the Acre state, spanning more than 1,000 kilometres (de Souza et al., 2018; Iriarte et al., 2020b; Saunaluoma et al., 2019). Mound villages are generally located on the top of small, flat plateaus overlooking a stream to which they are typically connected by a road. In southeastern Acre state, mound villages emerged as geoglyphs declined. The modelling of the available radiocarbon dates from nine mound villages sites in south-eastern Acre state, Brazil, establishes the beginning of this archaeological tradition in this region of south-western Amazonia to be around 952–1216 CE and its demise about 1650 CE (Iriarte et al., 2021).

Currently, fifty-one mound villages have been documented using lidar and satellite remote sensing in Acre alone. Circular/elliptical ones are locally called Sóis (suns) (e.g. Sol de Iquiri, Sol de Campinas) because, when seen from the sky, the elongated mounds arranged around a circle look like the marks of a clock and the sunken roads that depart from the circle of mounds resemble the rays of the sun. Circular mound villages are comparable to other circular villages across lowland South America (Heckenberger et al., 2008; Iriarte et al., 2004; Neves, 2022; Wüst and Barreto, 1999), but they exhibit several idiosyncratic features that set them apart from other known circular village traditions. Their singular features include ranked, paired, cardinally-oriented radial sunken roads, exhibiting high embankments and elongated mounds (among other mound shapes), positioned around the circle like the marks of a clock. Within a certain variability, they exhibit a strikingly uniform and consistent construction (Figure 7.9). The arrangements, shapes and sizes of the mounds in conjunction with radial road structures are repetitive and remarkably similar. The diameter of circular mound villages ranges from 40–153 metres (average of 86 metres; n=23), with the area enclosed by the central plaza ranging from ~0.12–1.8 hectares. Site size variation shows no trend toward a bimodal distribution, which could indicate a hierarchical settlement pattern. The number of mounds ranges from 3–32 – with lower numbers most likely corresponding to sites that have been partly destroyed. A diversity of mound shapes exists in the villages. Elongated, dome-shaped mounds are 20–25 metres long and 1.5–3 metres high, with their major axis radiating outwards from the centre of the circle of mounds. The mound slopes are steeper towards the village plaza and gradually fade away from the circle, forming what appear to be access ramps to the top of the mounds. Along with the elongated mounds, these sites exhibit larger platform and conical mounds, whose construction history and uses need further investigation (Iriarte et al., 2020b). Paired circular mound villages connected to each other by a road, such as the Donha Maria site (Figure 7.9), are emerging as a common occurrence in the region (e.g., Sol de Campinas and Fonte Boa, Nakahara 230 I and II, Sol de Nakahara and Nakahara 228). These are reminiscent of the dual patterns of architecture seen in other regions of lowland South America (Iriarte et al., 2013) and the Andes (e.g., Moore, 1995; Netherly and Dillehay, 1986).

The distinct architectural layout of rectangular mound villages clearly places them into a category of their own. Called 'villages' for the present, future archaeological excavations will provide further detail about their function. Besides the villages' rectangular shape, their diagnostic features include elongated, rectilinear mounds. These mounds define the perimeter of the structure, forming a rectangular enclosure with openings, some of which connect to roads. The diameter of rectangular mound villages ranges from 22–77 metres (average of 26 metres). The number of mounds ranges from 5–16 mounds, with lower numbers most likely corresponding to sites that have been partly destroyed.

Excavations of the mounds have revealed discrete layers, interpreted as alternating episodes of construction and occupation (clear occupation strata with domestic features). This evidence and the presence of adjacent middens confirms the nature of these sites as settlements (Iriarte et al., 2021; Saunaluoma et al., 2018). Construction layers are

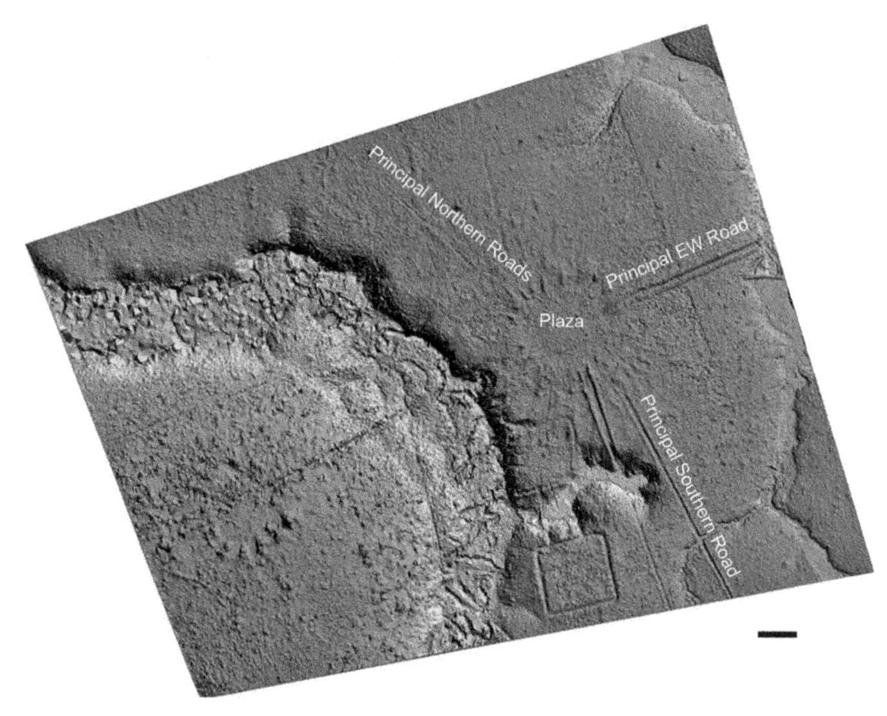

Figure 7.9 Following the ceasement of Aquiry geometric enclosures construction, the circular mound villages ('Suns') emerged in south-eastern Acre state, Brazil. Lidar map of the Donha Maria site (scale = 100 metres).

generally thicker and consist of laterite, the typical topsoil of tropical regions, which is clayey, reddish, and rich in Fe and Al. They lack charcoal, ceramics and macrobotanical remains, and are less compacted than occupation layers, which are thinner, darker and contain larger quantities of artefacts and ecofacts. Mounds may contain more than ten occupation layers intercalated with construction events, with a 250-year temporal span (Figure 7.10) (Iriarte et al., 2021).

Since research in mound villages is still in its beginnings, little is known about their material culture. But, preliminary data show differences relative to the ceramics of the geoglyphs and other ring-ditch traditions. For example, in neighbouring Riberalta, Bolivia, to the south of Acre, ceramics from a diversity of ring ditch sites are distinguished by red-painted geometric designs on a white-slipped surface (Saunaluoma 2010).

Subsistence plant remains include maize (*Zea mays*), Brazil nuts (*Bertholletia excelsa*), passion fruit (*Passiflora edulis*), *muruci* (*Byrsonima crassifolia*), *tucumã* or *murumuru* palms (*Astrocaryum* sp.) and Chenopodioideae seeds (Saunaluoma et al., 2021). An increase in maize fragment frequency is associated with an increase in charcoal macro remains on occupation surfaces, while both maize and charcoal decrease in construction layers.

Kistler et al. (2018) have proposed that mound villages could also be related to the second major west-to-east cultural expansion of maize traditions that appear to have taken place ~800–1000 CE. The authors suggest that during this time, mound villages

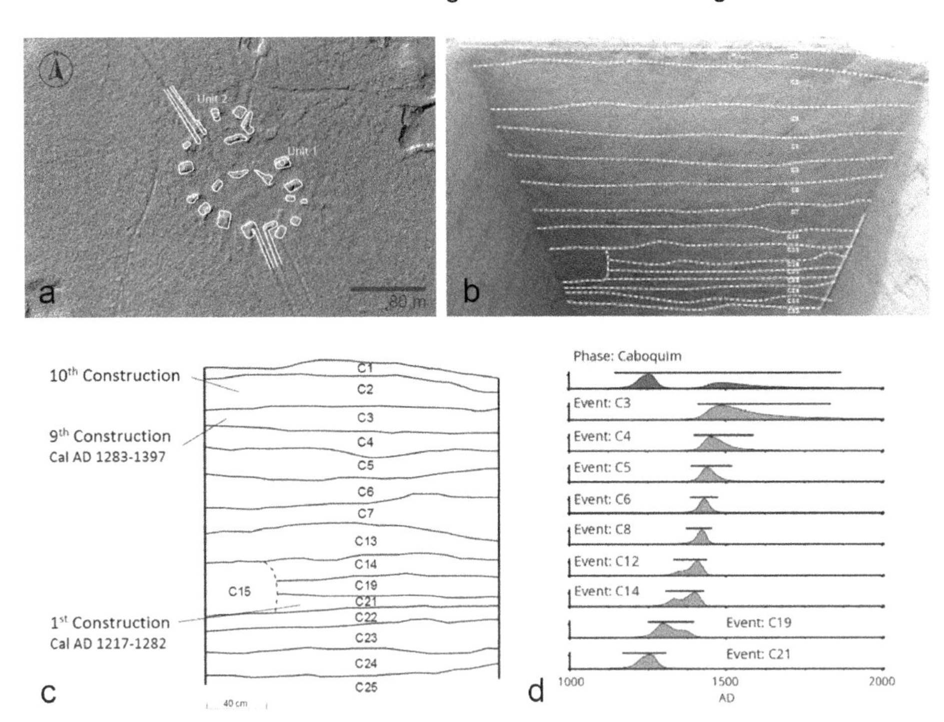

Figure 7.10 Stratigraphy of mounds showing intercalation of occupation and construction layers. *a*. Lidar map of Caboquinho site showing mounded architecture and location of excavated test units. *b* and *c*. Picture and drawing of sketched stratigraphic diagram of Unit 1. *d*. Graph of calibrated radiocarbon dates displaying more than ten occupation layers intercalated with construction events, indicating that the site was used over a 250-year temporal span.

and fortified villages spread throughout southern Amazonia, while ring villages spread through the central Brazilian savannahs and along the Atlantic coast. They also propose that Arawak speakers likely brought non-local Andean/Pacific maize lineages into a landscape where maize was an established component of long-term land management and food production strategies.

Mound villages are interconnected by roads that show a hierarchy and can be divided into principal and minor roads. Principal roads are deeper, wider (3–6 metres) and exhibit higher banks. Most mound villages exhibit two principal roads leaving northward (principal northern roads) and two principal roads leaving southward (principal southern roads). The roads generally run between 310–320 and 30–40 degrees range, coming closer to each other as they approach the village, but without joining. Generally, when the roads make contact with the village, their banks become higher and wider. They cut through the mounds producing a rather straight mound profile and/or creating a double-L-shaped feature as a prolongation of the banks. These mounded features are generally taller than the banks. Circular mound villages are also often cut by an east-west road. Principal roads become narrower as they move away from the site. Although they run separately close to the village, away from the village they can reconnect, forming a single trail. Minor roads are shorter. In the Dona Maria transect, lidar data have also allowed us to document roads that link Dona Maria to Boa Esperança (see Figure 7.7). The road passes through Caboquinho and extends over a distance of more than 5 kilometres, clearly showing that these villages were interconnected by roads. Dated structures from Caboquinho and Boa Esperança show that these settlements were broadly contemporaneous.

These networks of roads are hardly a surprise for Amazonian archaeologists. Historical accounts attest to the ubiquity of road networks across the Amazon, the earliest being the sixteenth-century account by Friar Gaspar de Carvajal (1984), who observed wide roads leading from the riverine villages of the Amazon River to the interior. Later, the explorer Antônio Pires de Campos (1862), crossing the headwaters of the Tapajós River in the nineteenth century, described a vast population inhabiting the region, with villages connected by straight, wide roads that were constantly kept clean. Numerous historical accounts in the Llanos de Mojos, Bolivia, describe elevated roads connecting villages and cultivated fields (Eder, [1772] 1985). 'Old Indian roads' were also reported by Nimuendaju in his work in the Santarém area in 1925 (Nimuendajú, 2004). Closer to our study area, the account of Colonial Antonio Labre (1889: 496–502), who travelled from the Madre de Dios River to Acre in the nineteenth century, is revealing. He mentions '[...] many very old abandoned villages, roads crossing each other in all directions, and small cultivated fields [...] a small temple with a clean courtyard in a circular form [...]'. The patterns described above comprising northern, southern and east-west principal roads appear to be unique to this sector of Amazonia.

Regarding settlement patterns, an examination of site size distribution, elaboration and standardization of their mounded architecture point to a lack of clear differences between sites, with no apparent signs of centralization or hierarchical settlement patterns. Taking the study region as a whole, mound villages do not show a regular spatial distribution. Some small groups of villages positioned along streams, however, do appear to be regularly spaced, with distances of 2.5–3 kilometres and 5–6 kilometres between sites. Where lidar data are available on sectors of the landscape that have not been modified by modern settlement and agriculture, villages are shown to be interconnected by roads with low banks that extend up to 5 kilometres long (Iriarte et al., 2020b).

Mound villages exhibit distinctive and rather consistent arrangements, suggesting that ancient Acreans had a very particular mental model for how they viewed community layout and village organization. The uniform spatial layout of the mound villages, like many contemporaneous ring villages of the Neotropics, is likely to represent physical representations of the Native American cosmos (e.g., Heckenberger, 2005; Siegel, 1999). The villages' sun-like appearance from above is intriguing given the sun's significance in Amazonian myths and cosmologies (e.g., Santos-Granero, 1988; Liebenberg, 2017).

Some dynamics relating to village movement may be reflected in the archaeological record exposed by lidar. This may especially be the case with 'twin' or superimposed mound villages. Many Amazonian forest farmers relocate their settlements 500–1,000 metres every couple of years in order to be closer to newly opened gardens, or because of rotting houses, frequent deaths, internal disputes, warfare or sanitary conditions (e.g., Craig and Chagnon, 2006; Gross, 1983; Hames, 1983). Longer movements happen every ten years to one generation, often relocating to previously occupied spots. Both 'micro' moves and returns to former territories may potentially account for the archaeological superimposition of mound villages and/or settlements that are located in close proximity ('twin' villages). More work is needed to clarify these patterns.

The overall settlement patterns observed in these nucleated circular mound villages of Acre have parallels in the archaeology of other parts of the southern rim of the Amazon and clearly correlate with ethnographic and archaeological circular villages. In lowland South America, circular villages began during the middle Holocene in disparate regions as far apart as Ecuador (Lathrap et al., 1977) and Uruguay (Iriarte et al., 2004). Ring villages along the southern rim of the Amazon during the late Holocene, mostly built by Arawak speakers, but also by other populations influenced by them, are relatively permanent settlements (Heckenberger, 2005; Hornborg et al., 2005; Wüst and Barreto, 1999). In the Upper Xingu, villages rarely move, except when dividing – in which case, they tend to remain within the catchment of the mother village (Heckenberger, 2005). Archaeological settlements and ethnographic villages in the Upper Xingu are usually separated by distances of 5–10 kilometres following rivers (Heckenberger, 2005), matching the pattern found among mound villages of Acre and reinforcing the hypothesis of their contemporary occupation. Similarly, the road network found in the archaeology and ethnography of the Upper Xingu is replicated in Acre. Contemporary village organizations can shed light on some of the patterns found in the archaeological settlement layouts. Xinguano villages, for example, are reported to have their main entrances aligned with the cardinal directions, with chiefs' houses built next to the northern and southern roads (Heckenberger, 2005). Although the circular mound villages of Acre share many commonalities with the Upper Xingu and the basic circular village template (circle of domestic units around a clean plaza-like interior), they possess distinctive characteristics that set them apart from all other archaeological traditions. For example, although they are reminiscent of the Upper Xingu settlements in terms of their standardized layout and formal road architecture connecting villages (Heckenberger et al., 2008), they are distinguished by their smaller size, idiosyncratic mounded architecture and patterned system of roads. More work along the southern rim of the Amazon will bring further clarification to these emerging patterns.

Southern rim of the Amazon

Over the past two decades, significant archaeological research along the southern rim of the Amazon has begun to document a diversity of pre-Columbian earth-building traditions between the Upper Xingu and the Upper Purus rivers. It is now apparent that this region of Amazonia was inhabited by earth-building societies involved in landscape engineering, landscape domestication and probable low-density urbanism, as will be described in the next chapter (Blatrix et al., 2018; de Souza et al., 2018; Heckenberger et al., 2008; Iriarte et al., 2020b; Levis et al., 2017; Pärssinen et al., 2009; Prümers et al., 2022; Schaan, 2012b). The southern rim of Amazonia is the location of some of the most important discoveries currently taking place in Amazonian archaeology. However, this is unfortunately happening because of deforestation. The red dots representing deforestation and the black circles representing archaeological sites in Figure 10.2 show how the majority of the sites have been discovered as a result of recent deforestation.

The Ring ditches: Conflict at the turn of the second millennium CE

In this section, I describe one type of earthwork found along the southern rim of the Amazon: the ring ditches. Ring ditches are circular to irregularly shaped ditched enclosures that date between 1250–1550 AD. Recent remote sensing, survey and compilation of current data by Souza et al. (2018) show that these enclosures spread over an 1,800 kilometres stretch of southern Amazonia. Unlike the 'geoglyphs' of Acre, it appears that encircling an area with a ditch was more important than achieving geometrical perfection. The enclosures can be elliptical, circular, D-shaped or completely irregular. The ditches can have different depths and extensions. Usually, the enclosures surround a village or habitation area, and were presumably built as a fortification. Ditches can be up to 10 metres wide and 4 metres deep, and the enclosed areas covers 1–5 hectares on average, with some larger sites covering 10–12 hectares. They were most likely built by people from various cultures. Below I present two regions where work on ring ditches has been conducted more intensively.

Bolivian Zanjas

One region where work on this type of site has been carried out is NE Bolivia (Figure 7.11). Here, ring ditches, which are locally known as 'Zanjas', are found on scattered, naturally elevated forest islands. These islands, from several hectares to many square kilometres in area, are natural formations produced by the upwelling of the Brazilian Shield. They are surrounded by seasonally flooded savannahs covering a region of at least 2,500 kilometres^2. Ring ditched archaeological sites occur in all forest islands larger than 1 kilometres^2. The sites are of diverse sizes and shapes: octagons, hexagons, squares, rectangles, 'D' shapes, circles, ovals and irregular shapes (Erickson et al., 2008). The ditches are often several metres deep and steep sided, with some extending for 1–2 kilometres. Some ditches are double, while some sites have concentric rings of ditches.

When Jesuits arrived in the region, they were impressed by the Baure people living in this region, who they linked with ornate clothing, huge towns, political structure, intense agriculture and massive earthworks, which the Jesuits acknowledged as a remarkable civilization (Eder, [1772] 1985; Métraux, 1942).

One of the best excavated sites in this region, known as 'Granja del Padre', site BV-2, is located to the north of Bella Vista town. Open area excavations covering 600 metres^2 revealed a single occupation layer, greyish-brown in colour with a thickness of approximately 0.2–0.4 metres, dating between ~1300–1500 CE. No post holes or hearths were found. All the pits corresponded to rubbish pits and urn burial pits. The sixteen burials unearthed were the most noticeable features of the site. Most of the urn burials were of children. In most cases, the deceased's body was laid in a large globular vessel placed upside down in a pit. In order to lay the body in the globular vessel, its base was

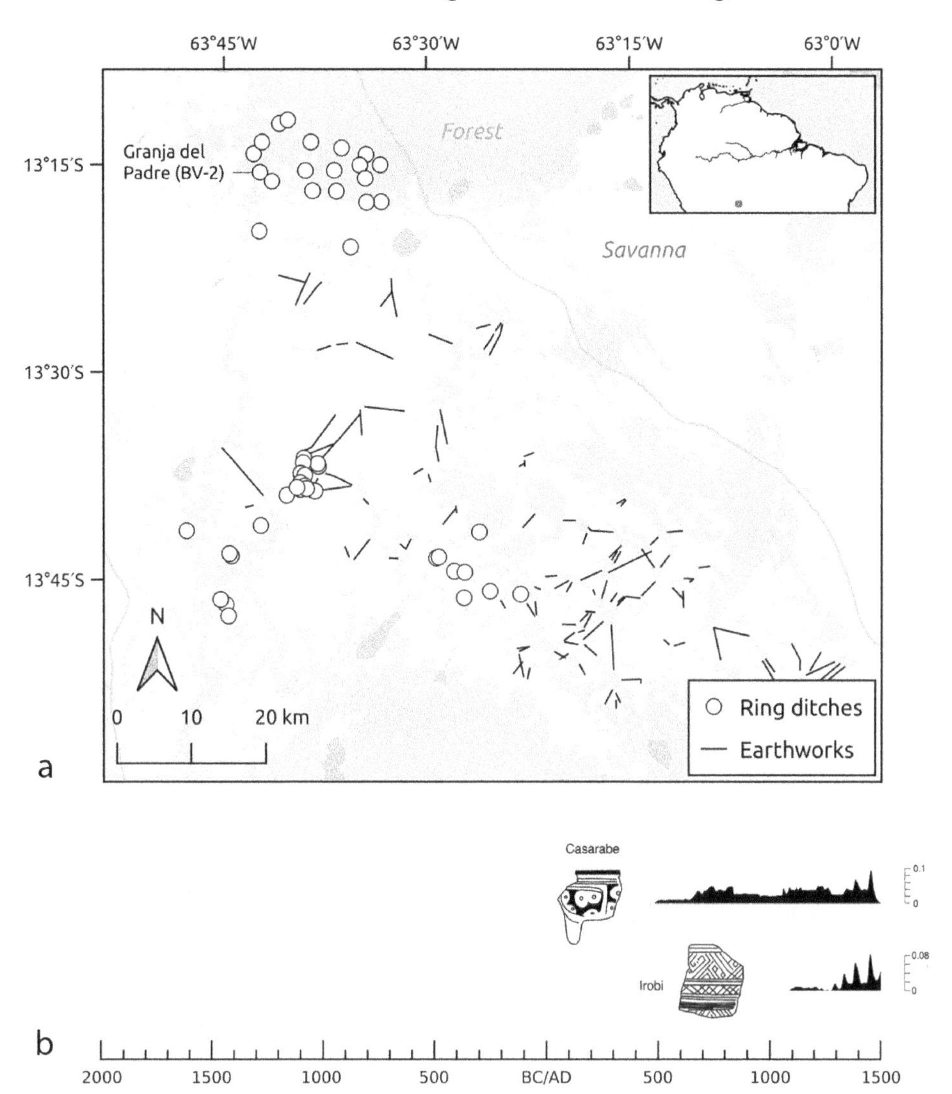

Figure 7.11 The ring ditch region of NE Llanos de Mojos, Bolivia. *a.* Site distribution map showing earthworks. *b.* SPDs of radiocarbon dates along with major ceramic phases for this region and the Casarabe culture (see more detailed map in Chapter 8).

removed by breaking it along a groove milled into the circumference of the bottom of the vessel. The base taken from the large globular vessel and large fragments of other vessels were used to cover the burial. Most of the burial goods are polished stone pendants. BV-2 is part of a larger system of ditches. Lidar data have revealed a system of ditches in an approximate 200 kilometres^2 area (Prümers and Jaimes Betancourt, 2014) showing that these ditched systems are located at moderate elevations in intermittent streams. Seven of the twenty systems of ditches detected contain areas greater than 200 hectares, which are located near the high banks of the San Simon and Baures rivers (Figure 7.12).

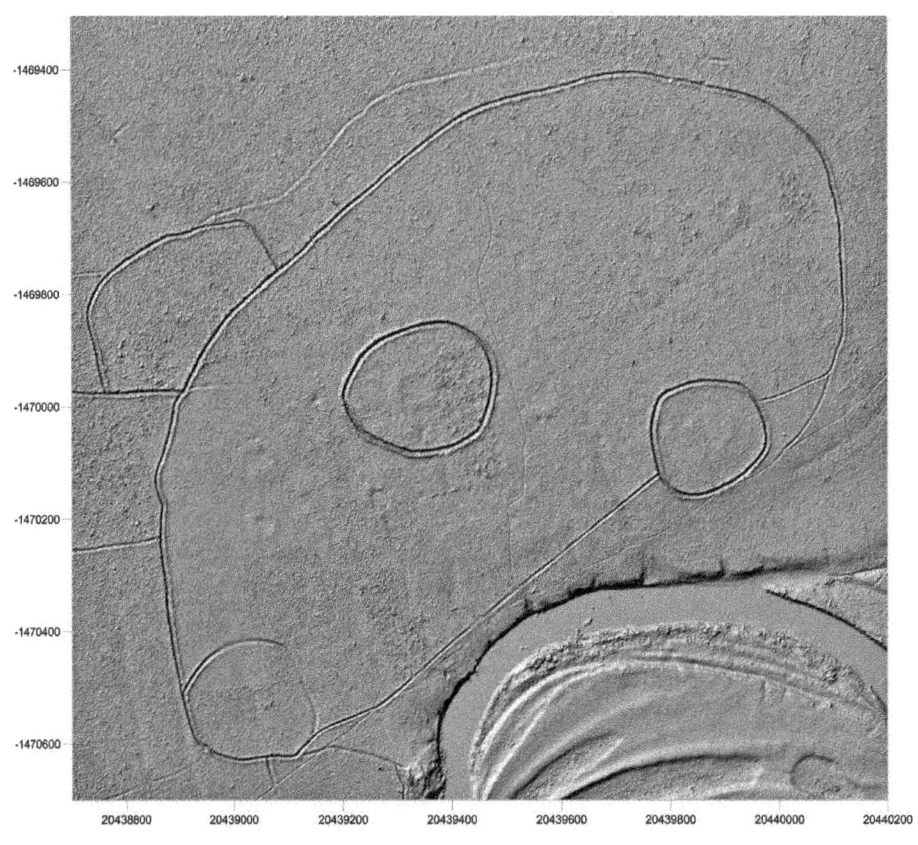

Figure 7.12 Lidar map of the surroundings of interconnected circular ditches along the San Simón River in the vicinity of Bella Vista town, Itenéz Province, Bolivia. Courtesy Heiko Prümers.

Ceramics from BV-2 present similarities to the contemporaneous Irobi Phase (1200–1500 AD) from the Jasiaquiri ring ditch a few kilometres south of Bella Vista. This ceramic is distinguished mainly by its fine incised decoration, with spirals, fretwork, concentric lozenges, concentric diamonds and reticulated triangles (Jaimes Betancourt, 2016). Vessel shapes exhibit straight walls, thickened and everted rims, and basketry imprints on the outer surface of the base. There are a wide range of necked vessels, most of them with straight rims and thinned lips, and with a slight curvature in the central part of the neck. These vessels are also decorated with fine incised lines of triangles with contrasting fretwork, along with spirals and triangles with hatching.

To the north, in the vicinity of Versalles village, contemporaneous ring ditches are associated with the Late Versalles phase (1200–1700 CE), showing very different ceramic styles, pointing to regional variability. The most common shapes in the Late Versalles phase are open vessels with straight walls and thickened or coiled rims. The primary decorative characteristic is two lines of dots on the lip or around the rim of the vessel. This decoration is also present on the rim of globular pots with open necks. The fairing bowls have a band applied with elongated dots on the apex of the vessel or on the fairing (Maezumi et al., 2022).

Ring ditches have been commonly interpreted as fortified settlements. Historical accounts of fortified villages across Amazonia are commonplace. For example, along the Negro River, the transcription of Medina, in Carvajal's account, describes the existence of very large settlements, and one of them is fortified with a wall of very thick wood (Carvajal, 1984: 39). Betendorf (cited in Nimuendajú, 2004) indicates the existence of walled towns among the Arawak Indians of the Urubu River in the lower Amazon towards the end of the seventeenth century. Alfred Métraux (1942: 63) cites comparable constructions for the Baure people in this study region: 'The Baure villages were surrounded by palisades with archer holes, and a ditch; for greater protection traps were hidden in the paths.'

Some researchers believe that fortified villages corresponding to the final phase of the pre-Columbian period could be the product of the continuous waves of migrations and ethnic expansions by Tupi-Guarani groups (de Paula Moraes and Neves, 2012; Lathrap, 1970; Wüst and Barreto, 1999). This hypothesis is supported by the descriptions written by the Jesuit priest Francisco Javier Eder ([1772] 1985: 106) at the beginning of the eighteenth century: 'The Guarayo (Tupi) having terrorized the whole region, they got the Baures to provide them annually a certain number of boys and girls: but even then they were not safe from their frequent and unexpected assaults. So, in order to solve their problems in another way, they decided to surround their islands with moats (which survive to this day and show how large the population must have been at that time). I have known islands whose circumference reached up to 5 kilometres and which were surrounded by two or three moats. These are so wide and deep, that they can be compared with those of Europe. They were piling up the earth by digging in the backs of the moat, forming a wall of very steep slope and difficult for a man to climb. In this way they made their assaults more difficult for the enemy.'

To the south of the above region, ring ditches form part of an impressive, interconnected architectural system that also includes causeways, canals and zigzag earthwork structures associated with ponds in the savannahs. Early work by Erickson (2000) revealed the remarkable scale and integration of this infrastructure in broad domesticated landscapes, including causeways, fish weirs and ponds, and forest islands bearing ring-ditch villages. Erickson et al. (2008), using Google Earth and ground truthing, recorded seventy-nine ditched enclosures in this region. The low-lying savannahs are crisscrossed by linear causeways and canals, usually connecting forest islands in radial patterns. Over a region of about 525 kilometres^2 in this area, Erickson has documented more than 1,000 individual artificial linear features totalling 994 kilometres. These causeways can be many kilometres long and vary in elevation (0.2–2 metres) and width (1–20 metres) (Figure 7.13). They are generally found in seasonally inundated areas of poor drainage but are rarely found in permanent wetlands, deeply flooded zones, or well-drained gallery forests and forest islands. They connect the ring-ditched archaeological settlements, raised fields, resources, rivers, wetlands and other causeways, forming physical networks at local and regional scales. Causeways can be used during both the rainy and dry season. They remain dry during the floods, and during the dry season the water-filled ditches created by the construction of the causeways can be used by canoes, allowing for easy transportation of agricultural produce and other goods. At present, there is only a single date for these causeways from 1490–1630 CE (Erickson, 2000). A similar network of causeways has been documented in the Llanos de Barinas in the Venezuela savannahs (Redmond and Spencer, 2007).

The zigzag earthworks particularly intrigued Erickson, since their changing orientations did not make sense as roads between settlements. Upon closer look during fieldwork, Erickson noted that there were small funnel-like openings where the earthworks changed direction, similar to those described as part of fish weirs in the ethnographic and historical literature on Amazonian peoples. Common in the flooded savannahs of Baures, fish weirs occur as zigzag structures with linear segments of raised earth (up to 5 kilometres long, 1–2 metres wide and 0.2–0.5 metres tall) that typically change direction every 10–30 metres. The linear segments are interrupted by V-shaped structures (1–3 metres tall and 1–2 metres wide): funnel-shaped channels where fish could be trapped, which are associated with small circular ponds (0.5–2 metres deep, 10–30 metres in diameter), where fish could be stored live until needed. These ingenious fish weirs provided a means to manage and harvest the fish that migrated into and spawned in these seasonally inundated savannahs, and that were then trapped during their out-migration in V-shaped structures and ponds as the flood waters receded. Although huge, these zigzag structures are similar to fish weirs built by Amazonians across the basin, where barriers of stones, rock or branches are constructed across shallow bodies of water, with V-shaped openings where fish are trapped in baskets (see for example summary of Noelli 1993 for Tupi groups).

Detailed topographic, remote sensing and ground-truthing by Blatrix et al. (2018) demonstrates that the V-shaped feature (Vs) of weirs points downstream for outflowing water and that ponds are associated with the V-shaped feature. Ponds are predominantly located on the upstream side of the weir, and the V often forms the pond's downstream wall. Because many Vs (244 out of 270 surveyed) surprisingly lack fishways, hydraulics cannot explain how Vs channelled fish into ponds. Berms are absent from the upstream rim of ponds, making it easier for out-migrating fish to swim into them, and berms are highest on the downstream rim of ponds, making it more difficult for these fish to swim out of them. Blatrix et al. (2018) envisioned the system working as follows. Although the water was still high enough to flow over the weir, out-migrating bottom-hugging fish followed the current downstream into Vs where they stayed in deeper, slower-moving water. As the floodwaters receded, the ponds on the upstream side of the weir appear to have served as traps, where fish could be contained and stored predictably. For the ones that have a gap, it is typically too big for a basket or trap to fit in, so the authors reasoned that some of these gaps were used to direct water into a pond, while others may have formed because of erosion of the weir.

What makes these pre-Columbian systems unique is that they appear to have combined weir-fishing and pond-fishing. In the savannahs, fish weirs and ponds are located between domestic sites on forest islands. As a result, in addition to trapping fish in conjunction with weirs, the ponds, as proposed by Erickson (2000), likely functioned

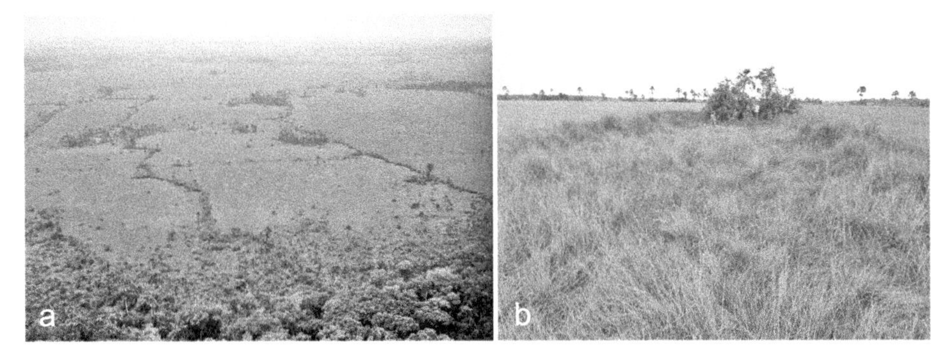

Figure 7.13 *a*. Aerial view of landscape-scale fish weirs in the San Simón region, Baures, Bolivia. *b*. Ground view of V-shaped structure with a pond on the inside at the end of the V. Courtesy Doyle McKey.

to keep the fish alive after they had been captured by the weirs, for some time after the water receded during the dry season.

The weirs must have been valuable property as a permanent food-producing infrastructure. The networks of causeways and canals may have facilitated communication and alliances among the many groups who used the fish weirs. (Erickson and Walker, 2009) Riverine fisheries, rich resources possibly owned and inherited by chiefly lineages, were likely zealously protected and guarded by groups in the Bolivian Amazon.

Ring ditches of the Upper Tapajós

Until recently, the Upper Tapajós basin in the Brazilian state of Mato Grosso was entirely unexplored. Recently, we carried out remote sensing and ground-truthing in a 800-kilometre stretch of this region, recording some new eighty-eight archaeological sites, the majority of which are ring ditches (de Souza et al., 2018). In this region, ditched enclosures of varying diameters (11–363 metres) and layouts, and containing different types and numbers of associated earthworks (such as mounds and avenues), are situated on the tops of small plateaus, overlooking rivers and streams. The layouts of the ditches at these sites are not perfectly circular, but irregular and often wavy, as if built in several independent segments. Ditches vary from 1–3 metres deep with 1 metre high internal and external embankments (Figure 7.14). Similar to other fortified villages in other areas along the southern rim of the Amazon, the majority of them contain superficial ceramics and ADE soils. Test excavations conducted at a single site, Mt-04, with 0.5 metre deep ADE soils in the interior of the structure, provided dates between 1410–1460 CE. Based on these new data, we have been able to model the potential full geographical extent of ditched enclosures in the southern rim of the Amazon, incorporating extant archaeological sites, as well as climate and environmental variables. Results of the modelling predict that ~1,000–1,500 ditched enclosures will be found in a 400,000 kilometres^2 area along the whole southern rim of Amazonia. Using ethnographic data and empirical archaeological data we estimate that the regional populations in this area could have been between 500,000–1 million during late Pre-Columbian times (1250–1500 CE) (de Souza et al., 2018). The fact that the predicted area of earthworks along the

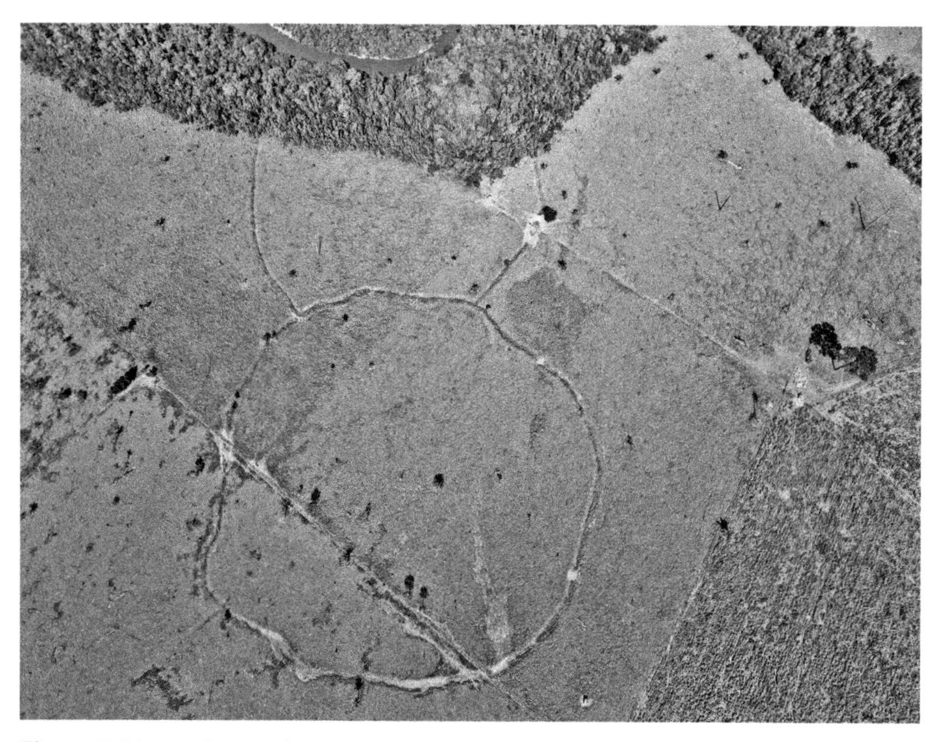

Figure 7.14 Aerial view of a ring ditched village in Mato Grosso state, Brazil. Note how the perimeter of the ditch wiggles, which could be breaks representing multiple screened entrances similar to the ones used for defence by the Guarani village as depicted in engravings during the sixteenth century (Schmidl, 1567).

southern rim of Amazonia, an area comprising merely 7 per cent of the Amazon, could have sustained a population in the hundreds of thousands (even if one accepts the lower threshold of our estimate), definitively discredits early low estimates of 1.5–2 million inhabitants for the whole basin (Meggers, 1996). The study by De Souza et al. (2019) further reinforces the significance of seasonal transitional forests for cultural developments in the Amazon basin (see also Bush et al., 2008).

Much is still to be investigated in this largely uncharted region. However, the ditched enclosure of the Upper Tapajós River adds to the diversity of traditions and socio-political trajectories for the southern rim of Amazonia, along with the 'geoglyphs' of Acre, the 'Garden Cities' of the Upper Xingu and the 'Zanjas' of NE Bolivia, all with their particular earthen architecture, ceramic styles and settlement patterns.

Amazonian Regions II: The Central Amazon

Where the white and black waters collide

The area around the modern city of Manaus in the central Amazon, where the Negro and Amazonas rivers meet, has been one of the poles of development of Amazonian

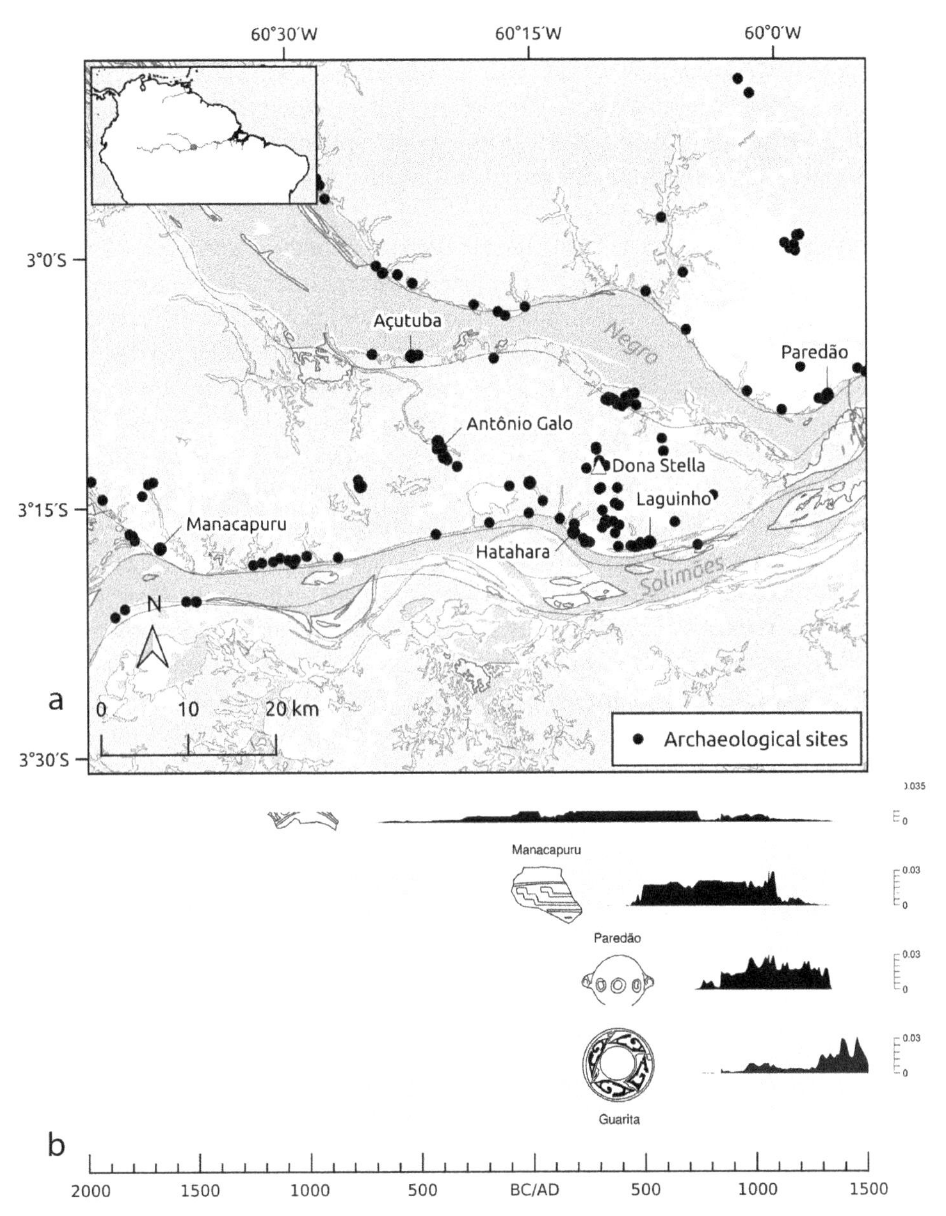

Figure 7.15 Central Amazon region. *a*. Site distribution map of ADE sites. *b*. SPDs of radiocarbon dates along with major ceramic phases.

archaeology in the past three decades (Figure 7.15). A large *várzea* floodplain is inundated on a yearly basis in this region. As the water table rises and falls, various ecosystems are formed, from flooded forests to sandy beaches, seasonal lakes and temporary river streams (*igarapés*).

Peter Hilbert and Mário Simões conducted the earliest archaeological surveys in the 1950s and 1960s, but more systematic research did not begin until 1995, with the launch of the Central Amazon Project (CAP) led by Eduardo Neves (2022). The CAP has documented 378 archaeological sites over an area of about 900 kilometres[2], defining a cultural chronology for this region. The region has a long history, beginning around 8.5 ka at the pre-Ceramic site of Dona Stella (Costa, 2009), followed by a middle Holocene hiatus, and finally, around 2 ka, the arrival of ADE sites associated with larger and more permanent sites.

After the middle Holocene hiatus, human occupation in the region resumed with the Açutuba phase (*c.* BCE 200 to 300 CE), distinguished by ceramics with *cariapé* temper and pots decorated with curvilinear incisions or zoomorphic figures, alternately covered with red or white slip and, in some cases, polychrome paint. The chromatic repertoire of the Açutuba phase is unique in the context of Amazonian archaeology. The abundant use of polychromy is one of the most striking decorative features, with black, yellow, orange, red, burgundy and white, generally used as slip, although red slip is also common. Rectangles, squares, circles, bands and lines are common geometric motifs used in the formation of complex graphic patterns. Incisions, modelling, excisions and brushed pointers, along with less common techniques, such as scraping, tracing and corrugation, are highlighted in plastic decoration. Incision motifs include straight and curved lines with an emphasis on volutes, which are frequently associated with lobed edges. Zoomorphic modelling is typically achieved through the addition of appliqués to the labial flanges, but it can also occur directly on the vessel walls. Zoomorphic models included naturalistic representations, such as jaguars, bats, turtles and frogs (Neves et al., 2014).

These are the first ceramics to appear in the region, and there are no technological or decorative similarities with the oldest known ceramics from the Amazon (e.g., Taperinha, Mina, Bacabal ceramics) reviewed in Chapter 5. They have similarities with the Incised Rim Tradition, also called Barrancoid, which for several authors marks the dispersion of groups speaking languages of the Arawak family into the region (Gregorio de Souza et al., 2020; Heckenberger, 2002; Neves et al., 2014). Sites with ADE soils are located along large river banks and lake margins. Large ADE sites, such as Hatahara and Acutuba, are located along 30–40 metre high river bluffs. For Neves et al. (2014) the Pocó-Açutuba occupations represent the ADE dispersers, the oldest and most widespread visible markers of the anthropization of nature in this sector of the Amazon.

The Axinim period (*c.* 1–800 CE) ceramics had elaborate, almost baroque ceramic styles, with sophisticated technologies employing incisions and excisions to highlight different fields on the slipped surfaces of the pottery, creating a distinct ceramic tradition. The Manacapuru phase (300–700 CE) is characterized by the use of *cauixi* temper and red slip, and various decorations consisting of incised lines, punctations, zoomorphic appendages and flanged rims. The following Paredão phase (700–1250 CE) comprises ceramics that appear to be a local development, where they emerged out of complexes related to the broader Incised Rim Tradition. Paredão pottery is very thin, well-fired and tempered with *cauixi*. Some vessels exhibit handles and pedestals. Decoration includes fine incisions and painting, as well as red slip. Funerary urns associated with this phase are recognizable by the presence of fine-line incisions, delicately painted lines and stylized modelled anthropomorphic appendages (Neves et al., 2014).

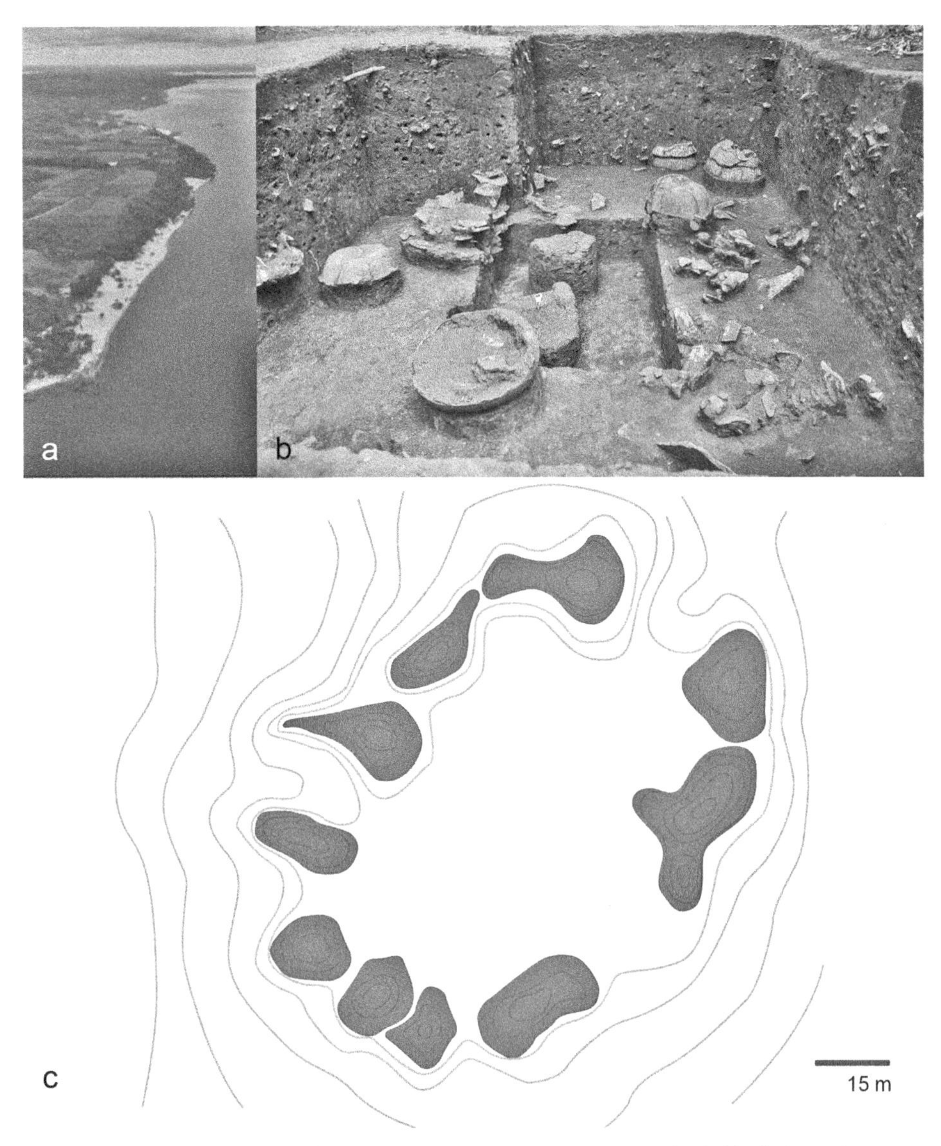

Figure 7.16 *a*. Aerial view of Açutuba site located on a 30-metre high bluff along the Negro River, typical of ADE sites located on strategic, stable and non-flooded sectors of the landscape. In the middle of the site is a large, sunken plaza resembling an amphitheatre (400 × 100 metres). Surrounding this central area are several mounds that served as living spaces for people. These mounds also contain burials and are accompanied by ramps, ditches and wetlands that were carefully managed. *b*. Excavations at the Hatahara site. Ceramic vessels left *in situ* are different-period funerary urns. Note features filled with darker sediments originating higher in the deposit. *c*. Plan of circular village at the Laginho site. *a* and *b*. courtesy Eduardo Neves; *c*. modified from de Paula Moraes and Neves (2012: 134).

Sites of this phase are constituted by rings of house mounds surrounding central plazas, indicative of well-planned village layouts. The Antônio Galo site is a case in point, exhibiting twelve mounds arranged in a circle in an area of approximately one hectare (Figure 7.13c). These villages, similar to the ones of Central Brazil (Wüst and Barreto, 1999) or the first Arawak speakers in the Caribbean (Heckenberger, 2002), were occupied for long periods of time, sometimes centuries, and are associated with the construction of small artificial house mounds and deep ADE soils. During this period, individuals were buried on these platforms, most likely inside the houses as well as in pyriform ceramic urns with anthropomorphic and zoomorphic modelled lateral appendages (PY-Daniel, 2016). The chronology shows overlapping and mixed occupations, which suggests extensive interaction and ethnic diversity.

The appearance of polychrome ceramics coincides with the disintegration of the Paredão complex in 1000 CE. The Guarita phase (700–1500 CE) is characterized by ceramics tempered with crushed potsherds and decorated with a profusion of bold and fine geometric motifs painted in red and black over a white-slipped surface. Plastic decoration with grooves forming the same geometric designs is also present. Vessels present thickened rims and mesial flanges, and include anthropomorphic funerary urns. As in the case of the Marajoara iconography, the painted motifs on Guarita ceramics can be read as stylized zoomorphic motifs (serpents, vultures), intertwined so as to convey anthropomorphic figures. The homogeneity and rapid spread of polychrome ceramics points to demographic expansions. Alternatively, it is possible that the style was diffused as a prestige technology among groups with access to floodplain resources. What is clear is that the process of transition from Paredão to Guarita polychrome was not peaceful, as evidenced by defensive ditches and palisades built around Paredão sites, which were later reoccupied by the Guarita tradition.

For de Paula Moraes and Neves (2012), the Guarita polychrome ceramic occupations are manifestations of groups speaking Tupi trunk languages that expanded into western Amazonia from the upper Madeira River basin, at the beginning of the second millennium CE. During the Guarita phase, settlement patterns change from circular plaza villages to linear settlements.

The Guarita is part of the APT. Let's take a moment to explore the ATP in more detail. ATP ceramics are typically distinguished by red and/or black paint on a white slip. These elements are often combined with other decorative techniques, such as incision, excision, fluting and retouching, on both simple and slipped surfaces. The ceramics may also feature thick edges, external reinforcement, holes and anthropomorphic urns (Barreto et al., 2016). The APT's fine ware ceramics are a clear example of the valuable goods traded throughout the Amazon floodplains. As noted by McEwan et al. (2001), along with ceramics, these trading economies also likely included other luxury items, such as shells, stones, perishable wood, baskets, feathers and other commodities,

APT has a broad geographic reach, spanning from the Amazon's mouth to the foothills of the Andes, with regional variations occurring from 400 CE to the colonial period. Meggers and Evans (1957) initially proposed that the APT originated in the circum-Caribbean region. However, Lathrap (1970) proposed that it actually originated in the region of the central Amazon. More recent evidence, dating back to the colonial period, suggests that these groups were pushed towards the mouth of the Solimões during the conquest. According to Porro (1994), the Amazon River channel and some of its main tributaries, from Peru, Ecuador and Colombia to the mouth of the Madeira River, were occupied in the sixteenth century CE by groups producing ceramics now associated with the APT.

Numerous investigations conducted across the Amazon region have uncovered more than 300 ceramic sites. Although they share similarities, each site has unique characteristics and is categorized into phases or local names. The most well-known examples of APT include the following: Guarita in the central Amazon discussed in this section; Marajoara phase in the Amazon delta (from 400–1400 CE); Tefé near the city of Tefé; Borba in the Lower Wood; Jatuarana, São Joaquim and Pirapittinga in the Upper Solimões; Zebu in Leticia, Colombia; Nofurei in the Caquetá River in Colombia; Caimito in the upper Amazon and Ucayali; and Napo on the Napo River in Ecuador (Barreto et al., 2016). Between 800–1000 AD, there was a noticeable increase in APT sites. As summarized above, Moraes and Neves (2012) argue that this expansion was likely driven by conflict, as evidenced by the defensive structures discovered in the central Amazon and across the southern rim of Amazonia (see ring ditched section above).

What do we know about the subsistence of the groups that inhabited the Central Amazon during the late Holocene? Phytolith analysis from an artificial mound context built with surrounding ADE soils at the Hatahara site documented the presence of maize, squash (*Cucurbita* sp.), gourd (*Lagenaria* sp.) and *Calathea*, in addition to *Heliconia* and *Bactris*-type palm phytoliths ~1000 CE (Bozarth et al., 2009). Maize and yam (*Dioscorea* sp.), starch grains and maize, *Cyperus* sp. and palm phytoliths were recovered from plant processing tools collected in a peripheral area of the Hatahara site, associated with two occupations between 600–1100 CE (Fernandes Caromano et al., 2013). Manioc carbonized stems and roots were recorded in sediments from the same context (Caromano, 2010). Macro-remains of maize have been recovered at the Osvaldo site, central Amazon, with associated dates of ~700 CE (Shock et al., 2014). Carbon and nitrogen stable from human bones associated with the formation of ADE sites suggest a 'maize-existing but not maize-reliant diet' (Arroyo-Kalin, 2010).

Anthracology (charcoal analysis) has also provided new insights into landscape and cultural practices. For example, in the pre-ADE context of the Hatahara site (~BCE 200–500 CE) and ADE Paredão phase (~800–300 CE) in the central Amazon, a predominance of early successional stage taxa (e.g., Melastomataceae) has been identified, indicating that the collection of firewood took place in secondary forest vegetation surrounding settlements, but also in fallows (Scheel-Ybert et al., 2016). The plant taxa identified using charcoal also suggests practices of succession management, resource use and the creation of areas of secondary vegetation around the settlement since ~BCE 200 at the Hatahara site. Despite recent advances in the taxonomic resolution of some crops, we should bear in mind that many indigenous plant foods used by pre-Columbian Amazonian people, including large numbers of perennial tree crops, will be invisible in the fragmentary archaeobotanical record.

Faunal analysis of Paredão contexts at the Hatahara site shows that fish was the primary animal resource consumed, followed by Amazon aquatic turtles. This underscores the importance of aquatic resources in the subsistence of the site residents. Thirty-seven fish taxa were identified. Particularly prominent among the fishes are three groups: the arapaimids (*pirarucu/paiche*), the doradids and the serrasalmids (*pacu*). Reptiles include turtles, followed by crocodilians, snakes (including anaconda, *Eunectes murinus*) and lizards. Despite the diversity of turtles in the Amazon, only the large (body mass 90 kilograms) South American river turtle, *Podocnemis* spp., was recovered in the bone assemblage. Evidence of burnt dorsal carapace shell elements suggests that they were probably turned upside down and roasted in their shells as commonly described in Amazonian ethnography (Prestes-Carneiro et al., 2016). Curiously, there is a lack of large mammals recovered at the site. This study found that 90 per cent of the species were caught in aquatic or semi-aquatic environments, such as *igapós*, lakes, the Amazon River bed, streams and sandy beaches, indicating that fisherfolk exploited a diverse range of aquatic niches. The results of this analysis contrast with other ADE sites along the Lower Xingu River, where preliminary faunal analysis documented a variety of faunal taxa, including tapir (*Tapirus* sp.), *paca* (*Cuniculus paca*), *agouti* (*Dasyprocta* sp.), *capybara* (*Hydrochoerus hydrochaeris*), Brazilian rabbit (*Silvilagus brasiliensis*), monkeys (Primates), deer (Cervidae), turtles (Testudines), alligators (Alligatoridae), nine-banded armadillo (*Dasypus novemcinctus*), sloth (*Bradypus* sp.) and fish such as the Vampire Fish/Cachorra (*Hydrolycus scomberoides*) (Müller et al., 2022). To what extent the lack of large terrestrial mammals at Hatahara is related to cultural practices, such as taboos, or to the depletion of game around the site, needs further studies. Modelling of large terrestrial game depletion by hunting based on ethnography and archaeological data suggest that the confluence of the Negro and Solimões River would have been depleted during the late Holocene (Shepard Jr et al., 2012). Collectively, the data from the central Amazon suggest an overall general pattern of riverine adaptations from fisher folks practising polyculture agroforestry.

Amazonian Regions III: The lower Amazon and the Guiana coast

The Tapajós

The area where Richard Ford wanted to accomplish the American dream (Grandin, 2009) was the location of one of the largest and most sophisticated societies in Amazonia, known as the Tapajós or Santarém culture, hereafter called the Late pre-Columbian Tapajo Period (LPTP), which developed between 1000–1600 CE.

The Tapajós River, a southern tributary of the Amazon, is a clear-water river that drains from the central Brazilian highlands (Figures 7.17–18). As with many other rivers in the Amazon basin, the rise in sea level from the beginning of the Holocene created a large 'green-coloured' lake at its mouth. The region is characterized by a large number of lakes and islands that make it extremely productive. The area surrounding what is today Santarém city, at the confluence of the Tapajós and Amazon Rivers, is the alleged site of the LPTP chiefdom's capital.

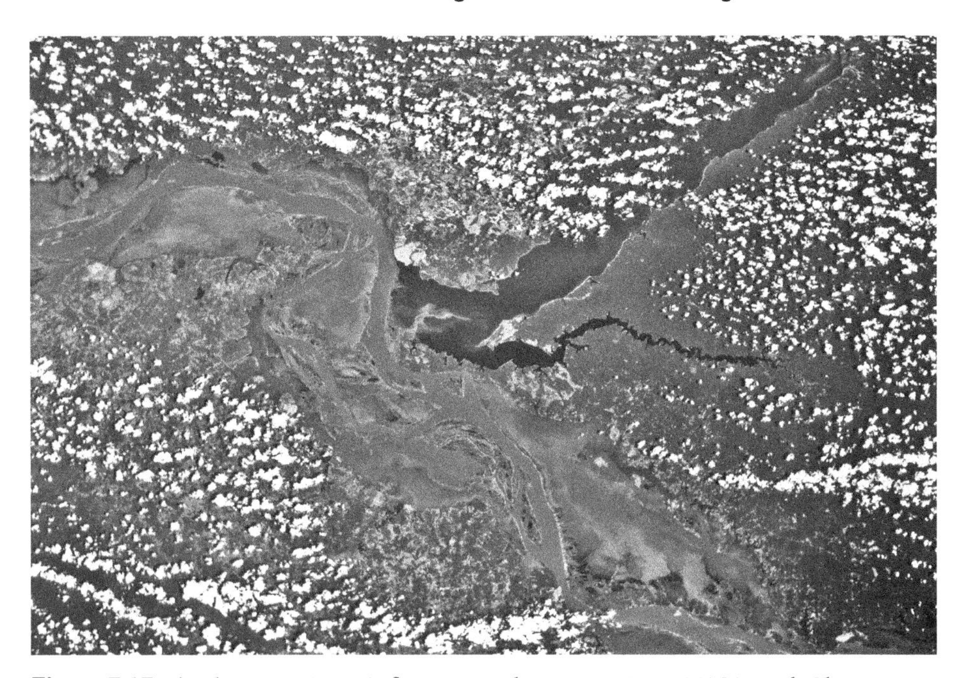

Figure 7.17 The clear water Tapajós flowing into the Amazon River. NASA Earth Observatory.

Early historical accounts of the region describe Tapajós hierarchical societies honouring the ancestors, and being based on maize agriculture. In the early-seventeenth century, Heriarte (1874 [1662]) described the city of Santarém as '. . . the largest village and settlement that we have discovered so far in this district. It raises 60,000 bowmen, when war is afoot and since there are so many Tapajo they are feared by the other Indians and nations and thus became the sovereign power in this district'. Regarding Tapajo's politics, he noted how 'these Indians are governed by principals, one in each hut of twenty or thirty couples, and all are governed by a great Principal over all of them, who they very much obey'. Early historical reports also describe religious activities centred on the veneration of pictures and mummies of chiefs and ancestors, which helped to enhance and affirm the prestige of chiefs, priests and lineage heads. The aesthetic similarities identified between Santarém pottery and other varieties from distant locations of northern South America may be explained by the interchange of ideas and trade items via networks linking these riverine chiefdoms.

Archaeological investigations in the Santarém region started in the early 1870s when Charles Hart associated the ADE with ancient indigenous settlements (Schaan, 2012b). In the 1920s, Curt Niemuendaju located sixty-five archaeological sites in the Santarém area while conducting archaeological surveys for the Ethnographic Museum of Gothenburg in Sweden (Nimuendajú, 2004). His expedition was important because sites along the Tapajós and Trombetas Rivers were mapped and recorded for the first time. His survey also demonstrated that Santarém-style pottery associated with the Tapajó group was distributed over a large geographic area thereby seemingly corroborating the

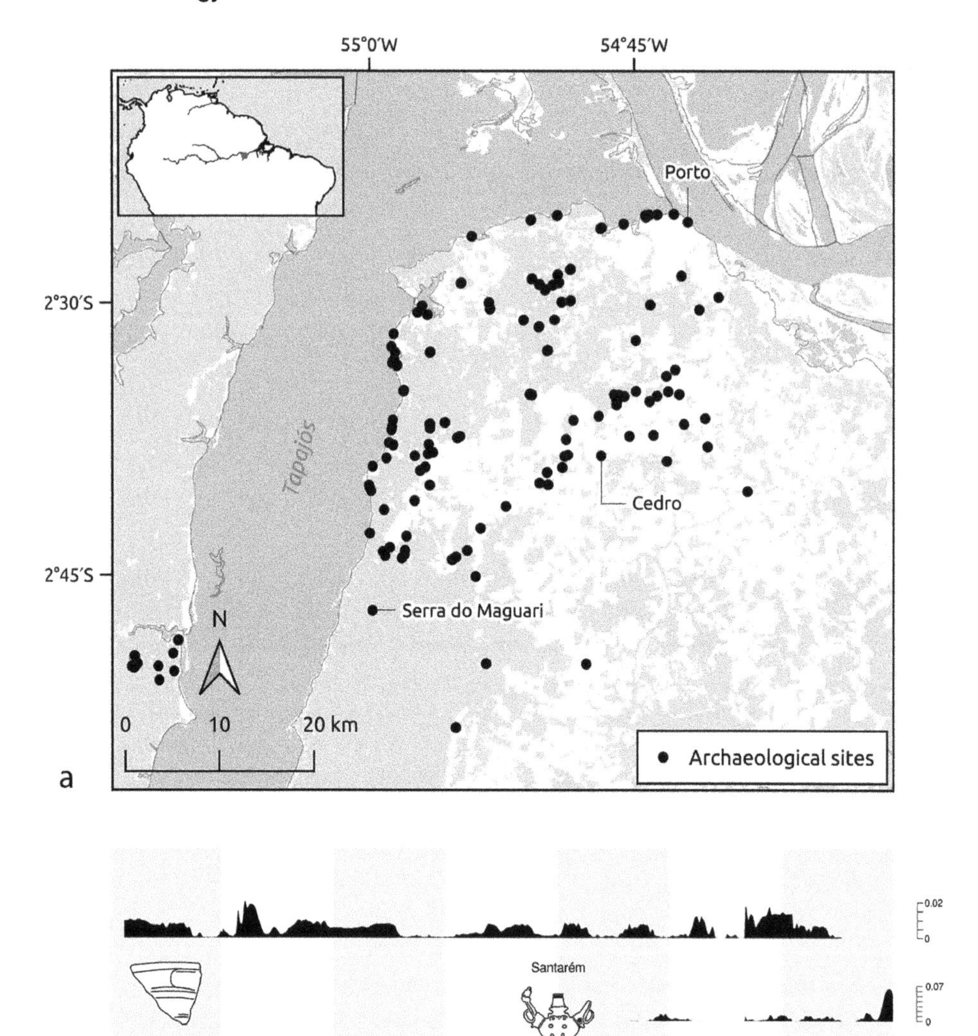

Figure 7.18 The Lower Tapajós River region. *a*. Site distribution map of ADE sites. *b*. SPDs of radiocarbon dates along with major ceramic phases.

ethnohistorical accounts of long-distance trade. Furthermore, he noticed the existence of connecting roads from one ADE site to another within the sites situated on the plateau, the construction of ponds in areas far from large rivers and the possible existence of a settlement hierarchy centred in the Santarém region (Schaan, 2012b). He also noted the presence of a large indigenous riverine population that had existed before the arrival of the Europeans, based on differences in the size of the settlements, quantity of archaeological material recovered and ADE soil concentrations (Nimuendajú, 2004). In the late 1980s, Roosevelt carried out the first systematic excavations at the Porto site in Santarém city based on a geophysical survey documenting *bolsões* (see below) and floors (Roosevelt, 1999; Roosevelt, 2007), as well as the Formative components in this location. Further work in the Porto and Aldeia site in Santarém was carried out by Gomes (2007; Gomes and Luiz, 2013) and Schaan (2012b), starting in 2006. Later, the Brazilian-Swedish 'Cultivated Wilderness Project' (Stenborg, 2016; Stenborg et al., 2012) carried out systematic surveys and excavations across the region.

Although we focus on the Santarém culture in this chapter, we must bear in mind that it is part of a much larger and more complex region that includes the Konduri and other cultures, which could represent yet another multilingual regional system of Amazonia. See Guapindaia (2009) and Schaan (2012b) for a more detailed review of the archaeology of the region and the Konduri tradition. As reviewed in previous chapters, this is the region where current information indicates the first people arrived in Amazonia ~13.1 ka at Caverna da Pedra Pintada, and where the earliest ceramics of the Amazon have been documented, at the Taperinha shell-midden ~7.9 ka. Like in some regions of the Amazon, this is followed by a 4-millennia hiatus until the appearance of the Formative period between 4,500–1,000 years ago, followed by the LPTP from ~1000–1600 CE. Interestingly, as described in Chapter 5, several pollen records in eastern Amazonia, including the one on the Tapajos River, show signs of forest disturbance during this gap of human occupation (Bush et al., 2007; Irion et al., 2006). Additional archaeological work is necessary to locate these middle Holocene sites potentially linked to human activity.

Evidence for the Formative period comes from the ceramics of the Aroxi phase made with crushed rock temper at Pedra Pintada Cave, which date back to 3.6–3.2 ka. Formative ceramic artifacts were discovered at the Porto site excavation dating between 2.9–2.3 ka (Roosevelt, 2007). Similar dates for Incised Rim, Formative ceramics have been found on the western margin of the Tapajós River by Gomes (2011). The pollen record from Caranã Lake shows maize cultivation during the Formative period since around 4.3 ka (Maezumi et al., 2018a).

Regional intensification begins at 500 CE and peaks at 1500 CE. In this section, I concentrate on describing in more detail the LPTP. The territory of the LPTP extends over an area of about 20,000 kilometres^2, with the northern outskirts of Almerim on the Amazon River, the mouth of the Xingu River to the east, the region of the Trombetas River to the west and to the south the community of Boim, situated on the left bank of the Tapajós River, about 100 kilometres from Santarém (Palmatary, 1960).

Hundreds of ADE sites have been recorded along the major waterways (Tapajós and Amazon rivers) and *terra firme* settings along the Belterra plateau (130–180 masl). The Brazilian-Swedish team (Stenborg et al., 2012) conducted a survey of 104 sites along the Tapajo River and the Belterra plateau, the majority of which are ADE sites. Site size ranges from small sites covering 1 hectare (Guari) to large sites, such as Santarém Aldeia, spread over 16 hectares. Based on this survey, the authors have classified the sites into three main categories: (i) large sites located close to the main watercourse, which contain high concentrations of artefacts and deep ADE deposits occurring in few numbers (e.g., Santarém Aldeia); (ii) large sites, which may or may not be located close to main watercourses and contain lower concentrations of artefacts, thinner ADE deposits (in many cases of lighter colour corresponding to ABEs) occurring in low numbers (e.g. Labras site); and (iii) small sites, often located on hills with limited access to water, which contain high concentrations of artefacts and anthrosol deposits of varying depth (e.g., Bom Futuro).

The Porto site is the largest site in the region. A systematic transect survey by Gomes and Luiz (2013) at the Porto site revealed an area of 2 x 0.7 kilometres of contiguous ADE. If the Porto and Aldeia sites are combined together, we have an area of 4 kilometres long of continuous ADE, reaching a depth of 2 metres in some sections. Santarém's big capital town is made up of a core area with dense archaeological deposits (100 hectares) amid a larger populated landscape up to 25 kilometres in size, rivalling many significant towns in the Americas (e.g., Cahokia, Chan Chan), as Heckenberger and Neves (2009) remind us.

Opportunistic inspection of profiles exposed by development projects at the Porto site area has revealed what appear to be floor structures, running north to south and ranging in width from 8–12 metres. Geophysics and excavations by Roosevelt (2007) have also revealed these floors as composed of many thin superimposed clayey-silty laminations, occasionally associated with a post base while containing very scarce cultural and biological remains. The structures are stacked, forming layers reaching a depth of up to 2 metres. It is understood that hard dirt floors were periodically renovated, causing a gradual elevation of the house floors.

In other parts of the site, where stack floors are not present, several projects have found pockets of black earth, called *bolsões*. *Bolsões* are round with diameters between 0.5–0.8 metres in size, and their depth is between 0.7–1 metre. Soil found within *bolsões* typically has a much darker colour than its exterior, indicating the presence of organic matter and charcoal. The ceramic assemblage discovered inside typically includes LPTP ceramics with red-slipped, incised and zoomorphic appendages; broken figurine pieces; large, broken spindle whorls; fragments of ordinary plates and bowls; bone fragments including fish, shells, river turtles; maize and tree-fruits; charcoal; lithic artefacts; rocks; and burned clay. *Bolsões*, as purposefully dug structures designed to house artefacts used in collective rituals and then discarded, with obvious signs of purposeful breakage and intentional arrangements, have been generally interpreted as representing 'termination' ceremonies (Gomes and Luiz, 2013). That is, the practice of breaking and burying objects in order to isolate and terminate whatever agency or power they were imbued with. Gomes (2013) has also detected midden refuse areas with domestic refuse, simple ceramics and lithic workshops characterized by small lithic debitage at the Porto site. Circular villages are present during the LPTP. A ~15 hectares mounded village with a central plaza surrounded by a mosaic of ADE sites dated between ~1420–1500 CE was documented at the Maguari site, ~50 kilometres south of Santarém located at the edge of the Belterra plateau overlooking the Tapajos River (Alves, 2017; Maezumi et al., 2018a).

The LPTP is also characterized by a network of ditch and causeway trails in addition to natural, large, crater-like enclosed depressions, locally known as *poços de água* (water holes). These reservoirs range from 15–30 metres in diameter, but could be as large as 100 metres. It is common for the latter to be artificially enhanced through the construction of berms, as reservoirs capable of storing considerable amounts of water (Stenborg et al., 2018). Of the sixty-eight recorded archaeological sites in the Belterra plateau, thirty-five have artificial or natural ponds principally located near streams, far from large rivers (Stenborg, 2016; Stenborg et al., 2018).

Santarém is described by Roosevelt as the epicentre of the LPTP chiefdom, the apogee of which lasted from 1000–1600 CE. Her model suggests the presence of a centralized political or ritual hierarchy where various chiefs controlled and integrated a large area of densely populated settlements comprising 23,000 kilometres^2. She interpreted the settlement data as a reflection of the presence of political elites who extracted tribute and labour from the mass of lower status commoners. She argues that the elite oversaw community construction of housing and defensive works (Roosevelt, 1999).

Pollen and phytolith data from the Maguari and Cedro sites document the presence of maize, manioc, sweet potato and squash, along with a diversity of palms (*Mauritela*, *Attalea* and *Astrocaryum*) and fruit trees, such as cacao and *pequi* (Alves, 2017; Maezumi et al., 2018a; Troufflard and Alves, 2019). Gomes (2013) also identified maize, manioc, *Bactris* sp. and *Mauritia flexuosa* from the starch grains and phytolith residues on plant processing tools at two ADE sites in Santarém, dated to 700–1100 CE.

LPTP ceramics are associated with the 'Incised Punctate' regional tradition (Gomes, 2007), which has affinities with the coeval APT, and also resemblances with the Orinoco and Guianas Arauquinoid ceramic complexes, implying that Carib-speaking peoples likely expanded into the middle-lower Amazon between 500–1000 CE (Figure 7.19) (Lathrap, 1970). The Incised Punctuate Tradition is characterized by its elaborate pottery vessels with representational and geometric plastic and painted designs, figurines, and a variety of polished-stone tools and sculptures. They are typically decorated with representational and geometric plastic and painted designs, in particular anthropomorphic and zoomorphic *adornos* displayed in the unique caryatid and *gargalo* bottleneck vessels. Caryatid vessels are unique to the Santarém ceramic inventory (Figure 7.19a). These vessels are named after the small crouching figures that support the bowl, resembling classic Greek architecture. They are made by coiling and modelling clay into three parts: a hollow base, a middle level with three modelled anthropomorphic 'caryatid' supports, and a bowl with modelled zoomorphic and anthropomorphic appendages. The caryatid vessels are surprising and distinctive because of their human-like zoomorphic figures, with two heads that resemble transformations experienced in a shamanic trance. The three caryatid supports are typically using their hands either to cover their eyes, ears or mouth. Although the figurines' positions vary between vessels, they are always identical within the same vessel. The ceramics have a volumetric capacity of 700 millilitres on average and could have been used as a kind of cup for the consumption of beverages. Gomes (2011) attributes the tripartite division of the vase to the representation of the structure of the cosmos, with heaven, earth and the underground world common to some Amazonian cultures today.

Bottleneck bases are vessels with a narrow neck and a globular body that has extensions on both sides (Figure 7.19e). They feature an anthropomorphic face and small figures of beings on opposite sides. They are placed on a pedestal base and have a reduced

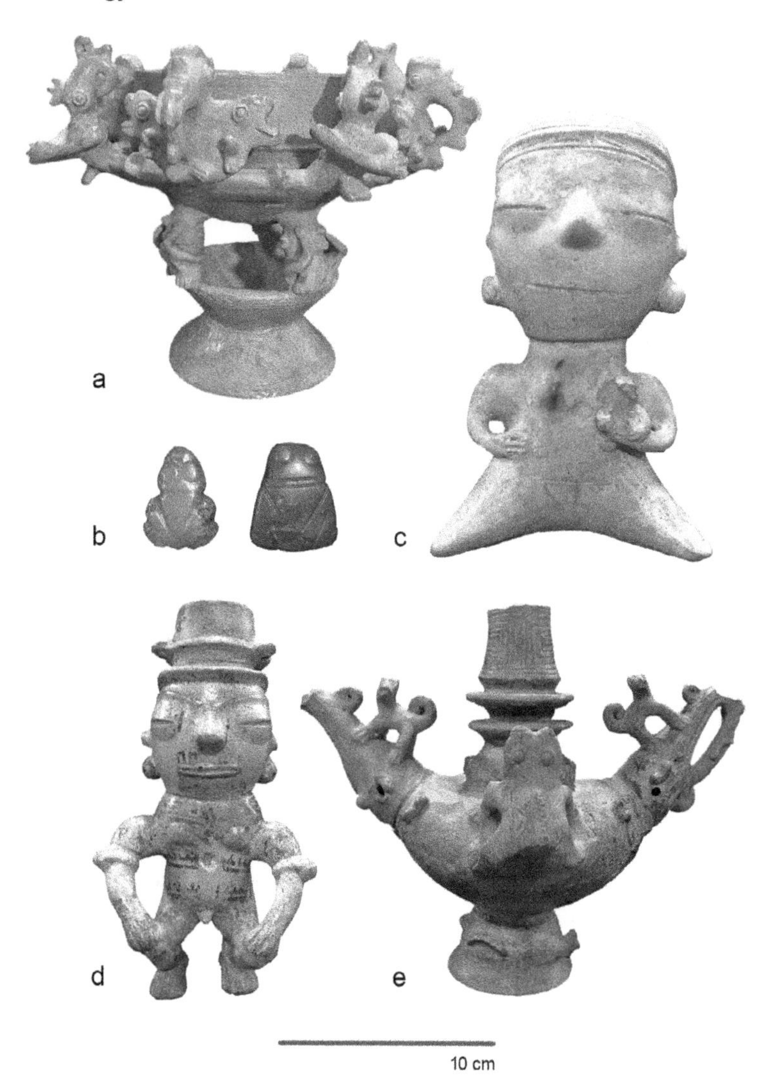

Figure 7.19 Selected ceramics and polished stones. *a.* Carytiad vessel (T-364, Collection Frederico Barata). *b.* Muiraquitãs. *c.* Female figurine (T-498, Collection Frederico Barata). *d.* Male figurine (T-502). *e.* Bottleneck vessel (T-377, Collection Frederico Barata). MCTI/Museu Paraense Emílio Goeldi, Reserva Técnica Mário Ferreira Simões, photographs by Brenda Bandeira. Courtesy Daiana Alves.

volume capacity (~300 millilitres), suggesting ceremonial use. They are typically decorated with plastic techniques, including faces and zoomorphic figures. The narrative iconography is standardized with various animals, such as the royal condor, other birds, frogs and hybrid beings with caiman heads (Figure 7.16e).

The Incised Punctate Tradition (IPT) was first defined by Meggers and Evans (1957). IPT ceramics are known for their incised and stippled decorations, which often include modelled elements of anthropomorphic, zoomorphic or geometric figures. These ceramics are commonly treated with red slip, and their tempering agents include *cauixi*, ground pottery, crushed rock and/or *caraipé*. Ceramics of the IPT have been dated back to around 1000–1500 CE in various regions, including Venezuela, the Orinoco, the Amazon, Guyana and Amapá. According to Meggers and Evans, this tradition originated in Colombia and spread through the mouth of the Orinoco to the Amazon River basin. Examples of this tradition include the Arauquín ceramic complex in the Orinoco, the Mabaruma phase in Guyana, Konduri in the lower Amazon and the Mazagão phase in Amapá (Barreto et al., 2016).

Figurines, small ceramic sculptures depicting human, animal or hybrid bodies, are very distinctive of the LPTP (Figure 7.19c–d). As Barreto (2017) has described, the creation of figurines has a long tradition in lowland South America. Stone figurines from the Valdivia complex were found in south-western Ecuador 3,000 years ago, while miniaturized pottery figures of humans and animals have a long history in greater Amazonia. These figurines date back to early styles of the Saladoid and Barrancoid series in the Orinoco basin, where small, modelled appendages were common on vessel rims. Although the influence of these styles can be seen in formative ceramic complexes, figurine traditions in the Amazon basin proper appeared later, during the first millennium before the European conquest, and are largely concentrated in the lower Amazon.

Human figurines range in height from 0.1–0.3 metres and are almost entirely female, although males are occasionally included. Figurine shape is typically stylized and conventional. Typically, in LPTP female figurines, the head occupies over half the total height and retains richly patterned facial features of eyebrows, eyes, nose and mouth. Eyes are either closed and swollen (shaped as coffee beans), or wide open (a double circular incision) as if in different stages of drug induced or altered state. Small holes are common behind earlobes and on top of the head. Other details include ear lobe perforation and ear plugs, and a head band binding a carefully braided coiffure falling over the neck and back of the body.

The bodies of Santarém figurines are depicted squatting or seated with the legs spread wide open and modelled as two cones and the pubis sometimes demarcated by incised triangles. Breasts, arms and hands (usually clasped to the stomach) are more naturalistically displayed. Some figurines seem to be pregnant, while others have a baby in hand. They typically exhibit body painting and adornments, such as earplugs, headdresses, bracelets and collars. The body is commonly ornamented with incised lines, which according to Barata (1950) may represent body painting or scarification. Models and overall body ornamentation are very standardized, seeming to signal depiction of a particular female person, perhaps an important chiefly woman or a mythological ancestral character. Gomes (2001) suggests that the muiraquitãs on female headdresses suggests that those figurines portrayed elite women.

As mentioned, among many lowland South American peoples the capacity to transform one's own body is often an important knowledge acquired by shamans in order to communicate with spirits and beings of other worlds. This communication is sought for calling upon the help of small spirit beings, birds or little people, who act as mediators between the society represented by the shaman and that in which he aims to intervene. Following this, Stahl (1986) argues that figurines in lowland South America are commonly used in shamanistic rituals during the ecstatic stage. They serve as visual aids to help communicate with helper spirits and also act as receptacles for them. Through this transformation, these figurines gain guiding, divinatory and curing powers. His research on ethnographic examples shows that figurines have been used in shamanistic and hallucinogenic practices as part of an ancient cosmological belief system shared by lowland South American Amerindians since formative times. Certain characteristics of figurines suggest that they were used in shamanic rituals. Ceramic figurines from Santarém and Marajó have small pellets inside them that create a rattling sound when shaken. These figurines resemble maracas, which are commonly used by shamans in Amazonia to induce curing trances. Some of the figurines even imitate the shape of a person holding a maraca, with a long, single-footed body serving as the handle and a round head mimicking the gourd case.

In Santarém, figurines and other ceramic artefacts were deliberately broken and buried as evidenced by the *bolsões* context of the Porto site (e.g., Gomes and Luiz, 2013), indicating their significance in rituals. Guapindaia's study (1993) analysis of figurines from collections shows that 52 per cent of all figurines had severed heads.

LPTP is also characterized by polished-stone figurines, locally called 'muiraquitãs', likely representing small amulets, which were fashioned from a variety of semi-precious gemstones, and represent various animals and humans (Figure 7.19b) (see Schaan, 2012b). They were probably an important exchange item along the Amazon's waterways and beyond. Green stones, also known as *muiraquitãs*, are commonly found in the Amazon and the Lesser Antilles. They are usually pendants shaped like animals, such as frogs, birds, fish, turtles or geometric figures. The production and exchange of these stones started around BCE 400 and continued until the beginning of European arrival. There are four known zones for the manufacture of green stones in the Amazon: the Lower Amazon (Palmatary, 1960), the central coast of Suriname (Boomert, 1987), around Valencia Lake on the coast of Venezuela and the north of the Lesser Antilles (Antczak and Antczak, 2006).

The snake people: Marajoara

The Lower Amazon region is widely regarded as one of the most diverse in terms of ceramic styles in pre-Columbian Amazonian history (Neves, 2006), and people from Marajó island crafted some of the most sophisticated ceramics ever known to have been made in this period. Because of the abundance of snake motifs in Marajoara ceramics, Denise Schaan (2012b) called them the snake people.

The estuary running from the Xingú River's mouth to Marajó island at the Amazon's mouth is unique in terms of environment and land use by Amazonian people (Figure 7.20). This area experiences twice-daily fluctuations in river levels and significant influence from salty water, unlike other areas that only experience yearly fluctuations. Clayish soils in these floodplains support a limited number of palm species that have adapted to estuarine cycles and waterlogged conditions, such as *murumuru* (*Astrocarium muru-muru*), *jupati* (*Raphia taedigera*), *açai* (*Euterpe oleracea*), *inajá* (*Maximiliana martiana*), *buriti* (*Mauritia* sp.) and *ubim* (*Geonoma* sp.). When managed properly, these highly productive agroforestry systems have the potential to support a large number of people, up to 48 people per kilometre^2 (Anderson and Loris, 1992). As will be seen below, the region has a rich history of successful fishing and agroforestry practices that led to one of the most sophisticated societies in Amazonia.

Marajó island constitutes ~50,000 kilometres^2 of a maze-like archipelago at the mouth of the Amazon. It is divided into two distinct ecological zones: rainforest in the southwest and savannah grasslands in the northeast – along with gallery forest following river courses and mangroves on the coast. A tropical equatorial climate regime of alternating wet and dry seasons governs life on the island. These seasonal fluctuations and the influence of the Amazon's yearly rise and fall dramatically affect the landscape. As with other savannah environments, the Marajó savannahs have fine-textured, clayey soil with low infiltration capacity, which tends to become saturated during the rainy season and overly dry during the dry season. Most low-lying grasslands are continually submerged under floodwater for half of the year, leaving only tiny dispersed islands of vegetation visible. During the dry season, the terrain dries up, and many minor watercourses evaporate, transforming the grasslands into an arid desert.

As Prümers (2017) summarized, three significant studies have contributed to our understanding of Marajó's archaeological history. The first study was conducted by Betty J. Meggers and Clifford Evans (1957), along with Mario Simões, who investigated archaeological sites in the island's northern and central regions. Following them were Anna Roosevelt's (1991) investigations of the artificial mounds named Teso dos Bichos and Guajará. Finally, Denise Schaan's work between 1999–2003 in the upper areas of the Anajás River and the artificial mounds of the Camutins River, has greatly contributed to our understanding of Marajó's past (Schaan, 2012b).

Marajó Island has a 5,000-year-old history. In this chapter, I am mainly concerned with the Marajoara, who flourished between ~700–1100 CE. The first ceramic societies appeared on the island around 1500 BCE (the Ananatuba and Mangeuras phases, 1500–850 BCE). After a hiatus of almost 800 years, which Meggers and Danon (1988) argue is because of climatic changes unfavourable to human settlement, the following ceramic phases follow: Formiga (~0–800 CE), Marajoara (700–1100 CE) and, lasting until the arrival of the Portuguese, the Aruan and Cacoal phases (~1300–1600 CE). Unlike Meggers and Evans (1957), who hypothesized that the complex Marajoara culture immigrated from the Andes, it is now widely accepted that the Marajoarans derived from populations living on the island from indigenous predecessors (see Roosevelt, 1991; Schaan, 2012b). According to Schann (2012b), the proper Marajoara phase begins around 500 CE, as evidenced by population growth and the emergence of mound clusters in the island's centre.

The Marajoara phase has distinct prestige ceramics, in particular the funerary urns, which are one of the most iconic styles of pre-Columbian Amazonia belonging to the Polychrome Tradition (Figure 7.21). They comprise spectacular funerary urns, plates, bowls, stools and a range of figurines, including also unusual ceramic female pubic covers known as *tangas*. Researchers such as Barreto (2017) talk about the 'corporization' of Marajoara ceramics, since many of them appear to represent a body and have a tail, ears and other body parts.

The prestige and ceremonial vessels of the so-called 'Joanes Painted style' stand out. They were manufactured via excision, incision, modelling and painting, characterized by the widespread use of white and red slip, resulting in sophisticated patterns.

The decorative elements on the Marajoara fine wares include depictions of caimans, lizards, scorpions, owls, king vultures, monkeys, turtles, jaguars, manatees, ducks and other birds, while snakes are some of the most abundant motifs. Most of these exquisite ceramics have been discovered in funerary contexts, prompting Schaan (2012b) to argue for the significance of ancestor cults and strong belief in the afterlife. Given their intricacy and time-consuming nature, she contends that groups of trained craftspeople, most likely part-time professionals, produced them.

Highly decorated stools are common (Figure 7.21 d–e). In general, in Amazonian societies, stools are badges of a differentiated status. They are the seats of the chiefs, of the shamans, who sit on stools to think, to speak deferentially to others or to connect with the world beyond. It is not surprising, therefore, that Marajoara statues depict seated figures holding rattles.

Like Santarém, Marajoara also exhibits distinct figurines, which vary in size from 0.9–0.18 metres and are made of either hollow or solid materials. They are typically handcrafted in shapes that combine the features of a phallus and a human body. Most hollow figurines contain small pebbles or broken pottery, which create sound when shaken. They resemble the rattles used by shamans throughout the Amazon. The majority of these figurines depict female bodies, often with a pubic triangle, breasts and sometimes a pregnant belly. They are usually shown in a squatting position, as if giving birth. Head adornments, such as bands and ear pools, as well as cranial deformation, are visible in the shape of the head. In Marajó there is also a typical symbiosis between the phallic form and the human body, generally female, while in Santarém some characters are portrayed in more detail and in a canonical way, highlighting the body adornments, including muiraquitãs, and women with swollen bellies indicating pregnancy (Barreto, 2017).

For Roosevelt (1991: 89–94), female representation in Marajoara pottery, especially in figurines, symbolizes female empowerment, mythical worship of female ancestors and the emergence of agrarian societies organized under a matriarchal system. It is also common for Marajoara figurines to have a breakage at the neck, separating the body and head. Such figurines are commonly found in trash middens. The extent to which they represent a deliberate decapitation of ceramic figurines as 'termination' (closing of a life cycle of living, powerful ceramic people-objects) is still uncertain. They may be shamanic aids, or connected to war practices. Another well-known ceramic piece of Marajoara are the famous '*tangas*' (thongs). These are triangular pubic covers that women wear around their waists. They have holes at the corners for cords that appear to have been used to hold them in place. *Tangas* can be found in both decorated and plain versions. Many *tangas* have body painting motifs that are similar to those observed on figurines. Additionally, they may indicate belonging to certain groups.

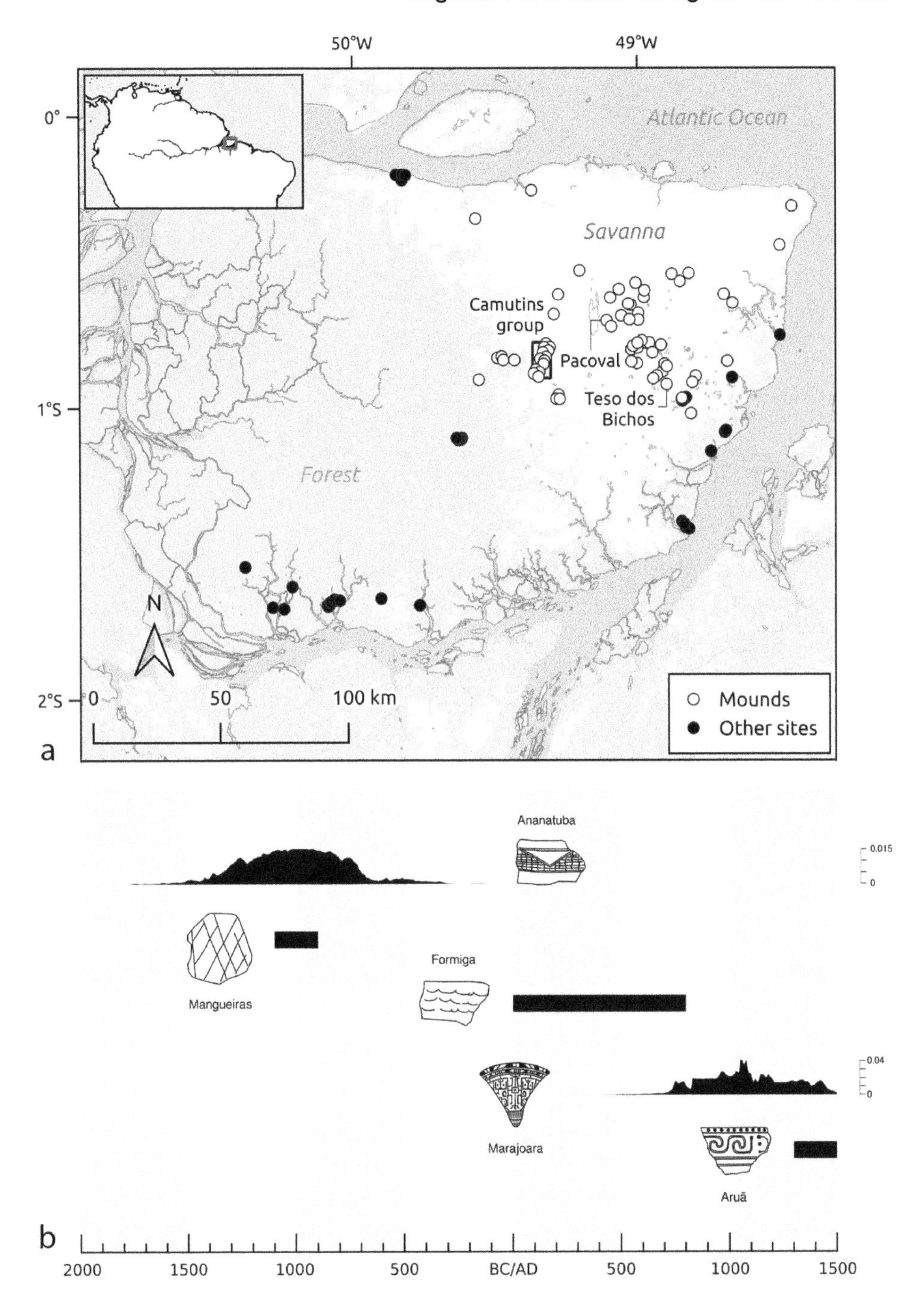

Figure 7.20 The Marajó region. *a*. Site distribution map. *b*. SPDs of radiocarbon dates along with major ceramic phases. Bars represent ceramic phases defined by ceramic seriation.

Figure 7.21 Marajó people were exceptionally gifted potters. *a.* Funerary urn from Camutins (T-1598, Meggers and Evans collection) displaying the 'smiling face' so commonly depicted in Marajoara artefacts. The Marajoara potters were known for using the 'Mona Lisa effect' in their funerary urns, which gives the impression that the eyes on the ceramics are following you. The urns were designed for interaction, that is, both to see and to be seen. *b.* 'Pacoval inciso' funerary urn (Paes de Carvalho collection). *c.* Joanes Pintado funerary urn with 'bean-shaped eyes' so frequent in figurines of this ceramic tradition. *d–f.* Decorated stools displaying a variety of geometrical elements, such as scrolls and T-shapes, which are combined to produced complex bipartite and cuadripartite mirror, inverted and reflected images following what appear to be very specific rules by the craft specialists. MCTI/Museu Paraense Emílio Goeldi, Reserva Técnica Mário Ferreira Simões, photographs by Brenda Bandeira and drawings courtesy of Daiana Alves.

Denise Schaan (2012a) has conducted one of the most informative studies on Marajoara iconography. She based her research on the anthropological understanding that art holds a vital role in communicating social, moral and ethnic values in illiterate societies. From this it follows that the decoration of objects (in this case, the iconography) is closely linked to their social function, and conveys the mythology and cosmology of societies. That is, art is intrinsically related to conveying cosmological concepts related to a particular mythical repertoire, serving to record, convey and perpetuate the culture. Following Levi-Strauss (1978), she reasoned that in the same way that myths are organized in minimal units called mythemes, the significant and conducting units of the mythical narratives, so are their iconographic representations moulded and painted in

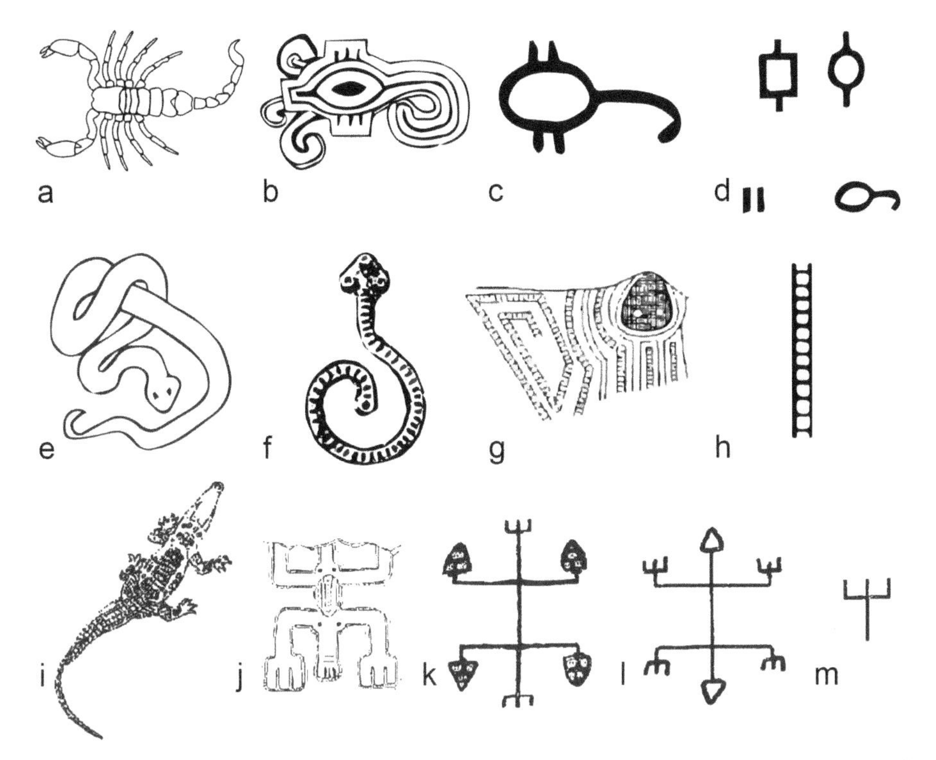

Figure 7.22 Natural to stylized representations in Marajoara ceramics: *a–d.* scorpions are usually associated with the representation of eyes, *e–h.* snakeheads are commonly represented as a spearhead and *i–m.* caimans are typically represented by a trident. Modified from Schaan 2012a.

ceramics. To this end, Denise Schaan analysed in detail the Johannes Pintado collection of Marajoara ceramics, trying to understand the development of these iconic simplified forms, these minimally meaningful units. She identified the existence of minimal structures that could be linked, not only to a total zoomorphic representation, but also to part of it. Figure 7.22 shows examples of these structures, from the natural to the iconic, including serpents, caimans and scorpions.

Where did the people that created these amazing ceramic live? Marajoara people lived on large settlement mounds located along major rivers and lakes in the savannah section of the island, which spread over an area of 23,000 kilometres^2. Settlement mounds can reach ~3 hectares in area and 7 metres in height. They are accretional mounds built with soil carried in from adjacent areas, as well as from the bottom of nearby streams. Geoarchaeological work by Rosetti et al. (2009) has shown that some of the largest ones are not entirely human-made, but that Marajoarans took advantage of the natural, pre-existing elevated surfaces and added on top of those to build their earthworks. One-hundred-and-thirty mounds have been recorded, but much more are suspected. They can form clusters of three, seven and fourteen, and in some cases, such as the Camutin locality, they appear in clusters of up to forty mounds. Excavations show that mounds served many purposes and were used as a defence against seasonal flooding, for habitation, as cemeteries and maybe for militaristic defence (Roosevelt, 1991).

One of the most informative sites of the Marajoara culture is Teso dos Bichos. There, archaeologist Anna Roosevelt conducted a geophysical survey, finding twenty-nine anomalies that were revealed to be hearths upon testing. Roosevelt has interpreted these hearths, which are spatially arranged in the periphery of the mound and enclosing a central space, as the remains of multi-family, communal houses, *malocas*. Hearths are lined up along the centre of the structure, each hearth likely representing one nuclear family. Hearths are assemblages of semi-tubular structures of fired clay that typically occur in horizontal groups in an east to west direction. These features have been interpreted as stoves based on comparisons with ethnographic data from Indonesia and modern Marajó tenants (Roosevelt, 1991). Similar to Amazonian villages, the *malocas* were arranged in a concentric oval pattern from east to west. They were likely constructed with earth, wooden poles and thatch roofs. More work is needed to determine the precise form, size and orientation of the dwellings as Roosevelt recognizes (1991: 334–5). At the Camutin mound, evidence of superimposed layers of structures, with up to twenty structures built atop one another at some locations, suggest that they were constantly reoccupied (Figures 7.23 and 7.24).

Hierarchical settlement systems, public projects such as fishponds and other earthworks, craft specialization and differential burial treatments evidence Marajoara's social complexity. For example, in the Camutin locality, one or two huge mounds (8–12 metres tall) occur with a number of smaller ones, creating groupings that appear to define hierarchical settlement patterns. The abundance of ceremonial and funerary remains on the higher mounds has led Schaan (2012b) to believe that these are political and ceremonial centres to which the smaller mounds were subordinated. Elaborately decorated urns containing the remains of important individuals are buried in the floors of houses built on top of the mounds. After the flesh was removed from the bones of the deceased, their remains were placed in the urns and covered with a bowl or platter.

High-status mounds are closely associated with the headwater of the rivers and water-management facilities, suggesting that they played a key role in the access to prestige ceramics and water-management systems, which suggests monopolization of resources and surplus production by the elite. Roosevelt has estimated a population of up to 2,000 for a mound group.

Around 500 CE, at the onset of the Marajoara phase proper, the island population seems to increase, in terms of both the number and size of the settlements. Schann (2012b) has argued that approximately 1,600 years ago, independent societies known as 'simple chiefdoms' emerged and thrived in the island's central region. This is supported by significant evidence, including the regional clustering of mound sites, varying site sizes, intricate ceremonial pottery, ancestor worship, the differential treatment of the dead and the presence of long-distance trade items.

What did the Marajoara eat? Carbonized plant remains recovered by Roosevelt in Teso dos Bichos site were comprised mainly of palms, such as *açaí* (*Euterpe oleracea*) and *tucumã* (*Astrocaryum vulgare*), as well as tree fruits, including *ingá* (*Inga* sp.), *muruci*

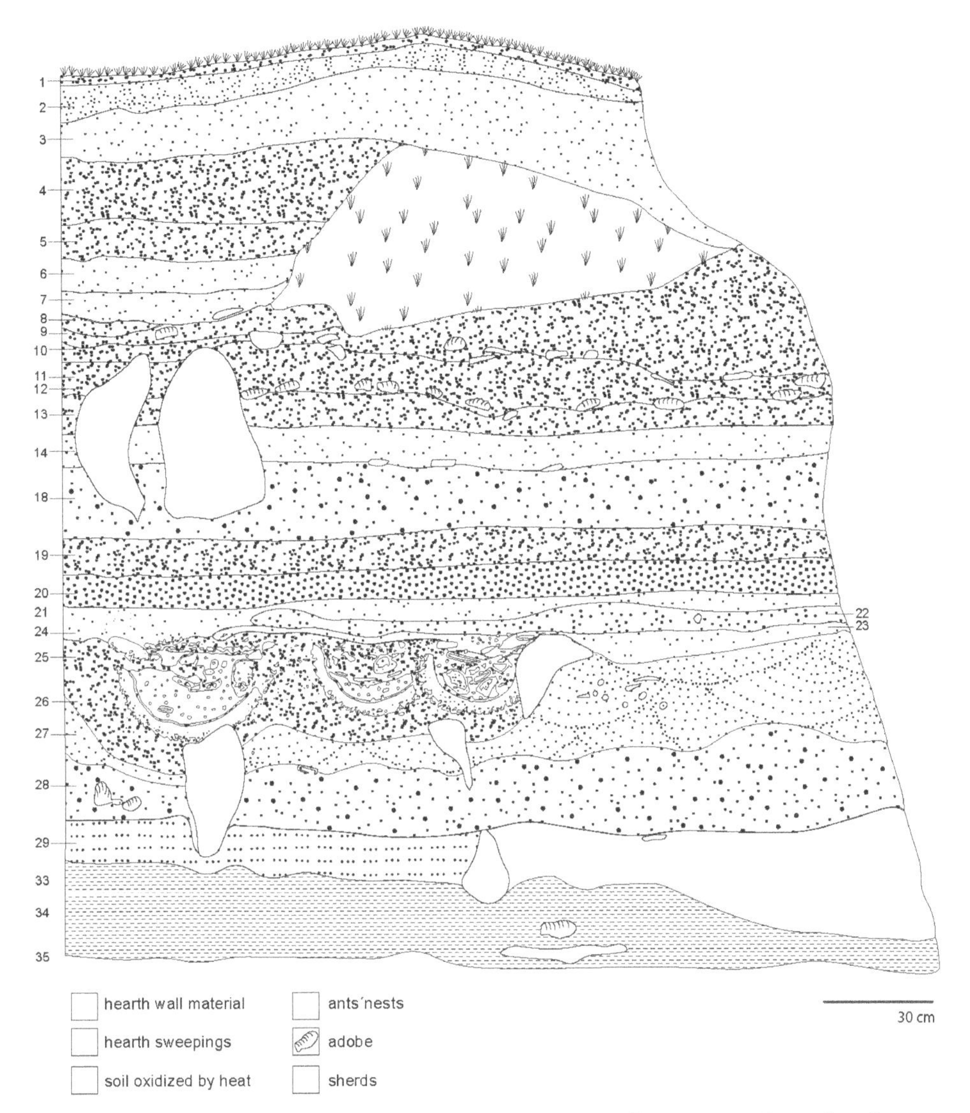

Figure 7.23 Sketch stratigraphic diagram of Excavation 1, Profile A at Tesos dos Bichos showing the complex construction history of Marajoara platform mounds including of prepared house floors, stoves made of clay plastered into troughs in the ground and burnt surfaces. Modified from Roosevelt (1991: Figure 5.4).

(*Byrsonima crassifola*) and taperebá (*Spondias lutea*) and are among the species identified (Roosevelt, 1991). Early historical accounts mention the consumption of wild rice, which would not be surprising since we now have evidence that rice was cultivated during the middle Holocene in SW Amazonia.

Large quantities of fish can be harvested in these savannahs, which are the natural nurseries for millions of fishes every year. Seasonally flooded savannahs encompass more

Figure 7.24 Excavations in progress at Mound M-17, Camutins Group, Marajó island. Courtesy Daiana Alves.

than 40 per cent of the island, and as Schaan (2012b) has argued, they seem to have been efficiently managed in the past to be the main staple of this sophisticated culture. Like in the Ring Ditch Region described above, the flooded savannahs are well-known for their abundance of aquatic resources. After the first rains of the rainy season, fish migrate to the rivers' headwaters in search of a safe area to spawn, away from predators. They spread out from there throughout the flooded savannahs, grazing on the riparian woodland and floating meadows. Seasonal and permanent lakes water levels recede during the dry season concentrating fish and making them more accessible to people. If handled appropriately, fish harvesting may be fruitful during the transition between the two seasons. No zigzag fish weirs, such as those in the Llanos de Mojos, have been found in Marajó. However, there is ample evidence for ponds. The soil used in constructing the artificial mounds was likely taken from borrow pits (locations where soil to build mounds was taken) located nearby (Roosevelt, 1991; Schaan, 2004). When floodwaters rise, they fill these ponds, and when they recede, a great many fish are left behind, providing an unrivalled source of protein during the dry season. Settlement patterns show that Marajoarans chose river headwaters, abundant in seasonally migrating fish, to establish their settlements.

It is not surprising that faunal remains mainly represent fishes. Faunal remains recovered from Teso dos Bichos excavated by Roosevelt (1991), show an almost complete absence of terrestrial fauna, but an abundance of fish. Large fish, such as the Osteoglossids *pirarucu* (*Arapaina gigas*) and *aruana* (*Osteoglossum bicirrhosum*), were recovered, while mammals and birds were rare. The majority of the assemblage recovered consisted of small aquatic fauna, including the small shells of *mussuã* turtles (*Kinosternon scorpioides*), teeth of *piranhas* (*Serrasalmus* sp.), bones of *traíra* (*Hoplias malabaricus*) and *tamoatá*, and an armored catfish (*Hoplosternum littorale*).

Bone isotope data by Colonese et al. (2020) shows that Marajó people relied primarily on freshwater fish/reptiles and/or terrestrial mammals for protein, although it is unclear how much of their diet came from each source. The model estimates suggest that terrestrial mammals and plants, rather than freshwater resources, provided the majority of calories. The researchers conclude that while fish may have been the primary source of protein, significant resources were also devoted to hunting, forest management and plant cultivation. Even though the C4 crop maize was not a staple food for Marajoara people, and maize macrobotanical remains are rare, it was likely consumed as part of the wide range of resources exploited by various agroforestry practices. Importantly, a few of the human bones analysed appear to contain a disproportionately high amount of C4 plants, most likely maize, which warrants further investigation. More work in this region will certainly clarify these patterns.

Maracá: Sitting with the ancestors

Although discovered in the late 1800s, this culture was not excavated until 100 years later. Despite some basic ceramic dating and occasional finds of these fascinating objects, they have only recently received the scientific attention they deserve, and their cultural and chronological context is only now beginning to be properly understood.

The Maracá sites are situated around 80 kilometres from the north bank of the Amazon River, within a 1-kilometre range of the Igarape' do Lago, a small tributary of the Amazon River. This area is known for its diverse and dynamic environment, featuring lakes, islands and wetlands. The most abundant vegetation in the region is wild rice (*Oryza* sp.) and *buruti* (*Mauritia flexuosa*) palms. The evergreen forest in the area grows on *terra firme*, which now hosts Brazil nut stands.

Habitation sites can be identified by open-air ADE sites with cultural stratigraphies that are no more than 0.6 metres deep. These sites are typically located 20–500 metres from the lake's edge, on higher, *terra firme* ground. Maracá sites range in length from 60–200 metres, are located parallel to the river and are spaced 2–6 kilometres apart. They are currently dated by a single radiocarbon date ranging from 1445–1645 CE. Domestic and utilitarian ceramics can be found at these sites (Guapindaia, 2001). Little is known about the subsistence economy of the Maracá people. No archaeobotany or faunal remains analysis has been carried out at the site, but bone collagen results obtained from the sixteen human burials from Maracá suggest a predominately C3-based diet substantially supported by animal protein (Hermenegildo et al., 2017).

The Maracá cemeteries are on higher ground in protected and hidden locations, such as caves or rock shelters. They contain groups of urns depicting imposing human figures,

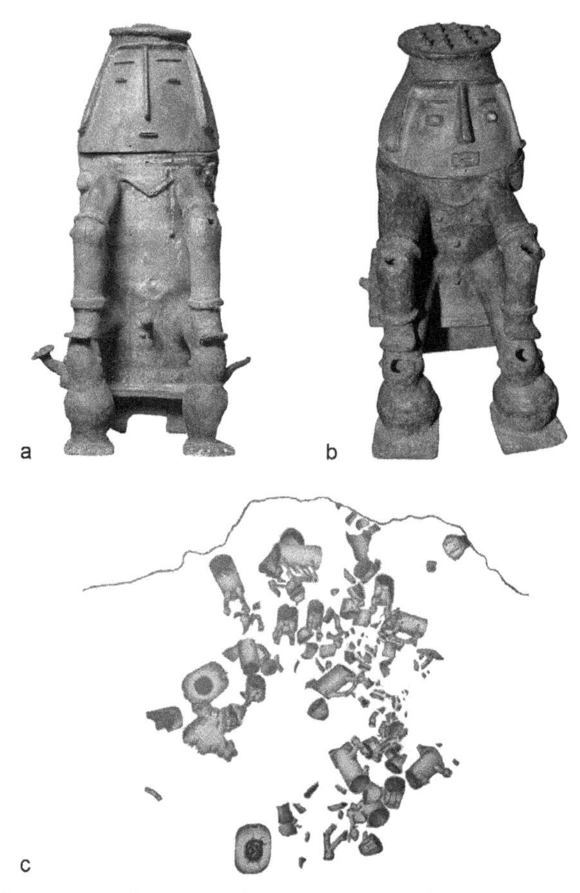

Figure 7.25 *a–b.* Maracá anthropomorphic urns. *c.* Floor plan of Gruta da Jaboti displaying the layout of anthropomorphic urns found on the cave's floor, which were likely part of elaborate mortuary practices. *a–b.* Museu Paranaense Emilio Goeldi, courtesy of Cristiana Barreto; *c.* modified from Guapindaia (2001: Figure 6.6).

men or women sitting on stools or small four-legged animals (Figure 7.25). Typical urns are 0.7 metres in height. Straight lines dominate the elaborate motifs in the polychrome paintings of the ceramic urns. The urn's lid is the head, with simple but elegant facial features that as Hemming (2009) puts it '. . . would have inspired sculptors from Matisse to Brancusi'. The sex of the deceased, many of whom were women, is clearly shown by stylized body parts. Seated figures have lengthy arms with hands on their knees, but their elbows are characteristically inverted. The urns were not buried but instead were left on the ground. Secondary urn burials reveal no evidence of cremation, but rather of bones recovered after the body has decomposed. According to Guapindaia (2001), close ties between the living and the dead were maintained, as evidenced by the proximity of cemeteries to habitation sites and the placement of urns on the ground surface for maximum visibility.

Amazonian stonehenges: The megaliths of Amapá

From 1100–1800 CE, the coastal forests of Amapá saw the emergence of ceremonial/burial megalithic sites featuring burial pits and associated with the Polychrome Tradition. The region has a long history of sporadic archaeological investigations mainly focused on the creation of ceramic chronologies (see summary in Cabral and Saldanha, 2008). It is only recently that Cabral and Saldanha (2008) have conducted a systematic regional survey, with extensive excavations at these sites producing a wide range of contextual information. As is the case of many other largely unexplored regions of the Amazon, this renewed research is revealing a much more complex picture than was previously thought.

The megaliths are located in a strip of land within the dynamic northern sector of the state of Amapá, Brazil, between the coastal forests, the seasonally flooded savannahs and *terra firme* evergreen forest. The large majority of these sites are located on natural knolls, representing islands within the seasonally flooded savannahs, which overlook *igapó* streams with fluvial forests (Figure 7.26).

Currently, forty-one megalithic sites have been documented. The sizes and compositions of megalithic structures differ. Some are small, less than 10 metres in diameter, and made up of blocks less than a metre in size. Others are large, reaching up to 30 metres in diameter and made up of blocks that can be as tall as 3 metres. The stones can be flat, vertical or slanted, and the number of stones can range from less than 10 to more than 100. Most megalithic enclosures are not perfectly circular, but are rather irregular and often oblong, as if built in stages to increase their size.

The megaliths contain funerary pits, some in the form of funerary chambers, excavated in the laterite crust. It is not unusual to find them below horizontally-placed stone slabs. Their interior contains ceramic vessels, often anthropomorphic, containing human bones, sometimes more than one individual. Besides funerary urns, other ceramic vessels – whole or fragmented – are also found inside or on the burial pits, as well as granite blocks of various sizes. Some pits are composed of a few vessels, while others may have more than 100 (Cabral, 2020). Some funerary pits correspond to a single event of deposition, while others were reused over time with the removal of the original deposition and deposition of new assemblages, which was observed in another burial pit from the same site studied here (Cabral, 2020).

The best-studied megalith so far, is Calçoene (dubbed by the BBC as the Brazilian Stonehenge), constituted by a 30-metre diameter circular structure composed of hundreds of granite blocks, some standing 3 metres high, which enclose chambered tombs containing polychromic funerary urns with zoomorphic and anthropomorphic appendages (Figure 7.27c–d) (Cabral and Saldanha, 2009). A set of radiocarbon dates places the start of construction of this site around the eleventh century CE, with a duration that may reach the eighteenth century CE (Saldanha et al., 2016).

Excavation at the site shows that this structure was used for multiple functions, including a variety of funerary practices. Four funerary pits were excavated at the site. The excavation of two funerary pits underneath horizontally placed stone slabs within the circle structure is particularly revealing. One of them, funerary pit 1, contains a side chamber, oriented north-east, containing three intact vessels that seem to be related to

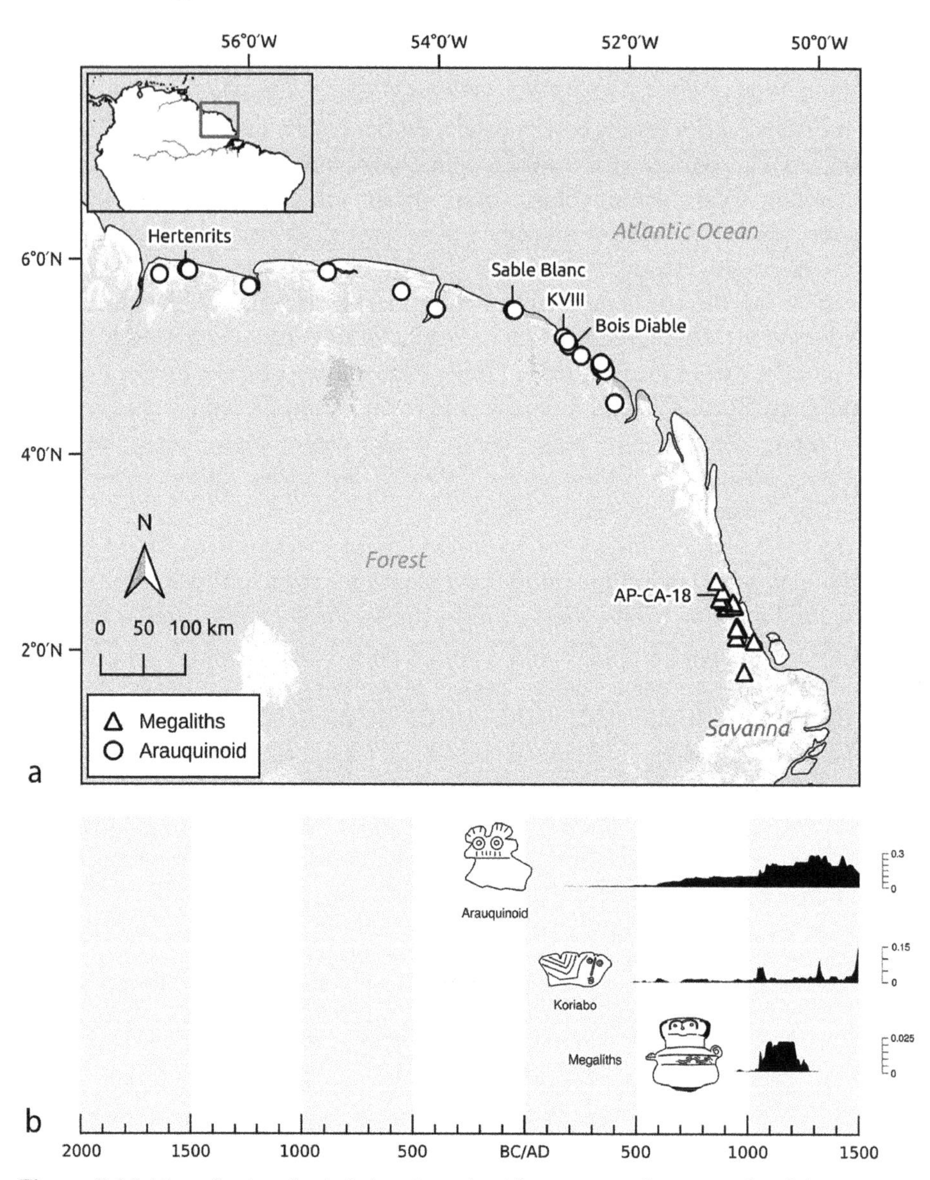

Figure 7.26 Map of archaeological sites along the Atlantic coast of NW Brazil and the Guianas.

the reuse of the funerary shaft (Figure 7.27b). In contrast, funerary pit 2 of 1.5 metres in diameter does not exhibit a chamber and contains eleven intact vessels.

The Aristide tradition includes anthropomorphic urns that feature various decorative elements, such as crescent shapes, intertwined spirals, *grecas*, semi-circles and volutes (Figure 7.27a). They include ornaments representing the human body, including faces, hair dresses, facial painting, pierced earlobes and headbands. Some exhibit some sort of mosaic decoration that resembles a fabric made from materials, such as woven bark, reed or other fibres (Bel, 2009).

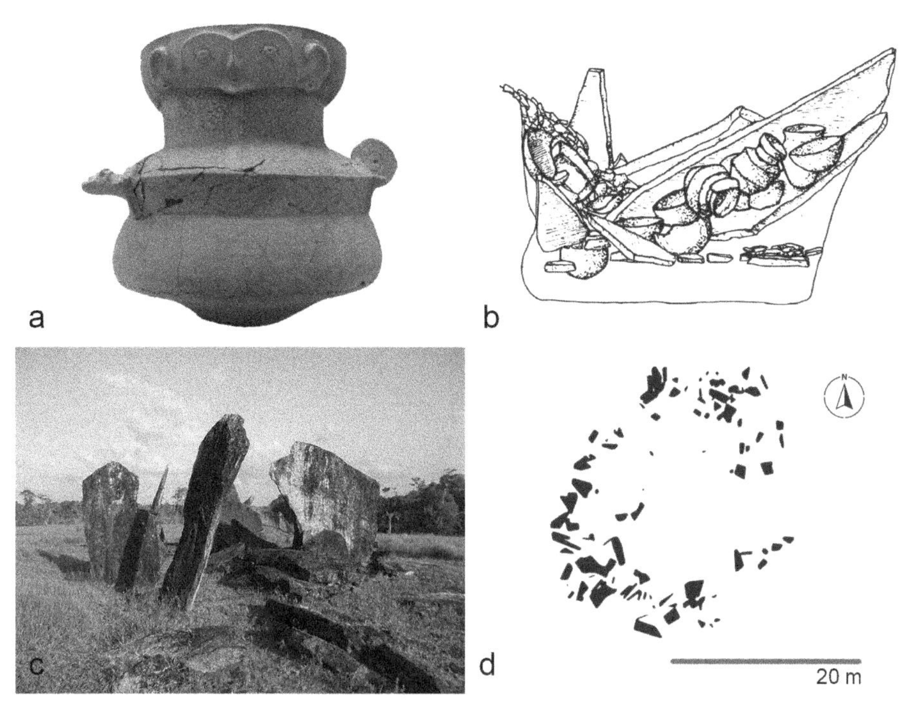

Figure 7.27 Calçoene megalith. *a.* Anthropomorphic urn from Pit 3, which was deposited with its face turned to the pit's wall. Observe the *appliqué* of an animal that crosses the main body of the funerary urn. The checkerboard pattern is typical of Aristé urns. *b.* Schematic profile drawing of Pit 4. *c.* Photo of standing stones at the site. *d.* Plan of stone structures. *a* and *b.* courtesy of João Saldanha; *d.* modified from Saldanha and Petry Cabral (2008: Figure 2).

The existence of a wide variety of ceramic deposits with a ritual appearance suggests that the megalith served multiple purposes beyond being a cemetery. For example, entire vessels as well as *in situ* broken vessels around the monoliths are a common occurrence. Excavators discovered pits, dug for erecting the stone blocks, in which small blocks of granite and laterite were used to wedge the monoliths to align them with the sun's path during the winter solstice. During the evening of the solstice, the trajectory of the sun would follow the inclination of the monolith. This could be related to ceremonial and astronomical functions, marking agricultural or foraging cycles.

There are other sites in the region related to the megaliths. Caves or rock shelters, formed in the laterite crust or granite outcrops, are another type of ceremonial/funeral site associated with Aristé pottery further inland from the coast. At these sites, ceramics are found on the surface of the sheltered areas in these cases (Saldanha et al., 2016).

Village sites associated with megalithic structures are small, measuring no more than 1 hectare. They are located along the coast, mangroves, savannahs and upland forests. Open-area excavations at three of these village sites reveal shallow archaeological deposits, a few ceramic artefacts and simple archaeological features, such as post holes and clay-moulded floors. Saldanha et al. (2016) argue that they represent short-term occupation sites, occupied seasonally in order to have a complementary subsistence activity, such as collecting palm tree fruits. The savannahs have large stands of palm (such as *açai and moriche*), along with abundant aquatic resources.

What happened to these cultures? Indigenous populations declined, the land was depopulated and earthworks ceased to be constructed because of the introduction of Old World illnesses, enslavement and battles between Spain and Portugal over this territory.

Arauquinoid raised-field farmers of the Guianas coast

The Guianas are geographically and culturally distinct regions of Amazonia, which bounded to the north by the Orinoco, to the east by the Atlantic, and to the west by the Rio Negro and the Casiquiare Canal (Figure 7.26). The Atlantic coast is a plain that spans 1,600 kilometres from the mouth of the Amazon River to the Orinoco Delta and is made up of Quaternary sediments. In the area from Suriname to French Guyana, there is a strip stretching for about 600 kilometres where the Arauquinoid tradition terraformed entire landscapes in these coastal savannahs starting at around 700 CE (Rostain, 2012b). Settlements of the Arauquinoid tradition can be found on top of sandy ridges that run parallel along the coast, which are the natural elevations of the landscape. At the peak of the Arauquinoid occupation, the coast was divided into territories centred around large platform mounds with ceremonial and domestic functions. Residential mounds were surrounded by a network of roads and raised-field agricultural landscapes that extended for up to 5 kilometres, with an estimated population of more than 1,000 inhabitants, such as the Hertitis site (Boomert, 1976; Versteeg, 2003). In some regions, such as the Hertenrits mound, they built large habitation mounds surrounded by causeways and raised-fields. The Arauquinoid pottery is characterized by ceramic bowls, jars and griddles exhibiting diagnostic decoration, including zoomorphic and anthropomorphic adornos decorated with thin incision punctuation. Arauquinod sites also display the iconic polished muiraquitãs described for the Tapajos above.

Pre-Columbian agricultural landscapes along the Guianan coast are characterized by raised fields, canals and ponds, which spread more than *c.* 600 kilometres, from the Berbice River in Guyana to near Cayenne. This region shows considerable diversity of raised-field types (see description in Chapter 6, Figure 10.5). As we will describe in more detail in Chapter 10, phytolith, starch grain and stable isotope evidence documents the cultivation of maize, squash and manioc (Iriarte et al., 2010; McKey et al., 2010b). Charcoal records suggest that fire was used to a limited extent in land management before the arrival of Europeans to the region (Iriarte et al., 2012).

The disruption of the Arauquinoid regional organization began in ~1300 CE, a period of upheaval marked by the spread of the Koriabo tradition. The earliest Koriabo sites are inland, with a progressive expansion toward the coast. Synchronicity between the Arauquinoid demise and the Koriabo expansion is clear across the Guianas Coast, especially along its western extent, where Arauquinoid earthwork density and complexity

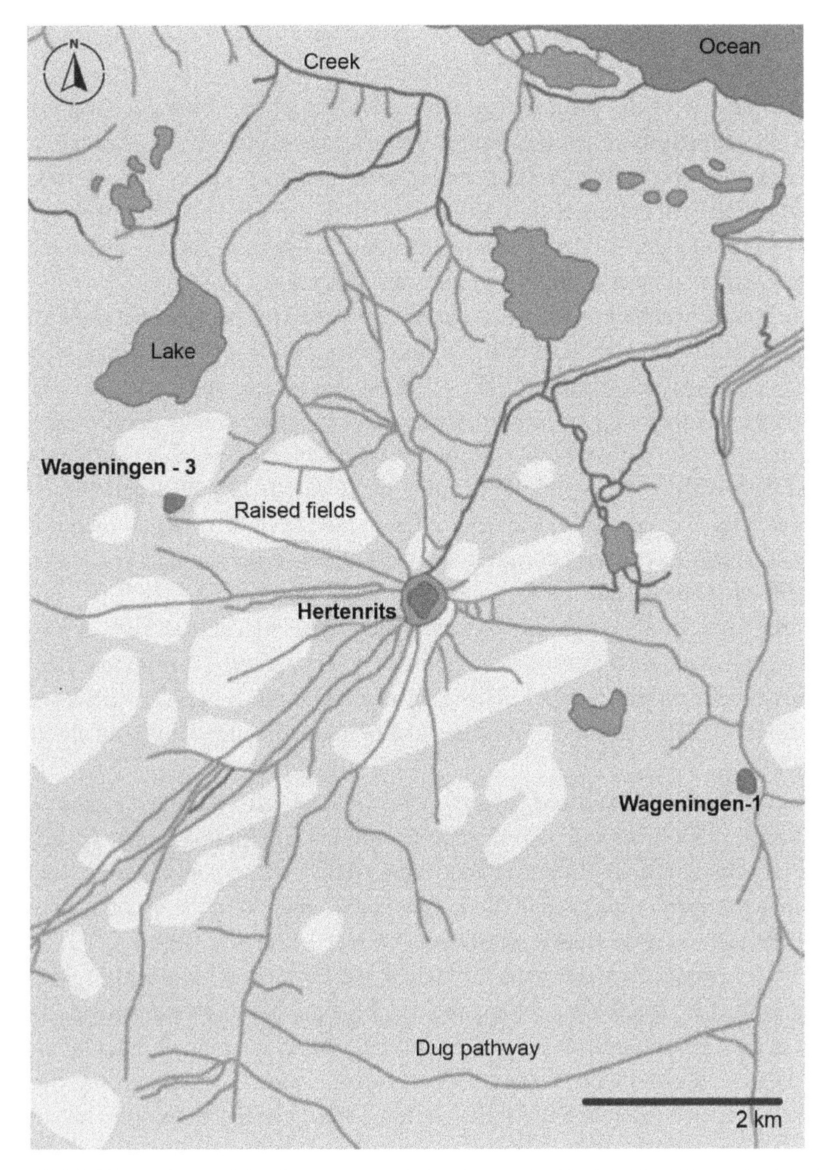

Figure 7.28 The engineered landscape around the Hertenrits site. Modified from Rostain (2012: Figure 54).

had been highest. In the eastern sector, there is continuity, interaction and emergence of hybrid traditions. The decline of mound centres at ~1300 CE could have been instigated by the prolonged droughts documented in the palaeoclimate records (De Souza et al., 2019). Alternatively, pressure from the Koriabo expansion itself could have been responsible for conflicts leading to the Arauquinoid demise, or could have accelerated a process already triggered by climate change.

Concluding remarks

This brief review of the complex late Holocene cultures of Amazonia shows that this period is characterized by population growth, an explosion of regional cultures expressing socio-political complexity and terraforming projects on a previously unseen scale. The variety of cultures that developed in the Late Holocene is a prime example of how we can no longer speak of a single Amazonia but how we must begin to subdivide it into cultural regions with their own historical trajectory.

Significant investment in *landesque* capital, as seen in the complex networks of roads, agricultural anthrosols and raised fields, and waterscapes, such as the landscape-scale fish weirs, took place at this time. When we assess these major infrastructure projects, we must remember that, in contrast to the peoples of the Andes and Central America, the Amazonian peoples did not build with stones, lacking in many regions of Amazonia, but instead built with earth, as did the peoples of the Rio de la Plata Basin (Iriarte et al., 2004), and the Venezuelan Llanos (Spencer and Redmond, 1998) to mention a few examples. This does not detract from the huge amount of work and feats of engineering that went into these terraforming projects.

As reviewed in this and the previous chapter, these cultures have a variety of land uses and depend on domesticated plants to different degrees. Integrated archaeology and palaeoecology show that polyculture agroforestry systems became a dominant form of land use on ADE sites, such as in the Tapajos and ring-ditch villages of the Bolivian Amazon.

During the late Holocene, Amazonian people also became master potters, manufacturing sophisticated ceramics rich in symbols. Another significant advancement is that beyond continuing to define and refine relative chronologies, archaeologists are using material culture studies and theories of embodiment to understand and provide a more nuanced and contextual interpretation of the ceramic assemblages.

Lidar is helping us reveal both individual site layouts and regional organizations. Entire systems of roads are now apparent in regions, such as Baures in the Bolivian Amazon, the circular mound villages of Acre, the Xinguano region of Brazil, as well as in the Upano in the montane forests of Ecuador (Chapter 8). With certain variability, cardinal orientation of roads and radial patterns appear to be common in the southern rim of the Amazon. At a regional level, some sites, such as the circular mound villages or the Maracá ADE sites, are spread along major waterways in regular intervals of 2–5 kilometres apart. Some show hierarchical settlement patterns, such as the Marajoara, while others, such as the Tapajos, have been proposed to be heterarchical. More research is needed to advance on these interpretations.

During this period, Amazonia also witnessed the emergence and dissemination of major ceramic traditions, each displaying significant regional variations and reaching out of Amazonia. These include the Amazonian Barrancoid or Incised Rim Tradition, dating back to BCE 500 and lasting until 900 CE, the Incised Punctuated Tradition, and the APT, which became widespread by 1000–1250 CE (Figure 7.1) (e.g., Gregorio de Souza et al., 2020; Neves, 2013).

Current research shows that the SW Amazonia and the southern rim of the Amazon were densely populated, and mounting evidence shows that we should expect a similar scenario in the largely archaeologically unexplored Western Amazon where work along the Ucayali, Upano and middle Caquetá rivers is revealing densely populated areas, some of them reaching urban-scale proportions.

In the next chapter, we turn to the late Holocene societies that reached urban-scale proportions urban-scale proportions, compelling us to reconsider the nature of complex Amazonian societies.

CHAPTER 8
GREEN CITIES: TROPICAL URBANISM IN AMAZONIA

Processes of social aggregation and the emergence of urban societies have, for a long time, been fundamental topics in archaeology and other human sciences (e.g., Cowgill, 2004; Smith, 2014). New methodological and conceptual advances are leading to a rethinking of the nature of pre-industrial societies, with multiple pathways to aggregation and urbanization being revealed. The implications of urbanization for social dynamics and resilience are being reassessed (see summary in Roberts, 2019). Early societies across the globe and in a diversity of environments, including the city of Anuradhapura, Sri Lanka (Coningham et al., 2007), the cities of the middle Niger River in Africa (McIntosh and McIntosh, 2005), and examples in temperate regions, such as Cahokia in SE North America (Pauketat, 2007) and the Oppidas in Eastern Europe (Fernández-Götz and Ralston, 2017; Moore, 2017), are being re-evaluated and reclassified as urban, thus calling into question traditional socio-evolutionary paradigms (Moore, 2017). This is particularly true for tropical regions, where it has been shown that traditional Eurasian models of urbanism fail to capture the diversity of early urban settlement networks. In contrast to the compact, bounded and densely populated settlements of Eurasian desert oasis civilizations, commonly seen as a dense grid of masonry and rarely exceeding an area of 100 kilometres^2, tropical urbanism is extensive. It is characterized by dispersed settlement and the incorporation of large amounts of open space and water management networks, in what have been termed 'agrarian low-density cities' (Arensberg, 1980; Fletcher, 2011; Graham, 1999).

Significantly, the development of these early urban tropical societies, in regions with seasonal flooding and a pronounced dry season, led in many cases to a growing reliance on increasingly elaborate, complex and intricately linked systems to manage the flow of water. In this way, intensive agricultural and aquacultural landscapes were created (Canuto et al., 2018; Erickson, 2000; Fletcher, 2011; McKey et al., 2016). These highly productive water management systems permitted population growth, and influenced the distribution of communities in the landscape, as well as the development and maintenance of political power. However, the functioning of these hydraulic systems, in landscapes with striking seasonal contrasts, was highly susceptible to external factors, such as climate change. Such factors would have posed challenges to the very survival of the socio-political systems these systems sustained (e.g., Lucero et al., 2015).

In this chapter, I will present three case studies from Amazonia that add to our growing knowledge of low-density agricultural urbanism: Casarabe, Upano and Xinguano. I will argue that these societies represent a *tour de force* in the conceptualization of Amazonian cultures. Examining ancient green low density in Amazonia provides valuable insights for developing sustainable cities in tropical regions. Any lessons we can learn from the past are especially important, as almost half of the world's population will live in the tropics, mega-urbanization is a common feature of the tropical global south and urban areas worldwide are moving towards low-density models (Penny et al., 2020).

The Casarabe culture

Fresh lidar data from the German-Bolivian-UK team (Prümers et al., 2022), from the SE sector of the Llanos de Mojos, home of the Casarabe culture, has rekindled discussion about urban societies in Amazonia. As seen in the previous chapter, research in the past three decades has begun to reveal the complexity of Amazonian societies. But apart from the 'Garden Cities' of the Upper Xingu (Heckenberger et al., 2008), Amazonia has, until very recently, remained an outsider in discussions of early urbanism. However, most scholars in the human and natural sciences now agree that some areas of pre-Columbian Amazonia show evidence of complex, hierarchical and regionally integrated societies.

During the late Holocene, at the same time as the Byzantine Empire was starting to flourish, a number of groups in the Llanos de Mojos, in the Bolivian Amazon, were living in dispersed urban communities and transforming one of the most extensive Amazonian seasonally flooded savannahs – an area roughly the size of England – into productive agricultural and aquacultural landscapes. The transformation was accompanied by the growth of diverse socio-political organization, economic bases and systems of water control, and the construction of some of the largest monuments in Amazonia. During historic times, the region was an ethnic enclave of various languages, and the diversity of archaeological cultures documented recently shows that these languages likely have deeper time roots.

Mojos is an exceptional landscape in Amazonia. The low and flat relief of the Llanos de Mojos basin, combined with thick, hard-packed Quaternary clays, gives rise to seasonally inundated grassland savannahs, while forest grows on fluvial levees (Figure 8.1). These vast plains are limited by the Andean piedmont to the south-west and the Brazilian Shield to the east and northeast. Four major rivers, all tributaries of the Madeira River, drain the Llanos de Mojos. The Mamoré cuts through the centre, with the Madre de Dios and Beni Rivers to the west, and the Guaporé-Itenéz River to the east. This is a region where seasonality takes a pronounced and dramatic form, with more than half the territory submerged beneath a thin sheet of water during the passage of the South American summer monsoon. Today's annual precipitation ranges from 2,000 millimetres (north) to 1,200 millimetres (south), with two marked seasons: the rainy season from October–April, when precipitation can reach 500 millimetres/month, and the dry season lasting approximately five months from May–September, with monthly precipitation <50 millimetres/month.

The savannahs are dotted with forest islands, which, as described in Chapter 3, are largely human-made and date to the earliest arrival of humans to the region (Lombardo et al., 2020). The area also exhibits hundreds of perennial lakes, known as 'savannah lakes', noted for their rectangular shape and markedly uniform SW–NE orientation.

Figure 8.1 Down under the marshes. Aerial photo of the Llanos de Mojos showing gallery forests, savannahs and oriented lakes. Courtesy Umberto Lombardo.

Although the lakes vary considerably in size, they are characterized by having a flat bottom and being very shallow, usually less than 2 metres deep. The genesis of these lakes has been a matter of controversy. Recent research suggests that the lakes were shaped and oriented by a combination of processes, including neotectonics, sediment compaction and water ponding, followed by wind/wave action (Lombardo and Veit, 2014).

The Llanos de Mojos is home to a diversity of archaeological cultures (see Walker, 2020b). Within them, the Casarabe Tradition region is unique. Located in the SE sector, its mounded architecture and hydraulic works extend more than ~4,500 kilometres^2 (Figure 8.2, Figure 7.1). The region is covered by savannahs closely interwoven with forested levees of paleo-rivers, and lies on top of a middle Holocene sedimentary lobe, formed by the paleo-Rio Grande River. The topography is convex and the soils are relatively well-drained. The lobe makes the region relatively high, allowing it to experience less flooding during the rainy season. Originating in the Andes, the Rio Grande River brings base-rich, fertile soils that give the region an exceptionally good agricultural potential (Lombardo et al., 2013a). The influence of the Chaco region on the southern border results in lower rainfall: for two to four months of the year, rainfall is less than 50 millimetres, while at times there is no rainfall at all for a month – no wonder most sites have water reservoirs. Agricultural raised fields, ubiquitous elsewhere in the Llanos de Mojos, are absent in the region of the Casarabe Tradition.

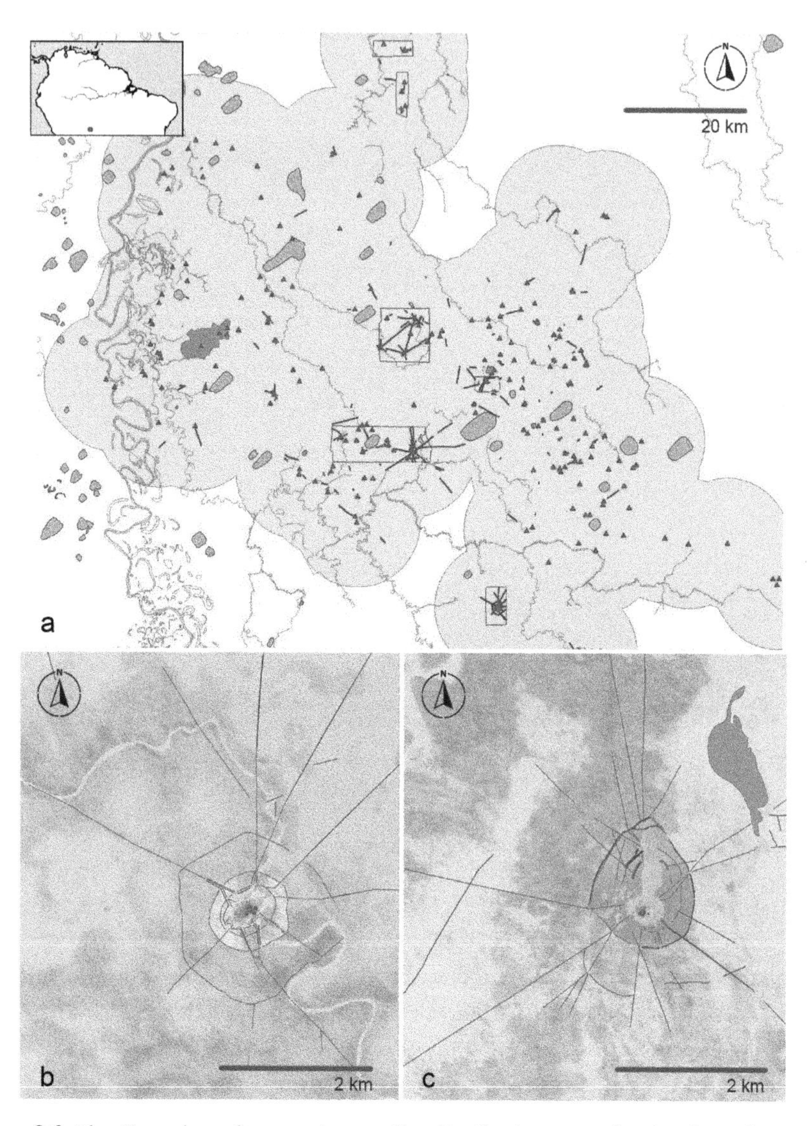

Figure 8.2 The Casarabe culture region. *a.* Site distribution map showing how these civic-ceremonial centres were integrated into a low-density urban landscape across a region of 4,500 kilometres^2. *b.* Detail of Loma Landivar with radiating causeways, polygonal enclosures and meander of palaeochannel passing through site. *c.* Similar detail of Loma Cotoca.

From the earliest excavations of Erland Nordenskiöld (1913) at the start of the twentieth century, the Casarabe Tradition has been the subject of occasional archaeological investigation by several national and international projects. Geographer William Denevan (1966; 2001) provided the first bird's-eye view approximation, revealing the sheer size and elaboration of terraforming in the region, while an Argentinian-Bolivian team constructed

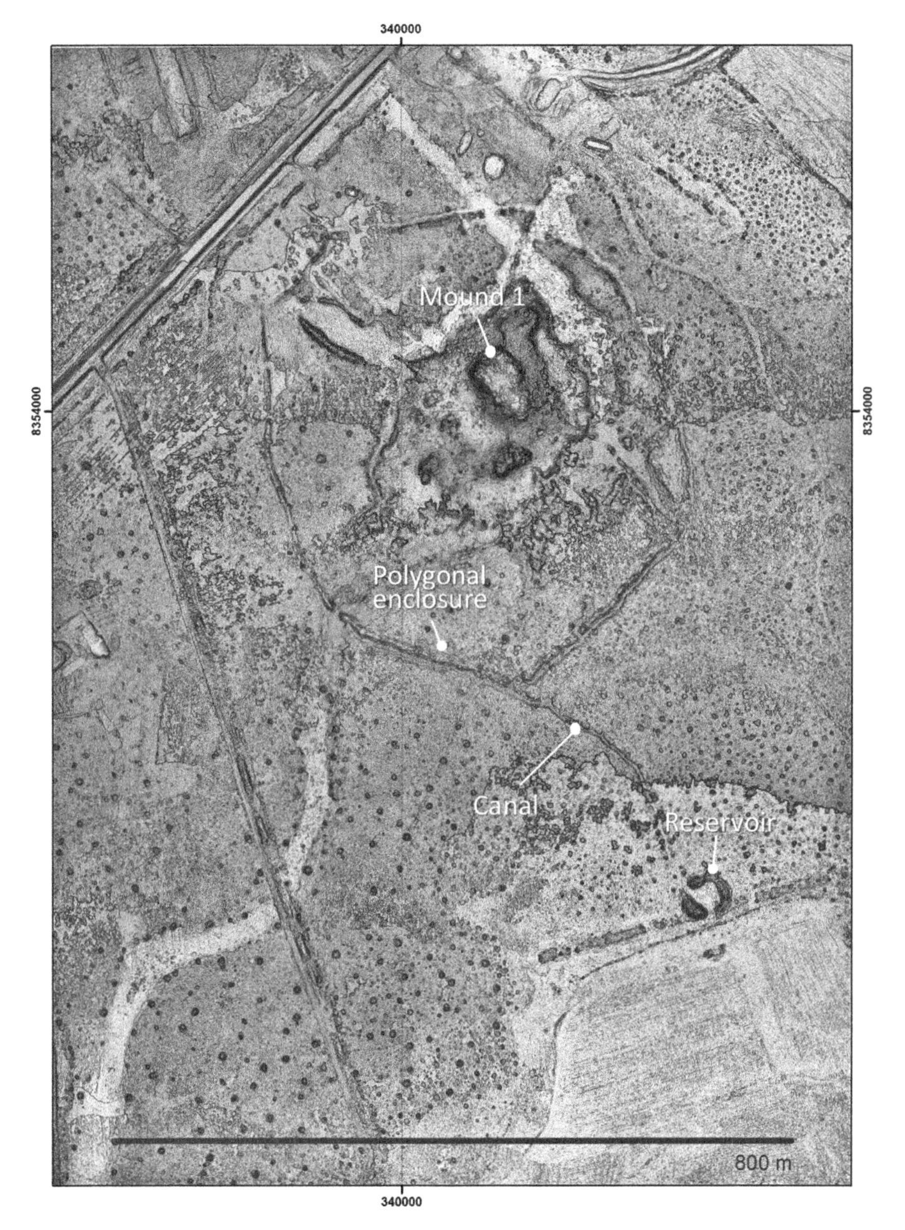

Figure 8.3 Lidar map of Loma Salvatierra showing palaeochannel passing through the site, U-shaped mound, polygonal enclosure and system of canals leading to reservoirs. *Mojos prehispánico en 3D* project.

the first regional chronology (Dougherty and Calandra, 1984). However, it is only during the past two decades that a German-Bolivian team, led by Heiko Prümers and Carla Jaimes Betancourt, have carried out large-scale excavations and material culture studies. They have investigated burial patterns, determined the economic basis and constructed precise chronologies for this region (Prümers and Jaimes Betancourt, 2014). Their large-scale excavations focused on two monumental sites (locally called 'lomas'), Salvatierra and Mendoza, and revealed that the construction and use of such sites can be dated to between ~500 and 1400 CE.

Subtle variations in the morphological and decorative attributes of the ceramics recovered from Loma Salvatierra allowed Jaimes Betancourt (2010) to distinguish five occupation phases for the Casarabe Tradition (Figure 8.4). Each phase is differentiated by changes in the shapes of the vessels, as well as in the motifs and decoration techniques. Prümers (2017) argues that the vessels belong to a single tradition, in which characteristic elements have survived, thus demonstrating the existence of a 'Casarabe culture'. As we will see below, within certain limits of variability, the known cultural uniformity of the Casarabe ceramic tradition is also apparent in the replication of monumental architecture across the region.

The excavations exposed deep and extensive refuse middens, indicating that these monumental sites were not vacant ceremonial centres but were inhabited throughout the year (Prümers, 2009; Prümers, 2015). Mounds show a complex stratigraphy. Taking advantage of the exposed profile from a road cut, Prümers (2015) showed that these massive mounds grew through slow accretion processes, with mass additions of construction fill. He was also able to demonstrate how sections of the mound were built and abandoned over time as the settlement shifted horizontally, with thick layers of construction fill added at various times to raise and level the living surface. Similarly, the domestic refuse that accumulated on the flanks of the platforms, and on other parts of the mound, contributed to the mounds' growth.

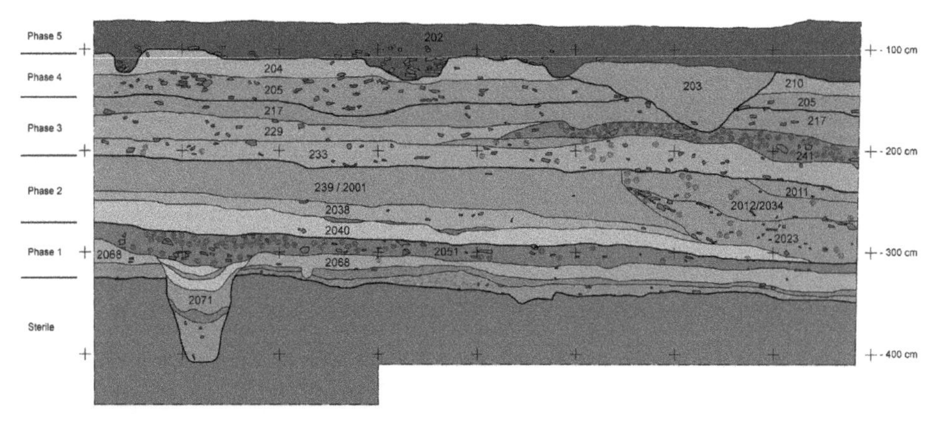

Figure 8.4 Detail of Loma Salvatierra stratigraphy showing the five phases of occupation at the site. Courtesy Heiko Prümers.

Figure 8.5 Excavations on the central plaza mounds of Loma Salvatierra. Courtesy of Heiko Prümers.

Independent lines of evidence indicate that the Casarabe people had a food production economy. Macro and microscopic plant remains (Dickau et al., 2012), as well as carbon and nitrogen isotopes on eighty-six human skeletons dug from Loma Salvatierra (Prümers and Jaimes Betancourt, 2014), show the Casarabe people were agriculturalists who cultivated a diversity of crops, including manioc (*Manihot esculenta*), yam (*Dioscorea* spp.), squash (*Cucurbita* spp.), peanut (*Arachis hypogaea*), cotton (*Gossypium* sp.) and palm fruits (Arecaceae), with maize (*Zea mays*) as the primary staple. Pollen recovered from coring in Laguna San José indicates that maize was cultivated in the savannahs. The pollen record also shows that during the Casarabe times there were no major shifts in forest abundance or composition, indicating that there was no major deforestation of the gallery forest found in higher areas of the landscape (Whitney et al., 2013). The high frequency of charcoal particles from this record shows that people were periodically burning the savannahs at this time, presumably to clean the land of pests and prepare it for the next cycle of cultivation, as well as to avoid an accumulation of dry vegetation that could encourage catastrophic fires at the end of the dry season – a common practice of indigenous groups who inhabit Amazonian savannahs (e.g., Mistry et al., 2005).

Faunal analysis shows that various terrestrial and aquatic resources were consumed year-round. Deer species (*Mazama* spp.), otter (*Myocastor coypu*), crab-eating fox (*Cerdocyon thous*), six-banded armadillo (*Euphractus sexcinctus*) and Muscovy duck

(*Cairina moschata*), along with lizards and caimans, were among the most common vertebrate taxa recovered at the site (von den Driesch and Hutterer, 2011). Interestingly, the Loma Salvatiera analysis shows that ducks were likely domesticated, while the high number of duck bones found with pathologies is striking. These pathologies include a bulbous exostosis at the proximal end of the carpometacarpus, which typically develops when the flight feathers of birds are pulled out to prevent them from flying. Anomalies were also recorded in the tarsometatarsal of ducks, with one possible explanation being that the birds were tied by the feet, with a string passing through the interdigital membrane between the toes, which caused irritation of metatarsals over time (von den Driesch and Hutterer, 2011). Finally and more telling, carbon and nitrogen isotopes from duck bones indicate that they were fed maize. This evidence corroborates missionary reports from this region (Eder, [1772] 1985), which mention the ubiquitous presence of domesticated duck in indigenous villages as a staple food combined with maize. Ducks certainly were a source of food, but Angulo (1998) has also raised the possibility that ducks were brought under domestication primarily for pest control in cultivated fields, as they were in the rice paddies of Asia.

Fish also played a significant role in the diet of the Casarabe people. At Loma Salvatierra, thirty-five fish genera were identified, in which four taxa were dominant: swamp-eels (*Synbranchus* spp.), armoured catfishes (*Hoplosternum* spp.), lungfish (*Lepidosiren paradoxa*) and tiger-fish (*Hoplias malabaricus*). These fishes are typical of shallow and lentic waters, suggesting that these seasonal environments were the most probable fishing spots exploited. Most of these species are quite tolerant of aquatic environments with low oxygen conditions and are often found in modern artificial ponds in the region. This has prompted Prestes-Carneiro et al. (2019; 2021) to hypothesize that one of the functions of artificial ponds in the region was to breed and store fish, in particular eels. Gastropods of the genus *Pomaceae*, locally called 'turos', which thrived during the rainy season, were also recovered in large numbers at Loma Salvatierra.

Funerary evidence points to a stratified society, with lavish burial goods reserved for a few individuals. A total of 103 burials corresponding to all phases of occupation of the Casarabe Tradition were excavated in Loma Salvatierra. Their analysis shows that most of the tombs lack burial goods, and that adults were always buried in shallow graves, with new-borns and infants usually placed in urns characterized by large globular vessels sealed with a cover plate. The position of the body was varied (decubitus dorsal, decubitus ventral, sideways, in the foetal position, seated or kneeling). However, the burials exhibit a recurrent orientation of the body at 300^0 W, with the head towards the NW and feet to the SE, which coincides with the orientation of the platforms (Prümers et al., 2022). Undoubtedly, this orientation must have had a core symbolic reference. Some of the burials received special treatment, which most likely reflects the individuals' elevated status within a stratified society. The most notable is the burial of a man between thirty-five and forty years of age, found 3 metres deep in the centre of Mound 2 at Loma Salvatierra, which was presumably built to commemorate this important person (Figure 8.6) (Prümers, 2009).

Ceramics also appear to point to the social differentiation of the Casarabe people. Potsherds recovered on top of the largest mound, Mound 1, are richly decorated

Figure 8.6 The Lord of Casarabe. Male burial in the central sector of Mound 2 at Loma Salvatierra shows personal adornments with which the individual was dressed: *a.* plate of copper, *b.* earpieces with pearls of sodalite (likely originating from Cochabamba) and armadillo shell, *c.* a collar of jaguar teeth, *d.* shell beads and *e.* bracelet of shell. Photos courtesy Heiko Prümers.

compared to those from the rest of the site. They possibly indicate the area where the elite lived, or that the area was used for special activities, such as communal feasts or rituals (Jaimes Betancourt, 2010).

When taken as a whole, all the evidence points to the conclusion that these artificial mounds were places of habitation, rather than ceremonial centres where gatherings took place sporadically for celebrations or cultural activities. Burials documented from every level of every excavation unit demonstrate that death was a part of the mound dwellers' 'daily life'.

At a regional level, it has long been suggested that these large sites were part of a well-planned complex that included civic-ceremonial architecture, polygonal enclosures, causeways, canals and reservoirs (Prümers et al., 2022). Remote sensing data hints that these monumental sites were centres of a broader, hierarchical political unit, constituting important nodes in the network of canals and causeways (Lombardo and Prümers, 2010). The new lidar capture for the region has not been disappointing and has allowed Prümers

(2022) to define a four-tiered hierarchy of sites, based on the dimensions of the different sites and the elaboration of their civic-ceremonial architecture. The occurrence of large-scale features, such as pyramids and U-shaped structures, which presumably had a public, municipal or religious function, has also been considered, along with the number of polygonal enclosures encircling the sites and the causeways radiating from them.

Primary centres, known as large settlements, have the largest base platforms (Cotoca) (Figure 8.7). They also possess a diversity of monumental architecture, including U-shaped platforms with conical pyramidal structures, and two to three ranked concentric polygonal enclosures surrounding areas up to 314 hectares. They have a minimum of seven radiating straight causeways that appear to show similar orientations. La Cotoca is a prime example of a 'large settlement', or ritual-administrative centre (Figure 8.7). Its core area is a base platform of irregular shape, covering about 22.5 hectares, approximately the size of thirty football fields, and standing 4 metres high above the immediate surrounding ground. On top of the base platform civic-ceremonial U-shaped structures and smaller platform mounds were identified, as well as a 21-metre tall conical pyramid. The U-shaped structures are oriented to the SW, as is the case at most of the sites in the region, and in burials. Beyond the core area, the SW sector of the site contains a series of smaller platforms with U-shaped structures and other architecture. Three polygonal

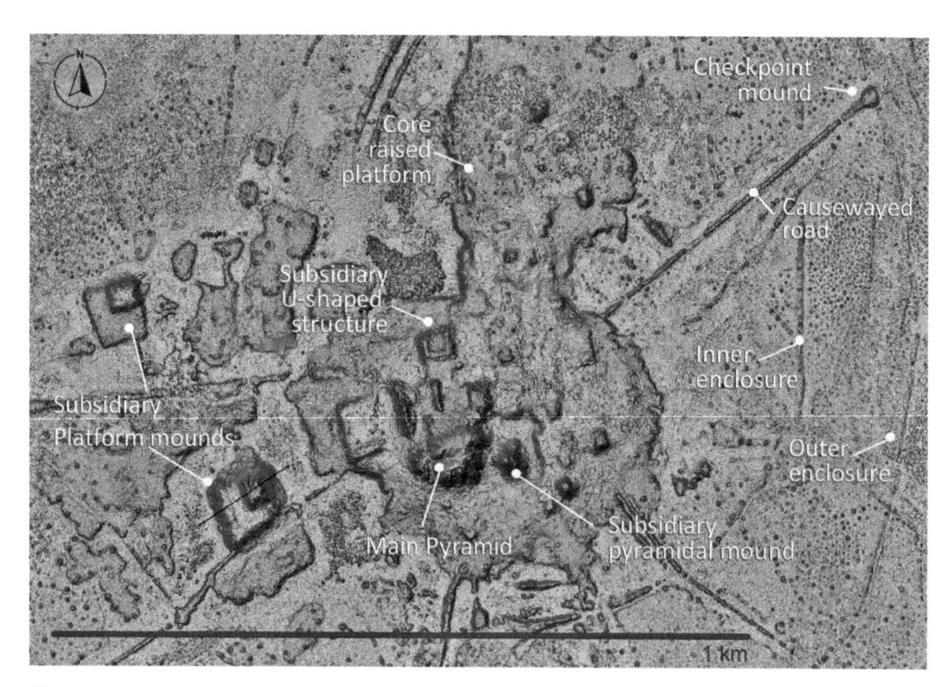

Figure 8.7 The lidar map of Cotoca shows a scale of monumental architecture that has no precedents in Amazonia. Built on a 4–5-metre-high artificial terrace covering ~22 hectares, with its 21-metre tall conical pyramid, U-shaped structures, subsidiary platforms, multiple polygonal enclosures and radiating causeways. Loma Cotoca show the sophistication and interconnectedness of Casarabe culture architecture. *Mojos prehispánico en 3D* project.

enclosures encircle the entirety of the site, enclosing a total area of 147 hectares. Numerous high, straight causeways radiate from the central core area to the outer perimeter and beyond. These broad avenues are 6–9 metres wide and typically 1 metre tall. Many of the causeways are broken up, which could represent the building of defensive screened entrances, or later destruction. Notably, platform mounds are particularly common where the causeways meet the polygonal enclosures, or where they fork or finish (Prümers et al., 2022), which could be representing checkpoints of access to the site.

Secondary centres, such as Loma Salvatierra, are characterized by base platforms ranging from 6–12 hectares and one still visible polygonal enclosure that circumscribes an area of 41–21 hectares. Civic-ceremonial architecture atop the base platform consists of one to several platform mounds. Tertiary centres comprise a base platform of ~0.5 hectares, with a single platform situated on it and a circular ditch enclosing an area of up to 2.5 hectares (Figure 8.3). In addition to these built sites, there is a diversity of small (average 0.34 hectares) elevated sites, known as forest islands, which were likely used as temporary campsites or sites for specialized activity. In some areas, like in the vicinity of Cotoca, forest islands appear in the form of clustered pockets, which may have represented house mounds for agricultural populations labouring the fields. It is important to remember that a large majority of these forest islands are artificial landscape features with a long history dating back to the early Holocene (Lombardo et al. 2020). A potential fifth tier of small hamlets exists but without mounded architecture they cannot be captured with lidar data. Within these broad patterns, the civic-ceremonial architecture within each tier of the hierarchy is variable, which could be related to chronology as well as to the function of the sites – a matter to clarify with future studies.

There is no precedent in Amazonia for the scale of the monumental architecture of the Casarabe people, and the amount of labour involved. It must also be remembered that at such large civic-ceremonial centres the archaeologist faces the end-product of hundreds of years of building, expansion and remodelling. The 4–5 metre high base platform of Landivar, which has a base area of ~500 x 240 metres (Figure 8.8), has a volume of about 276,000 metres^3 (Figure 8.8) (Prümers et al., 2022). The 570,690 metres^3 calculated for the centre of Cotoca is even more impressive (Figures 8.2 and 8.7). Cotoca is ten times bigger than the famous Akapana pyramid constructed at the capital of the Tiwanaku empire, and just a fifth smaller than Cahokia's Monks Mound (the largest earthen structure in the Western Hemisphere). Based on the precise calculations only possible with the digital terrain model produced by lidar, a conservative estimate show that La Cotoca must have taken 570,690 person/days to construct, implying labour and planning on a scale that can only be compared with the Archaic states of the central Andes. The scale, monumentality and labour involved in the construction of Amazonian civic-ceremonial architecture, water management infrastructure and spatially dispersed settlements, compares favourably to Andean cultures. Additionally, it needs to be remembered that no Tier 1 site has been excavated thus far, so there is still much to learn about the nature and function of these sites.

Regionally, sites are spatially clustered, interconnected by causeways and canals to form clusters spanning areas that range from 100 kilometres^2 to more than 500

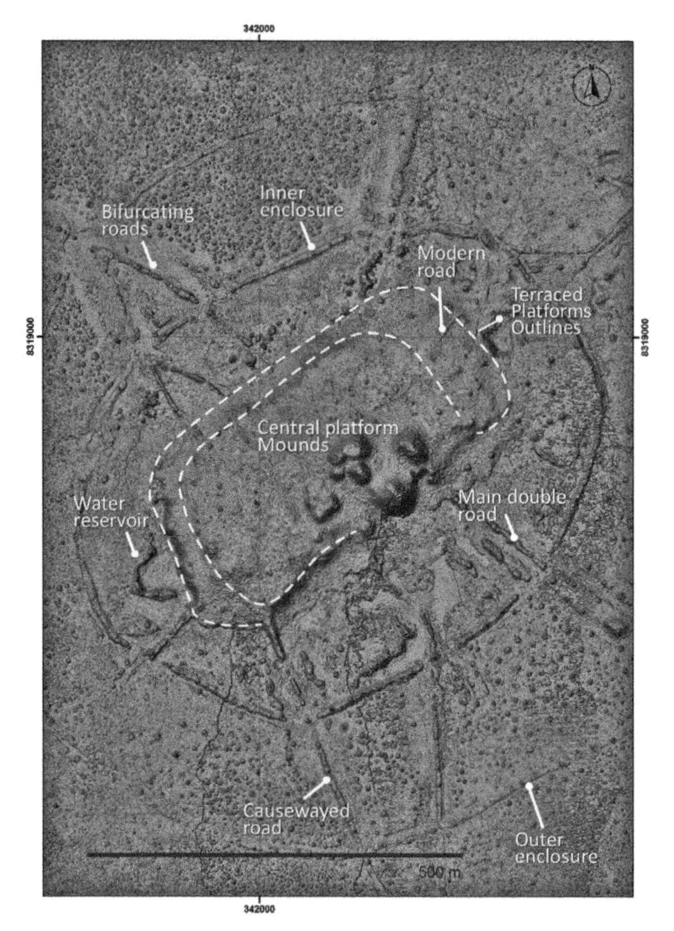

Figure 8.8 Loma Landivar spreads over 200 hectares. Its two-stepped terraced platforms lead to the civic ceremonial architecture at the core of the site. *Mojos prehispánico en 3D* project.

kilometres^2, with lower-tiered sites typically connected to higher-tier sites. Loma Cotoca, for example, appears to be the centre of an area of approximately 500 kilometres^2. It displays an impressive system of canals and causeways that radiate from the site in all cardinal directions, connecting with lower-tier sites, the Ibaré River to the south, and lakes to the east. A ~4-kilometres canal connects the topographically higher Laguna San José with the Loma Cotoca, likely built to bring water for drinking and irrigation of gardens in this site.

Combined with evidence from previous archaeological reconnaissance and remote sensing, the lidar data has shown that the Casarabe Tradition incorporated a highly integrated, continuous and dense settlement system. Across the 4,500 kilometres^2 of the Casarabe Tradition region, there is an average of ten Tier 1 to Tier 3 sites within a 10-kilometre radius of each settlement (i.e., within a two-hour walk). Density is higher in the eastern sector, with an average distance of 1,800–3,970 metres between settlements (Figure 8.2).

Mapping, using satellite images and field checks, has led Lombardo and Prümers (2010) to propose that the Casarabe people dammed, or bermed, natural depressions to capture rainwater runoff, as well as building canals of several kilometres in length, and draining fields to manage excess water. Canals connected the mounds to each other, and rivers and lakes to mounds and reservoirs. The system must have also played a crucial role in the mitigation of stagnant water. In the savannahs, most of the canals do not appear to be connected to settlement sites. Since they are often arranged within an interconnected network of right and acute angles, ultimately draining into modern rivers, they have been interpreted by Lombardo and Prümers (2010) as part of a system to drain the savannahs for cultivation.

Water scarcity must have been a major issue in the savannahs during the dry season. The problem was addressed through the construction of water reservoirs, with the region's clayey soils providing a natural watertight lining. Circular reservoirs identified next to sites with monumental architecture can be up to 40 metres in diameter and are usually surrounded by a pair of semi-circular dams. In some cases, it is easy to see how the reservoirs were planned to drain water towards the ponds, one of the best recorded examples being in the Loma Salvatierra. Here, a set of canals (about 300 metres long) were built to connect the mound to an excavated pond, which was itself connected to a second set of canals flowing into another pond. This system probably acted as a funnel, draining the rainwater towards ponds and canals during the period of receding waters (Lombardo and Prümers, 2010). The reservoirs may have also been used for the breeding of fish and turtles (Prestes-Carneiro et al., 2019) (Figure 8.3).

The scale and complexity of the regional systems of the Casarabe Tradition, along with the elaboration of its public-ceremonial architecture and the investment in water management infrastructure, has no parallels in lowland Amazonia.

How did the Casarabe Tradition come to an end? The anthropologist Holmberg (1950) writing in *Nomads of the Long Bow*, described the indigenous people of the region, the Sirionó, as one of the simplest cultures in the Amazon, with their quest for food so time-consuming as to preclude elaboration of most aspects of culture. They were identified by Meggers as one of five groups representing the cultural ecology of Amazonian *terra firme* adaptations. But ethnographic revisions (Isaac, 1977) and the advances of the archaeology of the region described in this chapter, led to a complete reassessment of the pre-Columbian cultural complexity of the region, documenting thriving, agricultural, low density urban societies that dedicated time and resources to building large settlements, and for whom ritual and an elaborate cultural life were important.

This complexity is unsurprising, given that the region witnessed some of the earliest episodes of human occupation in Amazonia. During the early Holocene it was the cradle of crops of global importance, such as manioc (Lombardo et al., 2020) (Chapter 3), and the location of the third global rice domestication event (Hilbert et al., 2017) (Chapter 5). The construction of landscape-scale fish weirs (Chapter 7) (Erickson, 2000), the likely domestication of duck (von den Driesch and Hutterer, 2011) and a reliance on maize agriculture from the late Holocene (Dickau et al., 2012; Prümers and Jaimes Betancourt,

2014), as shown by isotopic analysis of skeletal remains, are further evidence of this region being one of the hubs of cultural development in Amazonia.

The abandonment of the landscape systems at ~1400 CE precedes contact with Europeans. The Jesuits who traversed the Casarabe region in the seventeenth century found an empty landscape, the hydraulic systems abandoned and the Casabare society apparently gone. Significantly, their decline seems to have been accompanied by land use changes, with a coeval decrease in savannah burning (Whitney et al., 2013). One of the likely factors contributing to these shifts in land use, and ultimately to the demise of the Casabare people, is the protracted period of climate change experienced by the region during the late Holocene. The Torotoro record, which reflects the climate in the southern, drier, portion of the Llanos de Mojos, shows a prolonged drought in the centuries between the Medieval Climatic Anomaly (MCA) and the Little Ice Age (LIA), which reached its peak ~1300–1500 CE (De Souza et al., 2019). This prolonged dry period, in a region with striking seasonal contrasts, must have severely impacted the water management systems of the Casarabe culture.

In Souza et al. (2019), we argue that intense land use systems, like those of the Casabare people, with large investments in *landesque* capital and specialized technologies, were vulnerable to the changing climate of the late Holocene. As cross-cultural studies have found, intensification occurs in tandem with the evolution of complex political institutions, which increase inequality and centralization. Although political complexity may lead to rapid growth in the short term, it may also increase vulnerability in the long term because of the high interdependency of the constituent parts of the social system. Changes in any component are likely to compromise the system as a whole and lead to major transformations (e.g., Shehaan et al., 2018; Turchin et al., 2017).

Complex societies tend to promote and depend on the production of constant yields and surpluses, through intensification and specialization in resource exploitation. By doing so, they lose their ability to absorb unforeseen disturbances. An unstable climate could have serious consequences for large-scale water management, which, by providing the means to integrate dispersed subjects, was likely a key foundation of political power. Long-term and drastic change would disrupt planning, management and mobility flows to and from centres.

In such rainfall-dependent communities, accustomed to a long, dry season, predicting when the rains would commence was critical for agricultural scheduling and reservoir replenishment. If the Casarabe people relied on two harvests a year, they may have been especially vulnerable to reductions in precipitation in the late Holocene, particularly during the dry season. This vulnerability was possibly compounded by the fact that flooded ecosystems are prone to fire and erosion during periods of drought.

The demise of the Casarabe was likely not immediate. Casarabe may have shown resilience to the adverse conditions brought on by climate change. One possibility may have been the spread of low-density agrarian land use, and a rise in local – rather than centralized – hydraulic management and subsistence control. Both these measures would reduce resource pressure. Additionally, an increased reliance on a diversity of tuber and tree crops reduced the dependency on maize, thus alleviating the effects of adverse climate conditions. Furthermore, the construction of canals from lakes to habitation and agricultural sites, for example the ~4 kilometres canal that brought water from Laguna San José to the large settlement of Cotoca, may have mitigated the consequences of the decline in precipitation. An increase in the construction of reservoirs, taking advantage of the clayey soils of the region, may have also helped mitigate the drier climate. However, all these strategies appear not to have been maintained during the centuries-long period of drought.

Overall, the available data suggest that societies, such as the Casarabe, with their intensive, specialized land-use systems, were vulnerable to decreases in precipitation. This is in contrast with ADE land-use systems that relied primarily on polyculture agroforestry, which appear to be more resilient to climate change over long time periods (Souza et al., 2019).

Under the shade of volcanoes: The Upano cities

The Upper Amazon is characterized by great geographical and ecological diversity along the Upano River, at an elevation of about 1,300 masl. The Upano valley is home to the active Sangay volcano, which stands at an altitude of 5,230 masl. This area, known as *ceja de selva*, features irregular terrain, including subtropical valleys (approximately 1,000 masl) in the central region, the high Andean cordillera (more than 4,000 masl) to the west and the Trans-Cutuc mountains (around 2,500 masl) to the east. The Upano River flows through the valley's heart, from north to south, through a canyon of montane rainforest. The valley is located at a cultural crossroads, which likely served as a conduit for the exchange of goods and ideas between the Andes and the Amazon basin (Figure 8.9).

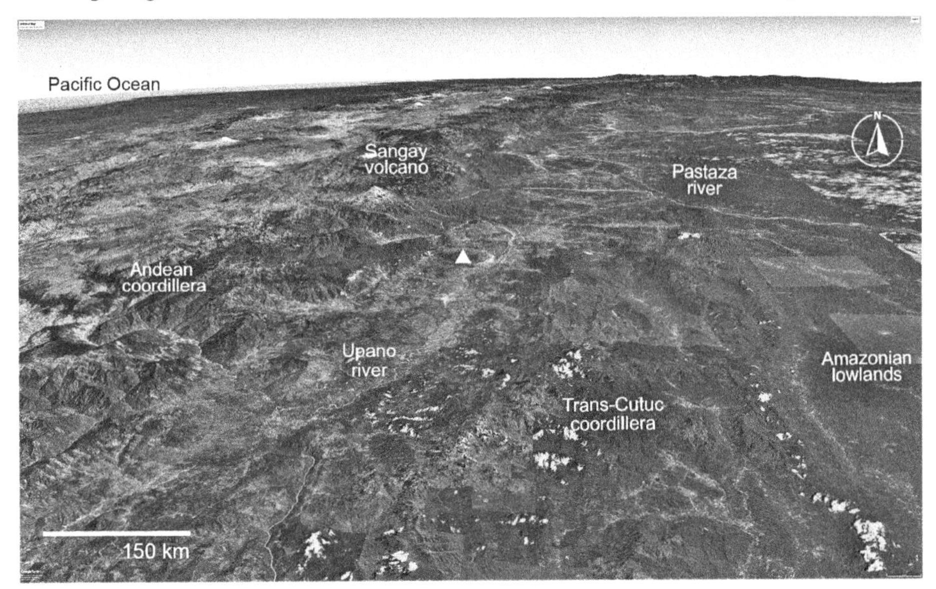

Figure 8.9 Satellite view of the Upano river region. White triangle shows approximate area shown in Figure 8.10. Google Earth.

The upper Upano River receives around 4,000 millimetres of precipitation per year, while the lower Upano valley receives progressively less precipitation towards the south. Temperatures average around 12°C and rarely go above 27°C. Sedimentary soils rest on top of both recent and ancient ash deposits formed from volcanic rocks (andesite and basalt). Native Shuar people and colonial farmers worked these soils without resorting to destructive slash-and-burn practices. The region is known for the practice of slash and mulch (*tapados*). According to Rostain (2012a), farmers in the area claim that today they can harvest maize as often as three times per year.

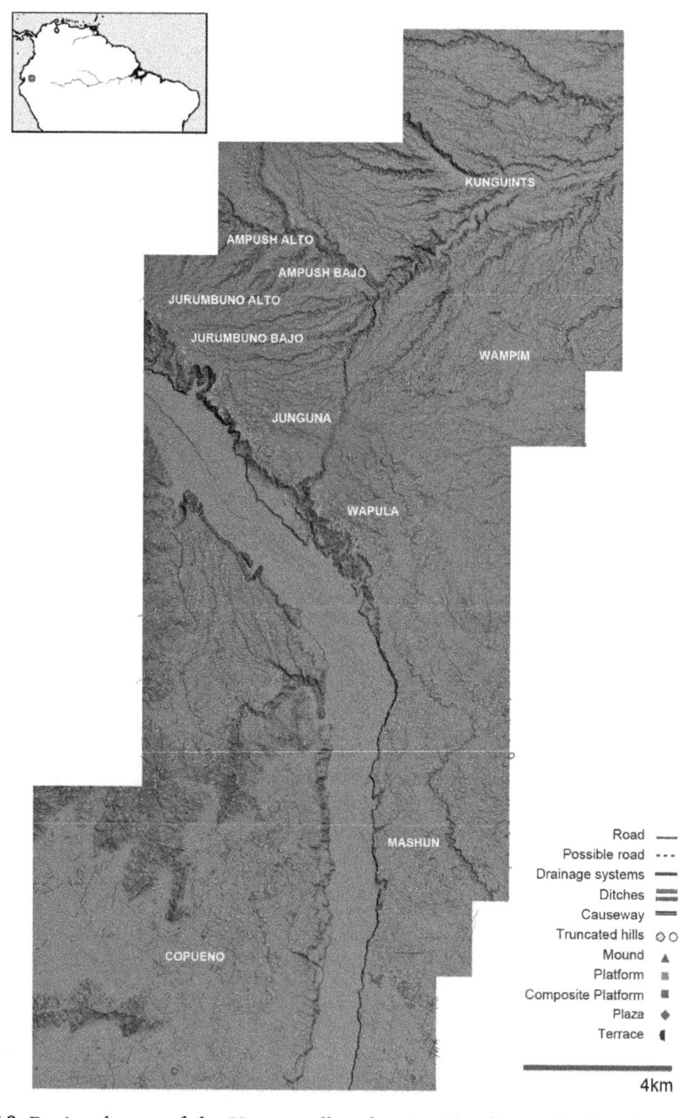

Figure 8.10 Regional map of the Upano valley showing the dispersal of settlements over 300 kilometre². Courtesy National Institute of Cultural Heritage (INPC), Ecuador.

In the 1970s, Porras (1989) conducted the first archaeological work in the region at the Huapala site (also known as Sangay), where he documented hundreds of monumental earthworks displaying an impressive level of planning. Lidar work carried out recently has further revealed that the site contains more than 474 structures, distributed over a 2.7 kilometres^2 area (Pazmiño, 2021).

The Upano culture is the most precocious of the urban developments of Amazonia and emerged between BCE 700 and 400 CE, lasting for more than 1,000 years. The most commonly accepted chronology includes four phases: Sangay (~ BCE 700–400), Upano (~ BCE 400–400 CE), Kilamope (~400–700 CE), and Huapula (~800–1200 CE) (Pazmiño, 2021). The Upano phase can be divided into two further phases: Upano 1 and Upano 2. Upano 1 occurred before the construction of earthworks, from BCE 400 to 65 CE, while Upano 2 coincided with the period of mound construction, from 65 to 400 CE. The exact time when the Upano Phase flourished is unknown, but it is believed to have occurred between BCE 700 and 400 CE. The start of monumental construction seems to be linked to changes in ceramic production, particularly the manufacturing of large jars and bowls, which may have been used in the consumption of fermented beverages (Figure 8.11) (Pazmiño, 2021). The decline of the Upano culture may have been caused by the eruption of the Sangay volcano between 400–600 CE, which deposited a layer of tephra throughout the region, making agriculture impossible for a long time. After a period of apparent abandonment, Huapula people repopulated the valley in 800–1200 CE (Pazmiño, 2021).

Lidar technology has uncovered an extensive and impressive landscape consisting of thousands of human-made structures, including platforms, mounds, flattened hills, terraces, plazas, roads and ditches, as well as drained fields likely used for agriculture (Figure 8.10) (Pazmiño, 2021; Rostain, 2012a; Sánchez-Polo and Litben, 2023). Initially, it was thought there was only one nucleated settlement, Huapala, but lidar along the valley more than 300 kilometres^2 has shown the presence of several clusters indicating large, nucleated settlements called *macro-asentamientos*, which contain more than 100

Figure 8.11 Ceramics of the Upano showing distinct red band decoration and globular corrugated vessel. Courtesy Stephen Rostain.

structures. These larger sites exhibit modular architecture with clusters that look as if they were designed on a board, with the delimitation of a square or rectangular, low, flat plaza area as the basis of the spatial pattern (Prümers, 2017). The largest of the newly mapped sites is Kunguints, which measures 5.9 × 1.7 kilometres and covers an area of 10 kilometres^2. It has 1,099 structures, consisting of 1,071 platforms, 10 mounds, 14 small plazas and 22.7 kilometres of roads, embankments and ditches. The density of structures in the area is 189/kilometres^2.

Key units in these large sites are 'platform plaza groups', consisting of four or six rectangular platforms, whose distribution is generally perfectly geometrical. The platforms enclose a central plaza (Figure 8.12) (Sánchez-Polo and Litben, 2023). A diversity of

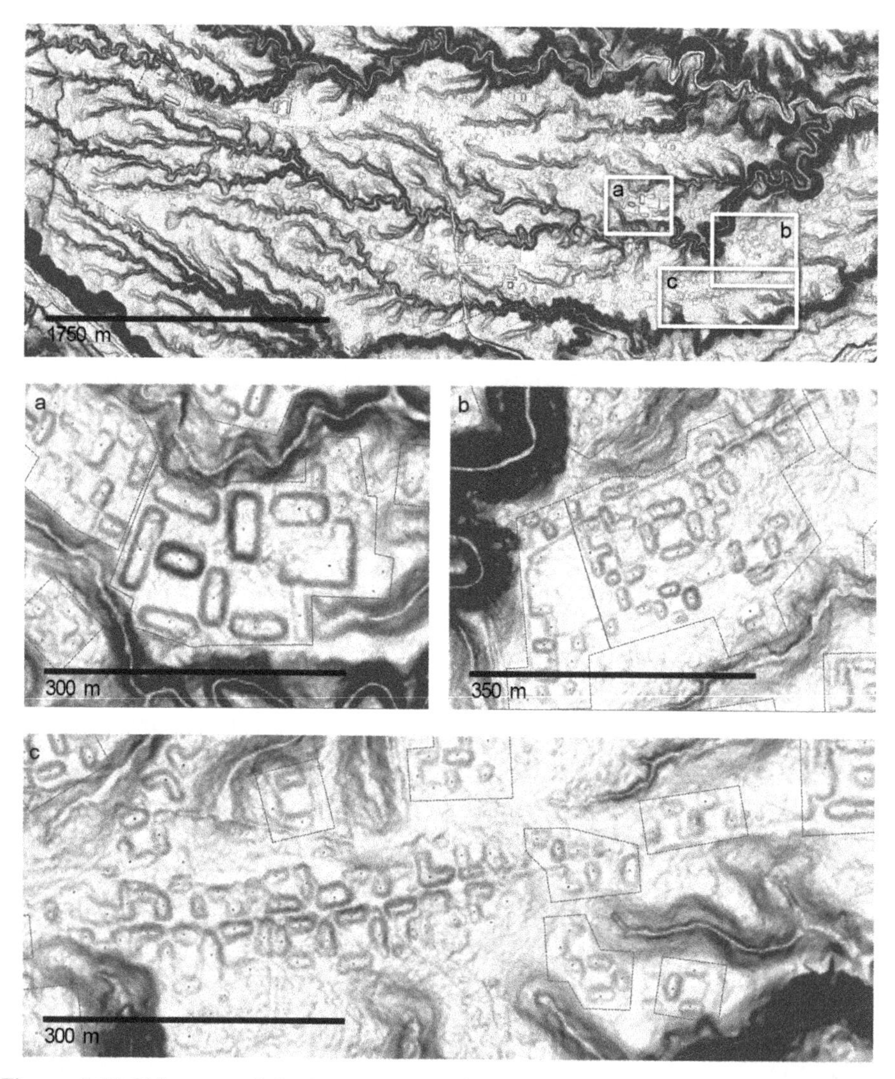

Figure 8.12 Lidar map of the Kunguints site showing different sectors of the site. Courtesy National Institute of Cultural Heritage (INPC), Ecuador.

simple rectangular platforms exist, along with a complex combination of platforms creating L-shaped, U-shaped and T-shaped structures. At Huapala, Porras (1989) distinguished three sizes of rectangular platforms: average (20 × 10 metres × 3 metres high), large (21–30 × 11 metres × 3–4 metres high) and monumental (31 × 15 metres × 4 metres high). Rostain's (2012a) excavations revealed flattened, levelled and burned plaza floors built to harden the floor surface for easier human traffic during the wet season when soils became slippery.

A complex network of ditched roads, U-shaped with sloping walls, complements the ancient urban layout. There are two distinct pathways, according to Rostain (2012a). Firstly, short, linear or slightly curved pathways connect complexes to nearby watercourses. They measure some tens of metres in length, 0.5–3 metres in width at the base and less than 3 metres in depth. Second are the larger, more substantial pathways, perfectly straight, bearing curbs and running alongside complexes to connect them. In the major settlements, these larger pathways appear to form axes that organize and connect the main plazas with minor groups of mounds in the village. They can have one or two side banks, measuring hundreds of metres in length, 2.5–13 metres in width at the base and more than 3 metres in depth. One example is the Huapala site, which is traversed from north-west to south-east by three major roads. The largest is 1.2 kilometres long, 13 metres wide and 3 metres deep.

Ditched fields were most likely built for cultivation, with a drainage system that would have prevented water retention in nutrient-rich soils. At the regional level, various sections of roads connected sites and settlements, shaping an integrated landscape.

Figure 8.13 Excavations in progress at an artificial mound of the Kilamope site. Courtesy Stephen Rostain.

To what extent these sites are contemporaneous is difficult to say, with only a few excavations and radiocarbon dates. However, the well-planned structure of the sites and the interconnecting roads points to their contemporaneity, at least during their final stages of construction.

Excavations at the central mound, 'Tola Central' of the Huapala site by Rostain (2012a), revealed a lack of stratification, indicating that at least these mounds may have been built in a single construction event. The top of the mound, corresponding to the Huapala people, contained a well-preserved domestic floor complete with hearths, pits, postholes, seeds and household tools related to domestic activities (Figure 8.13). The macrobotanical assemblage is dominated by maize, but also includes *guaba* (*Inga edulis*), cherry (*Prunus* sp.), blackberry (*Rubus* sp.) and passion fruit (*Passiflora* sp) (Pagán Jiménez and Rostain, 2014; Rostain, 2012a).

More research is required to uncover the intricate details of the chronology, economy and social structure of these complex societies that thrive in the tropical montane forests of Ecuador.

The Xinguano Garden Cities of Southern Amazonia

The Xinguano Garden Cities of Southern Amazonia have been proposed as yet another example of low-density urbanism in Amazonia during the late Holocene (Heckenberger et al., 2008). The region lies in what is now the Xingu Indigenous Park, in the headwaters of the Xingu River (Figure 8.14). It is home to various indigenous groups who speak Arawak, Carib, Tupian and other languages, and who are part of a regional society known as the Xinguano Nation. This region, along with the Upper Negro River, Mamoré-Guaporé rivers and Gran Chaco, is an example of the multi-ethnic regional systems that are common in lowland South America. Encompassing more than 25,000 kilometres^2, the region was Brazil's first demarcated indigenous reserve, founded in 1961 by the Villas Boas brothers, two Brazilian Indigenistas nominated for the Nobel Peace Prize. This is also the region where British explorer Colonel Percy Harrison Fawcett went missing in 1925 while searching for the legendary city of gold in the Amazon, whose tragic end inspired the novel and film The Lost City of Z.

The region is a uniquely productive area of study, since it is one of the few pre-Columbian areas of settlement in the Amazon where archaeological evidence can be directly linked to modern-day customs. Heckenberger and collaborators (2005; 2003; 2008) led the *Projeto Etnoarqueologico da Amazonia Meridional*, which established a pioneering collaborative project with the Kuikuro group. Using participatory mapping, they together documented dozens of settlements, fortified by ditches and connected by a regional network of roads, in what Heckenberger and collaborators (2008) named a 'galactic' system of regional polities extending over 20,000 kilometres^2. The system is unique, marked by its large settlement size (20–50 hectares) and road network, which likely supported a population up to 20 times greater than the indigenous population living in the region today. The study area encompasses a section of the Culuene River, as well as its smaller tributaries and tributary lakes. It is adjacent to the upland *terra firme*

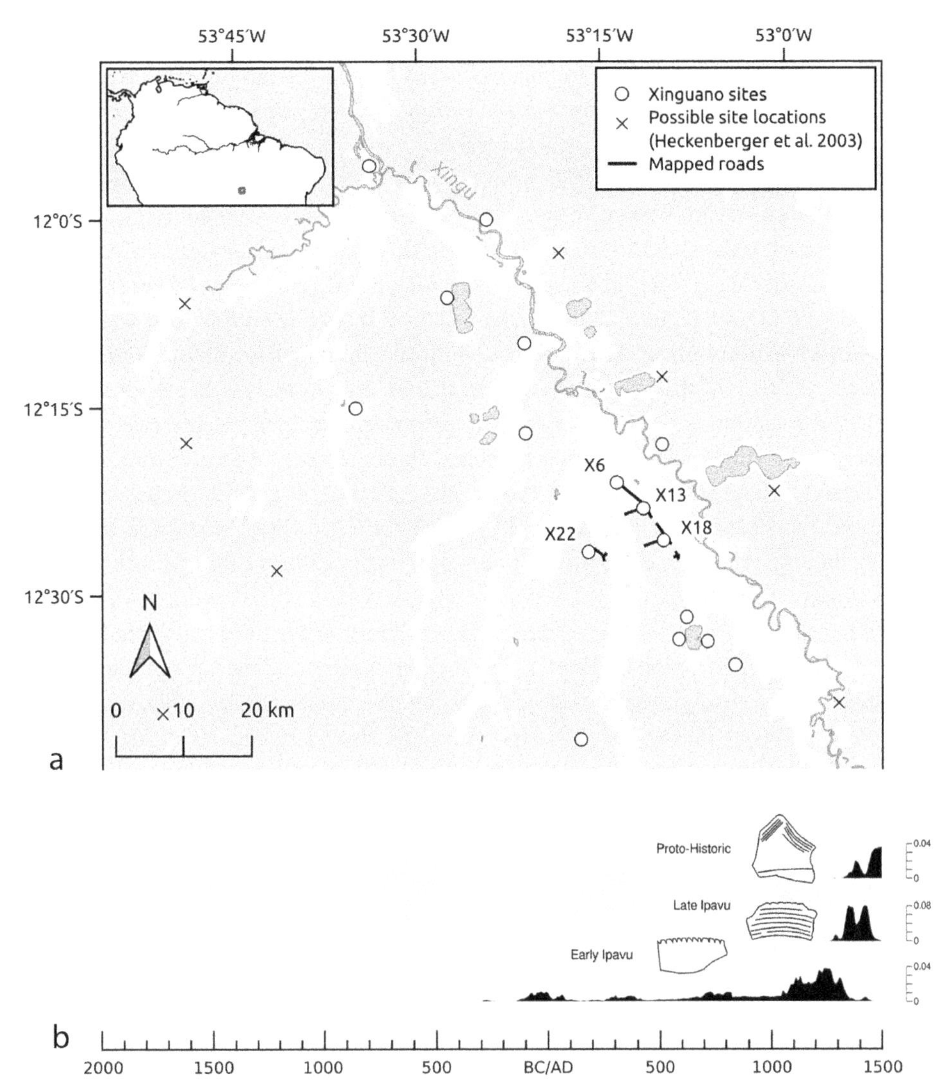

Figure 8.14 The Upper Xingu region. *a.* Site distribution map. *b.* SPDs of radiocarbon dates along with major ceramic phases.

forest and lacks *várzea* floodplains, constituting yet another 'unexpected' example of complex cultures in the upland forests of Amazonia.

As yet, no pre-ceramic sites are known from this area. The first settlements with ceramics appeared in the second half of the first millennium CE. The earlier ceramic phase belongs to the Early Ipavu phase, starting in 700 CE, which is part of the broader Barrancoid horizon in Amazonia, with influences from the Incised-Punctate and Polychrome Traditions. Heckenberger (1998) contends that this phase represents the ancestral foundation of today's Xinguano culture, when the region was colonized by Arawakan groups. Like other Barrancoid styles, the Early Ipavu phase is characterized by modelled appendages, incised lines forming parallel and curvilinear patterns, and red slip. The vessels have distinctive ungulate dots made with the thumb along the edge of the lip. Typically they are small and thin-walled, globular in shape and exhibit a pedestal base. They are mainly tempered with *cariapé*.

The Late Ipavu phase, which lasted from 1250–1350 CE, is marked by the development of circular villages with berms. Vessels from this period are larger, exhibit thicker walls and are mainly tempered with *cauxi*. Following this, the ceramic styles received Carib influences, ushering in a period of regional variation known as the Proto-historic period, which began around 1500 CE and was characterized by various styles, such as the local antecedent Ipavu Arawakan, Konduri and the so-called Oriental Complex (Toney, 2016).

Toney (2016) has observed that in general, and over time, vessels get increasingly larger in association with technological improvements, such as the increase in mean border size, lip thickness and border diameter, combined with a greater uniformity in vessel shapes. Changes in ceramic, Toney argues, reflect socio-political changes, such as increased food production necessitated by population growth. The manufacturing of vessels directly related to food production would thus gradually transform becoming increasingly larger.

Archaeological ceramics show remarkable similarity to the ones still manufactured by Upper Xingu people today. Three types of ceramics in particular are similar: firstly, *ahukugu* forms, corresponding to large to medium cooking pots; secondly, the *atangï*-like cooking pots, with everted and direct rims; and thirdly, manioc griddles. *Ahukugu* forms exhibit wide notches worn into the rim lips of large vessels, resulting from grater boards being placed over the pots during the processing of manioc (Heckenberger, 1998). Although forms show continuity over time, modern Xinguano ceramics differ from archaeological ones by including zoned red slip, black-painted designs and exterior white slip.

Heckenberger et al. (2008) argue that the Late Ipavu phase is an example of low-density urbanism forming 'galactic polities', a term coined by anthropologist Stanley Tambiah to describe traditional South East Asian kingdoms, in which the centripetal force of the centre was based as much on ritual and tradition as on centralized political, military and economic power. These regionally organized Late Ipavu societies peaked between 1250–1650 CE, before colonial arrival. Larger towns (20–50 hectares) formed a central point in an urban network and were surrounded by semi-circular ditches (up to 2 kilometres long and 3–4 metres deep), which possibly included a wooden palisade for defence. Systematic mapping at the Kuhikugu site revealed extensive ADE, occupation debris, house floors and middens (Figure 8.15) (see Chapter 6). Ditches appear to mark the extension of residential occupation, with areas of higher ceramic density around the central plaza. Mounded architecture is carefully planned around a concentric model of spatial organization, where domestic areas gravitate toward central plazas with spoke-like radial causeways. In these well-planned villages, linear ridges 0.5–2 metres high at the edges of central plazas and intra-village causeways are also prominent features (Figure 8.15). These larger villages were, in turn, surrounded by smaller satellite villages, connected by roads and pathways cleared through the forest. These roads are distinguished

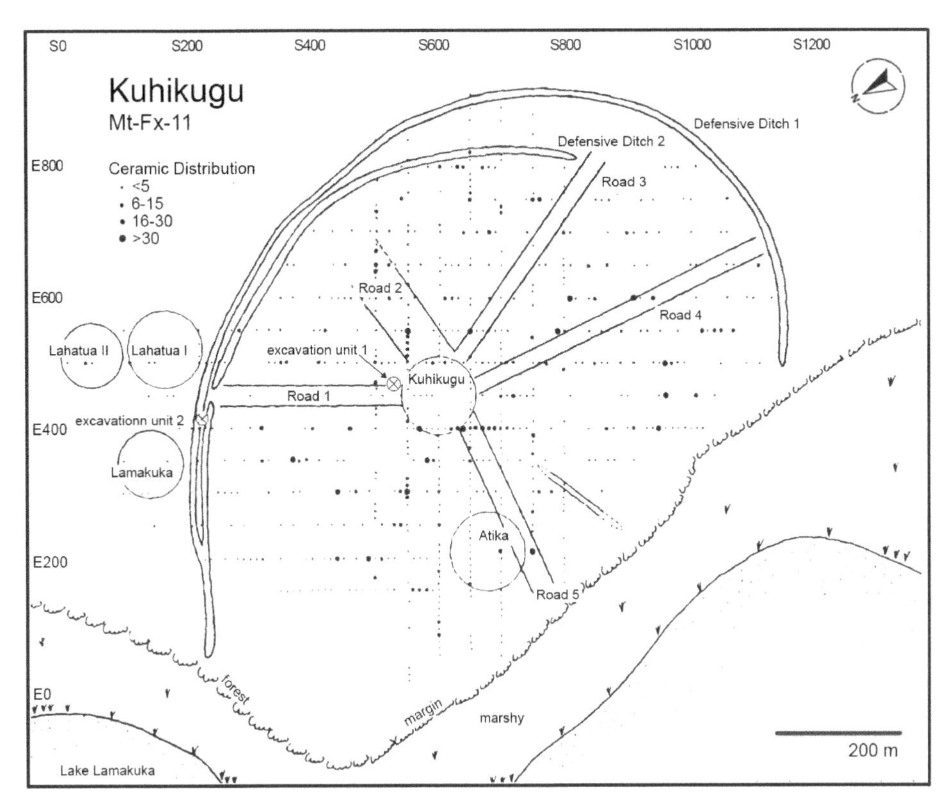

Figure 8.15 The Kuhikugu site showing defensive ditches, radial roads and ceramic density across the site. Modified from Heckenberger (2005: 99).

primarily by earthen curbs rather than raised roadways. The road network is based on the same fundamental principles as the current Kuikuro villages. Main roads run east–west, secondary roads branch out to the north and south, and smaller roads branch out in all directions. As we have seen in the previous chapters, the cardinal orientation of roads and the radial patterns appear to be common in the southern rim of the Amazon within certain variability.

Between these settlements, Heckenberger suggests there may have been a patchwork of fields of manioc, tree-fruit orchards and fields of *sape* grass (used for thatching), as well as artificial dams and ponds used to farm turtles and fish (Heckenberger and Neves, 2009; Heckenberger et al., 2008). According to Heckenberger (1998), manioc agriculture combined with rich aquatic resources was the key economic foundation for substantially larger villages and regional population aggregates in the region. However, beyond ethnographic analogy and the design of and use-wear marks of ceramics related to the processing of manioc, data on past diet is still lacking to corroborate this hypothesis.

Contemporary Xinguano villages are frequently found within or near ancient settlements, and the comparison is revealing (Figure 8.16). According to Heckenberger

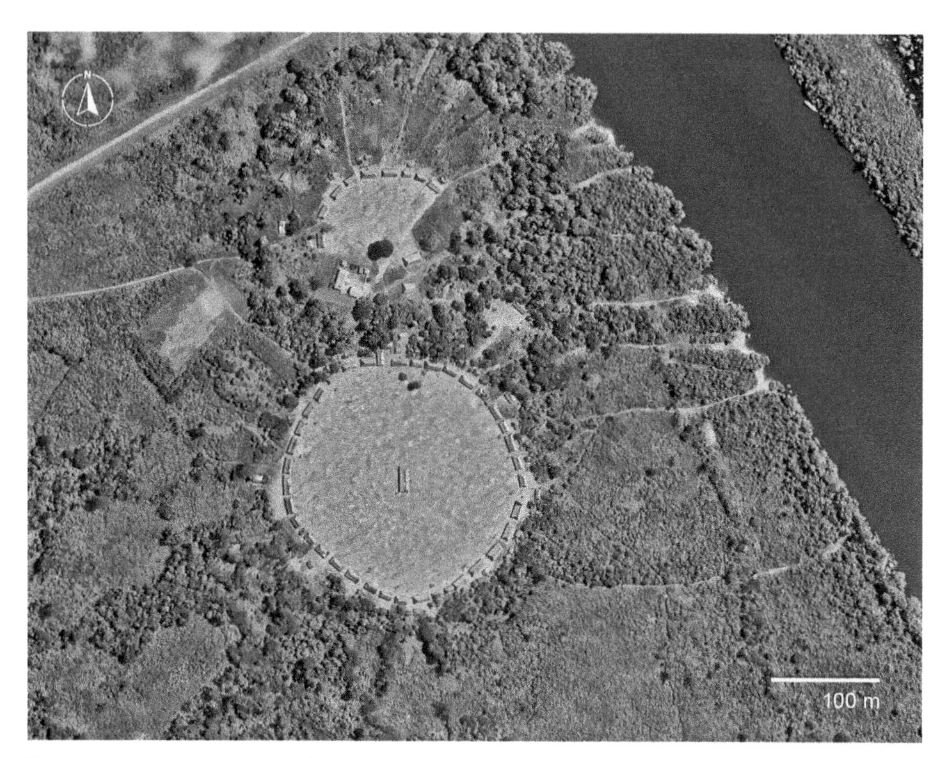

Figure 8.16 Satellite image of contemporary Kuikuro village. A ring of houses surrounds a large circular plaza in modern villages. Plazas are approximately 100–250 metres in diameter, and these villages typically house between 50 to 350 people. Google Earth.

(1998), contemporary Kuikuro villages are about 6 hectares in size and housed 320 people in 1994, whereas larger pre-Columbian plaza villages are 50 hectares. As a result, it makes sense to believe that pre-Columbian plaza villages were at least eight times larger than modern ones and could have housed up to 2,500 people.

The arrival of Europeans in the region shifted the historical trajectory of the Upper Xingu. Like in many other areas of Amazonia, diseases likely spread faster than people. The Portuguese had established sustained contact with the Lower Xingu by the early 1600s. A combination of epidemics, slave raiding and punitive expeditions well into the twentieth century resulted in a devastating decline in the Upper Xingu. For example, the 3,000 people who lived in the Upper Xingu in the 1890s – a much-reduced population from pre-contact – were further reduced to around 500 people by 1950 – a graphic depiction of the post-1492 population decline. Unsurprisingly, twentieth-century ethnographers discovered a social and political system fundamentally different from the 'galactic polities' believed to have emerged in the Upper Xingu between 1250–1650 CE. Despite these differences, Heckenberger (2005) demonstrates that there has been cultural continuity in this area for the past 800 years evident through the regional sociopolitical organization of hierarchical polities, as mainly seen in the surviving site layouts and ceramics.

CHAPTER 9
THE COLUMBIAN ENCOUNTER

The great dying

The voyages of Christopher Columbus to the Caribbean, along with later European voyages to the Americas, marked the beginning of some of the most profound transformations in human history (Figure 9.1) (e.g., Crosby, 1972; Dobyns, 1966; Turner and Butzer, 1992). The Columbian Exchange, also known as the Columbian Encounter or the Columbian Interchange, was characterized by the widespread transfer of plants, animals, precious metals, commodities, culture, human populations, technology, diseases and ideas between the Western Hemisphere's New World (the Americas) and the Eastern Hemisphere's Old World (Afro-Eurasia) in the late fifteenth and following centuries.

The first recorded interactions between Europeans and Indigenous Amazonians took place in 1498 CE. During this time, Christopher Columbus and his crew briefly landed on the coast of what is now Venezuela (Bergreen, 2011). A more significant contact occurred in 1500 CE, when Pedro Álvarez Cabral, who was seeking a route to India, accidentally discovered the coast of what would later become known as Brazil.

Figure 9.1 *Landing of Columbus at the Island of Guanahaní, West Indies* (1846), by John Vanderlyn. Wikimedia.

Shortly after the first contact with Europeans, the indigenous peoples of the Americas experienced what can, without exaggeration, be called one of the greatest demographic disasters in human history. Diseases that crossed the Atlantic with Europeans and hit populations with limited immunity to the new germs, mostly caused the rapid decline of indigenous populations. The deadliest Old World diseases in the Americas were smallpox, measles, whooping cough, chicken pox, bubonic plague, typhus and malaria (Figure 9.2). But this was not just a case of 'virgin-soil' epidemics. The violence of the European conquistadors, in the form of murder, slavery, military campaigns and relocation was another important factor.

Around the year 1500, the population of Amazonia was estimated to be between 5 and up to 20 million people (e.g., Denevan, 2001; Koch et al., 2019) and they spoke around 700 distinct languages (Rodrigues, 2001). In under a century, there was a significant reduction in population numbers, resulting in a catastrophic decline and the loss of linguistic and cultural diversity. Indigenous populations declined by an estimated 80–90 per cent, which (according to some estimates) is equivalent to 10–20 per cent of the world's population in the early-sixteenth century.

The population decimation following the Columbian Encounter poses significant challenges when trying to understand the pre-Columbian Amazonian societies described in the anthropological studies of the twentieth century (e.g., Roosevelt, 1999). Population decline had a significant impact on the agricultural labour force and as a result on land use systems. It is likely that some farmers became foragers (Balée, 1994; Fausto, 2001; Lévi-Strauss, 1952), while others switched from intensive to long-fallow shifting cultivation (Denevan, 2004).

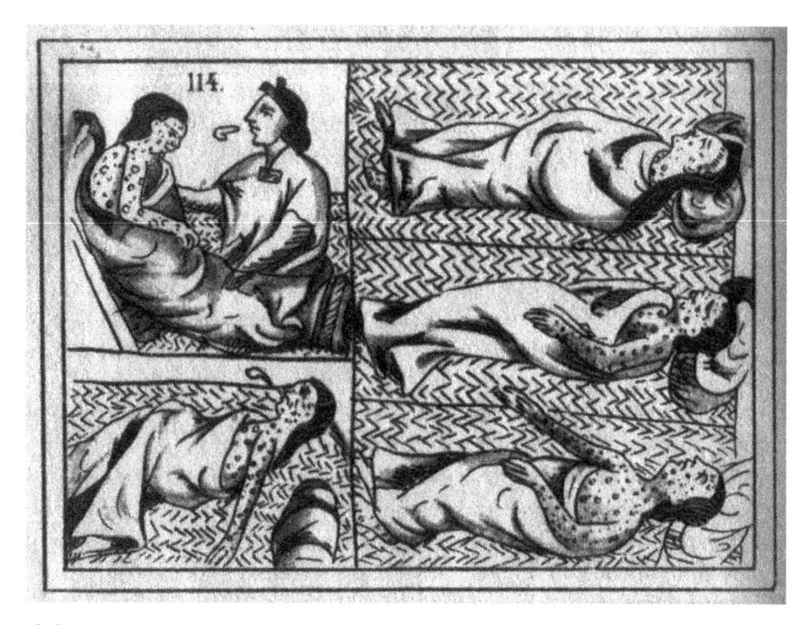

Figure 9.2 Sixteenth-century Aztec drawing of smallpox victims. Wikimedia.

The Columbian Encounter also started the Atlantic slave trade of the sixteenth to nineteenth centuries, which consisted of the involuntary movement to the Americas of 11.7 million Africans, predominantly from West Africa, who considerably outnumbered the approximately 3.4 million Europeans who travelled, mostly voluntarily, to the New World.

The exchange of crops, seeds and plants between the Old and New Worlds radically transformed agriculture in both regions. A wide range of crops arrived in the New World from the Old, including cereals, such as Old World rice, apple, banana, mango, coffee and sugar cane, to name but a few. Livestock from the Old World was also introduced. Meanwhile, crops, including maize, potatoes, tomatoes and tobacco were brought from the New to the Old World. For many authors, the Columbian Encounter represents a radical reorganization of life on Earth that marks the beginning of the 'world system'.

It is important to be cautious when trying to understand the past of Amazonian societies before the Columbian Encounter because of the significant changes caused by it. The absence of ethnographic records of the regional and complex societies that existed before the fifteenth century, challenges the accuracy of projections based on ethnographic records of the twentieth century, no matter how careful they may be.

The Columbian Encounter and the Anthropocene

Some authors (Koch et al., 2019; Nevle et al., 2011; Nevle and Bird, 2008) have taken the view that the Columbian Encounter had a global impact on climate, contributing to the start of the Little Ice Age. According to these authors, the 'Great Dying' and the abandonment of traditional slash-and-burn agriculture across the Neotropics led to dramatic forest re-growth. The authors estimate that afforestation at this time captured 7.4 Pg C (3.5 ppm CO_2 equivalent) from the atmosphere. The effect, known as the 'Orbis Spike', is detectable in ice cores by 1610 CE. It marks the lowest concentration of carbon dioxide in the atmosphere in the past 2,000 years, and precedes a period of global cooling. The dip is the footprint of the mass death, slavery and war that succeeded the events of 1492 CE. In other words, the decimation of Amazonian farmers transformed the Amazon from a net source of CO_2 (pre-Columbian agricultural fires) into a carbon sink for several centuries following the Columbian Exchange, which in turn contributed to the onset of the Little Ice Age.

Lewis and Maslin (2015) argue the impacts of the Columbian Exchange went far beyond the Americas, and that from ~1610 CE they were expressed on a planetary scale. Former farmlands reverted to forests, after the deaths by smallpox and warfare of an estimated 50 million Native Americans. But additionally, as a result of the Columbian Exchange, as many as 28 million Africans died or were taken for labour in the New World. In total, as much as three-quarters of the entire population of two continents died or were enslaved. The population of the regions of north-western Africa most affected by the slave trade did not begin to recover until the end of the nineteenth century. From 1600–1900, forest may have been recovering in vast swathes of that region, enough to draw down CO_2 and impact the climate in the same way as the regrowth of the Amazon forests and the great North American woods. Simply put, by 1610 CE, the growth of all those trees had sucked enough carbon dioxide out of the sky to cause a drop of at least seven parts per million in atmospheric concentrations of the most prominent greenhouse gas, and to start a Little Ice Age. Based on this dramatic shift, the authors have proposed a start date of 1610 CE for the new geological epoch, the Anthropocene, the recent age of humanity.

However, there are problems with this hypothesis. Traditionally, an exponential increase in pre-Columbian population and land use intensity up until the arrival of Europeans has been assumed. But recent analysis of radiocarbon dates suggests that population growth across the Amazon basin had begun to slow down well before this time, by around 1200 CE, perhaps nearing a carrying capacity (Arroyo-Kalin and Riris, 2020). Additionally, recent palaeoecological syntheses are showing that afforestation before and following the Columbian Encounter varied significantly across space and time, depending on social, economic and biogeographic contexts (Hamilton et al., 2021). The synthesis work by Bush et al. (2021), for example, shows that during the Great Dying period, the number of sites where forest pollen was increasing in abundance roughly equalled the number of sites where it was falling. Meanwhile, in the seasonally flooded savannahs of French Guiana, fires became a post-Colombian phenomenon (see next chapter) (Iriarte et al., 2012). Lastly, many land-use strategies employed in the tropics, such as the polyculture agroforestry systems used on ADEs across Amazonia, likely sustained forest cover rather than depleting it. This challenges the assumption that 'afforestation' in palaeoenvironmental records should be the only expected ecological signal of indigenous population decline and the arrival of European land-use.

In the following chapter, we will look at how archaeology's deep-time perspective can provide valuable lessons for sustainable Amazonian futures, and how working collaboratively with indigenous communities can benefit a better understanding of the past, traditional communities and forest conversation.

CHAPTER 10
LESSONS FROM THE PAST FOR A CHALLENGING FUTURE: REVITALIZING FOREST TRADITIONAL LIVELIHOODS

Archaeology matters

We are living in unprecedented times. Human-induced land change, habitat fragmentation, extinction and global warming have all come dangerously close to, or even crossed, important thresholds over the past few decades. Humans have become the dominant force in shaping the Earth's system, implying that our planet has entered a new geological epoch known as the Anthropocene (Crutzen, 2002). The Amazon is no exception, and its rapid disappearance is reaching a point of crisis. The protection of rainforests and the development of sustainable land use practices are of global significance. The Amazon rainforest is the largest reservoir of biodiversity in the world and is of crucial importance for the regulation of the Earth's climate. Tropical forests cover only 14 per cent of the Earth's surface but contain 68 per cent of the global living carbon stock, a large proportion of which is stored in Amazonian trees and Amazonian anthrosols. By 2050, 50 per cent of the global population will live in the tropics, while more than 90 per cent of the world's poorest people currently depend on forests for their livelihoods and the preservation of their culture (Penny et al., 2020).

However, the outlook is not very promising. Increasing challenges from economic demands, commercial interests, population growth and climate change threaten traditional indigenous identities and Amazonian biodiversity. The existence of indigenous lands is currently the most important factor in halting or slowing Amazonian deforestation (Nepstad et al., 2006) (Figure 10.2). In these areas, as Heckenberger (2009a) reminds us, saving tropical forests and protecting indigenous cultural heritage is, in many respects, one and the same thing. But indigenous and traditional communities living in the Amazon are increasingly turning to cattle ranching and commercial slash-and-burn agriculture for the potential economic rewards and because of the lack of alternative economic pathways. In many cases, they are encouraged to do so by modern states. This leads to widespread deforestation, with more trees being cut down for beef than for any other product. In the last two decades, the Brazilian Amazon has lost 197,000 kilometres^2 of forest, an area roughly the size of Uruguay, mainly because of pressure for increasing pastures. Now, 90 million cows graze on a cleared area the size of France in the Amazon. Regional precipitation is expected to decrease because of deforestation and reduced evapotranspiration (see Chapter 2), while natural- and human-caused fires are projected to increase fire activity across the Amazon, particularly across its southern rim.

Figure 10.1 Another day in the office under smoky skies in Lake Versalles, Bolivian Amazon. Ironically, this is not a cloudy day, it is smoke from a forest burning in the neighbouring Matto Grosso Brazilian state.

The areas that concentrate more cultivated and domesticated species (Figure 4.5) (Levis et al., 2017), are the areas where most forest degradation is occurring. They are biodiversity hotspots, and should be top conservation priorities as reservoirs of high-value forests for human populations.

The degradation of the world's largest rainforest is dangerously close to a point where it can no longer regenerate. The forest's ability to generate its own rain diminishes as more trees are cut down. As the land dries out, it becomes more susceptible to fire and lightning strikes, and eventually becomes a savannah. This completely different ecosystem is less diverse, less able to store carbon, and is less powerful in generating the rainfall and storms that keep weather systems moving. The study of Gatti and collaborators (2021) suggests that in some parts of the Amazon, emissions from the slashing and burning of trees – the preferred method for clearing fields in the Amazon – were exceeding the forest's capacity to absorb carbon, meaning that the lungs of the Earth are actually emitting carbon dioxide. The effects are particularly acute in eastern Amazonia, which has already lost a staggering 30 per cent of its forest. The dry season there used to be three months long; now it lasts more than four. During the driest months, rainfall has declined by as much as a third in four decades, while average temperatures have risen by as much as 3.1°C – triple the annual increase for the world as a whole in the fossil-fuel era. This, as we will see below, is leading to megafires associated with ENSO events (e.g., Aragão et al., 2018; Fonseca et al., 2017).

Already, along the southern rim of the Amazon, the forest is transforming into a savannah as it releases more carbon than it absorbs. The rest of the rainforest is following suit: 17 per cent has been cleared, and another 17 per cent is in a degraded state. The tipping point, according to some climate scientists, will occur when 20–25 per cent of the

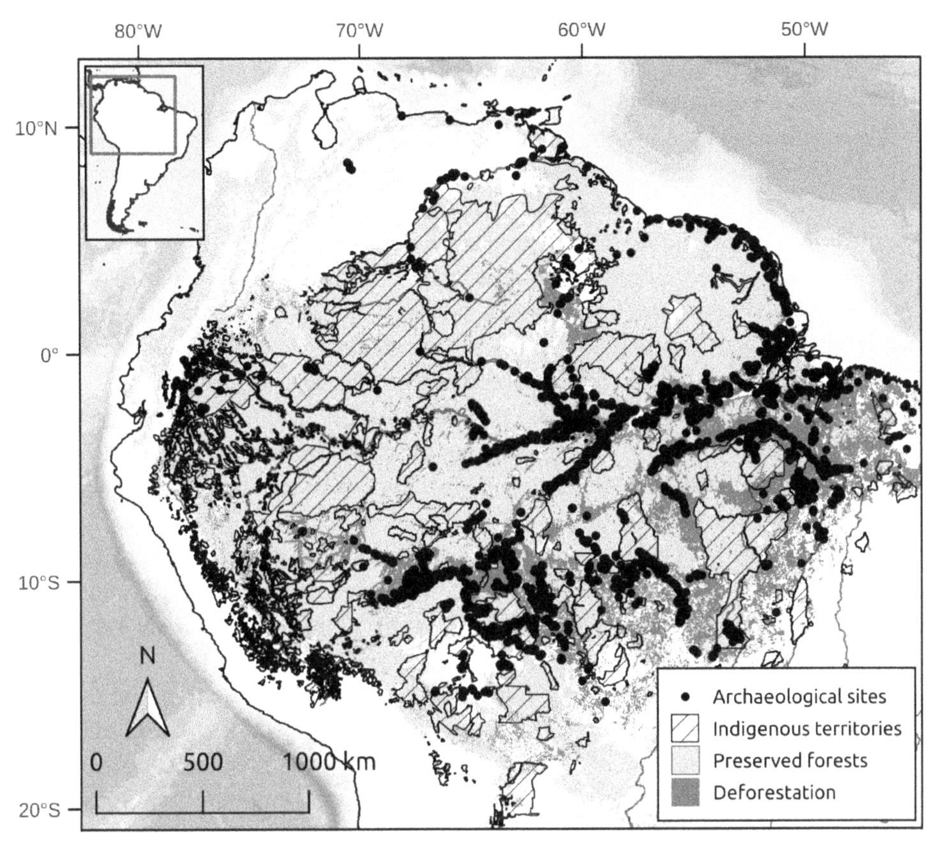

Figure 10.2 Keepers of the forest. Indigenous lands in the Amazon basin are the most forested as shown in this map comparing deforested areas, preserved forest and indigenous territories.

Amazon is lost, which, at the current rate of ecocide, is likely to be years rather than decades away (Lovejoy and Nobre, 2018). The loss of the forest is also having a dramatic impact on community identities. Therefore, looking for sustainable solutions that reduce deforestation, and developing alternative economic avenues, are key for Amazonian futures as well as helping meet UN Sustainable Development Goals.

In this chapter I will contend, along with many of my colleagues (e.g., Iriarte, 2017; Roberts, 2019; Willis 2007), that information from the long-term records of the past, provided by archaeology and palaeoecology, delivers a historical perspective on today's challenges, which can help improve the sustainability and resilience of our societies. In this regard, interdisciplinary archaeology can provide us with a unique deep-time perspective on the dynamics of coupled human-environment systems. This could be critical to understanding centennial- and millennial-scale change in human-natural systems, which are vital to debates regarding conservation, sustainable development and human rights in an era of unprecedented change across the region. In some ways, one of the best experiments we can conduct is to go back in time and see how people, vegetation and entire landscapes reacted to climate change. By studying how our ancestors adapted to major climatic shifts, we can learn from their experiences and prepare for the challenges that await us in the future, such as extreme weather, droughts and rising sea levels.

For example, knowing how resilient Amazonian forests were to past disturbances, along with understanding the historical role of humans in shaping Amazonian landscapes, is crucial for making policy decisions for a sustainable Amazonian future. Any work in restoration ecology necessitates finding an answer to the basic question – 'What landscape do we need to restore?' And for that, we need an understanding of the degree of change from baseline conditions. This is particularly important for the Amazon, where archaeological and palaeoecological data show a long history of indigenous management, as seen in the previous chapters. We should work hard to persuade conservationists and policymakers to embrace a novel ecosystems perspective that acknowledges that ecosystems created through long-term human management are equally valid conservation targets.

At present, tackling climate change may appear daunting. Some of us may feel helpless, thinking that our individual actions are insignificant. However, many studies show that it is precisely the actions we take at a local level that count. Furthermore, as argued by Boivin and Crowther (2021), some 'solutions from the past' have stood the test of time. They typically do not rely on fossil fuels, can be more easily implemented and managed at the local level, and, particularly, in the Global South, are often far more appropriate than modern solutions.

Archaeology can sometimes uncover old farming techniques that are more efficient and less harmful than modern ones. The engagement of archaeology with indigenous and local communities has resulted in a recognition of the importance to ecological conservation efforts of traditional ecological knowledge, customary practices, community values and cultural heritage sites.

In the following pages, I will delve into case studies from the deep Amazonian past that provide useful information for shaping the Amazon's future and bringing about a 'good Anthropocene'. Building on Amazonian archaeology and palaeoecology, I will examine how these historical case studies can strengthen ongoing initiatives in fields as diverse as conservation, food security and sustainable agriculture.

Polyculture agroforestry systems: Keepers of the forests

Throughout history, various societies have practised agricultural intensification using techniques that, despite vulnerable environments, allowed for sustained land use. By examining past methods of intensification, we can gain insights into the future sustainability, resilience and vulnerability of agricultural systems. Although not all ancient technologies are environmentally friendly, many older methods could be better suited than modern ones for developing countries.

Polyculture agroforestry systems implemented on ADEs have demonstrated that long-term food security and nutritional diversity can be achieved through soil fertilization, enrichment of closed-canopy forests, minimal clearing for crop cultivation and careful management of low-severity fires (Iriarte et al., 2020a).

These millennial-scale polyculture agroforestry systems supported large populations and were resilient to climate change (Souza et al., 2019). They have an enduring legacy in the form of persisting patches of highly fertile soil, as well as in the modern composition of the forest, including legacy plots of palms, Brazil nuts and cacao. These systems not only provide evidence of successful, sustainable subsistence strategies, but also highlight a rich cultural-ecological heritage. Scientifically grounded data can address the modern challenges faced by the rainforest and its marginalized indigenous inhabitants who still harbour and utilize much of the ecological knowledge accumulated over millennia.

The Bolivian Amazon

The Bolivian Amazon provides one of the most illustrative studies of how forest persisted, despite land use intensification, via ADE polyculture agroforestry systems. At the Triunfo ADE site, located on the ~5,000-kilometres^2 tract of forest located within the Iténez Forest Reserve, in the northeast of Beni Department, Bolivia, we designed a multi-proxy

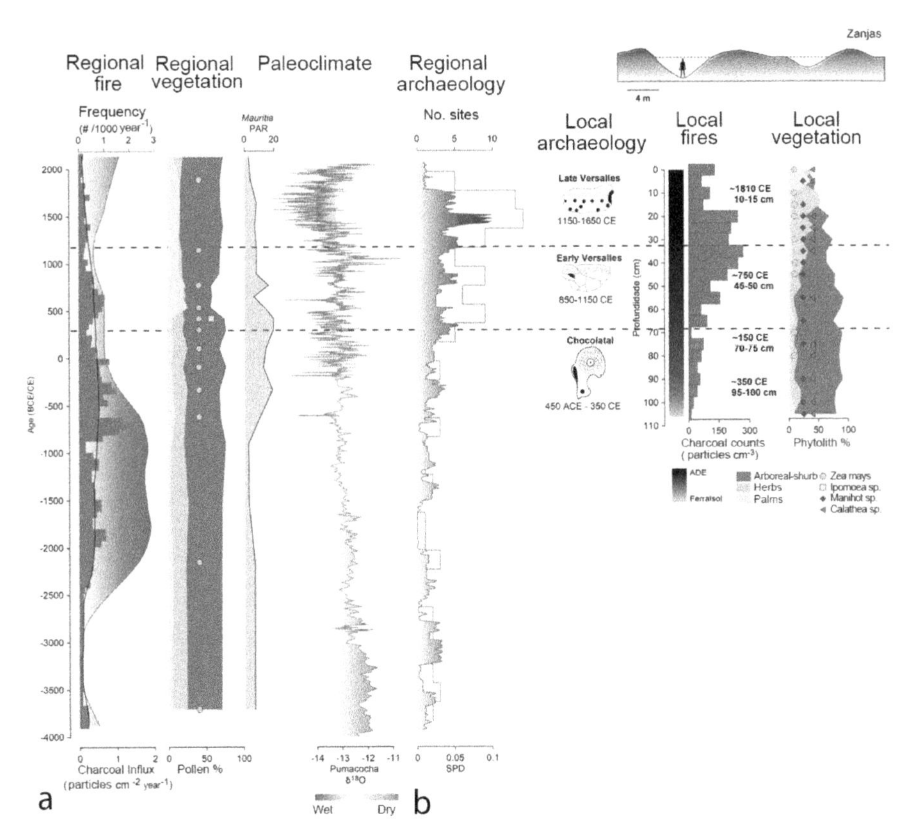

Figure 10.3 *a.* Charcoal and pollen data from the Versalles lake (Itenéz Forest Reserve, Bolivia) sediment core, along palaeoprecipitation data (δ^{18}O) from Pumacocha cave (Bird et al. 2011). *b.* SPD values from the region's archaeology local archaeological ceramic phases, charcoal and phytolith data from a soil profile located at the Triunfo site. Modified from Maezumi et al. (2022).

approach to compare local-scale land use, vegetation and fire histories (archaeological excavations/terrestrial archaeobotany) with broader regional-scale vegetation histories (lake palaeoecology) (Maezumi et al., 2022). Our environmental archive was the closed-basin, flat-bottomed Versalles lake, located ~3 kilometres south-west of the modern Itonama village of Versalles on the banks of the Iténez-Guaporé River. The Triunfo site, on the south-western shore of Laguna Versalles, is an ADE site surrounded by a ditch and embankment earthwork, known as a *zanja*, and a double ditch ring village. Preliminary excavations at the site and fifteen radiocarbon dates allowed us to define three ceramic phases: Chocolatal (before 2.4–1.6 ka), Early Versalles (~1.1–0.8 ka) and Late Versalles (0.8–0.3 ka) (Iriarte et al., 2020a; Maezumi et al., 2022; Robinson et al., 2020).

As the diagram in Figure 10.3 shows, the start of the pollen record during pre-ceramic times shows the presence of maize pollen ~5.7 ka, along with an onset of low levels of fire activity across the Amazon (Figure 4.1). The lake record documents an increase in biomass burning and fire frequency after ~4.5 ka, reaching record levels at ~2.8 ka. Between 3.0–2.4 ka, there is an 8 per cent decline in trees and shrubs, a ~3 per cent increase in palm pollen (*Mauritia/Mauritiella*, *Euterpe*, and *Oenocarpus*) and the continued presence of maize pollen. At this time, the phytolith data from the archaeological soil profiles also indicates the presence of manioc and leren (*Calathea* sp.) crops, along with maize.

ADE soil formation began ~2.3 ka during the Chocolatal ceramic phase. During this phase, the record shows an increase in biomass, a ~20 per cent decline in trees and shrubs, the continued presence of maize and sweet potato (*Ipomoea* sp.) pollen, as well as a >10 per cent increase in palms (*Mauritia/Mauritiella*, *Attalea*, *Euterpe* and *Oenocarpus*).

After 1.1 ka, with the start of the Early Versalles phase, the lake records show a decline in burning. Charcoal from the soil pits shows an increase in charcoal in line with the cultivation of manioc, maize and leren. The phytolith record from the ADE soil profiles shows a 20 per cent increase in herb phytoliths at the expense of trees and shrubs. However, change in vegetation composition is not large enough to be detected in the pollen record from the lake.

The following period, Late Versalles, shows low levels of biomass burning in the lake record. The phytolith record shows an intensification of ADE land use, evidenced by increased charcoal and a continuation of the increased proportion of herbs, as well as the continued cultivation of manioc, maize and leren. These changes happened when the regional SPD and site frequencies increased, in association with the development of fortification features – a pattern that appears to be pan-Amazonian at this time (see Chapter 7).

Towards the end of the record, the continued presence of maize pollen until ~0.2 ka, and maize and manioc phytoliths after 0.14 ka, suggests that this area did not experience immediate depopulation following the arrival of European settlers, and that indigenous populations did not abandon polyculture in this region following European contact.

Overall, one of the most significant findings of this record is that rainforest vegetation is persistent throughout, indicated by >40 per cent Moraceae/Urticaceae trees in the pollen record. This is despite the fact that after the formation of the ADE soils, there is a peak in land use intensification, indicated by record level erosion, peak forest clearance both locally (indicated by a 20 per cent increase in herb phytoliths) and regionally (indicated by a 30 per cent decrease in trees and shrubs), coupled with a 13 per cent increase in edible palms, along with maize, sweet potato, manioc and leren cultivation. Despite significant climate variability during the Medieval Climatic Anomaly (950–1250 CE), and the Little Ice Age (1650–1850 CE), social change and intensive human activity that influenced forest composition and structure, the rainforest ecosystems around Laguna Versalles maintained their integrity during the Holocene along this ecotonal boundary.

Along with the lower Amazon record of Caranã (Figure 6.4) (Maezumi et al., 2018a), the Peruvian Amazon (Kelly et al., 2018) and various ADE records across the Amazon (McMichael et al., 2012), the data from Versalles show that ADE land use was characterized by polyculture agroforestry systems that included the cultivation of multiple crops, such as maize, manioc, sweet potato and leren, as well as cultural burning and the enrichment of the forest with edible plants. Overall, and most importantly, these records show limited vegetation removal associated with ADE farming practices. It is worth noting that the record from other regions in the Amazon, such as the Casarabe culture, in the forest and savannah mosaic of the Llanos de Mojos, indicates similar patterns of limited vegetation clearing. The pollen record from Laguna San José, from the Casarabe culture period, shows a consistent presence of tree pollen, indicating that despite cultivating fertile savannahs and increased burning, the gallery forests' canopy remained largely unaffected (Whitney et al., 2013). Furthermore, research conducted in the southern Brazilian highlands using various methods such as archaeology, lake pollen records and carbon isotopes on soils, suggests that the southern Jê groups not only maintained by also afforested this region by replacing high-altitude grasslands with highly valued *Araucaria* forests (Robinson et al., 2018). Collectively, the data from these different regions indicate that pre-Columbian land use in them did not result in large-scale deforestation but rather maintained the canopy cover.

Lessons branded with fires

How to prevent a megafire: Lessons from the Tapajós

Humans may have been using fire as early as 1.5 million years ago. Archaeological, historical and ethnographic records show that societies have been shaping fire regimens globally for millennia through forest clearance, grazing promotion, plant dispersal, altering ignition patterns and active suppression of fires.

Located in the hinterland of the Tapajós culture, the fire record of Lake Caranã in the lower Amazon has revealed one of the most important lessons about fire management that we can learn from the paleorecords of Amazonia (Maezumi et al., 2018b). At this location, charcoal and pollen analysis indicate the onset of fire activity and crop cultivation ~4.5 ka (Figure 6.4). This increased local and regional fire activity occurred during the wettest period of the past 45,000 years, as shown by the Paraíso speleothem record (Wang et al., 2017). Further, pollen evidence suggests that this area was dominated by moist, fire-intolerant vegetation during this time. Collectively, the unusually wet conditions preceding the start of increased fires around 4.5 ka, the appearance of crop pollen from maize (4.3 ka) and sweet potato (3.1 ka), and the more intense occupation of the area (higher values for both SPD and site frequency) indicate that humans, rather than changes in climate, were responsible for increased fires in the region.

Pollen analysis shows that pre-Columbian people altered vegetation composition in ADE forests from 2,500 years ago, by enriching edible forest species at the expense of other trees, palms and herbs. The selective removal of vegetation, combined with frequent burning, most likely changed forest structure by increasing canopy gaps, decreasing fuel moisture and increasing forest flammability. Increased burning, combined with a more open canopy at this time, most likely played a role in the later development of ADE soils at this location, 2,000 years ago. Local fire activity rose between 1.2–0.4 ka during the Late Pre-Columbian Tapajó Period (Stenborg et al., 2012), paralleled by increased SPD and site frequency values. During this time, at the apogee of LPTP, Roosevelt (1999) estimates that the Santarém polity covered around 23,000 kilometres^2, with settlements spread over hundreds of kilometres along river bluffs and interior plateaus. The largest occupation in the modern city of Santarém is estimated to contain 500 hectares of ADE soils, of which 16 hectares comprise the pre-Columbian settlement core (see Chapter 7).

Despite increasing activity in the area throughout pre-Columbian times, rainforest taxa persisted. This suggests that widespread deforestation did not occur in the lake region. The simultaneous decreases in magnetic susceptibility values, indicating less erosion, are consistent with this understanding, since erosion is increased in a scenario where a lot of land is cleared. The combined multiproxy results suggest that low-severity fire management strategies were implemented within the rainforest to improve soil nutrient availability, and also to clear understorey vegetation, thereby decreasing fuel loads.

Fire activity remained low during European colonization (~0.3–0.03 ka) despite increased European settlement associated with Amazon rubber exploitation (Schroth et al., 2003). The record low levels of fire activity during the rubber boom, despite the prevalence in the region of a drier climate, suggest that traditional pre-Columbian fire management practices were abandoned, and that a fire suppression strategy may have been in place from the early 1800s. It is reasonable to suppose that rubber tappers were most likely keeping fires out of the forests in order to protect the valuable, fire-intolerant rubber plantations. The record ends when the rubber boom is over (0.03 ka), with a century of steadily rising rates of biomass burning and fire severity. Despite an aggressive fire prevention policy in the FLONA Reserve, the amount of biomass burned in the past decade was at record high levels (Cordeiro, 2004).

The widespread use of cultural burning associated with indigenous polyculture and anthrosol formation influenced key palaeofire regime components, such as fire severity, frequency and intensity. Fire management practices changed forest composition and structure in various ways. They promoted nutrient-demanding species, decreased competition for cultivated plants, lowered fuel loads and increased light availability. Many plants, such as palms (*Mauritia* and *Attalea*), have evolved fire adaptations that

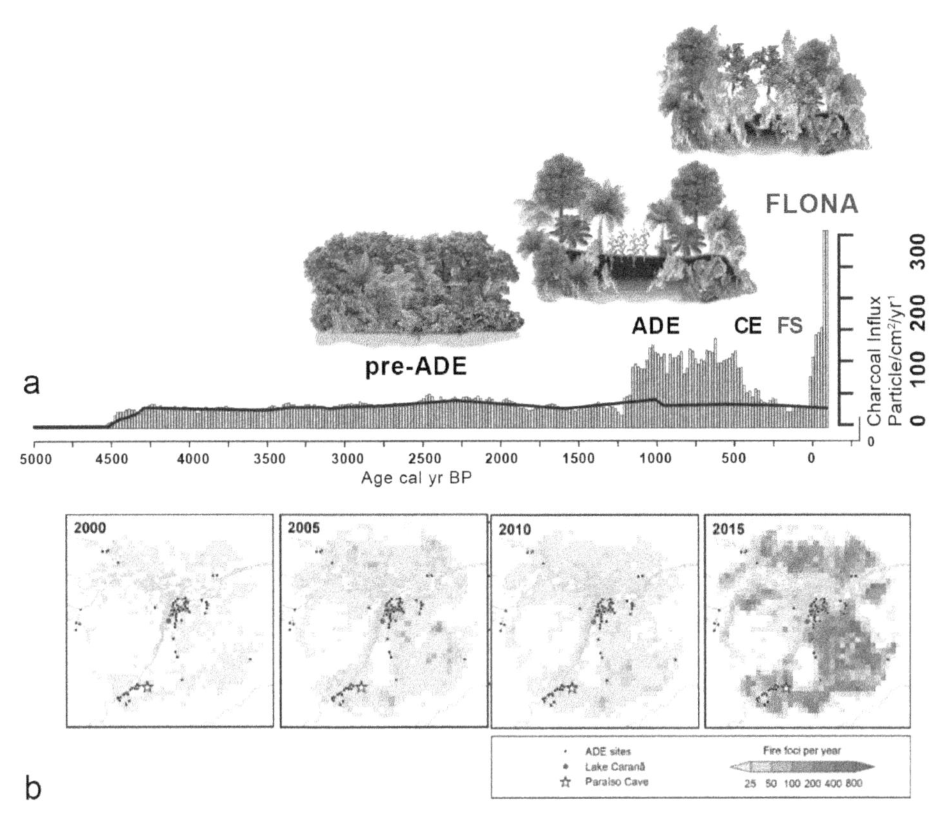

Figure 10.4 *a*. Fire record from Caranã Lake (Santarem, Lower Amazon). *b*. Figures showing the progressive increase in fire activity in the eastern Amazon from 2000–15. The total number of fire foci per 0.1 square decimal degree at five-year intervals between 2000–15 within a 100-kilometre radius around Lake Caranã. Data on fire activity for the period 1999–17 was obtained from the online database of the Brazilian National Institute of Spatial Research (INPE) (http://www.inpe.br/queimadas/portal). The raw data represent fire foci at least 30 metres^2 detected on satellite imagery of varying resolutions (CE=1492 Columbian Encounter; FS=Fire suppression). Modified from Maezumi et al. (2018).

allow them to persist over time in frequently burned areas, increasing the abundance of fire-tolerant plants while reducing the abundance of fire-intolerant seed banks.

Recently, anthropogenic climate change has lengthened and intensified the dry season, creating ideal conditions for large, frequent wildfires in the eastern Amazon (e.g., Aragão et al., 2018). This has led to a recent increase in biomass burning. Hotter, drier climates, coupled with longer dry seasons, create the 'perfect storm' of factors driving increased fire activity in the Amazon. The link between drought severity, fuel availability and fire activity has created optimal conditions for mega-fires in the eastern Amazon (Aragão et al., 2018). Furthermore, it is predicted that the length and severity of the dry season will increase because of increasing ENSO activity (Alencar et al., 2006; Cochrane et al., 1999; Soares-Filho et al., 2012). The eastern Amazon has some of the highest densities of ADE sites in the Amazon (see Chapter 7), which makes this area, and by extension all areas with an abundance of ADE across the basin, extremely vulnerable to fires induced by drought.

There are lessons to be learnt. Periodic, low-severity fires were likely used during pre-Columbian times to clear out much of the forest understorey fuels so crop cultivation could take place, leaving most edible fruit trees unaffected while reducing the risk of high-severity fires. After the pre-Columbian period, fire management was largely excluded from the landscape because of the abandonment of traditional fire management practices and because of the need to protect fire-adverse rubber groves. Despite FLONA's efforts to suppress fires, since its inception in 1974 (De Andrade and De Carvalho, 2011), fire severity has progressively increased, reaching record levels of annual fire activity in the past 15 years. The transition from 4,000 years of low-severity pre-Columbian fire management to a fire suppression policy, which still characterizes modern management policy, has most likely resulted in the accumulation of understorey fuels in ADE forests.

The results of our research have policy implications. In Maezumi et al. (2018b), we suggest the implementation of ADE fire management strategies during the off-peak fire season (e.g., the wet season, from January–April), prioritizing the reduction of fire use and more careful fire management for the farming of ADE soils (Aragão et al., 2018), which may help to reduce fuel loads. In turn, this will reduce the likelihood of high severity, stand-replacing fire events and prevent fires spreading to old-growth rainforests (Bowman et al., 2009). Studies have previously demonstrated that reducing fuel loads not only decreases fire severity and lowers the accidental spread of fires into neighbouring forests, but also improves the effectiveness of fire suppression efforts in subsequent fire seasons (Brando et al., 2014). Using an off-peak fire-reduction management policy may help reduce the risk and spread of mega-fires from ADE forests. Combined with sustainable ADE forest strategies by local farmers, this management policy may reduce fire-related carbon emissions and ultimately improve long-term forest conservation efforts in the eastern Amazon.

Fire free land use

This case study focuses on the coastal savannahs of French Guiana. The pre-Columbian agricultural landscapes along the coast of the Guianas are characterized by the presence of raised fields, canals and lagoons that stretch for 600 kilometres between the Berbice River in Guyana to near the town of Cayenne in French Guiana (Rostain, 2012b) (see description of these raised fields in Chapter 6).

To understand what type of agriculture was practised on these raised fields, and what kind of impact these systems had on the environment, an integrated interdisciplinary study was conducted. The study combined palaeoecological studies of a sediment column extracted from a wetland (combining pollen, phytoliths and charcoal analysis), soil analysis of a raised field profile located about 700 metres from the wetland core (Figure 10.5) and analysis of starch grains from nearby habitation sites (Iriarte et al., 2010; Iriarte et al., 2012; McKey et al., 2010b; Rostain, 2012b).

Analyses of charcoal particles, pollen and phytoliths provides a continuous record for the past 2,150 years before the present. In zone K-VIII-1, between ~2.2 ka (peat base) and ~0.8 ka, pollen and phytolith assemblages are dominated by wetland grasses, including Cyperaceae and Maranthaceae sedges. The percentage of grasses (Poaceae) and phytoliths are low, and macroscopic charcoal (>125 mm) is insignificantly represented throughout this period. Evidence from the various indicators shows that the local landscape was a

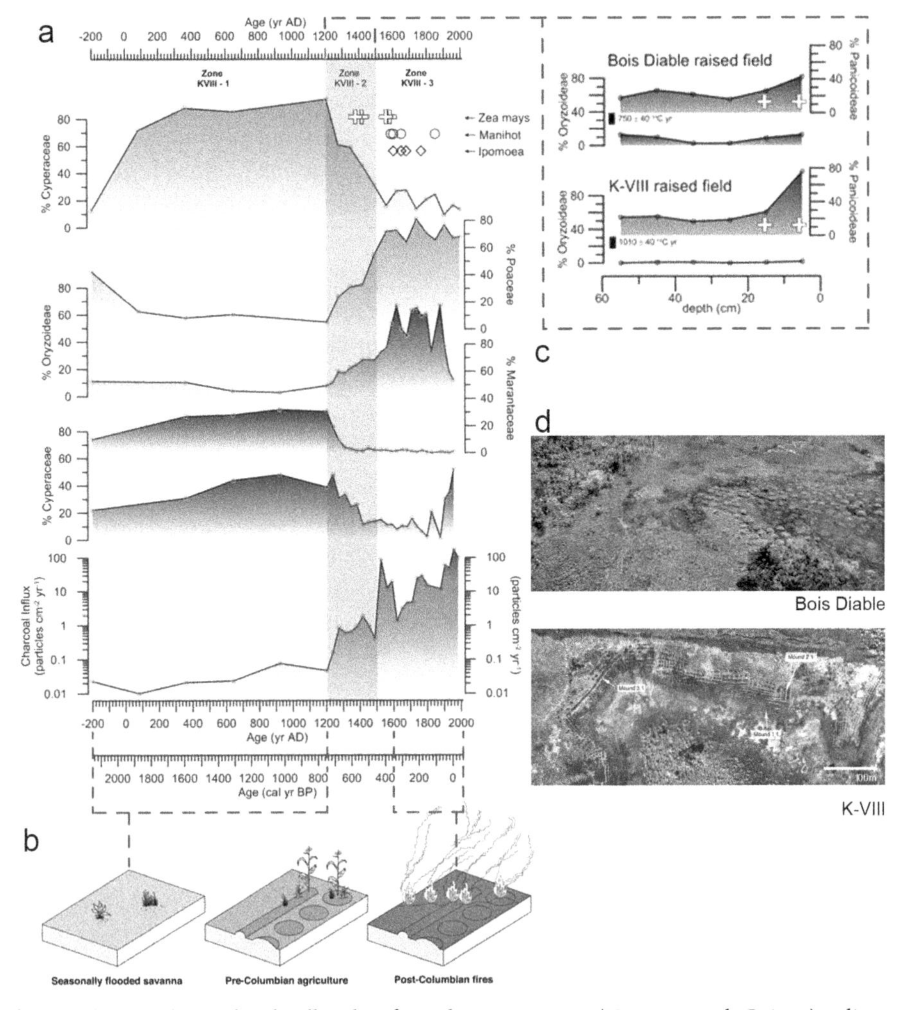

Figure 10.5 *a.* Charcoal and pollen data from the K-VIII core (Korou, French Guiana) sediment core. *b.* Schematic drawing of changing vegetation and disturbance regimes as inferred from analysis of pollen, phytoliths and charcoal from the K-VIII core. *c.* Percentage phytolith diagram of selected plant taxa from soil profiles from the K-VIII and Bois Diable pre-Columbian agricultural raised fields. The dates show the age of the uppermost levels of the buried A horizon (peat) immediately below the overlying raised-field soils. *d.* aerial views of Bois Diable and K-VIII raised-field sites shown in *c.* Modified from Iriarte et al. (2012).

seasonally flooded savannah that rarely had any fire. Around 0.8 ka, a marked decline in representative wetland taxa is coincident with a sharp increase in the abundance of grasses and the first appearance of maize pollen, suggesting that the initial construction of agricultural raised fields was primarily for maize cultivation (Iriarte et al., 2012).

One of the most important findings of this study comes from the macroscopic charcoal data, and challenges traditional assumptions about land use in pre-Columbian times. In general, palaeofire records show a trend towards increased burning in Neotropical forests during the late Holocene, reflecting the intensification of land use. This is usually followed by a sharp decline, associated with the collapse of the indigenous populations from 1492 CE, following European contact (Bush et al., 2008; Dull et al., 2010). However, the complete opposite trend was evident in the record from the savannahs of French Guiana.

The low charcoal abundance along zone K-VIII-2 (pre-Columbian raised-field farmers) is unexpected, since there is a significant increase in flammable grasses in this zone compared to the previous zone. The very low level of biomass burning in the more recent period is explained by the implementation of fire limitation practices by the raised-field farmers. Fire limitation must have presented advantages for raised-field agriculture, since fires cause soil nutrients, such as nitrogen and phosphorus, to be lost through the formation of gases and aerosols (Mahowald et al., 2005; Wan et al., 2001). In addition, fallows in the absence of fire were probably more effective in restoring plant biomass, soil organic matter and soil structure for the next crop cycle (Dezzeo and Chacón, 2005; Miranda et al., 2002). Moreover, fire control may have meant that the work of clearing the fields of fire-adapted weeds typical of Neotropical savannahs that proliferate after fires could had been avoided (Miranda et al., 2002).

In the third zone of our diagram, zone K-VIII-3 (Figure 10.5), the record shows a dramatic increase in charcoal influx around 1500 CE, signifying the return of fires to the region and demonstrating that this is a post-Columbian phenomenon. After 1500 CE, the charcoal frequency pattern for the savannah differs radically from reconstructions of palaeofires in the Neotropical forests, which decrease dramatically after 1500 CE. So once again, we must ask why these patterns are so different in savannah contexts relative to forest contexts. The record shows a clear correlation between the dramatic increase in charcoal abundance, which begins about 1500 CE, and the arrival of Europeans in the coastal region of the Guianas. It appears that only after the abandonment of raised fields in the flooded savannahs, and the adoption in colonial times of a different form of agriculture (raised beds in cleared forests in *terra firme* areas), (McKey et al., 2010) did fire begin to be used as an essential tool for land-use management.

The results of this study show that pre-Columbian raised-field farmers limited fires, which contrasts sharply with slash-and-burn farmers living in similar savannah and forest environments who regularly burn savannahs for a variety of reasons (e.g., to increase visibility, facilitate hunting and prevent catastrophic fires at the end of the dry season) (e.g., Mistry et al., 2005; Rodríguez, 2007). These data also call into question the hypothesis that anthropogenic fires have been a dominant feature of all Neotropical savannah ecosystems (Mann, 2005; Rodríguez, 2007), including those that were inhabited by pre-Columbian upland farmers (Balée and Erickson, 2006).

In the current climate of Amazonian development, the practice of using fire for agriculture in areas that have already been deforested releases more carbon into the atmosphere than is conserved by avoiding deforestation through programmes such as REDD (Aragão and Shimabukuro, 2010). Pre-Columbian fire-free land-use management practices along the coast of French Guiana should therefore be discussed as an alternative to current unsustainable practices. However, it should be noted that not all raised field farmers conduct fire suppression practices. Palaeoecological data from the Platform Ridge Region in the Llanos de Mojos show that human-caused fires were common during raised-field cultivation (Whitney et al., 2014) (see below).

Biochar: Amazonian black gold

In the past two decades, climate scientists have turned their attention to the mitigation potential of biochar. Biochar is a charcoal-like substance produced when organic material is burned in a controlled process with very little oxygen. Modern biochar technology has its roots in the ancient farming practices of the Amazon basin, where charred biomass was added to the soil to improve its quality (see Chapter 6). By sequestering large amounts of carbon in the soil, the impact of biochar on climate mitigation could be huge.

Biochar is a stable form of carbon that cannot easily escape into the atmosphere. This stability – time-tested on the 2,000-year-old ADEs – is one of biochar's main advantages. Although large amounts of carbon from decomposed plant matter are found in most soils, the carbon is relatively unstable, and the soil becomes a carbon source when disturbed, for example by ploughing. Biochar's ability to help absorb water is another advantage.

The amount of carbon stored is significant. Studies on ADEs (Schmidt et al., 2023) have shown that highly weathered Amazonian soils typically contain 6–10 kilograms/metres^2 SOC (soil organic carbon) in the upper 1 metre, while ADE deposits have densities of 9–22 kilograms/metres^2. Johannes Lehmann of Cornell University and others have calculated that biochar could remove between 5.5–9.5 billion tonnes of carbon from the air each year (Lehmann and Joseph, 2015). The procedure for making biochar is straightforward: take wood, straw or crop waste and heat it in the absence of oxygen. Traditionally, this was accomplished by heaping soil on top of the lighted biomass, allowing it to smoulder for an extended period. Modern kilns make the procedure more efficient, but the fundamentals remain the same. To speed up and scale up the process, researchers are turning to pyrolysis, which is a type of controlled thermal degradation of organic material in the absence of oxygen at temperatures ranging from 500–600°C (Manyà, 2012). However, the production of biochar is not without its problems. Biochar could be ideal for sequestering carbon, but on its own would not make soils fertile. Pre-Columbian ADEs contain nutrients from bone, excrement and other non-char vegetable materials, meaning they are highly fertile. The biochar undoubtedly plays a role in holding these nutrients together, ensuring they remain available to plant roots, but the nutrients must be provided by other means.

Another issue concerns finding suitable organic material for biochar production. In terms of climate change, destroying forests to make charcoal would be pointless. However, there is a wealth of other raw materials available. Agriculture generates considerable plant and animal waste, such as straw, husks and dung, while human waste, such as sewage sludge or other types of home garbage, could also be used. Using waste products saves twice as much carbon as not using them: rotting waste produces methane, a greenhouse gas twenty times stronger than carbon dioxide. This is especially relevant to the Amazon, where, as Aragão et al. (2010) demonstrated, most carbon emissions occur as a result of fires on agricultural lands that have already been deforested.

The challenge lies in collecting the waste products and making it profitable to do so. Farmers will need to be convinced that the effort of storing and converting their waste to charcoal is worthwhile, and they may require new equipment to do it. At the municipal level, the issue will be segregating the organic trash, which can be converted to char, from the rest of the garbage. It will need to be demonstrated that this is cheaper and more helpful than simply burying it. Several international groups are working on this promising venture informed by past land uses (e.g., International Biochar Initiative). Let us hope that these biochar initiatives succeed in addressing these critical issues to help shape a better Anthropocene.

Working alongside indigenous and traditional peoples: Saving the bio-cultural heritage

The partnership between archaeologists and indigenous peoples is particularly important in indigenous reserves, especially as these groups face political and economic forces that threaten their integrity and even their survival. The practice of participatory mapping, with a focus on issues such as protecting biodiversity and upholding the rights of indigenous communities, has garnered considerable attention in Amazonian research (Chapin et al., 2005). Participatory mapping in indigenous lands, both on the ground and through remote sensing technologies, provides a tangible mechanism for promoting dialogue between archaeologists and traditional communities.

There are several examples showing how archaeologists and indigenous people can work well together for the common good in Amazonia. As Heckenberger (2009b) argues, archaeologists, like anthropologists, are fascinated by the minutiae of debris in excavations, and the spatial relationships between settlements and other sites, and their distributions across larger landscapes and regions. In turn, the work of archaeologists as they investigate human-land relations and cultural heritage is intrinsically important to indigenous peoples, and is invariably of social, economic and political interest. Indigenous people are fascinated not only by the past and by the places where it occurred, but also by how archaeologists learn about it, map it and apply that knowledge in larger public arenas. Mapping and exploring old settlements is crucial, because it links people's oral histories with the actual locations where their ancestors lived. In Heckenberger's (2009b) work with the Kuikuro people of the Upper Xingu, for example, this process has revealed previously unknown information, such as the fact that many locations revered in ancestral time myths were actually significant as the birthplaces of individual Kuikuro people.

Figure 10.6 Archaeologist Carla Jaimes Betancourt and members of the Itonama community of Versalles (Guaporé-Itenéz River, Bolivian Amazon) carrying out participatory mapping in the context of the 'Cultural heritage tourism in the Versalles Itonama Indigenous Community' project by UKRI GCRF, University of Bonn and Wildlife Conversation Society.

Another example is provided by da Rocha and Vinicious (2020). Indigenous and traditional groups were fighting against the construction of a hydroelectric dam by a consortium of multinational corporations and the Brazilian federal government, along the Tapajós River and its tributaries. Construction of the dam would involve transforming free-flowing rivers into a series of lakes, irreversibly altering the landscapes and ecosystems on which the Munduruku and Beiradeiros rely. It would also lead to the destruction of their sacred places. The Munduruku are native Amazonians who speak the Munduruku language, which is the only surviving language of the Munduruku family, a branch of the Tupian language stock. The Beiradeiros are known as 'forest peasants' and have been living along the banks of the upper Tapajós for at least eight generations. From 2010, Rocha, collaborators and the Munduruku people conducted collaborative archaeological investigations along the middle and upper reaches of the Tapajós River in southern Brazilian Amazonia, in territories traditionally occupied by the Munduruku and riverine Beiradeiro communities.

From the start, the objective of the work was to use archaeological evidence to dispute the official claim that the area was unpopulated. In collaboration with the Brazilian Heritage Agency (IPHAN), the team first recorded and documented archaeological sites to prove that people had been present in the region throughout history. As part of the work, they engaged with the Beiradeiros, asking them about the location of Amazonian anthrosols, pottery sherds or polished axe heads. The work was conducted in various settings, including people's homes, manioc processing houses and house gardens. In community meetings, the team explained the purpose of our archaeological survey in relation to territorial claims.

Figure 10.7 Conducting collaborative archaeological excavations at the Munduruku lands. Archaeologist Bruna Rocha along with teacher Claudete Saw Munduruku checking the colour archaeological sediment to delimit the Sawre Muybu site (and village). Courtesy of Kuyjeat Etaybinap Program archive.

Excavation at one of the sites in the region, the Mangabal site, an ADE site occupied for 200 years between ~700–1100 CE, produced evidence for the exploitation of riverine and forest resources. Most importantly, the ceramic designs were strongly reminiscent of the Munduruku tattoos represented in the nineteenth century. One of the notable ceramic designs consisted of incised, oblique-oriented, criss-cross lines that follow the vessel body or everted griddle rims, forming lozenges. This design was observed to be present on both Munduruku pottery and tattoos. These findings, along with the mapping of ancient ADE habitation sites across Munduruku territory, were used by the federal public prosecution service to successfully argue for the cancellation of the São Luiz do Tapajós dam (Directive PRM/ STM/GAB1/330/2016), which was going to displace these groups from their ancestral territories.

Collectively, these case studies show how the deep time records of archaeology and palaeoecology can help inform policies for sustainable Amazonian futures and protect indigenous territories. In the upcoming final chapter of the book, I will provide a synopsis of the most important events in Amazonian history, along with some of the most important questions that still need to be answered.

CHAPTER 11
CONCLUSIONS

This book has delved into the human history of Amazonia, from the earliest foragers to the complex low-density urban societies of the later pre-Columbian period. Several decades of anthropological research have been dominated by the notion of Amazonia as a virgin wilderness, devoid of opportunities for the development of complex societies and cultures. By summarizing recent interdisciplinary research across the Amazon basin, I have presented a perspective on the region's history that suggests otherwise. As we have seen, archaeological evidence increasingly confirms the accounts of many early Amazon chronicles, previously dismissed as exaggerations and fables that bear witness to complex societies. Let me summarize some of the major findings to conclude the book.

Who were the first Amazonians? The timing and the routes taken by the first people to arrive in South America continues to be a matter of debate (Boëda et al., 2014; Borrero, 2016; Dillehay, 2000), although current archaeological and ancient DNA suggest that the Americas were colonized sometime between ~25–15 ka by anatomically modern humans who likely followed a Pacific Rim corridor from northeast Asia into the New World, reaching southern Chile by at least 14.3 ka (Braje et al., 2017; Dillehay et al., 2017). The first humans to arrive in NW South America were met with a great diversity of environments as well as large, now extinct, mammals. These early migrants have been traditionally portrayed as highly specialized, mobile hunter-gatherers, who exploited coastal resources and big savannah game while avoiding forest habitats because of the absence of large animals, and the difficulty of moving through this dense and unfamiliar environment (e.g., Lynch, 1990). But recent data, summarized in this book, show that these early South Americans did not avoid tropical rainforests, while evidence hinting at early plant cultivation suggests they were more than passive consumers of their resources (Aceituno and Loaiza, 2018; Iriarte, 2007; Piperno, 2011). From their first arrival in South America, these early modern humans successfully transited, and adapted to, sharply contrasting interior environments, including lowland, Sub Andean and Andean tropical forests, and savannahs (Bryan et al., 1978; Dickau et al., 2015; Mora, 2003; Ranere et al., 2002).

How did they get to Amazonia? The answer is unclear, but a possibility is that they travelled along the Magdalena and the Amazon Rivers, likely following the Caribbean coast, then entering inland or through the mouth of the Amazon. Perhaps some followed the dry corridor (Figure 3.1), the arch of lower precipitation stretching from the Guianas to the Lower Amazon. As people ventured into new surroundings, they likely had to backtrack and move laterally at times. With the little data we currently have to hand, we can only speculate on the outline of these potential routes (Figure 3.1).

What was the diet of early Amazonians? Archaeobotanical studies are providing a far greater appreciation of the role of plants in early colonists' diets in the tropics (Gnecco,

2003; Mora, 2003; Roosevelt et al., 1996) and elsewhere in SA (Dillehay and Rossen, 2002; Prous and Fogaça, 1999). Data from the montane forests of Colombia, the lowland evergreen forest of the Colombian Amazon and from the Lower Amazon, indicate a generalized subsistence with an early reliance on plant resources. In some regions, such as Colombia, the archaeobotanical evidence is supported by the appearance in the archaeological record of a distinct tool kit, including hoes and hand axes, which was likely used for managing and cultivating forest resources. Rather than the big-game hunting, narrow-spectrum foraging diet traditionally portrayed, the review carried out in this book shows that the earliest Amazon settlers relied instead on a broad-spectrum diet that included tropical roots and tubers, tree and palm fruits and nuts, in addition to the medium and small terrestrial and riverine fauna procured through hunting and fishing. Many medicinal/narcotic plants were also utilized. This data concurs with research over the past two decades that highlights the occupation and use of tropical rainforests by humans, including the manipulation of tree products, anthropogenic burning, the management of forest composition, the cultivation of edible plants and the detoxification of particular plants, along with the hunting of medium to small-sized arboreal, semi-arboreal and terrestrial tropical game. Evidence of the human manipulation of forest ecosystems begins in SE Asia from at least 50–45 ka, Near Oceania from 45 ka and now from at least 13 ka in South America (see summary in Roberts, 2019).

Intriguingly, many of the earliest plants consumed by humans are Amazonian hyperdominants, while edible plants have a five times greater chance of being hyperdominant than plants not consumed by humans (Levis et al., 2017; Ter Steege et al., 2013), which points to a possible very ancient human footprint on the forest. Palms (Arecaceae) were an essential food resource for these early tropical forest residents colonizing new environments (Robinson et al., 2021). Productive ecotones, particularly palm-dominated tropical forest-savannah-riverine mosaics, would likely have been attractive to early foragers for the construction of temporary or semi-permanent settlements, as in La Lindosa, Caverna de Pedra Pintada, Serra dos Carajás and Santa Elina.

Was the Amazon a centre of plant domestication? Recent evidence shows that plant cultivation and domestication emerged in the forest-savannah mosaics of SW Amazonia, as well as in the montane forests of NW Amazonia of the Colombian Andes, at the start of the Holocene. Amazonia is thus firmly established as a centre of plant cultivation and domestication. The evidence from the Llanos de Mojos shows that along with the beginnings of plant cultivation, the early settlers were involved in creating thousands of forest islands while managing savannah landscapes. Through these practices, communities increased resource abundance and heterogeneity for humans and animals. This further emphasises the strong relationship identified between plant and landscape domestication and the significant human footprint on Amazonian environments.

What happened during the middle Holocene? The middle Holocene is one of the least-studied periods of Amazonia. However, mounting evidence unearthed from shell-middens throughout the basin is shedding light on life at this time. Although radiocarbon databases suggest a decline in population, and although gaps in human occupation occur in some regions of Amazonia (e.g., Central Amazon and Santarém), recent research is revealing that it was actually a very dynamic period. The middle Holocene witnessed the domestication of important crops, such as cacao and rice, and the spread of Amazonian domesticates, such as manioc, as well as the arrival and spread of exotic cultigens, such as maize. Based on current genetic data, it has been determined that not only were there exchanges of cultivars between Central and South America during this period, but also movements of people from the south to the north. It is also at this time that the first ceramics in South America were manufactured, while Amazonian anthrosols began to be formed in the middle Madeira River.

As Neves (2013) has rightly pointed out there is a gap of several millennia between the first plant cultivation and domestication, and the emergence of the agricultural societies of the late Holocene. However, as I have previously argued (Iriarte, 2009), and the data presented in Chapter 5 tells us, new data is emerging to fill the long and uncharted gap of 'low-level food producers' (Smith, 2001) between initial plant cultivation and domestication and formative agriculture. Irrespective of the designations we employ for analytical reasons, characterizing the majority of middle Holocene societies as mobile hunters and gatherers, or as groups of foragers who augmented their diets with small portions of cultivated foodstuffs, is likely inappropriate (Iriarte, 2009).

What happened during the late Holocene? In the late Holocene, Amazonians started transforming the landscape on a large scale, and not only in the productive and agriculturally rich riverine areas. It is during this time that Amazonian anthrosols spread across the basin, with seasonally flooded savannahs transformed into productive raised-field agricultural landscapes. As food production became more important during the middle Holocene, the extent and pace of landscape modification increased, culminating in the major transformations that took place during the late Holocene, as seen in the radiocarbon databases. In turn, these changes likely generated a positive feedback effect on population growth (Arroyo-Kalin and Riris, 2020; De Souza et al., 2019).

By closely integrating archaeology and palaeoecology, we are able to document larger, regional populations in Amazonia, many of which relied on polyculture agroforestry systems supported by intensive cultivation in Amazonian anthrosols. These populations fall within the range of medium-sized pre-Columbian polities elsewhere in the Americas and pre-modern urbanized forested landscapes in most areas of the world. The data, along with soil science and micromorphology, show that these anthrosols, particularly ABEs, were used for high labour input cultivation, relying on organic amendments along with soil preparation and maintenance. Both annual and perennial crops were cultivated on ABEs. Plant remains show that these crops included maize, manioc, sweet potato, yams, squash, bottle gourd, arrowroot and leren. ABEs represent a long-term investment in the land, *landesque capital*, as well as in the labour required to cultivate trees with long multi-decadal productive cycles, such as the Brazil nut or the pequi, which are then productive for centuries.

The land use patterns on ADE and ABE soils indicate a similarity in the use of polyculture agroforestry in ADE systems throughout Amazonia, despite varying cultural, bio-geographic and climatic factors. This, along with the relatively rapid spread at the start of the second millennium CE, suggests a farming technology that was rapidly adopted by diverse cultures across the Amazon basin.

Despite not having access to writing, the wheel or domesticated animals beyond ducks and dogs, the ancient Amazonian civilizations still managed to engineer landscapes and create exquisitely manufactured ceramics. In contrast to the high Andean people who used stone, and the people of the Pacific Coast who used adobe masonry, Amazonians used soils for construction. Whether deliberately or as an unintended consequence of their cultural traditions, a variety of *terraforming* practices took place at this time. These included anthrosols, ditches, canals, landscape-scale fish weirs, reservoirs, causeways, raised enclosures, plazas, platform mounds and pyramids. All this activity had lasting effects on local ecology from the time of the earliest occupation in many regions, exemplified by the early Holocene forest islands of the Llanos de Mojos. Located well beyond the river and natural communication routes, a network of sunken and causewayed roads interconnecting regional polities also developed over time. The sophistication and monumentality of the urban-scale Casarabe and Upano societies are comparable to those of the so-called Archaic states of the Central Andes and the Pacific Coast of Peru.

Recent research indicates that some of the most complex late Holocene archaeological cultures developed in interfluvial areas of Amazonia, such as the mosaic of savannahs and forests in Llanos de Mojos, or in Ecuador's aseasonal montane forest, the latter which was previously considered peripheral or sparsely populated regions of Amazonia. Even more revealing of how recent archaeology is altering our perception of the Amazonian past is the fact that these interfluvial regions exhibit the greatest contrast between the relatively simple groups described in the ethnographies of the twentieth century, such as the Siriono (Mojos) and the Shuar (Upano), and the complex urban-like cultures of the distant past. It shows once again how inappropriate it could be to project the ethnographic present into the past.

The late Holocene also saw the expansion of language families, such as the Tupi, the Arawak and the Carib. However, the mosaic of archaeological cultures reflects to a certain extent the distribution of languages in historical times, indicating that no single sociopolitical formation was strong enough to expand its political influence on a large scale, as was the case during several episodes of Andean prehistory. Beyond these single-language families, the temporal depth and nature of multi-lingual interaction spheres is certainly a fascinating topic that deserves more focused research.

Unanswered questions and future directions

First and foremost, there is still a considerable need for intensive primary data collection across the Amazon basin for the different time periods. Because of the unexplored nature of Amazonia, every other year a new culture is 'discovered', which needs to be described, compared and classified. As a result, many regions of Amazonia are still on the 'classificatory-descriptive' stage (*sensu* Willey and Sabloff, 1974). This is particularly acute for certain regions, for example the Western Amazon. In this region, Levis et al.

(2017) identified this particular region as a hotspot of domesticated species, which the documentation of unprecedented cultural developments has somewhat begun to confirm. This is the case, for example, of the middle Holocene sophisticated Mayo-Chinchipe tradition, the complex societies described in the ethnohistory and archaeology of the Ucayali and Napo rivers beginning to be archaeologically documented, as well as the urban-scale societies of the Upano. Nonetheless, large portions of the vast Western Amazon remain unexplored. The same applies to many other regions, such as the Colombian Amazon, the Guiana coast interior and sectors of the southern rim of the Amazon, to mention a few.

In methodological terms, research programmes should strive for increasing integration of interdisciplinary, complementary multi-proxy approaches and techniques, combining archaeology, palaeoecology, paleoclimate studies, soil science, remote sensing and floristic inventories in an inclusive and collaborative manner. Integration of off-site and on-site locations should be done carefully and thoughtfully. Sample selection should include random locations as well as sites deliberately chosen because they are either close to, or some distance from, archaeological sites. Incorporating deep time records from the palaeo sciences into historical ecology approaches can help us to better understand past land uses in Amazonia with further implications for sustainable Amazonian futures. Accurate evaluation of the legacy of past indigenous people within current ecosystems can only be provided by appropriate research designs that integrate the long-term data from fossil records with the modern information provided by botanical inventories, ethnobotany and indigenous knowledge. This can help resolve the question of whether current vegetation derives from pre-Columbian activities or is the result of more recent historical land transformations.

Although an ever-growing number of important ecologically and economically important plant taxa are identifiable to the genus level in pollen, phytolith and charcoal analyses, taxonomic resolution needs further refinement to resolve long-standing issues (e.g., Piperno and McMichael, 2023). Current projects testing the accuracy of phytolith and other plant proxies identification using AI could certainly become game changers for the discipline. Similarly, more work along the lines of Whitney et al. (2019) to quantify the spatial scale of pollen and charcoal production and deposition is sorely needed. Although there has been considerable progress towards the creation of modern analogue pollen and phytolith assemblages from 'natural' vegetation formations, very little has been done to further our understanding of modern analogues for traditional Amazonian land use systems (but see Watling et al., 2023; Witteveen et al., 2023). Similarly, unlike in Europe and Asia where significant advances have been made towards identifying modern analogues of macrobotanical remains and phytolith assemblages of weeds associated with crops, with the aim of revealing specific agricultural practices (e.g., Weisskopf et al., 2015), no progress has so far been made in the Neotropics. Another major task ahead is to establish the phenotypic and genetic characterization of perennial tree fruits, to distinguish more precisely different degrees of morphogenetic modification. Molecular studies will continue to help clarify the genetic changes that constitute the domestication syndromes of crops.

The nature of regional systems should also be a focus of future research. Lidar, along with ground-truthing and excavations, is certainly playing a major role in this matter. Although some pre-Columbian polities, such as the Tapajós, have been proposed as being heterarchical in nature (Gomes, 2007), others, such as the Casarabe culture, appear to have been highly hierarchical, displaying four-tiered settlement patterns (Prümers et al., 2022). Research from historical accounts and ethnography reveals a strong connection between the Andes and Amazonia. The boundary between the two regions is becoming less distinct as further research is conducted along the eastern slope of the Andes, filling the voids of information with evidence from the lowland forest. Last but not least, it is time to begin unpacking Amazonia to apprehend the whole diversity of land use systems across the basin and in different periods. As we acquire more detailed data from different regions of Amazonia that underscores its diversity, it is becoming apparent how inappropriate it could be to extrapolate sub-regional data to the entire Amazon basin.

Chapter 10 highlighted the significant challenges faced by the Amazon's forests and people in the Anthropocene era. Addressing these challenges requires collaboration, cross-disciplinary engagement, action beyond academia and creativity. Archaeology, with its wealth of historical deep time knowledge, has a responsibility to assist humanity in utilizing all available information to improve the environment, and to promote equity and sustainability. The past may be a foreign country, but it is one we can visit and learn from. Through a combination of scientific endeavour, a humanistic approach and the involvement of traditional communities, we will continue to learn more about this fascinating and inspiring chapter of human history.

BIBLIOGRAPHY

Aalto, R., Maurice-Bourgoin, L., Dunne, T., Montgomery, D. R., Nittrouer, C. A. and Guyot, J.-L. (2003), 'Episodic sediment accumulation on Amazonian flood plains influenced by El Niño/Southern Oscillation', *Nature*, 425 (6957): 493–7.

Absy, M. L. (1979), *A Palynological Study of Holocene Sediments in the Amazon Basin*, PhD: University of Amsterdam.

Aceituno, F. J. and Lalinde, V. (2011), 'Residuos de almidones y el uso de plantas durante el Holoceno Medio en el Cauca Medio (Colombia)', *Caldasia*, 33 (1): 1–20.

Aceituno, F. J. and Loaiza, N. (2018), 'The origins and early development of plant food production and farming in Colombian tropical forests', *Journal of Anthropological Archaeology*, 49: 161–72.

Admiraal, M., Colonese, A. C., Milheira, R. G., da Rocha Bandeira, D., Demathe, A., Pereira dos Santos, A. M., Fossile, T., Talbot, H. M., Bondetti, M. and Lucquin, A. (2023), 'Chemical analysis of pottery reveals the transition from a maritime to a plant-based economy in pre-colonial coastal Brazil', *Scientific Reports*, 13 (1): 16771.

Aikhenvald, A. (2012), *Languages of the Amazon*, Oxford: Oxford Linguistics.

Alencar, A., Nepstad, D. and Diaz, M. C. V. (2006), 'Forest understory fire in the Brazilian Amazon in ENSO and non-ENSO years: Area burned and committed carbon emissions', *Earth Interactions*, 10 (6): 1–17.

Almeida de Oliveira, E., Marimon-Junior, B., Schwantes-Marimon, B., Iriarte, J., Morandi, P., Maezumi, S., Nogueira, D., Aragão, L. E. O., Brasil da Silva, I. and Feldpausch, T. (2020), 'Legacy of Amazonian Dark Earth soils on forest structure and species composition', *Global Ecology and Biogeography*, 29: 1458–73.

Alves, D. (2017), *Dark Earth plant management in the Lower Tapajós*, PhD: University of Exeter. Available online: https://ore.exeter.ac.uk/repository/handle/10871/34077 [Accessed.]

Anderson, A. B. and Ioris, E. M. (1992), 'Valuing the rain forest: Economic strategies by small-scale forest extractivists in the Amazon estuary', *Human Ecology*, 20 (3): 337–69.

Anderson, A. B. and Posey, D. A. (1989), 'Management of a tropical scrub savanna by the Gorotire Kayapó of Brazil', *Advances in Economic Botany*, 7: 159–73.

Andes, U. y. F. (2009), *Atlas sociolingüístico de pueblos indígenas en America Latina y el Caribe,* Cochabamba: FUNPROEIB Andes.

Angulo, E. G. (1998), 'Interpretación biológica acerca de la domesticación del pato criollo (Cairina moschata)', *Bulletin de l'Institut Français d'Études Andines*, 27 (1): 17–40.

Angulo, R. J., Lessa, G. C. and Souza, M. C. d. (2006), 'A critical review of mid- to late-Holocene sea-level fluctuations on the eastern Brazilian coastline', *Quaternary Science Reviews*, 25 (5–6): 486–506.

Antczak, M. M. and Antczak, A. T. (2006), *Los ídolos de las islas prometidas: Arqueología prehispánica del Archipiélago de Los Roques,* Caracas: Editorial Equinoccio.

Aragão, L. E., Anderson, L. O., Fonseca, M. G., Rosan, T. M., Vedovato, L. B., Wagner, F. H., Silva, C. V., Silva Junior, C. H., Arai, E. and Aguiar, A. P. (2018), '21st Century drought-related fires counteract the decline of Amazon deforestation carbon emissions', *Nature Communications*, 9 (1): 536.

Aragão, L. E. and Shimabukuro, Y. E. (2010), 'The incidence of fire in Amazonian forests with implications for REDD', *Science*, 328 (5983): 1275–8.

Araujo, A. G., Neves, W. A., Piló, L. B. and Atui, J. P. V. (2005), 'Holocene dryness and human occupation in Brazil during the "Archaic Gap"', *Quaternary Research*, 64 (3): 298–307.

Arroyo-Kalin, M. (2010), 'The Amazonian formative: Crop domestication and anthropogenic soils', *Diversity*, 2 (4): 473–504.

Arroyo-Kalin, M. (2012), 'Slash-burn-and-churn: Landscape history and crop cultivation in pre-Columbian Amazonia', *Quaternary International*, 249: 4–18.

Arroyo-Kalin, M., Marcote-Ríos, G., Lozada-Mendieta, N. and Veal, L. (2019), 'Entre La Pedrera y Araracuara: la arqueología del medio río Caquetá', *Revista del Museo de La Plata*, 4 (2): 305–30.

Arroyo-Kalin, M. and Rivas Panduro, S. (2019), 'La arqueología del río Napo: noticias recientes y desafíos futuros', *Revista del Museo de la Plata*, 4 (2): 331–52.

Arroyo-Kalin, M. and Riris, P. (2020), 'Did Amazonian pre-Columbian populations reach carrying capacity during the Late Holocene?', *SocArXiv*, 5 May, doi:10.31235/osf.io/ws8et.

Baker, P. A., Seltzer, G. O., Fritz, S. C., Dunbar, R. B., Grove, M. J., Tapia, P. M., Cross, S. L., Rowe, H. D. and Broda, J. P. (2001), 'The history of South American tropical precipitation for the past 25,000 years', *Science*, 291 (5504): 640.

Balée, W. (1989), 'The culture of Amazonian forests', *Advances in Economic Botany*, 7: 1–21.

Balée, W. (2006), 'The research program of historical ecology', *Annual Review of Anthropology*, 35 (1): 75.

Balée, W. (2013), *Cultural Forests of the Amazon. A Historical Ecology of People and Their Landscapes,* Tuscaloosa: University of Alabama Press.

Balée, W. L. (1994), *Footprints of the forest: Ka'apor ethnobotany – the historical ecology of plant utilization by an Amazonian people*, New York: Columbia University Press.

Balée, W. L. and Erickson, C. L. (2006), *Time and Complexity in Historical Ecology: Studies in the Neotropical Lowlands,* New York: Columbia University Press.

Balick, M. J. (1984), 'Ethnobotany of palms in the Neotropics', *Advances in Economic Botany*, 1: 9–23.

Barata, F. (1950), *A Arte Oleira dos Tapajós: Considerações Sobre a Cerâmica e Dois Tipos de Vasos Característicos*, Instituto de Antropologia e Etnologia do Pará 2, Belem.

Barnosky, A. D. and Lindsey, E. L. (2010), 'Timing of Quaternary megafaunal extinction in South America in relation to human arrival and climate change', *Quaternary International*, 217 (1–2): 10–29.

Barreto, C. (1998), 'Brazilian archaeology from a Brazilian perspective', *Antiquity*, 72 (277): 573–81.

Barreto, C. (2017), 'Figurine traditions from the Amazon', in Insoll, T. (ed.), *The Oxford Handbook of Prehistoric Figurines*, 417–40, Oxford: Oxford University Press.

Barreto, C., Lima, H. and Betancourt, C. J. (2016), *Cerâmicas Arqueológicas da Amazônia: Rumo a uma Nova Síntese*, Belem: IPHAN.

Barreto, C. and Machado, J. (2001), 'Exploring the Amazon, explaining the unknown: views from the past', in McEwan, C., Barreto, C., Neves, E. and Barreto, C. (eds), *Unknown Amazon,* 232–51, London: British Museum,.

Bates, J. (2022), 'The Fits and Starts of Indian Rice Domestication: How the Movement of Rice Across Northwest India Impacted Domestication Pathways and Agricultural Stories', *Frontiers in Ecology and Evolution*, 10: 924977.

Beach, T., Luzzadder-Beach, S., Krause, S., Guderjan, T., Valdez, F., Fernandez-Diaz, J. C., Eshleman, S. and Doyle, C. (2019), 'Ancient Maya wetland fields revealed under tropical forest canopy from laser scanning and multiproxy evidence', *Proceedings of the National Academy of Sciences*, 116 (43): 21469–77.

Bel, M. v. d. (2009), 'The Palikur Potters: an ethnoarchaeological case study on the Palikur pottery tradition in French-Guiana and Amapá, Brazil', *Boletim do Museu Paraense Emílio Goeldi, Ciências Humanas*, 4 (1): 39–56.

Bennett, K. and Willis, K. (2001), 'Pollen', in Smol, J. P., Birks, H. J., Last, W. M., Bradley, R. S. and Alverson, K. (eds), *Tracking Environmental Change using Lake Sediments. Volume 3: Terrestrial, Algal, and Siliceous Indicators,* 5–32, New York: Springer,.

Berger, A. and Loutre, M.-F. (1991), 'Insolation values for the climate of the last 10 million years', *Quaternary Science Reviews*, 10 (4): 297–317.

Bernal, R., Marmolejo, D. and Montes, M. E. (2007), 'Eastern Tukanoan Names of the Palm *Iriartea deltoidea*: Evidence of Its Possible Preagricultural Use as a Starch Source', *Journal of Ethnobiology,* 27 (2): 174–81.

Bernal, R., Torres, C., Garcia, N., Isaza, C., Navarro, J., Vallejo, M. I., Galeano, G. and Balslev, H. (2011), 'Palm Management in South America', *The Botanical Review*, 77: 607–46.

Bird, B. W., Abbott, M. B., Rodbell, D. T. and Vuille, M. (2011), 'Holocene tropical South American hydroclimate revealed from a decadally resolved lake sediment $\delta^{18}O$ record', *Earth and Planetary Science Letters*, 310 (3–4): 192–202.

Blaauw, M. and Christen, J. A. (2013), *Bacon Manual v2*.3.3.

Blatrix, R., Roux, B., Béarez, P., Prestes-Carneiro, G., Amaya, M., Aramayo, J. L., Rodrigues, L., Lombardo, U., Iriarte, J. and de Souza, J. G. (2018), 'The unique functioning of a pre-Columbian Amazonian floodplain fishery', *Scientific Reports*, 8 (1): 1–16.

Boëda, E., Clemente-Conte, I., Fontugne, M., Lahaye, C., Pino, M., Felice, G. D., Guidon, N., Hoeltz, S., Lourdeau, A. and Pagli, M. (2014), 'A new late Pleistocene archaeological sequence in South America: the Vale da Pedra Furada (Piauí, Brazil)', *Antiquity*, 88 (341): 927–41.

Boivin, N. and Crowther, A. (2021), 'Mobilizing the past to shape a better Anthropocene', *Nature Ecology and Evolution*, 5 (3): 273–84.

Boomert, A. (1976), 'Pre-Columbian raised fields in coastal Surinam', *Proceedings of the 6th international congress for the study of the Pre-Columbian cultures of the Lesser Antilles*, Gainesville: 134–44.

Boomert, A. (1987), 'Gifts of the Amazons: "green stone" pendants and beads as items of ceremonial exchange in Amazonia and the Caribbean', *Antropológica*, 67: 33–54.

Borem, A., Lopes, M., Clement, C. and Noda, H. (2012), *Domestication and breeding: Amazonian species*, Viçosa: Editora da Universidade Federal Viçosa.

Borrero, L. A. (2016), 'Ambiguity and Debates on the Early Peopling of South America', *PaleoAmerica*, 2 (1): 11–21.

Bortolotto, I. M., Amorozo, M. C. d. M., Neto, G. G., Oldeland, J. and Damasceno-Junior, G. A. (2015), 'Knowledge and use of wild edible plants in rural communities along Paraguay River, Pantanal, Brazil', *Journal of Ethnobiology and Ethnomedicine*, 11 (1): 1–15.

Bowman, D. M., Balch, J. K., Artaxo, P., Bond, W. J., Carlson, J. M., Cochrane, M. A., D'Antonio, C. M., DeFries, R. S., Doyle, J. C. and Harrison, S. P. (2009), 'Fire in the Earth system', *Science*, 324 (5926): 481–4.

Bozarth, S., Price, K., Woods, W., Neves, E. and Rebellato, R. (2009), 'Phytoliths and Terra Preta: The Hatahara Site Example', in Woods, W. I., Teixeira, W. G., Lehmann, J., Steiner, C., WinklerPrins, A. M. G. A. and Rebellato, L. (eds), *Amazonian Dark Earths: Wim Sombroek's Vision,* 85–98, New York: Springer,.

Braje, T. J., Dillehay, T. D., Erlandson, J. M., Klein, R. G. and Rick, T. C. (2017), 'Finding the first Americans', *Science*, 358 (6363): 592–4.

Brando, P. M., Balch, J. K., Nepstad, D. C., Morton, D. C., Putz, F. E., Coe, M. T., Silvério, D., Macedo, M. N., Davidson, E. A. and Nóbrega, C. C. (2014), 'Abrupt increases in Amazonian tree mortality due to drought-fire interactions', *Proceedings of the National Academy of Sciences*, 111 (17): 6347–52.

Bray, W. (2000), 'Ancient food for thought', *Nature*, 408 (6809): 145–6.

Brieger, F. G., Gurgel, J., Patemaniani, E., Blumenschein, A. and Alleoni, M. (1958), *Races of Maize in Brazil and Other Eastern South American Countries*, Washington, DC: National Academy of Sciences.

Brochado, J. P., Calderón, V., Chmyz, I., Dias Jr, O., Evans, C., Maranca, S., Meggers, B. J., Násser, N. A. d. S., Perota, C. and Piazza, W. F. (1969), 'Arqueologia brasileira em 1968: um relatório preliminar sobre o Programa Nacional de Pesquisas Arqueológicas', *Publicaçoēs Avulsas,* 12, Museo Paraense Emilio Goeldi, Belém.

Brugger, S. O., Gobet, E., van Leeuwen, J. F., Ledru, M.-P., Colombaroli, D., van der Knaap, W. O., Lombardo, U., Escobar-Torrez, K., Finsinger, W. and Rodrigues, L. (2016), 'Long-term man-environment interactions in the Bolivian Amazon: 8,000 years of vegetation dynamics', *Quaternary Science Reviews*, 132: 114–28.

Bryan, A. L., Casamiquela, R. M., Cruxent, J. M., Gruhn, R. and Ochsenius, C. (1978), 'An El Jobo Mastodon Kill at Taima-Taima, Venezuela', *Science*, 200 (4347): 1275–7.

Burger, R. (1995), *Chavin and the Origins of Andean Civilization*, London: Thames and Hudson.

Burn, M. J. and Mayle, F. E. (2008), 'Palynological differentiation between genera of the Moraceae family and implications for Amazonian palaeoecology', *Review of Palaeobotany and Palynology*, 149 (3): 187–201.

Bush, M., Silman, M., McMichael, C. and Saatchi, S. (2008), 'Fire, climate change and biodiversity in Amazonia: a Late-Holocene perspective', *Philosophical Transactions of the Royal Society B: Biological Sciences*, 363 (1498): 1795–802.

Bush, M. B., Correa-Metrio, A., McMichael, C., Sully, S., Shadik, C., Valencia, B., Guilderson, T., Steinitz-Kannan, M. and Overpeck, J. (2016), 'A 6900-year history of landscape modification by humans in lowland Amazonia', *Quaternary Science Reviews*, 141: 52–64.

Bush, M. B. (2017), 'Climate science: The resilience of Amazonian forests', *Nature*, 541 (7636): 167–8.

Bush, M. B., Correa-Metrio, A., McMichael, C., Sully, S., Shadik, C., Valencia, B., Guilderson, T., Steinitz-Kannan, M. and Overpeck, J. (2016), 'A 6900-year history of landscape modification by humans in lowland Amazonia', *Quaternary Science Reviews*, 141: 52–64.

Bush, M. B., De Oliveira, P. E., Colinvaux, P. A., Miller, M. C. and Moreno, J. E. (2004), 'Amazonian paleoecological histories: one hill, three watersheds', *Palaeogeography, Palaeoclimatology, Palaeoecology*, 214 (4): 359–93.

Bush, M. B., Dolores, R. P. and Colinvaux, P. A. (1989), 'A 6,000 year history of Amazonian maize cultivation', *Nature*, 340 (6231): 303–5.

Bush, M. B. and McMichael, C. N. (2016), 'Holocene variability of an Amazonian hyperdominant', *Journal of Ecology*, 104 (5): 1370–8.

Bush, M. B., Nascimento, M., Åkesson, C., Cárdenes-Sandí, G., Maezumi, S., Behling, H., Correa-Metrio, A., Church, W., Huisman, S. and Kelly, T. (2021), 'Widespread reforestation before European influence on Amazonia', *Science*, 372 (6541): 484–7.

Bush, M. B. and Oliveira, P. E. d. (2006), 'The Rise and Fall of the Refugial Hypothesis of Amazonian Speciation: A Paleoecological Perspective', *Biota Neotropica*, 6 (1): bn00106012006.

Bush, M. B., Silman, M. R., de Toledo, M. B., Listopad, C., Gosling, W. D., Williams, C., de Oliveira, P. E. and Krisel, C. (2007), 'Holocene fire and occupation in Amazonia: records from two lake districts', *Philosophical Transactions of the Royal Society B: Biological Sciences*, 362 (1478): 209–18.

Bush, M. B. and Weng, C. (2007), 'Introducing a new (freeware), tool for palynology', *Journal of Biogeography*, 34: 377–80.

Cabral, M. P. (2020), 'Sobre urnas, lugares, seres e pessoas: materialidade e substâncias na constituição de um poço funerário Aristé', *Boletim do Museu Paraense Emílio Goeldi, Ciências Humanas*, 15: e20190123.

Cabral, M. P. and Saldanha, J. D. M. (2008), 'Paisagens arqueológicas na costa norte do Amapá', *Revista de Arqueología*, 21: 1–14.

Caetano Andrade, V., Flores, B. M., Levis, C., Clement, C. R., Roberts, P. and Schöngart, J. (2019), 'Growth rings of Brazil nut trees (Bertholletia excelsa) as a living record of historical human disturbance in Central Amazonia', *PLoS ONE,* 14 (4): e0214128.

Callaway, E. (2014), 'Domestication: The birth of rice', *Nature*, 514 (7524): S58–S59.

Canuto, M. A., Estrada-Belli, F., Garrison, T. G., Houston, S. D., Acuña, M. J., Kováč, M., Marken, D., Nondédéo, P., Auld-Thomas, L. and Castanet, C. (2018), 'Ancient lowland Maya complexity as revealed by airborne laser scanning of northern Guatemala', *Science*, 361 (6409).

Capriles, J. M., Lombardo, U., Maley, B., Zuna, C., Veit, H. and Kennett, D. J. (2019), 'Persistent Early to Middle Holocene tropical foraging in southwestern Amazonia', *Science Advances*, 5 (4): eaav5449.

Carneiro, R. (1960), 'Slash-and-burn Agriculture: A Closer Look at its Implications for Settlement Patterns', in Wallace, A. (ed.), *Men and Cultures*, 229–34, Philadelphia: University of Pennsylvania.

Carneiro, R. (1998), 'What Happened at the Flashpoint? Conjectures on Chiefdom Formation at the Very Moment of its Conception', in Redmond, E. (ed.), *Chiefdoms and Chieftaincy in the Americas*, 18–41, Gainsville: University of Florida Press.

Carneiro, R. L. (1970), 'A Theory of the Origin of the State: Traditional theories of state origins are considered and rejected in favor of a new ecological hypothesis', *Science*, 169 (3947): 733–8.

Caromano, C. F. (2010), *Fogo no Mundo das Águas: Antracologia no sítio Hatahara, Amazônia Central*, Unpublished Master thesis, Departamento de Antropologia, Universidade Federal do Rio de Janeiro.

Carson, J. F., Mayle, F. E., Whitney, B. S., Iriarte, J. and Soto, J. D. (2016), 'Pre-Columbian ring ditch construction and land use on a "chocolate forest island" in the Bolivian Amazon', *Journal of Quaternary Science*, 31 (4): 337–47.

Carson, J. F., Whitney, B. S., Mayle, F. E., Iriarte, J., Prümers, H., Soto, J. D. and Watling, J. (2014), 'Environmental impact of geometric earthwork construction in pre-Columbian Amazonia', *Proceedings of the National Academy of Sciences*, 111 (29): 10497–502.

Carvajal, G. D. (1984), *Descubrimiento Del Río de Las Amazonas*, Sevilla: Imprenta de E. Rasco.

Carvalho, A. L. d., Nelson, B. W., Bianchini, M. C., Plagnol, D., Kuplich, T. M. and Daly, D. C. (2013), 'Bamboo-Dominated Forests of the Southwest Amazon: Detection, Spatial Extent, Life Cycle Length and Flowering Waves', *PLoS ONE*, 8 (1), e54852.

Castaño Uribe, C. (2019), *Chiribiquete: La maloka cósmica de los hombres jaguar*, Bogotá: Villegas Editores.

Cavalcante, P. B. (1991), *Frutas Comestíveis da Amazônia, 5ª Edição*, Museu Paraense Emílio Goeldi, Belém, Brazil.

Chapin, M., Lamb, Z. and Threlkeld, B. (2005), 'Mapping indigenous lands', *Annual Review of Anthropology*, 34: 619–38.

Church, W. (2021), 'A Record of Early Long-Distance Societal Interaction from Manachaqui Cave in Peru's Northeastern Andes', in Clasby, R. and Nesbitt, J. (eds), *The Archaeology of the Upper Amazon: Complexity and Interaction in the Andean Tropical Forest*, 38–61, Gainsville: University of Florida Press.

Clement, C. R. (1999a), '1492 and the loss of Amazonian crop genetic resources. I. The relation between domestication and human population decline', *Economic Botany*, 53 (2): 188–202.

Clement, C. R. (1999b), '1492 and the loss of Amazonian crop genetic resources. II. Crop biogeography at contact', *Economic Botany*, 53 (2): 203–16.

Clement, C. R., Cristo-Araújo, M. d., Coppens D'Eeckenbrugge, G., Reis, V. M. d., Lehnebach, R. and Picanço-Rodrigues, D. (2017), 'Origin and dispersal of domesticated peach palm', *Frontiers in Ecology and Evolution*, 5: 148.

Clement, C. R., de Cristo-Araújo, M., Coppens D'Eeckenbrugge, G., Alves Pereira, A. and Picanço-Rodrigues, D. (2010), 'Origin and domestication of native Amazonian crops', *Diversity*, 2 (1): 72–106.

Clement, C. R., Denevan, W. M., Heckenberger, M. J., Junqueira, A. B., Neves, E. G., Teixeira, W. G. and Woods, W. I. (2015), 'The domestication of Amazonia before European conquest', *Philosophical Transactions of the Royal Society B: Biological Sciences*, 282 (1812).

Clement, C. R. and Junqueira, A. B. (2010), 'Between a Pristine Myth and an Impoverished Future', *Biotropica*, 42 (5): 534–6.
Clement, C. R., McCann, J. M. and Smith, N. J. (2004), 'Agrobiodiversity in Amazonia and its relationship with dark earths', in Lehmann, J., Kern, D. and Woods, W. I. (eds), *Amazonian Dark Earths: Origins, Properties and Management,* 159–78, Amsterdam: Kluwer Academic Publisher.
Clement, C. R., Rodrigues, D. P., Alves-Pereira, A., Mühlen, G. S., Cristo-Araújo, M. d., Moreira, P. A., Lins, J. and Reis, V. M. (2016), 'Crop domestication in the upper Madeira River basin', Boletim do Museu Paraense Emílio Goeldi. *Ciências Humanas*, 11 (1): 193–205.
Cochrane, M. A., Alencar, A., Schulze, M. D., Souza Jr, C. M., Nepstad, D. C., Lefebvre, P. and Davidson, E. A. (1999), 'Positive feedbacks in the fire dynamic of closed canopy tropical forests', *Science*, 284 (5421): 1832–5.
Coe, S. D. and Coe, M. D. (2013), *The True History of Chocolate*, London: Thames and Hudson.
Coelho, S. D., Levis, C., Baccaro, F. B., Figueiredo, F. O., Pinassi Antunes, A., Ter Steege, H., Peña-Claros, M., Clement, C. R. and Schietti, J. (2021), 'Eighty-four per cent of all Amazonian arboreal plant individuals are useful to humans', *PloS ONE*, 16 (10): e0257875.
Cohen, M. C. L., Pessenda, L.C., Behling, H., Rossetti, D. F., França, M.C., Guimarães, J. T. F., Friaes, Y. and Beltrão Smith, C. (2012), 'Holocene palaeoenvironmental history of the Amazonian mangrove belt', *Quaternary Science Reviews,* 55: 50–8.
Coimbra Jr, C. E. A. (1989), *From shifting cultivation to coffee farming: The impact of change on the health and ecology of the Suruí Indians in the Brazilian Amazon*, PhD: Indiana University.
Colinvaux, P. A. (2008), *Amazon Expeditions: My Quest for the Ice-Age Equator*, New Haven: Yale University Press.
Colli-Silva, M., Richardson, J. E., Neves, E. G., Watling, J., Figueira, A. and Pirani, J. R. (2023), 'Domestication of the Amazonian fruit tree *cupuaçu* may have stretched over the past 8000 years', *Communications Earth and Environment*, 4 (1): 401.
Colonese, A. C., Winter, R., Brandi, R., Fossile, T., Fernandes, R., Soncin, S., McGrath, K., Von Tersch, M. and Bandeira, A. M. (2020), 'Stable isotope evidence for dietary diversification in the pre-Columbian Amazon', *Scientific Reports*, 10 (1): 1–11.
Coningham, R., Gunawardhana, P., Manuel, M., Adikari, G., Katugampola, M., Young, R., Schmidt, A., Krishnan, K., Simpson, I. and McDonnell, G. (2007), 'The state of theocracy: defining an early medieval hinterland in Sri Lanka', *Antiquity*, 81 (313): 699–719.
Coomes, O. T., Abizaid, C., Takasaki, Y. and Rivas Panduro, S. (2021), 'The Lower Ucayali river in prehistory: Cultural chronology, archeological evidence and a recently discovered Pre-Columbian site', *Geographical Review*, 111 (1): 145–67.
Cordeiro, A. (2004), *Floresta Nacional do Tapajós: plano de manejo*, Brasília, DF: IBAMA, 1.
Cornejo, O. E., Yee, M.-C., Dominguez, V., Andrews, M., Sockell, A., Strandberg, E., Livingstone, D., Stack, C., Romero, A., Umaharan, P., Royaert, S., Tawari, N. R., Ng, P., Gutierrez, O., Phillips, W., Mockaitis, K., Bustamante, C. D. and Motamayor, J. C. (2018), 'Population genomic analyses of the chocolate tree, *Theobroma cacao* L., provide insights into its domestication process', *Communications Biology*, 1 (1): 167.
Correal-Urrego, G. (1982), 'Restos de megafauna asociados a artefactos en la Sabana de Bogotá', *Caldasia*, 13 (64): 487–547.
Costa, F. (2009), *Arqueologia das Campinaranas do baixo rio Negro: em busca dos pré-ceramistas nos areais da Amazônia Central*, PhD Dissertation: MAE/USP.
Costa, J. A., da Costa, M. L. and Kern, D. C. (2013), 'Analysis of the spatial distribution of geochemical signatures for the identification of prehistoric settlement patterns in ADE and TMA sites in the lower Amazon Basin', *Journal of Archaeological Science*, 40 (6): 2771–82.
Cowgill, G. L. (2004), 'Origins and Development of Urbanism: Archaeological Perspectives', *Annual Review of Anthropology*, 33: 525–49.

Craig, N. and Chagnon, N. (2006), 'Locational Analysis of Yanomamö Gardens and Villages Observed in Satellite Imagery', in Sellet F, R, G. and P-L, Y. (eds), *Archaeology and Ethnoarchaeology of Mobility,* 44–74, Gainesville: University of Florida Press.

Crema, E. R. and Bevan, A. (2021), 'Inference from large sets of radiocarbon dates: Software and methods', *Radiocarbon*, 63 (1): 23–39.

Crosby, A. W. (2003), *The Columbian Exchange: Biological and Cultural Consequences of 1492*, Westport: Praeger.

Crutzen, P. J. (2002), 'The "anthropocene"', *Journal de Physique IV (Proceedings),* EDP Sciences.

Cruz, F. W., Burns, S. J., Karmann, I., Sharp, W. D., Vuille, M., Cardoso, A. O., Ferrari, J. A., Silva Dias, P. L. and Viana, O. (2005), 'Insolation-driven changes in atmospheric circulation over the past 116,000 years in subtropical Brazil', *Nature*, 434 (7029): 63–66.

Cunha, M. C. d. (2019), 'Antidomestication in the Amazon: Swidden and its foes', *HAU: Journal of Ethnographic Theory*, 9 (1): 126–36.

da Rocha, B. C. and de Oliveira, V. E. H. (2020), 'Historical ecology as an Instrument in Defence of Forest Peoples: reflections from the Tapajós River, Brazil', in Odonne, G. and Molino, J.-F. (eds), *Methods in Historical Ecology,* 153–61, London: Routledge.

Daggers, L., Plew, M. G., Edwards, A., Evans, S. and Trayler, R. B. (2018), 'Assessing the Early Holocene Environment of Northwestern Guyana: An Isotopic Analysis of Human and Faunal Remains', *Latin American Antiquity*, 29 (2): 279–92.

De Andrade, D. F. C. and De Carvalho, J. O. P. (2011), *Dinâmica da composição florística e da estrutura de uma floresta manejada, que sofreu incêndio acidental, na floresta nacional do Tapajós, Anais Do I Seminário De Pesquisas Científicas Da Floresta Nacional Do Tapajós,* Santarém: I Seminário de Pesquisas Científicas da Floresta Nacional do Tapajós.

de Fátima Rossetti, D., Góes, A. M. and Mann de Toledo, P. (2009), 'Archaeological mounds in Marajó Island in northern Brazil: A geological perspective integrating remote sensing and sedimentology', *Geoarchaeology*, 24 (1): 22–41.

de Freitas, H. A., Pessenda, L. C. R., Aravena, R., Gouveia, S. E. M., de Souza Ribeiro, A. and Boulet, R. (2001), 'Late Quaternary Vegetation Dynamics in the Southern Amazon Basin Inferred from Carbon Isotopes in Soil Organic Matter', *Quaternary Research*, 55 (1): 39–46.

de Paula Moraes, C. and Neves, E. G. (2012), 'OAno 1000: Adensamento populacional, interação e conflito na Amazônia Central', *Amazônica – Revista de Antropologia*, 4 (1): 122–48.

de Souza, J. G., Robinson, M., Maezumi, S. Y., Capriles, J., Hoggarth, J. A., Lombardo, U., Novello, V. F., Apaéstegui, J., Whitney, B. and Urrego, D. (2019), 'Climate change and cultural resilience in late pre-Columbian Amazonia', *Nature Ecology and Evolution*, 3 (7): 1007–17.

de Souza, J. G., Schaan, D. P., Robinson, M., Barbosa, A. D., Aragão, L. E., Marimon Jr, B. H., Marimon, B. S., da Silva, I. B., Khan, S. S. and Nakahara, F. R. (2018), 'Pre-Columbian earth-builders settled along the entire southern rim of the Amazon', *Nature Communications*, 9 (1): 1–10.

Deininger, M., Ward, B. M., Novello, V. F. and Cruz, F. W. (2019), 'Late Quaternary Variations in the South American Monsoon System as Inferred by Speleothems – New Perspectives using the SISAL Database', *Quaternary*, 2 (1): 6.

Denevan, W. (1966), *The Aboriginal Cultural Geography of the Llanos de Mojos of Bolivia*, Berkeley: University of California Press.

Denevan, W. M. (1976), *Estimating the Aboriginal population of Latin America in 1492: methodological synthesis,* Conference of Latin Americanist Geographers, 5:125–32.

Denevan, W. M. (1992), 'The Pristine Myth: The Landscape of the Americas in 1492', *Annals of the Association of American Geographers*, 82: 369–85.

Denevan, W. M. (1996), 'A Bluff Model of Riverine Settlement in Prehistoric Amazonia', *Annals of the Association of American Geographers*, 86 (4): 654–81.

Denevan, W. M. (2001), *Cultivated Landscapes of Native Amazonia and the Andes*, New York: Oxford University Press.

Denevan, W. M. (2004), 'Semi-Intensive Pre-European Cultivation and the Origins of Anthropogenic Dark Earths in Amazonia', in Glaser, B. and Woods, W. I. (eds), *Amazonian Dark Earths: Explorations in Space and Time,* 135–41, Berlin: Springer.

Denham, T. (2018), *Origin and Development of Agriculture in New Guinea, Island Melanesia, and Polynesia*, Oxford Research Encyclopedia of Environmental Science.

Denham, T. P., Iriarte, J. and Vrydaghs, L. (2007), *Rethinking Agriculture: Archaeological and Ethnoarchaeological Perspectives*, London: Routledge.

Denham, T. P. and Vrydaghs, L. (2007), 'Rethinking Agriculture: Introductory Thoughts', in Denham, T. P., Iriarte, J. and Vrydaghs, L. (eds), *Rethinking Agriculture: Archaeological and Ethnoarchaeological Perspectives,* 1–16, London: Routledge.

Descola, P. (1996), *In the Society of Nature: A Native Ecology in Amazonia*, Cambridge: Cambridge University Press.

Dezzeo, N. and Chacón, N. (2005), 'Carbon and nutrient loos in aboveground biomass along a fire induced forest-savanna gradient in the Gran Sabana, southern Venezuela', *Forest Ecology and Management*, 209: 343–52.

Dias, O. (1988), 'As estruturas de terra da arqueologia do Acre', *Série ArqueoIAB: Publicações avulsas*, 1.

Dick, C. W. and Pennington, R. T. (2019), 'History and Geography of Neotropical Tree Diversity', *Annual Review of Ecology, Evolution, and Systematics,* 50: 279–301.

Dickau, R., Bruno, M. C., Iriarte, J., Prümers, H., Jaimes Betancourt, C., Holst, I. and Mayle, F. E. (2012), 'Diversity of cultivars and other plant resources used at habitation sites in the Llanos de Mojos, Beni, Bolivia: evidence from macrobotanical remains, starch grains, and phytoliths', *Journal of Archaeological Science*, 39: 357–70.

Dickau, R., Ranere, A. J. and Cooke, R. G. (2007), 'Starch grain evidence for the preceramic dispersals of maize and root crops into tropical dry and humid forests of Panama', *Proceedings of the National Academy of Sciences*, 104 (9): 3651.

Dickau, R., Whitney, B. S., Iriarte, J., Mayle, F. E., Soto, J. D., Metcalfe, P., Street-Perrott, F. A., Loader, N. J., Ficken, K. J. and Killeen, T. J. (2013), 'Differentiation of neotropical ecosystems by modern soil phytolith assemblages and its implications for palaeoenvironmental and archaeological reconstructions', *Review of Palaeobotany and Palynology*, 193: 15–37.

Dillehay, T. and Rossen, J. (2002), 'Plant food and its implications for the peopling of the New World', in Jablonski, J. (ed.), *The First Americans: The Pleistocene Colonization of the New World,* 237–53, San Francisco: Wattis Symposium Series in Anthropology, Memoirs of the California Academy of Sciences.

Dillehay, T. D. (1997), *Monte Verde: A Late Pleistocene Settlement in Chile*, Volume: The Archaeological Context, Washington, DC: Smithsonian Institution Press.

Dillehay, T. D. (2000), *The Settlement of the Americas: A New Prehistory*, New York: Basic Books.

Dillehay, T. D., Rossen, J., Ugent, D., Karathanasis, A., Vásquez, V. and Netherly, P. J. (2010), 'Early Holocene coca chewing in northern Peru', *Antiquity*, 84 (326): 939–53.

Dillehay, T. D. (2017), *Where the land meets the sea: fourteen millennia of human history at Huaca Prieta, Peru*, Austin: University of Texas Press.

Dillehay, T. D., Goodbred, S., Pino, M., Vásquez Sánchez, V. F., Tham, T. R., Adovasio, J., Collins, M. B., Netherly, P. J., Hastorf, C. A., Chiou, K. L., Piperno, D., Rey, I. and Velchoff, N. (2017), 'Simple technologies and diverse food strategies of the Late Pleistocene and Early Holocene at Huaca Prieta, Coastal Peru', *Science Advances*, 3 (5): e1602778.

Dillehay, T. D., Ocampo, C., Saavedra, J., Sawakuchi, A. O., Vega, R. M., Pino, M., Collins, M. B., Scott Cummings, L., Arregui, I. and Villagran, X. S. (2015), 'New Archaeological Evidence for an Early Human Presence at Monte Verde, Chile', *PLoS ONE*, 10 (11): e0141923.

Dillehay, T. D., Rossen, J., Andres, T. C. and Williams, D. E. (2007), 'Preceramic adoption of peanut, squash, and cotton in northern Peru', *Science*, 316 (5833): 1890–3.

Dobyns, H. F. (1966), 'Estimating Aboriginal American Population: An Appraisal of Techniques with a New Hemispheric Estimate', *Current Anthropology,* 365: 395–416.

Dolmatoff, G. R. (1985), *Monsu: un sitio arqueologico*, Santa Fe de Bogota: Biblioteca Banco Popular.
Dougherty, B. and Calandra, H. A. (1984), 'Prehispanic human settlement in the Llanos de Moxos, Bolivia', *Quaternary of South America and Antarctic Peninsula*, 2: 163–99.
Doughty, C. E., Faurby, S. and Svenning, J. C. (2016), 'The impact of the megafauna extinctions on savanna woody cover in South America', *Ecography*, 39 (2): 213–22.
Doughty, C. E., Wolf, A. and Malhi, Y. (2013), 'The legacy of the Pleistocene megafauna extinctions on nutrient availability in Amazonia', *Nature Geoscience*, 6 (9): 761–4.
Dounias, E. (2001), 'The management of wild yam tubers by the Baka Pygmies in Southern Cameroon', *African Study Monographs,* 26: 135–56.
Duncan, N. A., Loughlin, N. J., Walker, J. H., Hocking, E. P. and Whitney, B. S. (2021), 'Pre-Columbian fire management and control of climate-driven floodwaters over 3,500 years in southwestern Amazonia', *Proceedings of the National Academy of Sciences*, 118 (40): e2022206118.
Dufour, D. L. (1990), 'Use of Tropical Rainforests by native Amazonians', *BioScience*, 40 (9): 652–9.
Duke, J.A. and Vasquez, R. (1994), *Amazonian ethnobotanical dictionary*, Boca Raton: CRC Press.
Dull, R. A., Nevle, R. J., Woods, W. I., Bird, D. K., Avnery, S. and Denevan, W. M. (2010), 'The Columbian Encounter and the Little Ice Age: Abrupt Land Use Change, Fire, and Greenhouse Forcing', *Annals of the Association of American Geographers*, 100 (4): 755–71.
Eder ([1772] 1985), *Breve Descripcion de las Reducciones de Mojos*, Cochabamba: Historia Boliviana.
Eisenberg, J. F. and Redford, K. H. (1989), *Mammals of the Neotropics, Volume 3: Ecuador, Bolivia, Brazil*, Chicago: University of Chicago Press.
Emperaire, L. (2001), *Elementos de discussão sobre a conservação da agrobiodiversidade: o exemplo da mandioca (Manihot esculenta Crantz), na Amazônia brasileira*, Capobianco J.-P., coord, 225–34, Biodiversidade da Amazônia, Estação Liberdade, ISA/São Paulo.
Epps, P. and Salanova, A. P. (2013), 'The languages of Amazonia', *Tipití*, 11 (1): 1–28.
Erickson, C. (2004), 'Historical Ecology and Future Explorations', in Lehmann, J., Kern, D. C., Glaser, B. and Woods, W. I. (eds), *Amazonian Dark Earths: Origins, Properties, Management*, 455–500, New York: Springer.
Erickson, C., Alvarez, P. and Calla, S. (2008), *Zanjas Circundantes: Obras Monumentales de Tierra de Baures en la Amazonia Boliviana*, *Informe de trabajo de campo de la temporada 2007.*
Erickson, C. L. (2000), 'An artificial landscape-scale fishery in the Bolivian Amazon', *Nature*, 408 (6809): 190–3.
Erickson, C. L. and Walker, J. H. (2009), 'Precolumbian causeways and canals as landesque capital', in Snead, J. E., Erickson, C. L. and Darling, J. A. (eds), *Landscapes of Movement: Trails, Paths, and Roads in Anthropological Perspective*, 235–69, Philadelphia: University of Pennsylvania Museum of Archaeology and Anthropology.
Eriksen, L. (2011), *Nature and Culture in Prehistoric Amazonia: Using GIS to reconstruct ancient ethnogenetic processes from archaeology, linguistics, geography, and ethnohistory*, PhD: Lund University.
Evans, D. H., Fletcher, R. J., Pottier, C., Chevance, J.-B., Soutif, D., Tan, B. S., Im, S., Ea, D., Tin, T. and Kim, S. (2013), 'Uncovering archaeological landscapes at Angkor using lidar', *Proceedings of the National Academy of Sciences*, 110 (31): 12595–600.
Ezell, K. C., Pearsall, D. M. and Zeidler, J. A. (2006), 'Root and tuber phytoliths and starch grains document manioc (*Manihot esculenta*), arrowroot (*Maranta arundinacea*), and llerén (*Calathea sp.*), at the real alto site Ecuador', *Economic Botany*, 60 (2): 103–20.
FAO and UNEP (2020), *The State of the World's Forests 2020: Forests, biodiversity and people*, Rome.
Fausto, C. (2001), *Inimigos Fieis: História, Guerra e Xamanismo na Amazônia*, São Paulo: EDUSP.

Fausto, C. and Neves, E. G. (2018), 'Was there ever a Neolithic in the Neotropics? Plant familiarisation and biodiversity in the Amazon', *Antiquity*, 92 (366): 1604–18.
Favero, A. P. and Valls, J. F. M. (2009), 'Domesticação e melhoramento de amendoim', in Borem, A., Lopes, M. T. G. and Clement, C. R. (eds), *Domesticação e melhoramento: espécies amazônicas*, 237–49, Viçosa, MG: Universidade Federal de Viçosa.
Feinman, G. and Neitzel, J. (1984), 'Too Many Types: An Overview of Sedentary Prestate Societies in the Americas', *Advances in Archaeological Method and Theory*, 7: 39–102.
Fernandes Caromano, C., Matthews Cascon, L., Góes Neves, E. and Scheel-Ybert, R. (2013), 'Revealing fires and rich diets: macro- and micro-archaeobotanical analysis at the Hatahara Site, Central Amazonia', *Tipití*, 11 (2): 40–51.
Fernández-Götz, M. and Ralston, I. (2017), 'The Complexity and Fragility of Early Iron Age Urbanism in West-Central Temperate Europe', *Journal of World Prehistory*, 30 (3): 259–79.
Fearnside, P. M. (1989) Extractive reserves in Brazilian Amazonia. *BioScience*, 39(6), 387–93.
Flantua, S., Hooghiemstra, H., Vuillle, M., Behling, H., Carson, J., Gosling, W., Hoyos, I., Ledru, M., Montoya, E. and Mayle, F. (2015a), 'Climate variability and human impact on the environment in South America during the last 2000 years: synthesis and perspectives', *Climate of the Past Discussions*, 11 (4): 3475–565.
Flantua, S. G., Hooghiemstra, H., Grimm, E. C., Behling, H., Bush, M. B., González-Arango, C., Gosling, W. D., Ledru, M.-P., Lozano-García, S. and Maldonado, A. (2015b), 'Updated site compilation of the Latin American Pollen Database', *Review of Palaeobotany and Palynology*, 223: 104–15.
Fletcher, R. (2011), 'Low-Density, Agrarian-Based Urbanism: Scale, Power, and Ecology', in Smith, M. E. (ed.), *The Comparative Archaeology of Complex Societies*, 285–320, Cambridge: Cambridge University Press.
Fonseca, M. G., Anderson, L. O., Arai, E., Shimabukuro, Y. E., Xaud, H. A., Xaud, M. R., Madani, N., Wagner, F. H. and Aragão, L. E. (2017), 'Climatic and anthropogenic drivers of northern Amazon fires during the 2015–2016 El Niño event', *Ecological Applications*, 27 (8): 2514–27.
Forest Trends (2017), http://www.forest-trends.org.
Franco-Moraes, J., Baniwa, A. F., Costa, F. R., Lima, H. P., Clement, C. R. and Shepard Jr, G. H. (2019), 'Historical landscape domestication in ancestral forests with nutrient-poor soils in northwestern Amazonia', *Forest Ecology and Management*, 446: 317–30.
Fraser, J., Cardoso, T., Junqueira, A., Falcão, N. P. S. and Clement, C. R. (2009), 'Historical Ecology and Dark Earths in Whitewater and Blackwater Landscapes: Comparing the Middle Madeira and Lower Negro Rivers', in Woods, W. I., Teixeira, W. G., Lehmann, J., Steiner, C., WinklerPrins, A. M. G. A. and Rebellato, L. (eds), *Amazonian Dark Earths: Wim Sombroek's Vision*, 229–64, Berling: Springer.
Fraser, J., Teixeira, W., Falcão, N., Woods, W., Lehmann, J. and Junqueira, A. B. (2011), 'Anthropogenic soils in the Central Amazon: from categories to a continuum', *Area*, 43 (3): 264–73.
Fraser, J. A., Alves-Pereira, A., Junqueira, A. B., Peroni, N. and Clement, C. R. (2012), 'Convergent adaptations: bitter manioc cultivation systems in fertile anthropogenic dark earths and floodplain soils in Central Amazonia', *PLoS ONE*, 7 (8): e43636.
Frikel, P. (1978), Áreas de arboricultura pré-agrícola na Amazônia. Notas preliminares. *Revista de Antropologia*, 21: 45–52.
Furquim, L. P., Watling, J., Hilbert, L. M., Shock, M. P., Prestes-Carneiro, G., Calo, C. M., Py-Daniel, A. R., Brandão, K., Pugliese, F. and Zimpel, C. A. (2021), 'Facing Change through Diversity: Resilience and Diversification of Plant Management Strategies during the Mid to Late Holocene Transition at the Monte Castelo Shellmound, SW Amazonia', *Quaternary*, 4 (1): 8.
Gassón, R. A. (2002), 'Orinoquia: The Archaeology of the Orinoco River Basin', *Journal of World Prehistory*, 16 (3): 237–311.

Gatti, L. V., Basso, L. S., Miller, J. B., Gloor, M., Gatti Domingues, L., Cassol, H. L., Tejada, G., Aragão, L. E., Nobre, C. and Peters, W. (2021), 'Amazonia as a carbon source linked to deforestation and climate change', *Nature*, 595 (7867): 388–93.

Gentry, A. H. (1988), 'Tree species richness of upper Amazonian forests', *Proceedings of the National Academy of Sciences*, 85 (1): 156–9.

Gentry, A. H. (1995), *Diversity and floristic composition of neotropical dry forests: Seasonally dry tropical forests*, Cambridge: Cambridge University Press.

German, L. (2003), 'Ethnoscientific Understandings of Amazonian Dark Earths', in Lehmann, J., Kern, D. C., Glaser, B. and Woods, W. I. (eds), *Amazonian Dark Earths,* 179–201, Dordrecht: Kluwer Academics.

Gerstel, D. U. and Sisson, V. A. (1995), 'Tobacco, Nicotiana tabacum (Solanaceae)', in Smart, J., Simmonds, J. and Norman, W. (eds), *Evolution of Crop Plants*, London: Longman.

Glaser, B. and Birk, J. J. (2012), 'State of the scientific knowledge on properties and genesis of Anthropogenic Dark Earths in Central Amazonia (*terra preta de Índio*)', *Geochimica et Cosmochimica Acta*, 82: 39–51.

Glaser, B. and Woods, W. (2004), *Amazonian Dark Earths: Explorations in Space and Time*, Berlin: Springer.

Gnecco, C. (2003), 'Against ecological reductionism: Late Pleistocene hunter-gatherers in the tropical forests of northern South America', *Quaternary International*, 109–10: 13–21.

Gomes, D. (2001), 'Santarém. Symbolism and Power in the Tropical Forest', in McEwan, C., Barreto, C. and Neves, E. (eds), *Unknown Amazon,* 134–55, London: The British Museum Press.

Gomes, D. (2007), 'The Diversity of Social Forms in Pre-Colonial Amazonia', *Revista de Arqueología Americana*, 25: 189–226.

Gomes, D. M. C. (2011), Cronologia e conexões culturais na Amazônia: as sociedades formativas da região de Santarém-PA. *Revista de Antropologia*, 54 (1): 269–314.

Gomes, D. M. C. and Luiz, J. G. (2013), 'Contextos domésticos no sítio arqueológico do Porto, Santarém, Brasil, identificados com o auxílio da geofísica por meio do método GPR', *Boletim do Museu Paraense Emílio Goeldi, Ciências Humanas*, 8: 639–56.

Gonda, R. (2018), *Pre-Columbian land use and its modern legacy in the Purus-Madeira Interfluve, Central Amazonia*, PhD: University of Exeter.

Goulding, M. (1980), *The Fishes and the Forest: Explorations in Amazonian Natural History*, Berkeley: University of California Press.

Gosling, W., Cornelissen, H. and McMichael, C. (2019), 'Reconstructing past fire temperatures from ancient charcoal material', *Palaeogeography, Palaeoclimatology, Palaeoecology*, 520: 128–37.

Gragson, T. L. (1992), 'Fishing the Waters of Amazonia: Native Subsistence Economies in a Tropical Rain Forest', *American Anthropologist*, 94 (2): 428–40.

Graham, E., Macphail, R., Turner, S., Crowther, J., Stegemann, J., Arroyo-Kalin, M., Duncan, L., Whittet, R., Rosique, C. and Austin, P. (2017), 'The Marco Gonzalez Maya site, Ambergris Caye, Belize: Assessing the impact of human activities by examining diachronic processes at the local scale', *Quaternary International*, 437: 115–42.

Grandin, G. (2009), *Fordlandia: The Rise and Fall of Henry Ford's Forgotten Jungle City*, New York: Henry Holt.

Gregorio de Souza, J., Alcaina Mateos, J. and Madella, M. (2020), 'Archaeological expansions in tropical South America during the late Holocene: Assessing the role of demic diffusion', *PLoS ONE*, 15 (4): e0232367.

Gregorio de Souza, J., Noelli, F. S. and Madella, M. (2021), 'Reassessing the role of climate change in the Tupi expansion (South America, 5000–500 BP)', *Journal of the Royal Society Interface*, 18 (183): 20210499.

Grobman, A., Bonavia, D., Dillehay, T. D., Piperno, D. R., Iriarte, J. and Holst, I. (2012), 'Preceramic maize from Paredones and Huaca Prieta, Peru', *Proceedings of the National Academy of Sciences*, 109 (5): 1755–9.
Gross, D. R. (1975), 'Protein Capture and Cultural Development in the Amazon Basin', *American Anthropologist*, 77 (3): 526–49.
Gross, D. R. (1983), 'Village Movement in Relation to Resources in Amazonia', in Hames, R. and Vickers, W. T. (eds), *Adaptive Responses of Native Amazonians,* 429–49, New York: Academic Press.
Guapindaia, V. (1993), *Fontes históricas e arqueológicas sobre os Tapajó: A coleção Frederico Barata do Museu Paraense Emílio Goeldi*, MA dissertation: Universidade Federal de Pernambuco.
Guapindaia, V. (2001), 'Encountering the ancestors: The Maracá Urns', in McEwan, C., Barreto, C. and Neves, E. (eds), *Unknown Amazon,* 156–73, London: British Museum.
Guapindaia, V. (2009), *Ocupação Konduri e Poco na Região de Porto of Archaeology*, PhD dissertation: University of São Paulo.
Haberle, S. G. and Maslin, M. A. (1999), 'Late Quaternary Vegetation and Climate Change in the Amazon Basin based on a 50,000 year Pollen Record from the Amazon Fan, ODP Site 932', *Quaternary Research*, 51 (1): 27–38.
Hames, R. (1983), 'The Settlement Pattern of a Yanomamo Population Bloc: A Behavioral Ecological Interpretation', in Hames, R. and Vickers, W. (eds), *Adaptive Responses of Native Amazonians*, New York: Academic Press.
Hamilton, R., Wolfhagen, J., Amano, N., Boivin, N., Findley, D. M., Iriarte, J., Kaplan, J. O., Stevenson, J. and Roberts, P. (2021), 'Non-uniform tropical forest responses to the "Columbian Exchange" in the Neotropics and Asia-Pacific', *Nature Ecology and Evolution,* 5: 1–11.
Hanelt, P., Buttner, R. and Mansfeld, R. (2001), *Mansfeld's Encyclopedia of Agricultural and Horticultural Crops: (Except Ornamentals)*, Berlin: Springer.
Harlan, J. R. (1995), *The Living Fields: Our Agricultural Heritage*, Cambridge: Cambridge University Press.
Harris, D. R. (2007), 'Agriculture, Cultivation and Domestication: Exploring the Conceptual Framework of Early Food Production', in Denham, T. P., Iriarte, J. and Vrydaghs, L. (eds), *Rethinking Agriculture: Archaeological and Ethnoarchaeological Perspectives,* 16–35. London: Routledge.
Hastie, A., Coronado, E. N. H., Reyna, J., Mitchard, E. T. A., Akesson, C. M., Baker, T. R., Cole, L. E. S., Oroche, C. J. C., Dargie, G. and Davila, N. (2022), 'Risks to carbon storage from land-use change revealed by peat thickness maps of Peru', *Nature Geoscience,* 15 (5): 369–74.
Haug, G. H., Hughen, K. A., Sigman, D. M., Peterson, L. C. and Rohl, U. (2001), 'Southward Migration of the Intertropical Convergence Zone through the Holocene', *Science*, 293 (5533): 1304–8.
Headland, T. N. and Bailey, R. C. (1991), 'Introduction: Have Hunter-Gatherers ever lived in Tropical Rain Forest independently of Agriculture?' *Human Ecology*, 19 (2): 115–22.
Hecht, S. (2009), 'Kayapó Savanna Management: Fire, Soils, and Forest Islands in a Threatened Biome', in Woods, W., Teixeira, W., Lehmann, J., Steiner, C., WinklerPrins, A. and Rebellato, L. (eds), *Amazonian Dark Earths: Wim Sombroek's Vision,* 143–62, Springer.
Hecht, S. B. (2003), 'Indigenous Soil management and the creation of terra mulata and terra preta in the Amazon Basin', in Lehmann, J., Kern, D., Glaser, B. and Woods, W. I. (eds), *Amazonian Dark Earths: Origin Properties and Management*, 355–72, Dordrecht: Springer.
Hecht, S. B. (2013), *The Scramble for the Amazon and the 'Lost Paradise' of Euclides da Cunha*, Chicago: University of Chicago Press.
Heckenberger, M. (2002), 'Rethinking the Arawakan diaspora: Hierarchy, regionality, and the Amazonian formative', in Hill, J. D. and Santos-Granero, F. (eds), *Comparative Arawakan Histories: Rethinking Language Family and Culture Area in Amazonia,* 99–122, Urbana: University of Illinois Press.

Heckenberger, M. (2005), *The Ecology of Power: Culture, Place and Personhood in the Southern Amazon, AD 1000–2000*, New York/London: Routledge.
Heckenberger, M. and Neves, E. G. (2009), 'Amazonian archaeology', *Annual Review of Anthropology*, 38: 251–66.
Heckenberger, M. J. (1998), 'Manioc agriculture and sedentism in Amazonia: the Upper Xingu example: Issues in Brazilian archaeology', *Antiquity*, 72 (277): 633–48.
Heckenberger, M. J. (2009a), 'Lost cities of the Amazon', *Scientific American*, 301 (4): 1009–64, doi:10.1038/scientificamerican.
Heckenberger, M. J. (2009b), 'Mapping Indigenous Histories: Collaboration, Cultural Heritage, and Conservation in the Amazon', *Collaborative Anthropologies*, 2 (1): 9–32.
Heckenberger, M. J., Kuikuro, A., Kuikuro, U. T., Russell, J. C., Schmidt, M., Fausto, C. and Franchetto, B. (2003), 'Amazonia 1492: Pristine Forest or Cultural Parkland?', *Science*, 301 (5640): 1710.
Heckenberger, M. J., Petersen, J. B. and Neves, E. G. (1999), 'Village Size and Permanence in Amazonia: Two Archaeological Examples from Brazil', *Latin American Antiquity*, 10 (4): 353–76.
Heckenberger, M. J., Russell, J. C., Fausto, C., Toney, J. R., Schmidt, M. J., Pereira, E., Franchetto, B. and Kuikuro, A. (2008), 'Pre-Columbian Urbanism, Anthropogenic Landscapes, and the Future of the Amazon', *Science*, 321 (5893): 1214–17.
Heijink, B. M., McMichael, C. N., Piperno, D. R., Duivenvoorden, J. F., Cárdenas, D. and Duque, Á. (2020), 'Holocene increases in palm abundances in north-western Amazonia', *Journal of Biogeography*, 47 (3): 698–711.
Heijink, B. M., Mattijs, Q. A., Valencia, R., Philip, A. L., Piperno, D. R. and McMichael, C. N. (2023), 'Long-term fire and vegetation change in northwestern Amazonia,' *Biotropica*, 55 (1): 197–209.
Hemming, J. (2009), *Tree of Rivers: The Story of the Amazon*, New York: Thames and Hudson.
Heriarte, M. d. (1874 [1662]), *Descripção do Estado do Maranhão, Pará, Corupá e Rio das Amazonas*, Vienna: Impresa do Filho de Carlos Gerold.
Hermenegildo, T., O'Connell, T. C., Guapindaia, V. L. and Neves, E. G. (2017), 'New evidence for subsistence strategies of late pre-colonial societies of the mouth of the Amazon based on carbon and nitrogen isotopic data', *Quaternary International*, 448: 139–49.
Herrera, L. F., Cavelier, I., Rodriguez, C. and Mora, S. (1992), 'The technical transformation of an agricultural system in the Colombian Amazon', *World Archaeology*, 24 (1): 98–113.
Hilbert, K. (1998), 'Nota sobre algumas pontas de projétil da Amazonia', *Estudos Ibero-Americanos*, 24 (2): 291–310.
Hilbert, L., Alves, D. T., Neves, E. G. and Iriarte, J. (2023), 'A glimpse into shell mound builders' diet during mid-to-late Holocene on Marajó island', *Vegetation History and Archaeobotany*, 1–10.
Hilbert, L., Neves, E. G., Pugliese, F., Whitney, B. S., Shock, M., Veasey, E., Zimpel, C. A. and Iriarte, J. (2017), 'Evidence for mid-Holocene rice domestication in the Americas', *Nature Ecology and Evolution*, 1 (11): 1693–8.
Hill, K., Hawkes, K., Hurtado, M. and Kaplan, H. (1984), 'Seasonal Variance in the Diet of Ache Hunter-Gatherers in Eastern Paraguay', *Human Ecology*, 12 (2): 101–35.
Hiraoka, M., Yamamoto, S., Matsumoto, E., Nakamura, S., Falesi, I., Ronaldo, A. and Baena, C. (2004), 'Contemporary Use and Management of Amazonian Dark Earths', in Lehmann, J., Kern, D., Glaser, B. and Woods, W. I. (eds), *Amazonian Dark Earths: Origins, Properties, Management*, 387–406, Dordrecht: Springer.
Hodell, D. A., Brenner, M. and Curtis, J. H. (2005), 'Terminal Classic drought in the northern Maya lowlands inferred from multiple sediment cores in Lake Chichancanab (Mexico)', *Quaternary Science Reviews*, 24 (12–13): 1413–27.
Hogg, A. G., Heaton, T. J., Hua, Q., Palmer, J. G., Turney, C. S., Southon, J., Bayliss, A., Blackwell, P. G., Boswijk, G. and Ramsey, C. B. (2020), 'SHCal20 Southern Hemisphere Calibration, 0–55,000 years cal BP', *Radiocarbon*, 62 (4): 759–78.

Holmberg, A. R. (1950), *Nomads of the Long Bow: The Siriono of Eastern Bolivia*, Washington, DC: Smithsonian Institution Press.
Hoorn, C. and Wesselingh, F. P. (2010), *Amazonia: Landscape and Species Evolution*, London: Blackwell.
Hornborg, A., Eriksen, L. and Bogadóttir, R. (2014), 'Correlating Landesque Capital and Ethnopolitical Integration in Pre-Columbian South America', in Håkansson, T. and Widgren, M. (eds), *Landesque Capital: The Historical Ecology of Enduring Landscape Modifications,* 215–31, Walnut Creek: Left Coast Press.
Hornborg, A. (2005), 'Ethnogenesis, Regional Integration, and Ecology in Prehistoric Amazonia: Toward a System Perspective', *Current Anthropology*, 46 (4): 589–620.
Huisman, S. N., Raczka, M. and McMichael, C. N. (2018), 'Palm phytoliths of mid-elevation Andean forests', *Frontiers in Ecology and Evolution*, 6: 193.
International Biochar Initiative – https://biochar-international.org/.
Iriarte, J. (2007), 'New Perspectives on Plant Domestication and the Development of Agriculture in the New World', in Deham, T., Iriarte, J. and Vrydaghs (eds), *Rethinking Agriculture: Archaeological and Ethnoarchaeological Perspectives*, 167–82, Walnut Creek: Left Coast Press.
Iriarte, J. (2009), 'Narrowing the Gap: Exploring the Diversity of Early Food-Production Economies in the Americas', *Current Anthropology*, 50 (5): 677–80.
Iriarte, J. (2017), 'Un futuro sostenible para la Amazonia: lecciones de la arqueología', in *Tropical Forest Conservation. Long-term Processes of Human Evolution, Cultural Adaptations, Cultural Practices*, 140–61, Mexico D.F.: UNESCO.
Iriarte, J., Aceituno, J., Robinson, M., Morcote-Rios, G. and Ziegler, M. (2022a), *The Painted Forest: Rock Art and Archaeology in the Colombian Amazon*, Exeter: University of Exeter.
Iriarte, J., Ziegler, M. J., Outram, A. K., Robinson, M., Roberts, P., Aceituno, F. J., Morcote-Ríos, G. and Keesey, T. M. (2022b), 'Ice Age megafauna rock art in the Colombian Amazon?', *Philosophical Transactions of the Royal Society B*, 377 (1849), 20200496.
Iriarte, J., De Souza, J. G., Robinson, M., Damasceno, A. and da Sivla, F. (2021), 'Refining the Chronology and Occupation Dynamics of the Mound Villages of South-Eastern Acre, Brazil', *Amazônica*, 13 (1): 153–76.
Iriarte, J. and Dickau, R. (2012), 'As culturas do milho? Arqueobotânica de las sociedades hidráulicas das terras baixas sul-americanas', *Amazônica*, 4 (1): 30–58.
Iriarte, J., Elliott, S., Maezumi, S. Y., Alves, D., Gonda, R., Robinson, M., de Souza, J. G., Watling, J. and Handley, J. (2020a), 'The origins of Amazonian landscapes: Plant cultivation, domestication and the spread of food production in tropical South America', *Quaternary Science Reviews*, 248: 106582.
Iriarte, J., Glaser, B., Watling, J., Wainwright, A., Birk, J. J., Renard, D., Rostain, S. and McKey, D. (2010), 'Late Holocene Neotropical agricultural landscapes: phytolith and stable carbon isotope analysis of raised fields from French Guianan coastal savannahs', *Journal of Archaeological Science*, 37: 2984–94.
Iriarte, J., Holst, I., Marozzi, O., Listopad, C., Alonso, E., Rinderknecht, A. and Montana, J. (2004), 'Evidence for cultivar adoption and emerging complexity during the mid-Holocene in the La Plata basin', *Nature*, 432 (7017): 614–17.
Iriarte, J., Moehlecke Copé, S., Fradley, M., Lockhart, J. J. and Gillam, J. C. (2013), 'Sacred landscapes of the southern Brazilian highlands: Understanding southern proto-Jê mound and enclosure complexes', *Journal of Anthropological Archaeology*, 32 (1): 74–96.
Iriarte, J., Power, M. J., Rostain, S., Mayle, F. E., Jones, H., Watling, J., Whitney, B. S. and McKey, D. B. (2012), 'Fire-free land use in pre-1492 Amazonian savannas', *Proceedings of the National Academy of Sciences*, 109 (17): 6473–8.
Iriarte, J., Robinson, M., de Souza, J., Damasceno, A., da Silva, F., Nakahara, F., Ranzi, A. and Aragao, L. (2020b), 'Geometry by Design: Contribution of Lidar to the Understanding of

Settlement Patterns of the Mound Villages in SW Amazonia', *Journal of Computer Applications in Archaeology*, 3 (1): 151–70.

Iriarte, J., Smith, R. J., Gregorio de Souza, J., Mayle, F. E., Whitney, B. S., Cárdenas, M. L., Singarayer, J., Carson, J. F., Roy, S. and Valdes, P. (2017), 'Out of Amazonia: Late-Holocene climate change and the Tupi–Guarani trans-continental expansion', *The Holocene*, 27 (7): 967–75.

Irion, G. (1984), 'Sedimentation and sediments of Amazonian rivers and evolution of the Amazonian landscape since Pliocene times', in Sioli, H. (ed.), *The Amazon*, 201–14, Dordrecht: Springer.

Irion, G., Bush, M., Nunes de Mello, J., Stüben, D., Neumann, T., Müller, G. and Junk, J. (2006), 'A multiproxy palaeoecological record of Holocene lake sediments from the Rio Tapajós, eastern Amazonia', *Palaeogeography, Palaeoclimatology, Palaeoecology*, 240 (3): 523–35.

Isaac, B. L. (1977), 'The Siriono of Eastern Bolivia: A Reexamination', *Human Ecology*, 5 (2): 137–54.

Jaimes Betancourt, C. (2010), *La Ceramica de la Loma Salvatierra*, PhD: Universidad de Bonn.

Jaimes Betancourt, C. (2016), 'Dos fases cerámicas de la cronología ocupacional de las zanjas de la provincia Iténez – Beni, Bolivia', in Barreto, C., Lima, H. and Betancourt, C. J. (eds), *Cerâmicas Arqueológicas da Amazônia: Rumo a uma nova síntesis*, 435–47, Belem: IPHAN.

Jezequel, C., Tedesco, P. A., Bigorne, R., Maldonado-Ocampo, J. A., Ortega, H., Hidalgo, M., Martens, K., Torrente-Vilara, G., Zuanon, J. and Acosta, A. (2020), 'A database of freshwater fish species of the Amazon Basin', *Scientific Data*, 7 (1): 96.

Jones, M. (2009), 'Moving North: Archaeobotanical Evidence for Plant Diet in Middle and Upper Paleolithic Europe', in Hublin, J. and Richards, M. (eds), *The Evolution of Hominin Diets*, 171–80, Dordrecht: Springer.

Junqueira, A. B., Shepard Jr, G. H. and Clement, C. R. (2011), 'Secondary Forests on Anthropogenic Soils of the Middle Madeira River: Valuation, Local Knowledge, and Landscape Domestication in Brazilian Amazonia', *Economic Botany*, 65 (1): 85–99.

Kanner, L. C., Burns, S. J., Cheng, H., Edwards, R. L. and Vuille, M. (2013), 'High-resolution variability of the South American summer monsoon over the last seven millennia: insights from a speleothem record from the central Peruvian Andes', *Quaternary Science Reviews*, 75: 1–10.

Kehoe, A. B. (1998), *The Land of Prehistory*, London: Routledge.

Kelly, T. J., Lawson, I. T., Roucoux, K. H., Baker, T. R., Honorio-Coronado, E. N., Jones, T. D. and Rivas Panduro, S. (2018), 'Continuous human presence without extensive reductions in forest cover over the past 2500 years in an aseasonal Amazonian rainforest', *Journal of Quaternary Science*, 33 (4): 369–79.

Kennett, D. J., Lipson, M., Prufer, K. M., Mora-Marín, D., George, R. J., Rohland, N., Robinson, M., Trask, W. R., Edgar, H. H. and Hill, E. C. (2022), 'South-to-north migration preceded the advent of intensive farming in the Maya region', *Nature Communications*, 13 (1): 1530.

Kennett, D. J., Prufer, K. M., Culleton, B. J., George, R. J., Robinson, M., Trask, W. R., Buckley, G. M., Moes, E., Kate, E. J. and Harper, T. K. (2020), 'Early isotopic evidence for maize as a staple grain in the Americas', *Science Advances*, 6 (23): eaba3245.

Kern, D., D'aquino, G., Rodrigues, T., Frazao, F., Sombroek, W., Myers, T. and Neves, E. (2003), 'Distribution of Amazonian Dark Earths in the Brazilian Amazon', in Lehmann, J., Glaser, B. and Woods, W. (eds), *Amazonian Dark Earths*, 51–75, Dordrecht: Springer.

Kern, D. C., Lima, H. P., da Costa, J. A., de Lima, H. V., Browne Ribeiro, A., Moraes, B. M. and Kämpf, N. (2017), '*Terras pretas*: Approaches to formation processes in a new paradigm', *Geoarchaeology*, 32 (6): 694–706.

Kistler, L., Maezumi, S. Y., De Souza, J. G., Przelomska, N. A., Costa, F. M., Smith, O., Loiselle, H., Ramos-Madrigal, J., Wales, N. and Ribeiro, E. R. (2018), 'Multiproxy evidence highlights a complex evolutionary legacy of maize in South America', *Science*, 362 (6420): 1309–13.

Kistler, L., Thakar, H. B., VanDerwarker, A. M., Domic, A., Bergström, A., George, R. J., Harper, T. K., Allaby, R. G., Hirth, K. and Kennett, D. J. (2020), 'Archaeological Central American maize genomes suggest ancient gene flow from South America', *Proceedings of the National Academy of Sciences*, 117 (52): 33124–9.

Labre, A. R. P. (1889), 'Colonel Labre's Explorations in the Region between the Beni and Madre de Dios Rivers and the Purus', *Proceedings of the Royal Geographical Society and Monthly Record of Geography*, 11 (8): 496–502.

Larson, G., Piperno, D. R., Allaby, R. G., Purugganan, M. D., Andersson, L., Arroyo-Kalin, M., Barton, L., Vigueira, C. C., Denham, T. and Dobney, K. (2014), 'Current perspectives and the future of domestication studies', *Proceedings of the National Academy of Sciences*, 111 (17): 6139–46.

Lathrap, D. W. (1970), *The Upper Amazon*, New York: Praeger.

Lathrap, D.W. (1977), 'Our Father the Cayman, Our Mother the Gourd: Spinden Revisited, or a Unitary Model for the Emergence of Agriculture in the New World', in Reed, C. A. (ed.), *Origins of Agriculture*, 713–51, The Hague: Mouton.

Lathrap, D. J., Marcos, J. and Zeidler, J. (1977), 'Real Alto: An Ancient Ceremonial Center', *Archaeology*, 30: 2–13.

Latrubesse, E. M. and Franzinelli, E. (2005), 'The late Quaternary evolution of the Negro River, Amazon, Brazil: implications for island and floodplain formation in large anabranching tropical systems', *Geomorphology*, 70 (3–4): 372–97.

Lehmann, J., da Silva Jr, J. P., Steiner, C., Nehls, T., Zech, W. and Glaser, B. (2003), 'Nutrient availability and leaching in an archaeological Anthrosol and a Ferralsol of the Central Amazon basin: fertilizer, manure and charcoal amendments', *Plant and Soil*, 249 (2): 343–57.

Lehmann, J. and Joseph, S. (2015), *Biochar for Environmental Management: Science, Technology and Implementation*, London/New York: Routledge.

Lehmann, J., Kern, D. C., Glaser, B. and Woods, W. I. (2004), *Amazonian Dark Earths: Origin, Properties, Management*, Dortdrecht: Springer.

Lévi-Strauss, C. (1952), 'The Use of Wild Plants in Tropical South America', *Economic Botany*, 6 (3): 252–70.

Lévi-Strauss, C. (1978), *Myth and Meaning*, London: Routledge.

Levis, C., Costa, F. R., Bongers, F., Peña-Claros, M., Clement, C. R., Junqueira, A. B., Neves, E. G., Tamanaha, E. K., Figueiredo, F. O. and Salomão, R. P. (2017), 'Persistent effects of pre-Columbian plant domestication on Amazonian forest composition', *Science*, 355 (6328): 925–31.

Levis, C., Flores, B. M., Moreira, P. A., Luize, B. G., Alves, R. P., Franco-Moraes, J., Lins, J., Konings, E., Peña-Claros, M. and Bongers, F. (2018), 'How People Domesticated Amazonian Forests', *Frontiers in Ecology and Evolution*, 5: 171.

Lewis, S. L. and Maslin, M. A. (2015), 'Defining the Anthropocene', *Nature*, 519 (7542): 171–80.

Liebenberg, D. (2017), 'Cosmology Performed, the World Transformed: Mimesis and the Logical Operations of Nature and Culture in Myth in Amazonia and Beyond', *Tipití: Journal of the Society for the Anthropology of Lowland South America*, 15 (2): 173–205.

Linares, O. F. (1976), '"Garden hunting" in the American tropics', *Human Ecology*, 4 (4): 331–49.

Linares, O. F. (2002), 'African rice (Oryza glaberrima): history and future potential', *Proceedings of the National Academy of Sciences*, 99 (25): 16360–5.

Lins, J., Lima, H. P., Baccaro, F. B., Kinupp, V. F., Shepard Jr, G. H. and Clement, C. R. (2015), 'Pre-Columbian floristic legacies in modern homegardens of Central Amazonia', *PLoS ONE*, 10 (6): e0127067.

Lombardo, U. (2010), 'Raised fields of northwestern Bolivia: a GIS based analysis', *Zeitschrift für Archäologie Außereuropäischer Kulturen*, 3: 127–49.

Lombardo, U., Canal-Beeby, E., Fehr, S. and Veit, H. (2011), 'Raised fields in the Bolivian Amazonia: a prehistoric green revolution or a flood risk mitigation strategy?', *Journal of Archaeological Science*, 38 (3): 502–12.

Lombardo, U., Denier, S., May, J.-H., Rodrigues, L. and Veit, H. (2013a), 'Human-environment interactions in pre-Columbian Amazonia: The case of the Llanos de Moxos, Bolivia', *Quaternary International*, 312: 109–19.

Lombardo, U., Iriarte, J., Hilbert, L., Ruiz-Pérez, J., Capriles, J. M. and Veit, H. (2020), 'Early Holocene crop cultivation and landscape modification in Amazonia', *Nature*, 581 (7807): 190–3.

Lombardo, U. and Prümers, H. (2010), 'Pre-Columbian Human Occupation Patterns in the Eastern Plains of the Llanos de Moxos, Bolivian Amazonia', *Journal of Archaeological Science*, 37 (8): 1875–85.

Lombardo, U., Ruiz-Pérez, J., Rodrigues, L., Mestrot, A., Mayle, F., Madella, M., Szidat, S. and Veit, H. (2019), 'Holocene land cover change in south-western Amazonia inferred from paleoflood archives', *Global and Planetary Change*, 174: 105–14.

Lombardo, U., Szabo, K., Capriles, J. M., May, J.-H., Amelung, W., Hutterer, R., Lehndorff, E., Plotzki, A. and Veit, H. (2013b), 'Early and middle holocene hunter-gatherer occupations in Western Amazonia: the hidden shell middens', *PLoS ONE*, 8 (8): e72746.

Lombardo, U. and Veit, H. (2014), 'The origin of oriented lakes: Evidence from the Bolivian Amazon', *Geomorphology*, 204: 502–9.

López-Zent, E. and Zent, S. (2004), 'Amazonian Indians as Ecological Disturbance Agents: The Hotï of the Sierra de Maigualida, Venezuelan Guayana', *Advances in Economic Botany*, 15: 79–112.

Lovejoy, T. E. and Nobre, C. (2018), 'Amazon tipping point', *Science Advances*, 4: eaat2340.

Lucero, L. J., Fletcher, R. and Coningham, R. (2015), 'From "collapse" to urban diaspora: the transformation of low-density, dispersed agrarian urbanism', *Antiquity*, 89 (347): 1139–54.

Lyon, P. (1974), *Native South Americans: Ethnology of the Least Known Continent,* Boston: Little, Brown and Co.

Lynch, T. F. (1990), 'Glacial-age man in South America? A critical review', *American Antiquity*, 55 (1): 12–36.

Maezumi, S. Y., Alves, D., Robinson, M., de Souza, J. G., Levis, C., Barnett, R. L., de Oliveira, E. A., Urrego, D., Schaan, D. and Iriarte, J. (2018a), 'The legacy of 4,500 years of polyculture agroforestry in the eastern Amazon', *Nature Plants*, 4 (8): 540–7.

Maezumi, S. Y., Elliott, S., Robinson, M., Betancourt, C. J., Gregorio de Souza, J., Alves, D., Grosvenor, M., Hilbert, L., Urrego, D. H. and Gosling, W. D. (2022), 'Legacies of Indigenous land use and cultural burning in the Bolivian Amazon rainforest ecotone', *Philosophical Transactions of the Royal Society B: Biological Sciences*, 377 (1849), 20200499.

Maezumi, S. Y., Robinson, M., de Souza, J., Urrego, D. H., Schaan, D., Alves, D. and Iriarte, J. (2018b), 'New Insights from pre-Columbian Land use and Fire Management in Amazonian Dark Earth Forests', *Frontiers in Ecology and Evolution*, 6: 111.

Maezumi, S. Y., Gosling, W. D., Kirschner, J., Chevalier, M., Cornelissen, H. L., Heinecke, T. and McMichael, C. N. (2021), 'A modern analogue matching approach to characterize fire temperatures and plant species from charcoal', *Palaeogeography, Palaeoclimatology, Palaeoecology*, 578: 110580.

Magalhães, M. P., Lima, P. G. C., Santos, R. d. S., Maia, R. R., Schmidt, M., Barbosa, C. A. P. and Fonseca, J. A. d. (2019), 'O Holoceno inferior e a antropogênese amazônica na longa história indígena da Amazônia oriental (Carajás, Pará, Brasil)', *Boletim do Museu Paraense Emílio Goeldi*, 14 (2): 291–326.

Mahowald, N. M., Artaxo, P., Baker, A. R., Jickells, T. D., Okin, G. S., Randerson, J. T. and Townsend, A. R. (2005), 'Impacts of biomass burning emissions and land use change on Amazonian atmospheric phosphorus cycling and deposition', *Global Biogeochemical Cycles*, 19, GB4030.

Major, J., DiTommaso, A., Lehmann, J. and Falcao, N. P. (2005), 'Weed dynamics on Amazonian Dark Earth and adjacent soils of Brazil', *Agriculture, Ecosystems and Environment*, 111 (1): 1–12.

Mann, C. C. (2005), *1491: New Revelations of the Americas Before Columbus*, New York: Alfred A. Knopf Inc.

Manyà, J. J. (2012), 'Pyrolysis for Biochar Purposes: A Review to Establish Current Knowledge Gaps and Research Needs', *Environmental Science and Technology*, 46 (15): 7939–54.

Martin, P. S. and Klein, R. G. (1989), *Quaternary Extinctions: A Prehistoric Revolution*, Tucson: University of Arizona Press.

Martinelli, L. A., Ometto, J. P. H. B., Ishida, F. Y., Domingues, T. F., Nardoto, G. B., Oliveira, R. S. and Ehleringer, J. R. (2007), 'The Use of Carbon and Nitrogen Stable Isotopes to Track Effects of Land-Use Changes in the Brazilian Amazon Region', *Terrestrial Ecology*, 1: 301–18.

Martínez, J. L. (2009), 'Registros andinos al margen de la escritura: el arte rupestre colonial', *Boletín del Museo Chileno de Arte Precolombino*, 14 (1): 9–35.

Martius, K. F. P. v. (1867), *Beiträge zur Ethnographie und Sprachenkunde Amerikas zumal Brasiliens, I. Zur Ethnographie*, Leipzig: Fleischer.

Matsuoka, Y., Vigouroux, Y., Goodman, M. M. and Sanchez, G. (2002), 'A single domestication for maize shown by multilocus microsatellite genotyping', *Proceedings of the National Academy of Sciences*, 99 (9): 6080.

Mayle, F. E., Burbridge, R. and Killeen, T. J. (2000), 'Millennial-scale dynamics of southern Amazonian rain forests', *Science*, 290 (5500): 2291–94.

Mayle, F. E. and Iriarte, J. (2014), 'Integrated palaeoecology and archaeology – a powerful approach for understanding pre-Columbian Amazonia', *Journal of Archaeological Science*, 51: 54–64.

McEwan, C., Barreto, C. and Neves, E. (2001), *Unknown Amazon: Culture in Nature in Ancient Brazil*, London: British Museum.

McIntosh, R. J. and McIntosh, R. J. (2005), *Ancient Middle Niger: Urbanism and the Self-Organizing Landscape*, Cambridge: Cambridge University Press.

McKey, D. and Beckerman, S. (1993), 'Chemical ecology, plant evolution and traditional manioc cultivation systems', *Man and the Biosphere Series*, 13: 83.

McKey, D., Cavagnaro, T. R., Cliff, J. and Gleadow, R. (2010a), 'Chemical ecology in coupled human and natural systems: people, manioc, multitrophic interactions and global change', *Chemoecology*, 20 (2): 109–33.

McKey, D., Rostain, S., Iriarte, J., Glaser, B., Birk, J. J., Holst, I. and Renard, D. (2010b), 'Pre-Columbian agricultural landscapes, ecosystem engineers, and self-organized patchiness in Amazonia', *Proceedings of the National Academy of Sciences*, 107: 7823–8.

McKey, D. B., Durécu, M., Pouilly, M., Béarez, P., Ovando, A., Kalebe, M. and Huchzermeyer, C. F. (2016), 'Present-day African analogue of a pre-European Amazonian floodplain fishery shows convergence in cultural niche construction', *Proceedings of the National Academy of Sciences*, 113 (52): 14938–43.

McMichael, C., Palace, M., Bush, M., Braswell, B., Hagen, S., Neves, E., Silman, M., Tamanaha, E. and Czarnecki, C. (2014a), 'Predicting pre-Columbian anthropogenic soils in Amazonia', *Philosophical Transactions of the Royal Society B: Biological Sciences*, 281 (1777): 20132475.

McMichael, C., Piperno, D., Bush, M., Silman, M., Zimmerman, A., Raczka, M. and Lobato, L. (2012), 'Sparse Pre-Columbian Human Habitation in Western Amazonia', *Science*, 336 (6087): 1429–31.

McMichael, C. H., Feeley, K. J., Dick, C. W., Piperno, D. R. and Bush, M. B. (2017), 'Comment on "Persistent effects of pre-Columbian plant domestication on Amazonian forest composition"', *Science*, 358 (6361).

McMichael, C. H., Palace, M. W. and Golightly, M. (2014b), 'Bamboo-dominated forests and pre-Columbian earthwork formations in south-western Amazonia', *Journal of Biogeography*, 41 (9): 1733–45.

McMichael, C., Levis, C., Gosling, W., Junqueira, A., Piperno, D., Neves, E., Mayle, F., Pena-Claros, M. and Bongers, F. (2023), 'Spatial and temporal abilities of proxies used to detect pre-Columbian Indigenous human activity in Amazonian ecosystems', *Quaternary Science Reviews*, 321: 108354.

Medina, J. T. (1934), *The discovery of the Amazon*, New York: American Geographical Society.

Meggers, B. J. (1982), in Prance, G. T. (ed.), *Biological Diversification in the Tropics: Proceedings of the Fifth International Symposium of the Association for Tropical Biology*, New York: Columbia University Press, 483–96.

Meggers, B. J. (1994), 'Archeological evidence for the impact of mega-Niño events on Amazonia during the past two millennia', *Climatic Change*, 28 (4): 321–38.

Meggers, B. J. (1996), *Amazonia: Man and Culture in a Counterferit Paradise (Revised Edition)*, Washington, DC: Smithsonian Institution Press.

Meggers, B. J. (2007), 'Mid-Holocene climate and cultural dynamics in Brazil and the Guianas', in Anderson, D. G., Maasch, K. A. and Sandweiss, D. H. (eds), *Climate Change and Cultural Dynamics*, 117–55, New York: Academic Press.

Meggers, B. J. and Danon, J. (1988), 'Identification and Implications of a Hiatus in the Archeological Sequence on Marajó Island, Brazil', *Journal of the Washington Academy of Sciences*, 78 (3): 245–53.

Meggers, B. J. and Evans, C. (1957), 'Archeological investigations at the mouth of the Amazon', *Bureau of American Ethnology Bulletin*, 167: 1–664.

Meggers, B. J. and Evans, C. (1969), *Como interpretar el lenguaje de los tiestos*, Washington, DC: Smithsonian Institution.

Meggers, B. J. and Evans, C. (1978), 'Lowland South America and the Antilles', in Jennings, J. D. (ed.), *Ancient Native Americans*, 543–91, San Francisco: Freeman.

Meggers, B. J., Evans, C. and Estrada, E. (1965), *Early Formative Period of Coastal Ecuador: The Valdivia and Machalilla Phases*, Washington, DC: Smithsonian Institution Press.

Métraux, A. (1942), 'The Native Tribes of Eastern Bolivia and Western Matto Grosso', *Bureau of American Ethnology*. Bulletin 134. Washington, DC: Smithsonian Institution.

Miller, E. T. (1987), 'Pesquisas arqueológicas paleoindígenas no Brasil Ocidental', *Estudios Atacameños*, 8: 37–61.

Miller, E. T. (1992), 'Adaptação agrícola pré-histórica no alto rio Madeira', in Meggers, B. J. (ed.), *Prehistoria Sudamericana: Nuevas Perspectivas*, 219–32, Washington: Taraxacum.

Miller, E. T. (2013), 'Algumas Culturas Ceramistas, do Noroeste do Pantanal do Guaporé à Encosta e Altiplano Sudoeste do Chapadão dos Parecis. Origem, Difusão/Migração e Adaptação – do Noroeste da América do Sul ao Brasil', *Revista Brasileira de Linguística Antropológica*, 5 (2): 335–83.

Miranda, H. S., Bustamante, M. M. C., Miranda, A. C., Oliveira, P. and Marquis, R. (2002), 'The Fire Factor', in Marquis, R. and Oliveira, P. (eds), *The Cerrados of Brazil: Ecology and Natural History of a Neotropical Savanna*, 51–68, New York: Columbia University Press.

Mistry, J., Berardi, A., Andrade, V., Kraho, T., Kraho, P. and Leonardos, O. (2005), 'Indigenous Fire Management in the *cerrado* of Brazil: The Case of the Krahô of Tocantins', *Human Ecology*, 33 (3): 365–86.

Montoya, E., Lombardo, U., Levis, C., Aymard, G. A. and Mayle, F. E. (2020), 'Human contribution to Amazonian plant diversity: legacy of pre-Columbian land use in modern plant communities', in Rull, V. and Carnaval, A. (eds), *Neotropical Diversification: Patterns and Processes*, 495–520, Cham: Springer.

Moore, J. D. (1995), The Archaeology of Dual Organization in Andean South America: A Theoretical Review and Case Study. *Latin American Antiquity*, 6 (2): 165–81.

Moore, T. (2017), 'Beyond Iron Age 'towns': Examining *oppida* as examples of low-density urbanism', *Oxford Journal of Archaeology*, 36 (3): 287–305.

Mora, S. (2003), *Early Inhabitants of the Amazonian Tropical Rain Forest: A Study of Humans and Environmental Dynamics,* Pittsburgh: University of Pittsburgh Latin American Archaeology Reports.

Mora, S., Herrera, L. F., Cavalier, I. and Rodríguez, C. (1991), *Cultivars, Anthropic Soils, and Stability: A Preliminary Report of Archaeological Research in Araracuara, Colombian Amazonia, Center for Comparative Archaeological Research*, Pittsburgh: University of Pittsburgh.

Moraes, C. d. P. (2015), O determinismo agrícola na arqueologia amazônica. *Estudos Avançados*, 29 (83): 25–43.

Moran, E. F. (1993), *Through Amazonian Eyes: The Human Ecology of Amazonian Populations*, Iowa City, University of Iowa Press.

Moran, E. F. and Brondizio, E. S. (eds) (2013), *Human-Environment Interactions*, Dordrecht: Springer, 371–88.

Morcote-Ríos, G., Aceituno, F. J., Iriarte, J., Robinson, M. and Chaparro-Cárdenas, J. L. (2021), 'Colonisation and early peopling of the Colombian Amazon during the Late Pleistocene and the Early Holocene: New evidence from La Serranía La Lindosa', *Quaternary International*, 578: 5–19.

Morcote-Ríos, G., Aceituno, F. J. and León Sicard, T. I. R. S. (2014), 'Recolectores del Holoceno Temprano en la Floresta Amazónica Colombiana', in Rostain, S. (ed.), *Antes de Orellana: Actas del 3er Encuentro Internacional de Arqueología Amazónica*, 39–50, Quito: Instituto Frances de Estudios Andinos.

Morcote-Ríos, G. and Bernal, R. (2001), 'Remains of Palms (Palmae), at archaeological sites in the New World: A review', *The Botanical Review*, 67 (3): 309–50.

Morcote-Ríos, G., Bernal, R. and Raz, L. (2016), 'Phytoliths as a tool for archaeobotanical, palaeobotanical and palaeoecological studies in Amazonian palms', *Botanical Journal of the Linnean Society*, 182 (2): 348–60.

Morcote-Ríos, G., Raz, L., Giraldo-Cañas, D., Franky, C. E. and León Sicard, T. T. (2013), 'Terras Pretas de Índio of the Caquetá-Japurá River (Colombian Amazonia)', *Tipití*, 11 (2): 30–39.

Moreira, P. A., Lins, J., Dequigiovanni, G., Veasey, E. A. and Clement, C. R. (2015), 'The Domestication of Annatto (Bixa orellana), from Bixa urucurana in Amazonia', *Economic Botany*, 69 (2): 127–35.

Moreno-Mayar, J. V., Potter, B. A., Vinner, L., Steinrücken, M., Rasmussen, S., Terhorst, J., Kamm, J. A., Albrechtsen, A., Malaspinas, A.-S. and Sikora, M. (2018), 'Terminal Pleistocene Alaskan genome reveals first founding population of Native Americans', *Nature*, 553 (7687): 203–7.

Motamayor, J. C., Lachenaud, P., Da Silva e Mota, J. W., Loor, R., Kuhn, D. N., Brown, J. S. and Schnell, R. J. (2008), 'Geographic and genetic population differentiation of the Amazonian chocolate tree (Theobroma cacao L)', *PloS ONE*, 3 (10): e3311.

Moy, C. M., Seltzer, G. O., Rodbell, D. T. and Anderson, D. M. (2002), 'Variability of El Niño/Southern Oscillation activity at millennial timescales during the Holocene epoch', *Nature*, 420 (6912): 162–5.

Munoz-Rodriguez, P., Carruthers, T., Wood, J. R., Williams, B. R., Weitemier, K., Kronmiller, B., Ellis, D., Anglin, N. L., Longway, L. and Harris, S. A. (2018), 'Reconciling Conflicting Phylogenies in the Origin of Sweet Potato and Dispersal to Polynesia', *Current Biology*, 28 (8): 1246–56, e12.

Müller, L. M., Kipnis, R., Ferreira, M. P., Marzo, S., Fiedler, B., Lucas, M., Ilgner, J., Silva, H. P. and Roberts, P. (2022), 'Late Holocene dietary and cultural variability on the Xingu River, Amazon Basin: A stable isotopic approach', *PloS ONE*, 17 (8), e0271545.

Myers, T. P. (1974), 'Spanish Contacts and Social Change on the Ucayali River, Peru', *Ethnohistory*, 21 (2): 135–57.

Myers, T. P. (2004), 'Dark Earth in the Upper Amazon', in Glaser, B. and Woods, W. I. (eds), *Amazonian Dark Earths: Explorations in Space and Time*, 67–94, Berlin: Springer.

Nepstad, D., Schwartzman, S., Bamberger, B., Santilli, M., Ray, D., Schlesinger, P., Lefebvre, P., Alencar, A., Prinz, E. and Fiske, G. (2006), 'Inhibition of Amazon Deforestation and Fire by Parks and Indigenous Lands', *Conservation Biology*, 20 (1): 65–73.

Netherly, P. and Dillehay, T. D. (1986), 'Duality in public architecture in the Upper Zaña Valley, Northern Peru', in Sandweiss, D. H. and Kvietok, D. (eds), *Perspectives on Andean Prehistory and Protohistory,* 85–114, New York: Cornell University.

Neves, E. G. (1998), 'Twenty years of Amazonian archaeology in Brazil (1977–1997)', *Antiquity*, 72 (277): 625–32.

Neves, E. G. (1999), 'O velho e o novo na arqueologia amazônica', *Revista USP,* 44: 86–111.

Neves, E. G. (2007), 'El Formativo que nunca terminó: la larga historia de estabilidad en las ocupaciones humanas de la Amazonía central', *Boletín de Arqueología PUCP,* 11: 117–42.

Neves, E. G. (2013), 'Was Agriculture a Key Productive Activity in Pre-Colonial Amazonia? The Stable Productive Basis for Social Equality in the Central Amazon', in Brondizio, E. S. and Neves, E. G. (2022), *Sob os tempos do equinócio: oito mil anos de história na Amazônia Central.* São Paulo: Ubu Editora.

Neves, E. G., Guapindaia, V. L. C., Lima, H., Costa, B. L. S. and Gomes, J. (2014), 'A tradição Pocó-Açutuba e os primeros sinais visíveis de modificações de paisagens na calha do Amazonas', in Rostain, S. (ed.), *Actas del 3er Encuentro Internacional de Arqueología Amazónica*, 137–58, Quito: Instituto Frances de Estudios Andinos.

Neves, E. G. and Heckenberger, M. J. (2019), 'The Call of the Wild: Rethinking Food Production in Ancient Amazonia', *Annual Review of Anthropology*, 48: 371–88.

Neves, E. G. and Petersen, J. B. (2006), 'Political Economy and Pre-Columbian Landscape Transformations in Central Amazonia', in Erickson, C. and Balée, W. (eds), *Time and Complexity in Historical Ecology: Studies in the Neotropical Lowlands,* 279–309, New York: Columbia University Press.

Nevle, R., Bird, D., Ruddiman, W. and Dull, R. (2011), 'Neotropical human–landscape interactions, fire, and atmospheric CO_2 during European conquest', *The Holocene*, 21 (5): 853–64.

Nevle, R. J. and Bird, D. K. (2008), 'Effects of syn-pandemic fire reduction and reforestation in the tropical Americas on atmospheric CO_2 during European conquest', *Palaeogeography, Palaeoclimatology, Palaeoecology*, 264: 25–38.

Nichols, J. (1992), *Linguistic diversity in space and time*, Chicago, University of Chicago Press.

Nielsen, R., Akey, J. M., Jakobsson, M., Pritchard, J. K., Tishkoff, S. and Willerslev, E. (2017), 'Tracing the peopling of the world through genomics', *Nature*, 541 (7637): 302–10.

Nimuendajú, C. (2004), *In pursuit of a Past Amazon: Archaeological Researches in the Brazilian Guyana and in the Amazon Region*, 45, Goteborg: Elanders Infologistik.

Nobre, A. D. (2014). *The Future of Climate of Amazonia*, Scientific Assessment Report, São José dos Campos: ARA.

Noelli, F. (1993), *Sem Tekohá não há Tekó (Em Busca de um Modelo Etnoarqueológico da Aldeia e da Subsistência Guarani e sua Aplicação a uma Área de Domínio no Delta do Rio Jacuí – RS)*, MA PUCRS: Porto Alegre.

Noelli, F. S. (1998), 'The Tupi: explaining origin and expansions in terms of archaeology and of historical linguistics', *Antiquity*, 72 (277): 648–63.

Nordenskiöld, E. (1930), *Ars Americana I. L'Archélogie du Bassin de l'Amazone*, Paris: Les ëditions G. Van Oest.

Nordenskiöld, E. (1913), 'Urnengräber und Mounds im bolivianischen Flachlande', *Baessler-Archiv*, 3 (6): 205–55.

Normile, D. (2017), 'Rice so nice it was domesticated thrice', *Science*, doi: 10.1126/science.aaq1816.

Oliver, J. (2001), 'The archaeology of forest foraging and agricultural production in Amazonia', in McEwan, C., Barreto, C. and Neves, E. (eds), *Unknown Amazon. London: The British Museum Press*, 50–85.

Olsen, K. M. and Schaal, B. A. (2001), 'Microsatellite variation in cassava (*Manihot esculenta*, Euphorbiaceae), and its wild relatives: further evidence for a southern Amazonian origin of domestication', *American Journal of Botany*, 88 (1): 131–42.

Oyuela-Caycedo, A. and Bonzani, R. (2005), '*San Jacinto 1. A Historical Ecological Approach to an Archaic site in Colombia*', Tuscaloosa: University of Alabama Press.

Pagán-Jiménez, J. R., Rodríguez-Ramos, R., Reid, B. A., van den Bel, M. and Hofman, C. L. (2015), 'Early dispersals of maize and other food plants into the Southern Caribbean and Northeastern South America', *Quaternary Science Reviews*, 123: 231–46.

Pagán Jiménez, J. R. and Rostain, S. (2014), 'Uso de plantas económicas y rituales (medicinales o energizantes), en dos comunidades precolombinas de la Alta Amazonia ecuatoriana: Sangay (Huapula), y Colina Moravia (c. 400 aC–1200 dC)', in Rostain, S. (ed.), *Actas del 3er Encuentro Internacional de Arqueología Amazónica. Quito: Instituto Frances de Estudios Andinos*, 313–22.

Palmatary, H. C. (1960), 'The archaeology of the Lower Tapajos valley, Brazil', *Transactions of the American Philosophical Society*, 50 (3).

Parsons, J. J. and Shlemon, R. (1987), 'Mapping and dating the prehistoric raised fields of the Guayas basin, Ecuador', in Denevan, W. M., Mathewson, D. and Knapp, G. (eds), *Pre-Hispanic Agricultural Fields in the Andean Region,* 207–16, Oxford: BAR International Series 359.

Pärssinen, M. (2021), 'Tequinho Geoglyph Site and Early Polychrome Horizon BC 500/300–AD 300/500 in the Brazilian State of Acre', *Amazônica*, 13 (1): 177–220.

Pärssinen, M., Ferreira, E., Virtanen, P. K. and Ranzi, A. (2020), 'Domestication in Motion: Macrofossils of Pre-Colonial Brazilian Nuts, Palms and Other Amazonian Planted Tree Species Found in the Upper Purus', *Environmental Archaeology*, 1–14.

Pärssinen, M., Schaan, D. and Ranzi, A. (2009), 'Pre-Columbian geometric earthworks in the upper Purús: a complex society in western Amazonia', *Antiquity*, 83 (322): 1084–95.

Pauketat, T. R. (2007), *Chiefdoms and Other Archaeological Delusions*, Lanham, Altamira Press.

Paz-Rivera, C. and Putz, F. E. (2009), Anthropogenic Soils and Tree Distributions in a Lowland Forest in Bolivia. *Biotropica*, 41 (6): 665–75.

Pazmiño, E. M. (2021), 'Monumentality and Social Complexity in the Upano Valley, Upper Amazon of Ecuador', in Clasby, R. and Nesbitt, J. (eds), *The Archaeology of the Upper Amazon: Complexity and Interaction in the Andean Tropical Forest,* 129–47, Gainsville: University of Florida Press.

Pearsall, D. (1995), '"Doing" paleoethnobotany in the tropical lowlands: adaptation and innovation in methodology', in Stahl, P. (ed.), *Archaeology in the Lowland American Tropics: Current Analytical Methods and Recent Applications,* 113–29, Cambridge: Cambridge University Press.

Pearsall, D. M. (2007), 'Modeling Prehistoric Agriculture through the Palaeoenvironmental Record: Theoretical and Methodological Issues, in Denham, T. P., Iriarte, J. and Vrydaghs, L. (eds), *Rethinking agriculture: archaeological and ethnoarchaeological perspectives,* 210–30, Walnut Creek: Left Coast Press.

Pearsall, D. M. (2008), 'Plant Domestication and the Shift to Agriculture in the Andes', in Silverman, H. and Isbell, W. (eds), *The Handbook of South American Archaeology,* 105–20, New York: Springer.

Pearsall, D. M. (2015), *Paleoethnobotany: A Handbook of Procedures,* London: Routledge.

Pearsall, D. M., Chandler-Ezell, K. and Zeidler, J. A. (2004), 'Maize in ancient Ecuador: results of residue analysis of stone tools from the Real Alto site', *Journal of Archaeological Science*, 31 (4): 423–42.

Pedersen, M. W., Overballe-Petersen, S., Ermini, L., Sarkissian, C. D., Haile, J., Hellstrom, M., Spens, J., Thomsen, P. F., Bohmann, K. and Cappellini, E. (2015), 'Ancient and modern environmental DNA', *Philosophical Transactions of the Royal Society B: Biological Sciences*, 370 (1660): 20130383.

Peltier, W. and Fairbanks, R. G. (2006), 'Global glacial ice volume and Last Glacial Maximum duration from an extended Barbados Sea level record', *Quaternary Science Reviews*, 25 (23): 3322–7.

Pennington, R. T., Lewis, G. P. and Ratter, J. A. (2006), *An overview of the plant diversity, biogeography and conservation of neotropical savannas and seasonally dry forests,* Boca Raton, CRC Press.

Penny, A., Templeman, S., McKenzie, M., Tello Toral, D. and Hunt, E. (2020), *State of the Tropics Report.*

Pereira, E. d. S. and Moraes, C. d. P. (2019), 'A cronologia das pinturas rupestres da Caverna da Pedra Pintada, Monte Alegre, Pará: revisão histórica e novos dados. Boletim do Museu Paraense Emílio Goeldi', *Ciências Humanas*, 14 (2): 327–42.

Peripato, V. et al (2023), 'More than 10,000 pre-Columbian earthworks are still hidden throughout Amazonia', *Science,* 382 (6666): 103–9.

Perry, L. (2004), 'Starch analyses reveal the relationship between tool type and function: an example from the Orinoco valley of Venezuela', *Journal of Archaeological Science*, 31 (8): 1069–81.

Perry, L., Dickau, R., Zarrillo, S., Holst, I., Pearsall, D. M., Piperno, D. R., Berman, M. J., Cooke, R. G., Rademaker, K. and Ranere, A. J. (2007), 'Starch fossils and the domestication and dispersal of chili peppers (Capsicum spp. L.), in the Americas', *Science*, 315 (5814): 986.

Pezo-Lanfranco, L., Eggers, S., Petronilho, C., Toso, A., da Rocha Bandeira, D., Von Tersch, M., dos Santos, A. M., Ramos da Costa, B., Meyer, R. and Colonese, A. C. (2018), 'Middle Holocene plant cultivation on the Atlantic Forest coast of Brazil?' *Royal Society Open Science*, 5 (9): 180432.

Pickersgill, B. (2007), 'Domestication of plants in the Americas: insights from Mendelian and molecular genetics', *Annals of Botany*, 100 (5): 925–40.

Pigati, J. S., Springer, K. B., Honke, J. S., Wahl, D., Champagne, M. R., Zimmerman, S. R., Gray, H. J., Santucci, V. L., Odess, D. and Bustos, D. (2023), 'Independent age estimates resolve the controversy of ancient human footprints at White Sands', *Science*, 382 (6666): 73–5.

Piperno, D., Moreno, J., Iriarte, J., Holst, I., Lachniet, M., Jones, J., Ranere, A. and Castanzo, R. (2007), 'Late Pleistocene and Holocene environmental history of the Iguala Valley, Central Balsas Watershed of Mexico', *Proceedings of the National Academy of Sciences*, 104 (29): 11874–81.

Piperno, D., Ranere, A., Holst, I., Iriarte, J. and Dickau, R. (2009), 'Starch grain and phytolith evidence for early ninth millennium B.P. maize from the Central Balsas River Valley, Mexico, *Proceedings of the National Academy of Sciences*, 106 (13): 5019–24.

Piperno, D. R. (1984), *Phytolith Analysis. An Archaeological and Geological Perspective,* New York: Academic Press.

Piperno, D. R. (2006), Phytoliths: *A Comprehensive Guide for Archaeologists and Paleoecologists,* San Diego: AltaMira Press.

Piperno, D. R. (2011), 'The Origins of Plant Cultivation and Domestication in the New World Tropics: Patterns, Process, and New Developments', *Current Anthropology*, 52 (S4): S453–S470.

Piperno, D. R. and Dillehay, T. D. (2008), 'Starch grains on human teeth reveal early broad crop diet in northern Peru', *Proceedings of the National Academy of Sciences*, 105 (50): 19622.

Piperno, D. R. and Flannery, K. V. (2001), 'The earliest archaeological maize (*Zea mays* L.), from highland Mexico: New accelerator mass spectrometry dates and their implications'. *Proceedings of the National Academy of Sciences*, 98 (4): 2101.

Piperno, D. R., Holst, I., Wessel-Beaver, L. and Andres, T. C. (2002), 'Evidence for the control of phytolith formation in *Cucurbita* fruits by the hard rind (*Hr*), genetic locus: archaeological and ecological implications', *Proceedings of the National Academy of Sciences*, 99 (16): 10923–8.

Piperno, D. R. and Jones, J. G. (2003), 'Paleoecological and archaeological implications of a Late Pleistocene/Early Holocene record of vegetation and climate from the Pacific coastal plain of Panama', *Quaternary Research*, 59 (1): 79–87.

Piperno, D. R. and McMichael, C. (2023), 'Phytoliths in modern plants from Amazonia and the Neotropics at large: II. Enhancement of eudicotyledon reference collections', *Quaternary International*, 655: 1–17.

Piperno, D. R. and Pearsall, D. M. (1998), *The Origins of Agriculture in the Lowland Neotropics*, San Diego: Academic Press.

Piperno, D. R., Ranere, A. J., Holst, I. and Hansell, P. (2000), Starch grains reveal early root crop horticulture in the Panamanian tropical forest. *Nature*, 407 (6806): 894–7.

Piperno, D. R. and Stothert, K. E. (2003), 'Phytolith Evidence for Early Holocene *Cucurbita* Domestication in Southwest Ecuador', *Science*, 299 (5609): 1054.

Pires de Campos, A. (1862), 'Breve notícia que dá o capitão Antônio Pires de Campos do gentio que há na derrota da viagem das minas do Cuyabá e seu recôncavo', *Revita Trimestral do Instituto Histótico, Geográfico, e Etnográfico do Brasil*, 5: 437–49.

Pires, J. and Prance, G. (1985), 'The vegetation types of the Brazilian Amazon', in Prance, G. T. and Lovejoy, T. E. (eds), *Key Environments: Amazonia*. Oxford: Pergamon Press.

Plowman, T. (1984), 'The Ethnobotany of Coca (Erythroxylum spp., Erythroxylaceae)', *Advances in Economic Botany*, 1: 62–111.

Pohl, M. D., Pope, K. O., Jones, J. G., Jacob, J. S., Piperno, D. R., deFrance, S. D., Lentz, D. L., Gifford, J. A., Danforth, M. E. and Josserand, J. K. (1996), 'Early Agriculture in the Maya Lowlands', *Latin American Antiquity*, 355–72.

Politis, G. (2009), *Nukak: Ethnoarchaeology of an Amazonian People*, Walnut Creek: Left Coast Press.

Porras, G. (1989), 'Investigations at the Sangay mound complex, Eastern Ecuador', *National Geographic Research*, 5 (3): 374–81.

Porro, A. (1994), 'Social Organization and Political Power in the Amazon Floodplain: The Ethnohistorical Sources', in Roosevelt, A. C. (ed.), *Amazonian Indians from Prehistory to the Present: Anthropological Perspectives*, 79–94, Tucson: University of Arizona Press.

Pöschl, U., Martin, S., Sinha, B., Chen, Q., Gunthe, S., Huffman, J., Borrmann, S., Farmer, D., Garland, R. and Helas, G. (2010), 'Rainforest aerosols as biogenic nuclei of clouds and precipitation in the Amazon', *Science*, 329 (5998): 1513–16.

Posey, D. A. (1984), 'A preliminary report on diversified management of tropical forest by the Kayapo Indians of the Brazilian Amazon', *Advances in Economic Botany*, 1: 112–26.

Posey, D. A. (1985), 'Indigenous management of tropical forest ecosystems: the case of the Kayapó indians of the Brazilian Amazon', *Agroforestry Systems*, 3 (2): 139–58.

Posey, D. A. and Balée, W. L. (1989), *Resource Management in Amazonia: Indigenous and Folk Strategies*, New York: New York Botanical Garden.

Posth, C., Nakatsuka, N., Lazaridis, I., Skoglund, P., Mallick, S., Lamnidis, T. C., Rohland, N., Nägele, K., Adamski, N. and Bertolini, E. (2018), 'Reconstructing the Deep Population History of Central and South America', *Cell*, 175 (5): 1185–97, e22.

Prestes-Carneiro, G., Béarez, P., Bailon, S., Py-Daniel, A. R. and Neves, E. G. (2016), 'Subsistence fishery at Hatahara (750–1230 CE), a pre-Columbian central Amazonian village', *Journal of Archaeological Science Reports*, 8: 454–62.

Prestes-Carneiro, G., Béarez, P., Pugliese, F., Shock, M. P., Zimpel, C. A., Pouilly, M. and Neves, E. G. (2020), 'Archaeological history of Middle Holocene environmental change from fish proxies at the Monte Castelo archaeological shell mound, Southwestern Amazonia', *The Holocene*, 30 (11): 1606–21.

Prestes-Carneiro, G., Béarez, P., Shock, M. P., Prümers, H. and Betancourt, C. J. (2019), 'Pre-Hispanic fishing practices in interfluvial Amazonia: Zooarchaeological evidence from managed landscapes on the Llanos de Mojos savanna', *PLoS ONE*, 14 (5).

Prestes-Carneiro, G., Sá Leitão Barboza, R., Sá Leitão Barboza, M., Moraes, C. d. P. and Béarez, P. (2021), 'Waterscapes domestication: an alternative approach for interactions among humans, animals, and aquatic environments in Amazonia across time', *Animal Frontiers*, 11 (3): 92–103.

Prous, A. (2019), *Arqueologia Brasileira: a pré-história e os verdadeiros colonizadores*, Cuiabá: Carlini & Caniato.

Prous, A. and Fogaça, E. (1999), 'Archaeology of the Pleistocene-Holocene boundary in Brazil', *Quaternary International*, 53: 21–41.

Prümers, H. (2009), '"Charlatanocracia" en Mojos? Investigaciones arqueológicas en la Loma Salvatierra. Beni, Bolivia', *Boletín de Arqueología PUCP*, 11, 103–16.

Prümers, H. (2014), 'Sitios prehispánicos con zanjas en Bella Vista, Provincia Iténez, Bolivia. Amazonía', in Rostain, S. (ed.), *Actas del 3er Encuentro Internacional de Arqueología Amazónica*, 73–89, Quito: Instituto Frances de Estudios Andinos.

Prümers, H. (2015), *Loma Mendoza. Excavaciones de los años 1999–2002*, La Paz: Editorial Plural.

Prümers, H. (2017), 'Los monticulos artificiales de la Amazonia', in Rostain, S. and Jaimes Betancourt, C. (eds), *Las siete maravillas de la Amazonia precolombiana*, 47–72, La Paz: Plural.

Prümers, H., Betancourt, C. J., Iriarte, J., Robinson, M. and Schaich, M. (2022), 'Lidar reveals pre-Hispanic low-density urbanism in the Bolivian Amazon', *Nature*, 606 (7913): 325–8.

Prümers, H. and Jaimes Betancourt, C. (2014), '100 años de investigación arqueológica en los Llanos de Mojos', *Arqueoantropológicas*, 4 (4): 11–54.

Pugliese, F. A., Augusto Zimpel Neto, C. and Neves, E. G. (2018), 'What do Amazonian Shellmounds Tell Us About the Long-Term Indigenous History of South America?', *Encyclopedia of Global Archaeology*, 1–25, Cham: Springer International Publishing.

Py-Daniel, A. R. (2016), 'Práticas Funerárias na Amazônia: a morte, a diversidade e os locais de enterramento', *Revista Habitus*, 14 (1): 87–106.

Ranere, A. J., Cooke, R. G. and Mercader, J. (2002), 'Late glacial and early Holocene occupation of Central American tropical forests', in Mercader, J. (ed.), *Under the Canopy: The Archaeology of Tropical Rainforests*, 219–48, New Burnswick: Rutgers University Press.

Ranzi, A. and Pärssinen, M. (2021), *Amazônia: Os Geoglifos e a Civilização Aquiry*, Florianopolis: Massiambooks/Officio.

Ranzi, T. J. (2011), *Geoglifos do Acre e a Proteção de Sítios Arqueológicos no Brasil*, Rio Branco: Printac.

Redford, K. H. and Robinson, J. G. (1987), 'The Game of Choice: Patterns of Indian and Colonist Hunting in the Neotropics', *American Anthropologist*, 89 (3): 650–67.

Redmond, E. and Spencer, C. (2007), *Archaeological Survey in the High Llanos and Andean Piedmont of Barinas Venezuela*, New York: Anthropological Papers of the American Museum of Natural History.

Reichel-Dolmatoff, G. (1971), *Amazonian cosmos: the sexual and religious symbolism of the Tukano Indians*, Chicago: University of Chicago Press.

Renard, D., Iriarte, J., Birk, J., Rostain, S., Glaser, B. and McKey, D. (2011), 'Ecological engineers ahead of their time: The functioning of pre-Columbian raised-field agriculture and its potential contributions to sustainability today', *Ecological Engineering*, 45: 30–44.

Ribeiro, D., Bouzek, J., Burridge, K., Galvao, E., Hicks, F., Leslie, C., Nelson, C. and Whiteford, A. H. (1970), 'The Culture-Historical Configurations of the American Peoples [and Comments and Reviews and Reply]', *Current Anthropology*, 11 (4/5): 403–34.

Rick, J. W. (1987), 'Dates as Data: An Examination of the Peruvian Preceramic Radiocarbon Record', *American Antiquity*, 52 (1): 55–73.

Riris, P. (2020), 'Spatial structure among the geometric earthworks of western Amazonia (Acre, Brazil)', *Journal of Anthropological Archaeology*, 59: 101177.

Riris, P. and Arroyo-Kalin, M. (2019), 'Widespread population decline in South America correlates with mid-Holocene climate change', *Scientific Reports*, 9 (1): 6850.

Rival, L. (1998), 'Domestication as a Historical and Symbolic Process: Wild Gardens and Cultivated Forests in the Ecuadorian Amazon', in Balée, W. (ed.), *Advances in Historical Ecology*, 232–48, New York: Columbia University Press.
Rival, L. and McKey, D. (2008), 'Domestication and Diversity in Manioc (*Manihot esculenta* Crantz ssp. *esculenta*, Euphorbiaceae)', *Current Anthropology*, 49 (6): 1119–28.
Roberts, N., Fyfe, R. M., Woodbridge, J., Gaillard, M.-J., Davis, B. A., Kaplan, J. O., Marquer, L., Mazier, F., Nielsen, A. B. and Sugita, S. (2018), 'Europe's lost forests: A pollen-based synthesis for the last 11,000 years', *Scientific Reports*, 8 (1): 1–8.
Roberts, P. (2019), *Tropical Forests in Prehistory, History and Modernity*, Oxford: Oxford University Press.
Robinson, M., De Souza, J. G., Maezumi, S. Y., Cárdenas, M., Pessenda, L., Prufer, K., Corteletti, R., Scunderlick, D., Mayle, F. E. and De Blasis, P. (2018), 'Uncoupling human and climate drivers of late Holocene vegetation change in southern Brazil', *Scientific Reports*, 8 (1): 7,800.
Robinson, M., Jaimes-Betancourt, C., Elliott, S., Maezumi, S. Y., Hilbert, L., Alves, D., de Souza, J. G. and Iriarte, J. (2020), 'Anthropogenic soil and settlement organisation in the Bolivian Amazon', *Geoarchaeology*, 36: 388–403.
Robinson, M., Morcote-Rios, G., Aceituno, F. J., Roberts, P., Berrío, J. C. and Iriarte, J. (2021), '"Moving South": Late Pleistocene Plant Exploitation and the Importance of Palm in the Colombian Amazon', *Quaternary*, 4 (3): 26.
Rodet, M. J., Duarte-Talim, D., Pereira, E. and Moraes, C. (2023), 'New Data from Pedra Pintada Cave, Brazilian Amazon: Technological Analyses of the Lithic Industries in the Pleistocene-Holocene', *Latin American Antiquity*, 1–21.
Rodrigues, A. D. I. (2001), 'Biodiversidade e Diversidade Etnolingüística na Amazônia', in Simões, M. d. S. (ed.), *Cultura e Biodiversidade entre o Rio e a Floresta*, 269–78, Belém: Edufpa.
Rodrigues, L., Sprafke, T., Moyikola, C. B., Barthès, B. G., Bertrand, I., Comptour, M., Rostain, S., Yoka, J. and Mckey, D. (2020), 'A Congo Basin ethnographic analogue of pre-Columbian Amazonian raised fields shows the ephemeral legacy of organic matter management', *Scientific Reports*, 10 (1): 1–12.
Rodrigues, L., Lombardo, U. and Veit, H. (2018), 'Design of pre-Columbian raised fields in the Llanos de Moxos, Bolivian Amazon: Differential adaptations to the local environment?', *Journal of Archaeological Science: Reports*, 17: 366–78.
Rodríguez, I. (2007), 'Pemon Perspectives of Fire Management in Canaima National Park, Southeastern Venezuela', *Human Ecology*, 35: 331–43.
Roosevelt, A. (1989), 'Resource Management in Amazonia before the Conquest: Beyond Ethnographic Projection', *Advances in Economic Botany*, 7: 30–62.
Roosevelt, A. C. (1987a), 'Chiefdoms in the Amazon and Orinoco', in Drennan, R. D. and Uribe, C. A. (eds), *Chiefdoms in the Americas*, 153–84, Lanham, Maryland: University Press of America.
Roosevelt, A. C. (1987b), *Parmana: Prehistoric Maize and Manioc Subsistence along the Amazon and Orinoco*, New York: Academic Press.
Roosevelt, A. C. (1991), *Moundbuilders of the Amazon: Geophysical Archaeology on Marajó Island, Brazil*, San Diego: Academic Press.
Roosevelt, A. C. (1995), 'Early Pottery in the Amazon: Twenty Years of Scholarly Obscurity', in Barnett, W. and Hoopes, J. (eds), *The Emergence of Pottery: Technology and Innovation in Ancient Societies*, 115–31, Washington, DC: Smithsonian Institution Press,.
Roosevelt, A. C. (1999), 'The Development of Prehistoric Complex Societies: Amazonia, A Tropical Forest', in Bacus, E. A. and Lucero, L. J. (eds), *Complex Polities in the Ancient Tropical World*, 13–33, Arlington: American Anthropological Association.
Roosevelt, A. C. (2007), 'Geophysical Archaeology in the Lower Amazon: A Research Strategy', in Wiseman, J. R. and El-Baz, F. (eds), *Remote Sensing in Archaeology*, 443–75, New York: Springer.
Roosevelt, A. C. (2013), 'The Amazon and the Anthropocene: 13,000 years of human influence in a tropical rainforest', *Anthropocene*, 4: 69–87.

Roosevelt, A. C., Douglas, J. and Brown, L. (2002), 'The Migrations and Adaptations of the First Americans: Clovis and Pre-Clovis Viewed from South America', in Jablonski, N. G. (ed.), *The First Americans: The Pleistocene Colonization of the New World*, 159–236, San Francisco: California University Press.

Roosevelt, A. C., Housley, R. A., Da Silveira, M. I., Maranca, S. and Johnson, R. (1991), 'Eighth millennium pottery from a prehistoric shell midden in the Brazilian Amazon', *Science*, 254 (5038): 1621–4.

Roosevelt, A. C., Lima da Costa, M., Lopes Machado, C., Michab, M., Mercier, N., Valladas, H., Feathers, J., Barnett, W., Imazio da Silveira, M. and Henderson, A. (1996), 'Paleoindian Cave Dwellers in the Amazon: The Peopling of the Americas', *Science*, 272 (5260): 373–84.

Rostain, S. (2012a), 'Between Sierra and Selva: Landscape transformations in upper Ecuadorian Amazonia', *Quaternary International*, 249: 31–42.

Rostain, S. (2012b), *Islands in the Rainforest. Landscape Management in Pre-Columbian Amazonia*, Waltnut Creek, CA: Left Coast Press.

Rostain, S. and Jaimes Bentancourt, C. (2017), *Las siete maravillas de la Amazonía precolombina*, La Paz: Plural.

Rouse, I. and Cruxent, J. (1963), *Venezuelan Archaeology*, New Haven: Yale University Press.

Rull, V. and Montoya, E. (2014), 'Mauritia flexuosa palm swamp communities: natural or human-made? A palynological study of the Gran Sabana region (northern South America), within a neotropical context', *Quaternary Science Reviews*, 99: 17–33.

Saldanha, J. D. M., Cabral, M. P., Nazaré, A. S., Lima, J. J. S. and Flores da Silva, M. B. (2016), 'Os complexos cerâmicos do Amapá: proposta de uma nova sistematização', in Barreto, C., Lima, H. and Betancourt, C. J. (eds), *Cerâmicas Arqueológicas da Amazônia: Rumo a uma nova síntese*, 86–96, Belem: IPHAN,.

Salick, J., Cellinese, N. and Knapp, S. (1997), 'Indigenous diversity of Cassava: Generation, maintenance, use and loss among the Amuesha, Peruvian upper Amazon', *Economic Botany*, 51 (1): 6.

Sánchez-Polo, A. and Litben, R. Á. (2023), 'Un paisaje monumental prehispánico en la Alta Amazonía ecuatoriana: primeros resultados de la aplicación de Lidar en el valle del Upano', *Strata*, 1 (1): e3–e3.

Sanjur, O. I., Piperno, D. R., Andrés, T. C. and Wessel-Beaver, L. (2002), 'Phylogenetic relationships among domesticated and wild species of *Cucurbita* (Cucurbitaceae), inferred from a mitochondrial gene: Implications for crop plant evolution and areas of origin', *Proceedings of the National Academy of Sciences*, 99 (1): 535–40.

Santos-Granero, F. (1992), *Etnohistoria de la Alta Amazonía*, Quito: Editorial Abya Yala.

Santos-Granero, F. (1998), 'Writing History into the Landscape: Space, Myth, and Ritual in Contemporary Amazonia', *American Ethnologist*, 25 (2): 128–48.

Santos, G. M. (2006), *Da cultura à natureza – um estudo do cosmos e da ecologia dos enawene-nawe*, PhD Thesis: Universidade de São Paulo.

Santos Mühlen, G., Alves-Pereira, A., Clement, C. R. and Losada Valle, T. (2013), 'Genetic Diversity and Differentiation of Brazilian Bitter and Sweet Manioc Varieties (Manihot esculenta Crantz, Euphorbiaceae), Based on SSR Molecular Markers', *Tipití*, 11 (2): 66–73.

Sauer, C. O. (1944), 'A Geographic Sketch of Early Man in America', *Geographical Review*, 34 (4): 529–73.

Sauer, C. O. (1952), *Agricultural Origins and Dispersals*, New York: The American Geographical Society.

Saunaluoma, S. (2010), 'Pre-Columbian Earthworks in the Riberalta Region of the Bolivian Amazon', *Amazônica*, 2 (1): 104–38.

Saunaluoma, S. (2016), 'Ceramicas do Acre', in Barreto, C., Lima, H. and Betancourt, C. J. (eds), *Cerâmicas Arqueológicas da Amazônia: Rumo a uma nova síntese*, 433–8, Belem: IPHAN.

Saunaluoma, S., Anttiroiko, N. and Moat, J. (2019), 'UAV survey at archaeological earthwork sites in the Brazilian state of Acre, southwestern Amazonia', *Archaeological Prospection*, 26 (4): 325–31.

Saunaluoma, S., Moat, J., Pugliese, F. and Neves, E. G. (2021), 'Patterned Villagescapes and Road Networks in Ancient Southwestern Amazonia', *Latin American Antiquity*, 32 (1): 173–87.

Saunaluoma, S., Pärssinen, M. and Schaan, D. (2018), 'Diversity of Pre-colonial Earthworks in the Brazilian State of Acre, Southwestern Amazonia', *Journal of Field Archaeology*, 43 (5): 362–79.

Saunaluoma, S. and Schaan, D. (2012), 'Monumentality in Western Amazonian formative societies: geometric ditched enclosures in the Brazilian state of Acre', *Antiqua*, 2 (1), e1.

Scaldaferro, M. A., Barboza, G. E. and Acosta, M. C. (2018), 'Evolutionary history of the chili pepper Capsicum baccatum L.(Solanaceae): domestication in South America and natural diversification in the Seasonally Dry Tropical Forests', *Biological Journal of The Linnean Society*, 124 (3): 466–78.

Schaan, D., Pärssinen, M., Ranzi, A. and Piccoli, J. (2007), 'Geoglifos da Amazônia ocidental: Evidência de complexidade social entre povos da terra firme', *Revista de Arqueología*, 20: 67–82.

Schaan, D., Pärssinen, M., Saunaluoma, S., Ranzi, A., Bueno, M. and Barbosa, A. (2012), 'New radiometric dates for precolumbian (2000–700 b.p.), earthworks in western Amazonia, Brazil', *Journal of Field Archaeology*, 37 (2): 132–42.

Schaan, D. P. (2004), *The Camutins Chiefdom: Rise and Development of Social Complexity on Marajó Island, Brazilian Amazon*, PhD: University of Pittsburgh.

Schaan, D. P. (2012a), 'Marajoara Iconography: A Structural Approach', *Naya*, 2 (13).

Schaan, D. P. (2012b), *Sacred Geographies of Ancient Amazonia: Historical Ecology of Social Complexity*, Walnut Creek: Left Coast Press.

Scheel-Ybert, R., Caromano, C. F. and de Azevedo, L. W. (2016), 'Of forests and gardens: landscape, environment, and cultural choices in Amazonia, southeastern and southern Brazil from c. 3000 to 300 cal yrs BP', *Cadernos do LEPAARQ*, 13 (25): 425–58.

Schmidl, U. (1950), *Derrotero y Viaje a Espana y las Indias*, Santa Fe: Universidad Nacional del Litoral.

Schmidt, M. (1917), *Die Aruaken: Ein beitrag zum problem der kulturverbreitungVeit and Comp.*

Schmidt, M. J., Goldberg, S. L., Heckenberger, M., Fausto, C., Franchetto, B., Watling, J., Lima, H., Moraes, B., Dorshow, W. B. and Toney, J. (2023), 'Intentional creation of carbon-rich dark earth soils in the Amazon', *Science Advances*, 9 (38): eadh8499.

Schmidt, M. J. and Heckenberger, M. J. (2009), 'Amerindian Anthrosols: Amazonian Dark Earth Formation in the Upper Xingu', in Woods, W. I., Teixeira, W. G., Lehmann, J., Steiner, C., WinklerPrins, A. M. G. A. and Rebellato, L. (eds), *Amazonian Dark Earths: Wim Sombroek's Vision*, 163–91, Berlin: Springer.

Schmitz, P., Rosa, A. and Bitencourt, A. (2004), *Arqueologia nos cerrados do Brasil Central*, Serranópolis III, 60, São Leopoldo: Instituto Anchietano de Pesquisas.

Schultes, R. E. and Raffauf, R. F. (1990), *The Healing Forest: Medicinal and Toxic Plants of the Northwest Amazonia*, Portland, Dioscorides Press.

Schroth, G., Coutinho, P., Moraes, V. H. and Albernaz, A. L. (2003), 'Rubber agroforests at the Tapajós river, Brazilian Amazon – environmentally benign land use systems in an old forest frontier region', *Agriculture, Ecosystems and Environment*, 97 (1–3): 151–65.

Sheehan, O., Watts, J., Gray, R. D. and Atkinson, Q. D. (2018), 'Coevolution of landesque capital intensive agriculture and sociopolitical hierarchy', *Proceedings of the National Academy of Sciences*, 115 (14): 3628–33.

Shennan, S., Downey, S. S., Timpson, A., Edinborough, K., Colledge, S., Kerig, T., Manning, K. and Thomas, M. G. (2013), 'Regional population collapse followed initial agriculture booms in mid-Holocene Europe', *Nature Communications*, 4 (1): 1–8.

Shepard, G., Jr. and Ramirez, H. (2011), '"Made in Brazil": Human dispersal of the Brazil Nut (Bertholletia excelsa, Lecythidaceae), in Ancient Amazonia', *Economic Botany*, 65 (1): 44–65.

Shepard Jr, G. H., Levi, T., Neves, E. G., Peres, C. A. and Yu, D. W. (2012), 'Hunting in Ancient and Modern Amazonia: Rethinking Sustainability', *American Anthropologist*, 114 (4): 652–67.

Shepard Jr, G. H., Neves, E., Clement, C. R., Lima, H., Moraes, C. and dos Santos, G. M. (2020), *Ancient and Traditional Agriculture in South America: Tropical Lowlands*, Oxford Research Encyclopedia of Environmental Science, https://oxfordre.com/environmentalscience/view/10.1093/acrefore/9780199389414.001.0001/acrefore-9780199389414-e-597.

Shock, M., de Paula Moraes, C., da Silva Belletti, J., Lima, M., da Silva, F. M., Lima, L. T., Cassino, M. F. and de Lima, A. M. A. (2014), 'Initial contributions of charred plant remains from archaeological sites in the Amazon to reconstructions of historical ecology', in Rostain, S. (ed.), *Antes de Orellana. Actas del 3er Encuentro Internacional de Arqueología Amazónica,* 291–304, Quito: Instituto Francés de Estudios Andinos.

Siegel, P. E. (1999), 'Contested Places and Places of Contest: The Evolution of Social Power and Ceremonial Space in prehistoric Puerto Rico', *Latin American Antiquity*, 209–38.

Sigmon, B. and Vollbrecht, E. (2010), 'Evidence of selection at the ramosa1 locus during maize domestication', *Molecular Ecology*, 19 (7): 1296–311.

Silveira, M., Daly, D. C., Salimon, C., Wadt, P., Amaral, E., Pereira, M. and Passos, V. (2008), *Ambientes físicos e coberturas vegetais do Acre. Primeiro catálogo da flora do Acre, Brasil*, Rio Branco: Edufac, 36–46.

Simões, M. F. and Correa, C. G. (1971), 'Pesquisas arqueologicas na regiao do Salgado (Para), – a fase Areao do litoral de Mariparim. *Boletim do Museu Paraense Emílio Goeldi*', 48L 1–30.

Simpson, B. B. and Haffer, J. (1978), 'Speciation Patterns in the Amazonian Forest Biota', *Annual Review of Ecology and Systematics*, 9 (1): 497–518.

Smith, B. D. (1997), 'The Initial Domestication of *Cucurbita Pepo* in the Americas 10,000 Years Ago', *Science*, 276 (5314): 932–4.

Smith, B. D. (1998), *The emergence of agriculture,* New York. Scientific American Library.

Smith, B. D. (2001), 'Low-Level Food Production', *Journal of Archaeological Research*, 9 (1): 1–43.

Smith, B. D. (2007), *Rivers of Encounters: Essays on Early Agriculture in Eastern North America,* Tuscaloosa: University of Alabama Press.

Smith, B. D. and Zeder, M. A. (2013), 'The onset of the Anthropocene', *Anthropocene*, 4: 8–13.

Smith, M. and Fausto, C. (2016), 'Socialidade e diversidade de pequis (Caryocar brasiliense, Caryocaraceae), entre os Kuikuro do alto rio Xingu (Brasil)', *Boletim do Museu Paraense Emílio Goeldi*, 11 (1): 87–113.

Smith, M. L. (2014), 'The Archaeology of Urban Landscapes', *Annual Review of Anthropology*, 43: 307–23.

Smith, R. J. and Mayle, F. E. (2018), 'Impact of mid-to late Holocene precipitation changes on vegetation across lowland tropical South America: a paleo-data synthesis', *Quaternary Research*, 89 (1): 134–55.

Soares-Filho, B., Silvestrini, R., Nepstad, D., Brando, P., Rodrigues, H., Alencar, A., Coe, M., Locks, C., Lima, L. and Hissa, L. (2012), 'Forest fragmentation, climate change and understory fire regimes on the Amazonian landscapes of the Xingu headwaters', *Landscape Ecology*, 27: 585–98.

Sombroek, W. (1966), *Amazon Soils: A Reconnaisance of the Soils of the Brazilian Amazon Region,* Wageningen: Center for Agricultural Publications and Documentation.

Sonnante, G., Stockton, T., Nodari, R., Becerra Velásquez, V. L. and Gepts, P. (1994), 'Evolution of genetic diversity during the domestication of common-bean (Phaseolus vulgaris L.)', *Theoretical and Applied Genetics*, 89 (5): 629–35.

Spencer, C. S. and Redmond, E. M. (1998), 'Prehispanic Causeways and Regional Politics in the Llanos of Barinas, Venezuela', *Latin American Antiquity*, 9 (2): 95–110.

Sponsel, L. E. (2021) Human impact on biodiversity, overview. *Encyclopedia of biodiversity*, 3, 430–48.

Stahl, P. W. (1986), 'Hallucinatory imagery and the origin of early South American figurine art', *World Archaeology*, 18 (1): 134–50.

Stahl, P. W. (2008), 'Animal Domestication in South America', in Silverman, H. and Isbell, W. (eds), *The Handbook of South American Archaeology*, 121–30, New York: Springer,.
Stahl, P. W. and Pearsall, D. M. (2012), 'Late pre-Columbian agroforestry in the tropical lowlands of western Ecuador', *Quaternary International*, 249: 43–52.
Stenborg, P. (2016), 'Archaeological research at hinterland sites on the Belterra Plateau, Pará', in Stenborg, P. (ed.), *Beyond Waters. Archaeology and Environmental History of the Amazonian Inland*, 113–26, Gothenburg: University of Gothenburg.
Stenborg, P., Schaan, D. P. and Figueiredo, C. G. (2018), 'Contours of the Past: LiDAR Data Expands the Limits of Late Pre-Columbian Human Settlement in the Santarém Region, Lower Amazon', *Journal of Field Archaeology*, 43 (1): 44–57.
Stenborg, P., Schaan, D. P. and Lima, M. A. (2012), 'Precolumbian land use and settlement pattern in the Santarém region, lower Amazon', *Amazônica*, 4 (1): 222–50.
Steward, J. H. (1946), *Handbook of South American Indians, Vol. 1*, Bulletin 143, Washington, DC: Smithsonian Institution.
Sutter, R. C. (2021), 'The Pre-Columbian Peopling and Population Dispersals of South America', *Journal of Archaeological Research*, 29: 93–51.
Tamm, E., Kivisild, T., Reidla, M., Metspalu, M., Smith, D. G., Mulligan, C. J., Bravi, C. M., Rickards, O., Martinez-Labarga, C. and Khusnutdinova, E. K. (2007), 'Beringian standstill and spread of Native American founders', *PLoS ONE*, 2(9), e829.
Taylor, A. C. (1999), 'The Western Margins of Amazonia from the Early Sixteenth to the Early Nineteenth Century', in Salomon, F. and Schwartz, S. B. (eds), *The Cambridge History of the Native Peoples of the Americas,* 188–256, New York: Cambridge University Press.
Teixeira, W. G. T., Kern, D. C., Madari, B. E., Lima, N. H. and Woods, W. I. (2010), *As Terras Pretas de Indio da Amazônia: Sua Caracterização e Uso deste Conhecimento na Criação de Novas Areas,* Manaus: Embrapa Amazônia Ocidental.
Tello, J. C. (1960), *Chavín, cultura matriz de la civilización andina,* Lima: Universidad de San Marcos.
Ter Steege, H., Pitman, N. C., Sabatier, D., Baraloto, C., Salomão, R. P., Guevara, J. E., Phillips, O. L., Castilho, C. V., Magnusson, W. E. and Molino, J.-F. (2013), 'Hyperdominance in the Amazonian Tree Flora', *Science*, 342 (6156): 1243092.
Ter Steege, H., Prado, P. I., Lima, R. A. F. d., Pos, E., de Souza Coelho, L., de Andrade Lima Filho, D., Salomão, R. P., Amaral, I. L., de Almeida Matos, F. D., Castilho, C. V., Phillips, O. L., Guevara, J. E., de Jesus Veiga Carim, M., Cárdenas López, D., Magnusson, W. E., Wittmann, F., Martins, M. P., Sabatier, D., Irume, M. V., da Silva Guimarães, J. R., Molino, J.-F., Bánki, O. S., Piedade, M. T. F., Pitman, N. C. A., Ramos, J. F., Monteagudo Mendoza, A., Venticinque, E. M., Luize, B. G., Núñez Vargas, P., Silva, T. S. F., de Leão Novo, E. M. M., Reis, N. F. C., Terborgh, J., Manzatto, A. G., Casula, K. R., Honorio Coronado, E. N., Montero, J. C., Duque, A., Costa, F. R. C., Castaño Arboleda, N., Schöngart, J., Zartman, C. E., Killeen, T. J., Marimon, B. S., Marimon-Junior, B. H., Vasquez, R., Mostacedo, B., Demarchi, L. O., Feldpausch, T. R., Engel, J., Petronelli, P., Baraloto, C., Assis, R. L., Castellanos, H., Simon, M. F., de Medeiros, M. B., Quaresma, A., Laurance, S. G. W., Rincón, L. M., Andrade, A., Sousa, T. R., Camargo, J. L., Schietti, J., Laurance, W. F., de Queiroz, H. L., Nascimento, H. E. M., Lopes, M. A., de Sousa Farias, E., Magalhães, J. L. L., Brienen, R., Aymard C, G. A., Revilla, J. D. C., Vieira, I. C. G., Cintra, B. B. L., Stevenson, P. R., Feitosa, Y. O., Duivenvoorden, J. F., Mogollón, H. F., Araujo-Murakami, A., Ferreira, L. V., Lozada, J. R., Comiskey, J. A., de Toledo, J. J., Damasco, G., Dávila, N., Lopes, A., García-Villacorta, R., Draper, F., Vicentini, A., Cornejo Valverde, F., Lloyd, J., Gomes, V. H. F., Neill, D., Alonso, A., Dallmeier, F., de Souza, F. C., Gribel, R., Arroyo, L., Carvalho, F. A., de Aguiar, D. P. P., et al (2020), 'Biased-corrected richness estimates for the Amazonian tree flora', *Scientific Reports*, 10 (1): 10130.
Terrell, J. E., Hart, J. P., Barut, S., Cellinese, N., Curet, A., Denham, T., Kusimba, C. M., Latinis, K., Oka, R. and Palka, J. (2003), 'Domesticated Landscapes: The Subsistence Ecology of Plant and Animal Domestication', *Journal of Archaeological Method and Theory*, 10 (4): 323–68.

Thomas, E., Alcazar Caicedo, C., McMichael, C. H., Corvera, R. and Loo, J. (2015), 'Uncovering spatial patterns in the natural and human history of Brazil nut (Bertholletia excelsa) across the Amazon Basin', *Journal of Biogeography*, 42 (8): 1367–82.

Timpson, A., Colledge, S., Crema, E., Edinborough, K., Kerig, T., Manning, K., Thomas, M. G. and Shennan, S. (2014), 'Reconstructing regional population fluctuations in the European Neolithic using radiocarbon dates: a new case-study using an improved method', *Journal of Archaeological Science*, 52: 549–57.

Toney, J. R. (2016), 'Ceramica e historia indigena do Alto Xingu', in Barreto C., Lima, H. and Betancourt, C. J. (eds), *Cerâmicas Arqueológicas da Amazônia: Rumo a uma Nova Síntese*, 235–48, Belem: IPHAN.

Towle, M. A. (1961), *The Ethnobotany of Pre-Columbian Peru*, Chicago: Aldine.

Troufflard, J. and Alves, D. T. (2019), 'Uma abordagem interdisciplinar do sítio arqueológico Cedro, baixo Amazonas', *Boletim do Museu Paraense Emílio Goeldi*, 14 (2): 553–80.

Turchin, P., Currie, T. E., Whitehouse, H., François, P., Feeney, K., Mullins, D., Hoyer, D., Collins, C., Grohmann, S. and Savage, P. (2018), 'Quantitative historical analysis uncovers a single dimension of complexity that structures global variation in human social organization', *Proceedings of the National Academy of Sciences*, 115 (2), E144–E151.

Turner, B. and Butzer, K. W. (1992), 'The Columbian Encounter and Land-Use Change', *Environment*, 34: 16–44.

Urban, G. (1992), 'A História da Cultura Brasileira Segundo as Línguas Nativas', in Carneiro da Cunha, M. (ed.), *História dos Indios no Brasil*, 87–102, São Paulo: Companhia da Letras.

Urbina, F. (1991), 'Mitos y Petroglifos en el río Caquetá. *Boletín del Museo de Oro*', 30: 1–41.

Urbina, F. and Peña, J. (2016), 'Perros de guerra, caballos, vacunos y otros temas en el arte rupestre de la serranía de La Lindosa (río Guayabero, Guaviare, Colombia): una conversación', *Ensayos: Historia y Teoría del Arte*, 20 (31): 7–37.

Valdez, F. (2021), 'The Mayo-Chinchipe-Marañón Complex: The Unexpected Spirits of the *Ceja*, in Clasby, R. (ed.), *The Archaeology of the Upper Amazon: Complexity and Interaction in the Andean Tropical Forest*, 62–82, Gainsville: University of Florida Press.

Vallebueno-Estrada, M., Rodríguez-Arévalo, I., Rougon-Cardoso, A., Martínez González, J., García Cook, A., Montiel, R. and Vielle-Calzada, J.-P. (2016), 'The earliest maize from San Marcos Tehuacán is a partial domesticate with genomic evidence of inbreeding', *Proceedings of the National Academy of Sciences*, 113 (49): 14151–6.

Vallejos, P. Q., Veit, P., Tipula, P. and Reytar, K. (2020), *Undermining Rights: Indigenous Lands and Mining in the Amazon*, World Resources Institute.

van der Merwe, N. J., Roosevelt, A. C. and Vogel, J. C. (1981), 'Isotopic evidence for prehistoric subsistence change at Parmana, Venezuela', *Nature*, 292: 536–8.

Versteeg, A. H. (2003), *Suriname before Columbus*, Paramaribo: Stichting Surinaams Museum.

Vialou, D., Benabdelhadi, M., Feathers, J., Fontugne, M. and Vialou, A. V. (2017), 'Peopling South America's centre: the late Pleistocene site of Santa Elina', *Antiquity*, 91 (358): 865–84.

Virtanen, P. K. and Saunaluoma, S. (2017), 'Visualization and Movement as Configurations of Human–Nonhuman Engagements: Precolonial Geometric Earthwork Landscapes of the Upper Purus, Brazil', *American Anthropologist*, 119 (4): 614–30.

Viveiros de Castro, E. (1996), 'Images of Nature and Society in Amazonian Ethnology', *Annual Review of Anthropology*, 25 (1): 179–200.

von den Driesch, A. and Hutterer, R. (2011), 'Mazamas, Patos criollos y anguilas de lodo', *Zeitschrift für Archäologie Außereuropäischer Kulturen*, 4: 341–67.

Von Hildebrand, E. (1975), 'Levantamiento de los petroglifos del río Caquetá entre La Pedrera y Araracuara', *Revista Colombiana de Antropología*, 19: 303–70.

Wahl, D., Byrne, R., Schreiner, T. and Hansen, R. (2006), 'Holocene vegetation change in the northern Peten and its implications for Maya prehistory', *Quaternary Research*, 65 (3): 380–9.

Walker, J. H. (2020a), 'People as Agents of Environmental Change', in Smith, C. (eds), *Encyclopedia of Global Archaeology*, Springer, Cham, https://doi.org/10.1007/978-3-030-30018-0_2129.
Walker, J.H. (2020b). 'Earthworks of the Llanos de Mojos', in Smith, C. (eds), *Encyclopedia of Global Archaeology*. Springer, Cham.
Walker, W., Baccini, A., Schwartzman, S., Ríos, S., Oliveira-Miranda, M. A., Augusto, C., Ruiz, M. R., Arrasco, C. S., Ricardo, B. and Smith, R. (2014), 'Forest carbon in Amazonia: the unrecognized contribution of indigenous territories and protected natural areas', *Carbon Management*, 5 (5–6): 479–85.
Walker, M. J., Berkelhammer, M., Björck, S., Cwynar, L. C., Fisher, D. A., Long, A. J., Lowe, J. J., Newnham, R. M., Rasmussen, S. O. and Weiss, H. (2012), 'Formal subdivision of the Holocene Series/Epoch: a Discussion Paper by a Working Group of INTIMATE (Integration of ice-core, marine and terrestrial records), and the Subcommission on Quaternary Stratigraphy (International Commission on Stratigraphy)', *Journal of Quaternary Science*, 27 (7): 649–59.
Walker, W. S., Gorelik, S. R., Baccini, A., Aragon-Osejo, J. L., Josse, C., Meyer, C., Macedo, M. N., Augusto, C., Rios, S. and Katan, T. (2020), 'The role of forest conversion, degradation, and disturbance in the carbon dynamics of Amazon indigenous territories and protected areas', *Proceedings of the National Academy of Sciences*, 117 (6): 3015–25.
Wan, S., Hui, D. and Luo, Y. (2001), 'Fire effects on nitrogen pools and dynamics in terrestrial ecosystems: a meta-analysis', *Ecological Applications*, 11: 1349–65.
Wang, S., Qianlai, Z., Outi, L., Draper, F. C. and Hinsby, C.-Q. (2018), 'Potential shift from a carbon sink to a source in Amazonian peatlands under a changing climate', *Proceedings of the National Academy of Sciences*, 115 (49): 12407–12.
Wang, X., Edwards, R. L., Auler, A. S., Cheng, H., Kong, X., Wang, Y., Cruz, F. W., Dorale, J. A. and Chiang, H.-W. (2017), 'Hydroclimate changes across the Amazon lowlands over the past 45,000 years', *Nature*, 541 (7636): 204–7.
Watling, J., Castro, M. T., Simon, M. F., Rodrigues, F. O., de Medeiros, M. B., De Oliveira, P. E. and Neves, E. G. (2020), 'Phytoliths from native plants and surface soils from the Upper Madeira river, SW Amazonia, and their potential for paleoecological reconstruction', *Quaternary International*, 550: 85–110.
Watling, J., Iriarte, J., Mayle, F. E., Schaan, D., Pessenda, L. C., Loader, N. J., Street-Perrott, F. A., Dickau, R. E., Damasceno, A. and Ranzi, A. (2017), 'Impact of pre-Columbian "geoglyph" builders on Amazonian forests', *Proceedings of the National Academy of Sciences*, 114 (8): 1868–73.
Watling, J., Iriarte, J., Whitney, B., Consuelo, E., Mayle, F., Castro, W., Schaan, D. and Feldpausch, T. (2016), 'Differentiation of neotropical ecosystems by modern soil phytolith assemblages and its implications for palaeoenvironmental and archaeological reconstructions II: Southwestern Amazonian forests', *Review of Palaeobotany and Palynology*, 226: 30–43.
Watling, J., Schmidt, M., Heckenberger, M., Lima, H., Moraes, B., Waura, K., Kuikuro, H., Kuikuro, T. W., Kuikuro, U. and Kuikuro, A. (2023), 'Assessing charcoal and phytolith signals for pre-Columbian land-use based on modern indigenous activity areas in the Upper Xingu, Amazonia', *The Holocene*, 09596836231183066.
Watling, J., Saunaluoma, S., Pärssinen, M. and Schaan, D. (2015), 'Subsistence practices among earthwork builders: Phytolith evidence from archaeological sites in the southwest Amazonian interfluves', *Journal of Archaeological Science: Reports*, 4: 541–51.
Watling, J., Shock, M. P., Mongeló, G. Z., Almeida, F. O., Kater, T., De Oliveira, P. E. and Neves, E. G. (2018), 'Direct archaeological evidence for Southwestern Amazonia as an early plant domestication and food production centre', *PLoS ONE*, 13 (7), e0199868.
Weisskopf, A., Qin, L., Ding, J., Ding, P., Sun, G. and Fuller, D. Q. (2015), 'Phytoliths and rice: from wet to dry and back again in the Neolithic Lower Yangtze', *Antiquity*, 89 (347): 1051–63.
Weng, C., Bush, M. B. and Athens, J. S. (2002), 'Holocene climate change and hydrarch succession in lowland Amazonian Ecuador', *Review of Palaeobotany and Palynology*, 120 (1–2): 73–90.

Whitehouse, N. J. and Kirleis, W. (2014), 'The world reshaped: practices and impacts of early agrarian societies', *Journal of Archaeological Science*, 51: 1–11.
Whitmore, T. M. and Turner, B. L. I. (2001), *Cultivated Landscapes of Middle America on the Eve of Conquest,* Oxford: Oxford University Press.
Whitney, B. S., Dickau, R., Mayle, F. E., Soto, J. D. and Iriarte, J. (2013), 'Pre-Columbian landscape impact and agriculture in the Monumental Mound region of the "Llanos de Moxos", lowland Bolivia', *Quaternary Research*, 80 (2): 207–17.
Whitney, B. S., Dickau, R., Mayle, F. E., Walker, J. H., Soto, J. D. and Iriarte, J. (2014), 'Pre-Columbian raised-field agriculture and land use in the Bolivian Amazon', *The Holocene*, 24 (2): 231–41.
Whitney, B. S. and Mayle, F. E. (2012), 'Pediastrum species as potential indicators of lake-level change in tropical South America', *Journal of Paleolimnology*, 47 (4): 601–15.
Whitney, B. S., Rushton, E. A., Carson, J. F., Iriarte, J. and Mayle, F. E. (2012), 'An improved methodology for the recovery of *Zea mays* and other large crop pollen, with implications for environmental archaeology in the Neotropics', *The Holocene*, 22 (10): 1,087–96.
Whitney, B. S., Smallman, T. L., Mitchard, E. T., Carson, J. F., Mayle, F. E. and Bunting, M. J. (2019), 'Constraining pollen-based estimates of forest cover in the Amazon: A simulation approach', *The Holocene*, 29 (2): 262–70.
Willerslev, E., Davison, J., Moora, M., Zobel, M., Coissac, E., Edwards, M. E., Lorenzen, E. D., Vestergård, M., Gussarova, G. and Haile, J. (2014), 'Fifty thousand years of Arctic vegetation and megafaunal diet', *Nature*, 506 (7486): 47–51.
Willey, G. R. and Sabloff, J. A. (1974), *A history of American Archaeology,* New York: W.H. Freeman.
Williams, D. (1992), 'El arcaico en el noroeste de Guyana y los comienzos de la horticultura., in Meggers', B. J. (ed.), *Prehistoric sudamericana: Nuevas perspectivas,* 233–51, Washington, D.C.: Taraxacum.
Willis, K. J., Gillson, L. and Brncic, T. M. (2004), 'Ecology. How 'virgin' is virgin rainforest?', *Science*, 304 (5669): 402–3.
Willis, K. J., Araujo, M. B., Bennet, K. D., Figueroa-Rangel, B., Froyd, C. A. and Myers, N. (2007), 'How can a knowledge of the past help to conserve the future? Biodiversity conservation and the relevance of long-term ecological studies', *Philos Trans R Soc Lond B Biol Sci*, 362 (1478): 175–87.
Witteveen, N., Hobus, C., Philip, A., Piperno, D. and McMichael, C. (2022), 'The variability of Amazonian palm phytoliths', *Review of Palaeobotany and Palynology*, 300: 104613.
Witteveen, N. H., White, C., Sanchez Martinez, B. A., Booij, R., Philip, A., Gosling, W. D., Bush, M. B. and McMichael, C. N. (2023), 'Phytolith assemblages reflect variability in human land use and the modern environment', *Vegetation History and Archaeobotany*, 1–16.
Woods, W. I. and McCann, J. M. (1999), 'The Anthropogenic Origin and Persistence of Amazonian Dark Earths', *Yearbook*, *Conference of Latin Americanist Geographers.* Austin: University of Texas Pres, 7–14.
Woods, W. I., Teixeira, W. G., Lehmann, J., Steiner, C., WinklerPrins, A. M. G. A. and Rebellato, L. (2009), Amazonian Dark Earths: Wim Sombroek's Vision, Berlin: Springer
Wüst, I. and Barreto, C. (1999), *The Ring Villages of Central Brazil: A Challenge for Amazonian Archaeology*. Latin American Antiquity, 10, 3–23.
Zarrillo, S., Gaikwad, N., Lanaud, C., Powis, T., Viot, C., Lesur, I., Fouet, O., Argout, X., Guichoux, E. and Salin, F. (2018), 'The use and domestication of Theobroma cacao during the mid-Holocene in the upper Amazon', *Nature Ecology and Evolution*, 2 (12): 1879–88.
Ziegler, C. and Leigh Jr, E. G. (2016), *A Magic Web: The Tropical Forest of Barro Colorado Island*, Washington, D.C.: Smithsonian Institution.
Zurita-Benavides, M. G. (2016), 'Cultivando las plantas y la sociedad waorani Cultivating plants and Waorani society', *Boletim del Museu Paranaense Emilio Goeldi*, 12 (2): 495–516.

INDEX

The letter *f* following an entry indicates a page with a figure.

Index